CW01187013

Domestic Violence

Sarah Hilder • Vanessa Bettinson
Editors

Domestic Violence

Interdisciplinary Perspectives on Protection, Prevention and Intervention

palgrave
macmillan

Editors
Sarah Hilder
Health and Life Sciences
De Montfort University
Leicester, United Kingdom

Vanessa Bettinson
Dept. Law
De Montfort University
Leicester, United Kingdom

ISBN 978-1-137-52451-5   ISBN 978-1-137-52452-2   (eBook)
DOI 10.1057/978-1-137-52452-2

Library of Congress Control Number: 2016944838

© The Editor(s) (if applicable) and The Author(s) 2016
The author(s) has/have asserted their right(s) to be identified as the author(s) of this work in accordance with the Copyright, Designs and Patents Act 1988.
This work is subject to copyright. All rights are solely and exclusively licensed by the Publisher, whether the whole or part of the material is concerned, specifically the rights of translation, reprinting, reuse of illustrations, recitation, broadcasting, reproduction on microfilms or in any other physical way, and transmission or information storage and retrieval, electronic adaptation, computer software, or by similar or dissimilar methodology now known or hereafter developed.
The use of general descriptive names, registered names, trademarks, service marks, etc. in this publication does not imply, even in the absence of a specific statement, that such names are exempt from the relevant protective laws and regulations and therefore free for general use.
The publisher, the authors and the editors are safe to assume that the advice and information in this book are believed to be true and accurate at the date of publication. Neither the publisher nor the authors or the editors give a warranty, express or implied, with respect to the material contained herein or for any errors or omissions that may have been made.

Cover illustration: © Anton Starikov / Alamy Stock Photo

Printed on acid-free paper

This Palgrave Macmillan imprint is published by Springer Nature
The registered company is Macmillan Publishers Ltd. London

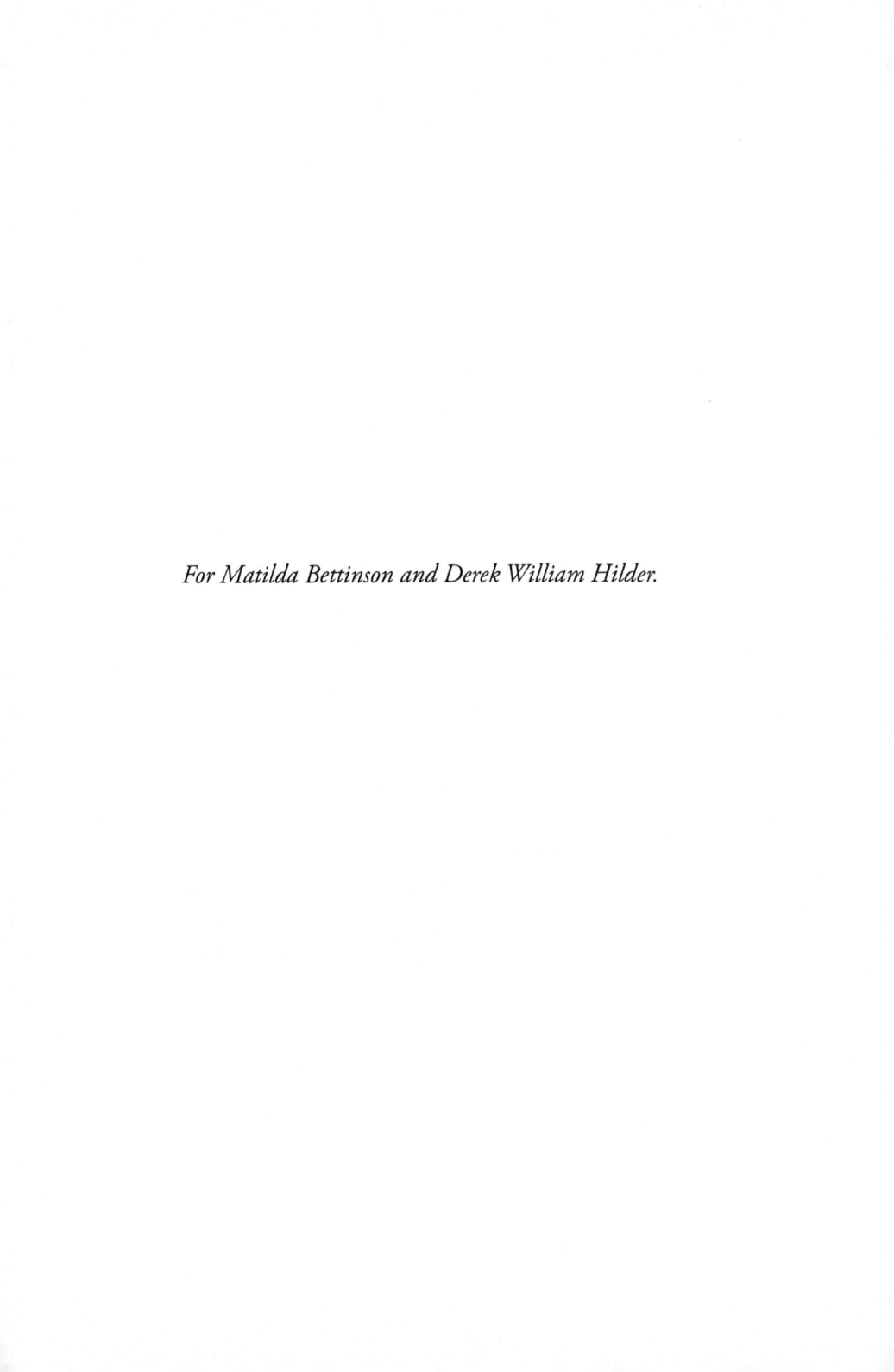

For Matilda Bettinson and Derek William Hilder.

Preface

We were introduced in 2012 by Professor Rob Canton, under the premise that we shared a common interest in Domestic Violence and Abuse (DVA) concerns. This was, indeed, the case, although we soon found that our social science and legal backgrounds resulted in some challenging debates and that whilst we shared an underpinning philosophy relating to a desire to see a reduction in the prevalence of and harm caused by DVA, our definitions, language and perceived priorities varied significantly. Our knowledge and analysis of policy developments, research activities and practice innovations within each other's subject discipline pertaining to DVA were also clearly restricted by our own subjective 'lens', shaped by our personal and professional perspectives. We knew our exchanges were not unique in this respect and that, despite the establishment of a myriad of DVA partnerships and networks nationally, retaining an insightful overview and informed understanding of the ever increasing diversity of activity and approach taken to protection, prevention and intervention strategies remains challenging. We also agreed that there appeared to be less appetite for a social and legal interface, with one discipline very happy to critique the other and vice versa, but currently with limited opportunities for mutual exchange and engagement. It had taken a semi-formal introduction for us to meet and our offices were only 100 yards apart across a university court yard! Since 2012, we have established a university-wide research network concerned with issues of sexual violence and domestic violence, with colleague members from a vast array of disciplines and professional roles, many engaged in sexual violence and DVA work with external partners across a wide variety of public service functions at regional, national and international levels. It leads to a lively discourse full of furrowed brows, raised eyebrows, sighs of relief, smiles of enthusiasm and some renewed vigour for the consideration of 'alternatives'. We are acutely aware, however, that for those experiencing DVA, the convergence of various professional disciplines in the 'real world' can often still feel far from congenial and collaborative. An important step for us was the delivery of the Interdisciplinary Domestic Violence Conference (IDVC) at De Montfort University in December 2013, supported by the Social Policy Association and attracting contributors nationally, many of whom are authors within this collection. This book continues our pursuit of an ongoing dialogue across disciplines, to encourage less rigid attachments to a particular perspective and a more holistic reflection on victims'/survivors' varied experiences of DVA protection, prevention and intervention strategies. We are grateful to all of the authors for their commitment to this project.

Contents

1 Introduction 1
  Sarah Hilder and Vanessa Bettinson

Part I Protection 13

2 Domestic Violence: Applying a Human Rights Discourse 15
  Ronagh McQuigg

3 A Fresh Approach to Policing Domestic Violence 37
  Mandy Burton

4 Domestic Violence: The Limitations of a Legal Response 59
  Charlotte Bishop

5 Surviving Times of Austerity: Preserving the Specialist Domestic Violence Court Provision 81
  Vanessa Bettinson

Part II Prevention and Intervention 105

6 Victim Support Services and the World of
   Commissioning 107
   Di Turgoose

7 Children and Domestic Violence: What Do Family
   Intervention Workers Have to Offer? 131
   Jo Little and Fae Garland

8 Building Healthy Relationships for Young People
   and the Prevention of Domestic Abuse 155
   *Christopher Crowther-Dowey, Terry Gillespie, and
   Kristan Hopkins*

9 Debates of Difference: Male Victims of Domestic
   Violence and Abuse 181
   Luke Martin

10 The Relationship Between Spiritual Abuse and Domestic
    Violence and Abuse in Faith-Based Communities 203
    Lisa Oakley and Kathryn Kinmond

11 Housing: More Than Just Bricks and Mortar. Domestic
    Abuse Interventions Within the Housing Sector 227
    Gudrun Burnet

12 Independent Advocacy and Multi-Agency Responses to
    Domestic Violence 249
    Amanda Robinson and Joanne Payton

13 Working with Perpetrators of Domestic Violence
  and Abuse: The Potential for Change   273
  Sarah Hilder and Caroline Freeman

14 Developing Interventions for Abusive Partners in Lesbian,
  Gay, Bisexual and/or Transgender Relationships   297
  Rebecca Barnes and Catherine Donovan

Index   321

Notes on Contributors

Rebecca Barnes is Lecturer in Criminology at the University of Leicester. She has been researching domestic violence in LGB and/or T relationships for the last 10 years. Her PhD, completed at the University of Nottingham in 2007, was one of the first in-depth, qualitative studies of survivors of partner abuse in women's same-sex relationships. Her articles have appeared in *Feminism & Psychology* and *Partner Abuse* on her doctoral research, in addition to chapters in two edited collections. With Professor Catherine Donovan, Barnes recently completed an ESRC-funded study called the Coral Project, which sought to understand the use of abusive behaviours in LGB and/or T relationships and inform the development of appropriate interventions. She is also co-leading a mixed-methods evaluation of provision for medium risk, repeat female victims/survivors of domestic abuse in Nottinghamshire. In addition to her academic role, Barnes is a member of the Management Committee at Leicester Rape Crisis.

Vanessa Bettinson is Senior Lecturer in Law at Leicester De Montfort Law School, De Montfort University. Her teaching spans across criminal law, human rights and immigration law. Her recent research has centred on legal responses to domestic violence, particularly in the context of criminal law, justice and human rights. As an academic criminal lawyer, she has published work on the ability of the substantive criminal law to capture coercive and controlling behaviour and is now exploring comparative approaches to this context. In addition to her domestic violence research, she has examined the human rights concerns surrounding imprisonment for public protection sentences. Her articles have appeared internationally, including the *Modern Law Review, Journal of Criminal Law, International Journal of Law, Crime and Justice, Northern Ireland Legal Quarterly* and the *Criminal Law Review*. She is a trustee of the charity New Dawn New Day, which provides support services for victim/survivors of domestic violence.

Charlotte Bishop is Lecturer and Researcher in Law at Exeter University. Her research interests are broad and interdisciplinary, crossing the boundaries of socio-legal research into psychology, sociology, philosophy and criminology. She has particular expertise in criminal law, gender studies and the gendered nature of the legal system and its institutions. Her doctoral research critiqued the legal response to domestic violence in England and Wales and more recently she published with Ms Vanessa Bettinson, examining the new criminal offence of coercive and controlling behaviour. She is researching how the harm of domestic violence, including coercive control, could be evidenced in criminal court proceedings. She is also interested in how understandings of coercive control could improve the criminal justice system's response to victims who kill their abusers.

Gudrun Burnet started her career as a volunteer for the National Domestic Violence Helpline. Her first professional role was as a Domestic Violence Support Worker with Refuge and then as a manager for outreach services in South London. Burnet is now a Senior Business Partner (Domestic Abuse) at Peabody Housing, where she has been working to improve the housing response to domestic abuse for the last 7 years. She has provided training on domestic abuse to more than 41 other housing providers nationally. She is also engaged in work on domestic abuse issues with the Home Office, Ministry of Justice, Mayor's Office of Policing and Crime (MOPAC) and the Welsh Housing Minister. Burnet is the housing sector representative for the national stakeholder panel for Violence Against Women and Girls. She has spoken at several international conferences and co-founded the Domestic Abuse Housing Alliance (DAHA), which supports a national accreditation process for housing providers seeking to improve their response to domestic abuse.

Mandy Burton is Professor of Socio-Legal Studies at the University of Leicester. Her research lies in the fields of criminal law, criminal justice and family law. She is particularly interested in police and prosecution decision making, criminal courts, victims' rights and domestic violence. She has considerable experience in carrying out empirical research into legal responses to domestic violence, producing a monograph and numerous research reports for UK government departments on the topic. Her work includes a study examining whether the police and other third parties should be empowered to apply for civil protection orders on behalf of victims of domestic violence and another project examining why, up until 2012, there was a decline in applications for non-molestation orders in domestic violence cases in England and Wales.

Chris Crowther-Dowey is Senior Lecturer in Criminology at Nottingham Trent University (NTU). He has a background in sociology and social policy and is the lead for the Crime Reduction and Policing Research Cluster. His research and expertise are in the fields of gender and violence, specifically the prevention of aggressive attitudes and behaviour amongst young people and the relationship between masculinities and violence. He also has a long-standing interest in the relationship between the police, policing and different forms of social exclusion. This is complemented by more general interests in criminal justice policymaking and criminological and social theory. Crowther-Dowey is the course leader for the MA Criminology at NTU and has extensive experience of teaching criminology and criminal justice to undergraduate and postgraduate students on a range of modules, but especially those relating to policing, gender and crime and comparative criminology.

Catherine Donovan is Professor of Social Relations at the University of Sunderland and lead of the Centre for Applied Social Sciences (CASS). She has conducted collaborative research in Lesbian, Gay, Bisexual and, more recently, Transgender communities for over 25 years, co-authoring *Same Sex Intimacies: Families of Choice and Other Life Experiments* (2001, Routledge). Since 2004, her focus has been on domestic violence and abuse and child sexual exploitation in LGB and/or T communities. With Professor Marianne Hester, Donovan conducted the first comprehensive study comparing love and violence in same-sex and heterosexual relationships, which culminated in *Domestic Violence and Sexuality: What's Love Got To Do With It?* (2014). With Dr Rebecca Barnes, the Coral Project explored the abusive behaviours of partners in LGB and/or T relationships and interventions to address them. Her work has also explored the heteronormative construction of risk in domestic violence and abuse practice and the impacts of austerity in the North East of England.

Caroline Freeman is the Service Manager at the Jenkins Centre, part of the Leicester-based charity FreeVA, which delivers a Community Domestic Violence Perpetrator Programme, accredited by RESPECT. She has worked in the domestic violence sector for the last four years, managing IDVAs and sexual violence services. In 2012, she established the Jenkins Centre. She also has over 20 years of experience of working in the voluntary sector as a qualified Youth &

Community worker. More recently, from 2009–2010, Freeman was a VSO volunteer in Sri Lanka working for a local charity as a consultant, to build capacity in the delivery of Sexual, Gender Based Violence Projects and co-ordinating a post-conflict humanitarian feeding project for internally displaced people. Her specific practice interests include developing best practice for working with women using violence, understanding abusive men and trauma and developing links with international perpetrator programmes. She is an active member of the Women's International League for Peace and Freedom.

Fae Garland is Lecturer in Law at the University of Exeter. Her research and teaching interests centre on family law and gender, with a growing expertise in empirical research. She completed an MRes in Socio-Legal Research in 2008 and was awarded her doctorate in 2013 on 'Valuing Domestic Contributions: A Search for A Solution in Family Law'. Her thesis used a range of empirical, feminist and comparative methodologies to explore the way in which the law should value caregiving at the end of a relationship. Garland has previously published work on issues relating to the gendered impact of the law and has been awarded a SLSA small grant for an empirical project entitled 'Exploring the Possibility of Being "X": Lessons from Australia's Legal Construction of Intersex'. She was also the co-investigator on a BCHA-funded qualitative project, which evaluated the effectiveness of a Family Intervention Worker working with children exposed to domestic violence in the South West.

Terry Gillespie is Senior Lecturer in Criminology at NTU, where she set up the successful BA Criminology degree course in 1994. Gillespie is Chair of the NTU School of Social Sciences Research Ethics Committee, Deputy Chair of the NTU College of Business, Law and Social Sciences Research Ethics Committee and sits on the British Society of Criminology Professional Ethics Committee. Her research and teaching expertise have focused on women and crime, gender and violence, domestic abuse, rape and sexual assault and honour abuse. Gillespie has published on feminist research methods and support services for rape victims and has recently conducted research projects on multi-agency approaches to honour abuse and young people's attitudes towards domestic abuse and appropriate interventions.

Sarah Hilder is Senior Lecturer and Researcher in Community and Criminal Justice at De Montfort University. Her research and teaching expertise have centred on working with victims, domestic abuse, issues of social justice, sex offender rehabilitation, supervision and surveillance. Previously, she worked for the National Probation Service, as both a main grade and then Senior Probation

Officer in various capacities from 1993–2004, where her work included the management of Court and Victim Services, domestic abuse perpetrator programmes and work with high risk violent and sexual offenders. Hilder has published work on risk assessment and safety planning in situations of domestic abuse, multi-agency working, desistance work and sexual offending and cross-border information exchanges on serious violent or sexual offenders travelling across the European Union (EU) community. She is well versed in comparative victim and criminal justice work across the EU, having worked as a senior researcher on two major EU-funded projects from 2010–2015.

Kristan Hopkins is Senior Lecturer in Criminology at NTU. Her research and teaching expertise have centred on research methods, crime and criminal justice and, more specifically, sexual offending, community-based responses to sexual offending, honour-based violence, domestic abuse and young people and, more recently, on students in higher education and sexual harassment. Hopkins has published work on research methods for health and social care, student engagement and the process of student feedback. Hopkins is researching sexual harassment and the experiences of young people in higher education and is preparing for a PhD in 2016.

Kathryn Kinmond is a Senior Lecturer and Faculty Chair of Ethics at Manchester Metropolitan University. Kinmond is a Chartered Psychologist, Chartered Scientist and Associate Fellow of the British Psychological Society and an accredited member of the British Association of Counselling & Psychotherapy (BACP). She has more than 20 years of experience in Higher Education. Her research and teaching expertise centre on issues of abuse and qualitative methods. Having been awarded a number of significant research grants and having published extensively herself and in collaboration with colleagues, she has also produced a text for final-year undergraduates on how to undertake a qualitative research project. Kinmond's work and research on the issue of spiritual abuse has resulted in a number of published papers and the co-authorship of a book with Lisa Oakley. She also counsels in private practice, working, in particular, with clients who have been abused. She is an executive member of the division of Spirituality with the BACP.

Jo Little is Professor of Geography and Gender at the University of Exeter in the UK. She has researched widely on gender issues in rural geography, focusing, in particular, on women's employment and rural gender identities. She has undertaken a number of studies on women's fear and is working on domestic violence in rural communities. In 2014, she received a Leverhulme fellowship for research on rural domestic violence. Little's research has been conducted mainly in the UK and New Zealand. Her articles have appeared in *Human Geography* and *Sociology* journals and she is the author and editor of a number of books on rural geography issues including *Contested Countryside Cultures* (with Paul Cloke), *Critical Studies in Rural Gender Issues* (with Carol Morris) and *Gender and Rural Geography*.

Luke Martin is a consultant, primarily focusing on work with male and LGBT victims of domestic abuse. His academic background is in Law, Gender, Sexuality and Human Rights. Historically, his work has included seven years working as a Male Independent Domestic Violence Advisor (IDVA) and he is CAADA/SafeLives accredited. He has also worked extensively for and with RESPECT, including the national helpline for male victims of abuse, The Men's Advice Line. Martin is a trainer for RESPECT's 'Working with Male Victims' training programme as well as the SafeLives IDVA accreditation course. Martin has worked as a consultant for organisations such as SurvivorsUK, the national male rape and sexual violence service. He has also been an active campaigner on projects such as the Home Office's 'This is Abuse' campaign. Martin has previously published a series of articles on legal issues pertaining to domestic abuse for the Law Society.

Ronagh McQuigg is a Lecturer in the School of Law at Queen's University, Belfast. Her research interests lie in the area of international human rights law, with a particular focus on an analysis of domestic violence through a human rights lens. She has published widely in this field, across a range of international publications. She also produced a monograph entitled *International Human Rights Law and Domestic Violence* (2011). McQuigg graduated with an LLB in 2002, an LLM in Human Rights Law in 2003 and a PhD in 2006, all from Queen's University Belfast. She qualified as a solicitor in 2008 and took up her lectureship in the School of Law at Queen's University in 2009. McQuigg has presented papers on Human Rights and domestic violence issues at conferences across a range of socio-legal disciplines. She also teaches at undergraduate and postgraduate levels.

Lisa Oakley is Senior Lecturer in Psychology at the Research Institute for Health and Social Change at Manchester Metropolitan University, where she is programme leader for the Abuse Studies academic programme at Manchester Metropolitan University. Her research is primarily focused on abuse in faith communities and specifically on the area of spiritual abuse. Oakley co-authored the first academic publication on the topic of spiritual abuse, with her colleague Kathryn Kinmond, *Breaking the Silence on Spiritual Abuse* (2015, Palgrave). She has also published work on effective safeguarding policies and practice in faith communities. She has spoken extensively at academic and practitioner conferences, most recently addressing the link between domestic violence and faith. Oakley also works alongside national organisations providing education, support and guidance in addressing allegations of spiritual abuse.

Joanne Payton has worked for more than 10 years with the Iranian and Kurdish Women's Rights Organisation (IKWRO), the UK's leading organisation supporting victims of domestic violence who have origins in the Middle East and Central Asia. Reflecting this background and experience, her PhD thesis, undertaken at Cardiff University, was on the topic of 'honour'-based violence and family structure in the Kurdistan Region of Iraq. She works with Norwegian artist, activist and documentary maker Deeyah Khan at the media company Fuuse as a researcher and writer.

Amanda Robinson is Reader in Criminology at Cardiff University. Her research generally includes a strong policy focus and it has made a significant policy impact. For example, she has conducted research on services that deliver advocacy to victims of domestic and sexual violence, multi-agency partnerships, specialist courts and risk-based approaches such as IDVAs and MARACs. Many of these initiatives have now become integrated into the mainstream response to domestic and sexual violence in the UK and Europe. Closer to home, she was directly involved in drafting the Welsh Government's White Paper proposals, which earlier this year were passed as the Violence against Women, Domestic Abuse and Sexual Violence (Wales) Act 2015. Her current projects include a review of the DASH risk tool in collaboration with the College of Policing and developing a new multi-agency process for the identification and management of priority domestic abuse perpetrators in Wales. She is an editor of the British Journal of Criminology.

Di Turgoose is a Senior Lecturer and early career researcher in the Division of Community and Criminal Justice at De Montfort University. She is the programme leader for the undergraduate Criminology and Criminal Justice Programmes and has previously led the Probation Qualifying Framework. Her research and teaching expertise are in work with perpetrators and victims of crime, with specific interests in the field of domestic violence, community safety and substance use. Turgoose worked in the specialist domestic violence women's sector during 1991–1994 as a refuge worker, steering group committee member and Director of North Nottinghamshire Women's Aid. She has also worked for the Probation Service, as both a Probation Officer and Practice Development Assessor in London and Nottingham from 1994–2007. Her work included specialisms in victim units, perpetrator programmes for high risk and mentally disordered offenders and secondments to both the male and female prison estates. She is a member of Women's Aid and the Fawcett Society.

1

Introduction

Sarah Hilder and Vanessa Bettinson

Moral and legal obligations to address issues of domestic violence and abuse (DVA) are now of global concern. At a regional level, the Council of Europe Convention on Preventing and Combating Violence against Women and Domestic Violence (Istanbul Convention), 2014, provides legally binding standards to improve the prevention of violence, the protection of victims, and the prosecution of perpetrators through a set of integrated policies, calling for a stronger coordination of legal and community-based responses (Council of Europe, 2011). Although at the time of writing this chapter, the UK had yet to ratify the Istanbul Convention, the last 10–15 years has also seen a powerful policy rhetoric materialize in the UK, advocating the need for more effective interdisciplinary, multi-agency working and coordinated community responses to

---

S. Hilder (✉)
Community and Criminal Justice Division,
De Montfort University, Leicester, UK

V. Bettinson
De Montfort Business and Law, De Montfort University, Leicester, UK

© The Editor(s) (if applicable) and The Author(s) 2016
S. Hilder, V. Bettinson (Eds.), *Domestic Violence*,
DOI 10.1057/978-1-137-52452-2_1

issues of DVA. From the late 1990s onwards, professional partnership networks have emerged, pursuing collective responsibilities for protection, prevention, and intervention. However, some of these groupings have remained narrow and self-referential in their outlook (Dobash & Dobash, 1998), with the ideologies of the larger leading organisations tending to dominate (Nash, 2010). The additional benefits of partnership working have also been differentially pursued by policymakers and service providers, which may, in turn, be viewed as: a strategy to ensure that a joint, prompt, and effective response is made to cases where victims/survivors and children may be in imminent danger; an opportunity to improve, coordinate, innovate, and expand the range of DVA services available; a strategy to address prior evaluations of poor practice by a single agency; a mechanism by which the resourcing of a particular service may continue; or an opportunity to streamline funding overall.

The various aspects of interdisciplinary work on DVA have, therefore, been pursued by a range of quite distinct agency alliances, although it is the case that some DVA specialist agencies are becoming increasingly compelled to work across borders in order to sustain any consistent level of resourcing. Larger organisations, particularly those within the criminal justice system, have primarily sought partners who are seen to complement their own core function, aims and responsibilities, rather than pursuing new opportunities for joint innovation. The legal world, both civil and criminal, whilst subject to some significant levels of external scrutiny and independent evaluation, is often notably disengaged from wider interdisciplinary discourses on DVA. As such, the law develops in practice primarily through the legal analysis of issues of definition, evidence, legal processes and procedures. Other agencies, such as the Probation Service, have seen their core functions and aims shift dramatically over the last two decades, with centralised management and public protection priorities taking hold (Burke & Collet, 2015). This, in turn, has resulted in a significant change in the organization's relationships with both voluntary and private sector partners (FitzGibbons & Lea, 2014).

The modernisation of public services through the development of a performance culture based on target setting and managerial control has been a central tenet of the successive labour, coalition, and conservative UK governments from 1997 onwards. Such developments have been promoted as a means of driving up standards via a mixed economy of service provision achieved through competitive tendering. Considerable efforts have been made by specialist DVA services to positively frame these developments as opportunities for greater creativity and more effective coordination between agencies. However, the pressures of commercial contracting and payments attached to statistical outcomes have resulted in increased fragmentation in the longer term (see Turgoose, Chap. 6). This has served to further exacerbate inconsistencies nationally in the support available to DVA victims/survivors and the interventions available for DVA perpetrators. A partnership ethos can quickly be replaced by one of suspicion and competition. Within this climate, achieving any comprehensive understanding of current strategies to address DVA and their effectiveness remains challenging and the need for a greater cross-fertilisation of concerns, evidence and ideas across different intellectual disciplines, identified by Dobash and Dobash (1998), remains obvious today. However, the contemporary request is clearly set against quite a different background and 'intellectual' debate is no longer reserved for the different schools of thought within academia, but traverses across a broad selection of professional roles and lobbying groups.

New campaigns have arisen, resulting in an ever widening recognition of the diverse nature of DVA, with a complex mix of vulnerabilities and experiences (Martin, Chap. 9; Oakley and Kinmond, Chap. 10; Barnes and Donovan, Chap. 14). The increasing public awareness of DVA has also seen the emergence of some exciting advancements, as those agencies that were not traditionally recognised as first responders realise their potential to do more (Burnet, Chap. 11). Other more established territorial boundaries have also started to shift. For example, DVA specialist agencies and social work teams are becoming increasingly more involved in work with DVA perpetrators (Hilder and Freeman, Chap. 13). The risk models that have underpinned more formal frameworks, such as Multi Agency Risk Assessment Conferences (MARACs), have come under increasing scrutiny (see Robinson and Payton, Chap. 12) and there is now a greater emphasis on early intervention and prevention work with children and young people. This has led to greater social care involvement in DVA issues (Little and Garland, Chap. 7; Crowther-Dowey, Gillespie and Hopkins, Chap. 8). Ascertaining thresholds for the criminalisation of DVA behaviours becomes increasingly challenging as a mixed economy of service providers continues to expand across the statutory, voluntary, and private sectors. Questions are raised, such as whether the ongoing legal pursuit of DVA as a violation of human rights (McQuigg, Chap. 2) is contradictory to developments which seek to place interventions within a family domain and if not, is it clear how and when different approaches may apply? The legal system itself appears to have some internal challenges to face, as the survival of specialist domestic violence court provisions remains uncertain (Bettinson, Chap. 5) whilst new substantive legal definitions of DVA, which include coercion and control, enter into force. The law will need to acquire a sophisticated understanding of the psychological impact of DVA, which it has traditionally struggled to address (Bishop, Chap. 4). New powers of policing have also emerged, based in civil law and again with potential implications for developments in policing practice as agents of prevention rather than prosecution (Burton, Chap. 3). Clearly, therefore, as knowledge of DVA in relation to the question 'who does what to whom?' (Hester, 2009) continues to expand, the questions of 'who should do what with whom, when, why and how?' are becoming increasingly complex to answer.

This edited collection does not profess to offer a solution to the aforementioned questions; rather, it provides a range of perspectives that inform the debate. There are some clear limitations to such a discourse without the full appraisal of those who have experienced DVA and the profile of the victim's/survivor's voice continues to remain stronger within some disciplinary perspectives more than others. There are, of course, also many other 'perspectives,' which may have been sought. However, in casting the net more widely, it is inevitable that some significant elements of the catch will slip by while others will remain reluctant to swim in shared waters. There is no exclusionary intention and the core priorities of the Istanbul Convention are all encompassed here.

The contributing authors take various positions on the benefits and limitations of addressing issues of DVA via a single unit of analysis, the most commonly applied being that of gender and reflections on the advantages of an intersectional approach to understandings of, and responses to, DVA experiences are apparent. Whilst overarching international activity continues to root the issue of DVA in the context of broader gender inequalities and patriarchal power relations, the potency of this framework varies across DVA service provider activities in the UK. A gender-neutral approach to the application of legal tools and protective measures, organisational policy, practice development, and the delivery of staff training is seen as a more palatable approach by some, which may lead to greater inroads in terms of increasing general awareness and sensitivity to issues of DVA. However, for others, any blanket dismissal of the clear potential for gender to be a matter of significance in the commission of DVA is also of great concern, to the detriment of the development of effective practice with victims/survivors and perpetrators, both male and female. However, examinations of individual, interactional, contextual and ideological issues pertaining to the occurrence of DVA are variably engaged with by those responsible for protection, prevention, and intervention measures. Compatible conclusions may not always be reached, but this may improve with a more open and more benign approach to interdisciplinary dialogue.

The conceptual issues pertaining to gender also clearly link to the varied definitions of DVA and the diverse use of terminology across disciplines. In particular, there are a range of views on the breadth or limitations of the term 'violence.' Legal perspectives tend to be more familiar with the term 'domestic violence,' which is used to encompass a range of physical and sexual acts of harm, but now also includes behaviours of harassment, sustained non-physical intimidation psychological and emotional abuse. However, for others it implies a reliance on the more tangible evidence of physical or sexual assault, and terms such as domestic, violence and abuse (DVA) and intimate partner violence and abuse are used elsewhere to represent a more nuanced understanding of a broader range of victim/survivor experiences. The usefulness of the term 'victim' is also contested, with preferences by some for the term 'survivor,' while others find this equally problematic in terms of imposing a status, which implies a level of ongoing vulnerability or recovery. The terms 'service user' and 'service providers' reflect the move towards consumerist frameworks for intervention and support, with an emphasis on achieving identified, quantifiable outputs. Similar issues of terminology and definition also arise in work with perpetrators of abuse and in particular the determination of thresholds of seriousness leading to the criminalisation of DVA, as highlighted previously. Arguments may also be made for a greater opportunity for self-determination and definition by those experiencing DVA, although this approach assumes that victims/survivors are a homogenous group who will reach a consensus. Rationales for these and other approaches are ideologically and politically motivated and every variation offered in this collection has its own benefits and limitations. They reflect the conceptualisation of DVA as a criminal or non-criminal matter and the various diverse stages of victim/survivor, perpetrator, or potential perpetrator engagement with mechanisms for protection, prevention and intervention. A matter of some reflection for the reader perhaps is which definitions appear to dominate in the wider public discourse on DVA and which remain more marginalised. It is also vital that the various disciplinary perspectives are willing to explore these conceptual differences and utilise them as an opportunity for refining and improving their own position and approach.

Structure of the Book

The authors provide a critical analysis of their core subjects informed by internal, practitioner-based perspectives, from those currently working in the DVA field with both perpetrators and victims/survivors and external perspectives from independent academic researchers across subject disciplines in law, socio-legal studies, applied social sciences, criminal justice, criminology, sociology, psychology, gender and abuse studies.

Part I

Contributions in Part I of this collection are written from a legal perspective and focus on legal processes and provisions for protection.

In Chap. 2, Ronagh McQuigg sets a broader context for a legal discourse of DVA and in particular the efforts made to secure the recognition of DVA as a human rights violation. With the advent of the Council of Europe Convention on Preventing and Combating Violence against

Women and Domestic Violence (2011), a renewed opportunity has occurred for a human rights approach to inform and strengthen national strategies for the prevention of and protection from DVA. For those less well versed in the overarching legal frameworks to address DVA, an overview is provided of the guidance supplied at both international and European levels. The chapter considers whether developments have extended beyond the symbolic function of a human rights discourse and explores the challenges of implementing and enforcing a human rights perspective to make real changes for victims/survivors of DVA.

The collection then turns to further legal and criminal justice concerns at a national level. In Chap. 3, Mandy Burton considers the enduring challenges of securing effective police responses to DVA in England and Wales. She considers the 2014 report undertaken by Her Majesty's Inspectorate of Constabulary (HMIC), which highlighted ongoing issues of poor evidence gathering, the persistence of a dismissive police culture towards DVA and a fundamental lack of understanding of the dynamics of DVA by frontline police officers. She considers whether the recently implemented Domestic Violence Protection Notices and Orders provide a positive innovation to assist with the challenges of policing in this area. Alternatively, is this a step towards preventative, diversionary actions by the police and to what extent might this also be seen as a step towards the decriminalisation of DVA?

In Chap. 4, Charlotte Bishop considers the limitations of a legal response and in particular, a perceived 'hierarchy of harms' where non-physical acts of DVA remain misunderstood and subject to poor legal redress. She highlights that systematic patterns of coercive and controlling behaviour aimed at disempowering the victim/survivor are frequently characterised by specific gendered expectations. However, despite recent legislative developments, the legal system often negates the enduring nature of DVA and the gendered significance of many DVA cases. It is stated that this is due, in part, to the legal system's own history as an institution steeped in broader social and cultural conditions of gender inequality. The chapter concludes by suggesting that the law would be a more effective tool to address DVA if the legal system is able to step beyond its current 'gender-neutral' approach, to engage more fully in the complexities of DVA and acknowledge the deprivation of autonomy as a central harm. One approach that may serve to address some of these issues is the survival and further development of the Specialist Domestic Violence Court (SDVC) provision. In Chap. 5, Vanessa Bettinson charts the inception and expansion of this, which sought to provide a victim-centred approach to the criminal justice system to improve victim/survivor satisfaction and increase the number of prosecutions for DVA-related offending. However, since 2010, the number of court houses across England and Wales has declined and the need to ensure that SDVC provision survives further budgetary cuts is advocated here. Comparisons are made with the development of specialist Domestic Abuse Courts in Scotland as a model of good practice, which preserve effective working relationships between the police, prosecution authorities and the independent victim's advocate. An expansion of the SDVC remit is argued for to address the increase in the use of police diversions and to oversee the use of police cautions and out-of-court disposals in situations of DVA.

Part II

Part II of the collection examines strategies for prevention and intervention, highlighting both new innovations and calls for increased diversity and expansion of service delivery within the challenging context of the current economic climate.

In Chap. 6, Di Turgoose sets the context for this element of the DVA discourse by exploring the impact of a competitive market ideology with its demands for quality, effectiveness and evaluation of outcomes. The chapter examines the extent to which these changes have maximised or hindered opportunities to address complex needs and increased DVA victim/survivor engagement. It is argued that the expansion of the competitive field, decreasing levels of autonomy, the time-consuming administration of tenders and the short-term nature of financial contracts have reduced the ability of DVA staff to develop good practice. The diverse spectrum of victims'/survivors' needs are not well served and the further dilution of funds cannot continue without further serious repercussions.

In Chap. 7, Little and Garland provide an example of the 'changing landscape' of DVA intervention work, focusing on the needs of children who have witnessed DVA in the family home. Drawing upon a small-scale study, they examine the role of a Family Intervention Worker (FIW) charged with providing support to families, primarily children and mothers, in situations of DVA. The value of an advocate for children who is independent from child protection concerns is highlighted, with benefits for both the children concerned and the primary victim/survivor. Crowther-Dowey, Gillespie, and Hopkins are also concerned with the impact of DVA on young people in Chap. 8. Their research, conducted with children and young people on a housing estate in the Midlands region, looks at the intergenerational transfer of negative values and attitudes that serve to support 'gendered' assumptions, and ultimately the commission of DVA. They focus on the relationship between gender, age and socio-economic environmental factors, which may serve to sustain a hyper masculine culture. They reflect on the nature of interventions that may serve as a 'firebreak' to inhibit the perpetuation of such a culture and reduce patterns of DVA in the longer term.

Chapter 9, by Luke Martin, is also concerned with gender and concepts of masculinity. However, here the discussion turns to the experiences of male victims/survivors of DVA. Whilst there is an increasing recognition of male victimisation by both female and male perpetrators, fundamental barriers to accessing appropriate support services remain. The extent to which this is also 'entangled' with concepts of gender is explored, with some observations of male victim/survivor experiences across heterosexual, bisexual, and/or transgender relationships. It is argued that assumptions that an extension of existing services for female victims/survivors is 'good enough' ignores the varied pathways and shaping factors, which result in a commission of DVA. It also results in unhelpful tensions, as existing resources for female victims/survivors of DVA are seen to be stretched even further. In Chap. 10, Oakley and Kinmond highlight another area of DVA victim/survivor experience, which remains on the margins of current mainstream service provisions and poorly understood. They highlight the importance of understanding spiritual abuse and the intersection with DVA in faith-based communities. A detailed discussion of the ways in which spiritual abuse and DVA may manifest is provided, together with observations on the role and responsibilities of faith leaders in providing a more constructive image of intimate partner relationships. The issues raised are pertinent to all faiths and highlight the reluctance of DVA specialist organisations to engage in issues of spirituality and faith identity, when such factors may be vital to many victims'/survivors' recovery.

In Chap. 11, Gudrun Burnet provides an optimistic note on the broadening awareness of different agency capacities to be proactive in responding to situations of DVA. Written from her experiences of working with Peabody Housing, she charts the historical developments and challenges faced by DVA victims/survivors engaging with the housing sector, where various strategies to manage demands for housing have impacted negatively on those seeking to rebuild their lives. However, Peabody has sought to fundamentally change perceptions of the role housing plays in the coordinated community response to DVA, shifting centre stage as a first responder with unique access into the realities of people's lives. Partnership working and multi-agency strategies are also the core focus of Amanda Robinson and Joanne Payton's discussion in Chap. 12, centering on the more formal, statutory arrangements for MARACs in high-risk cases of DVA. They examine the pivotal role of the Independent Domestic Violence Advisor (IDVA) and ongoing contentions regarding the danger of using of risk frameworks to rationalise resources. They also reflect on a fuller embracement of the concept of community as a process of protection, prevention and intervention.

The last two chapters in this collection examine theory, policy, and practice pertaining to DVA perpetrator interventions, a vital component of both European and national frameworks for the prevention and reduction of the harm caused by DVA, yet one which is often neglected in inter-disciplinary and multi-agency discourses. Hilder and Freeman, in Chap. 13, provide an overview of perpetrator programme developments in the UK and the theoretical works that underpin them. They highlight the current diverse array of referral pathways on to perpetrator programmes, as children services and the family courts become more involved in DVA work. They argue that an overemphasis on competing ideas regarding effective and relevant programme content as the core intervention, which will result in behavioural change, can result in both unrealistic and unrealised expectations. It also overlooks desistance frameworks that advocate a more comprehensive approach to perpetrator intervention, taking a much broader look at the various ways in which an individual can be encouraged to adopt a new, non-offending identity. Following this, and the themes that emerge throughout this book as a whole, including calls for a more sophisticated intersectional approach to protection, prevention and intervention strategies, Rebecca Barnes and Catherine Donovan complete this collection in Chap. 14. They make the case for the development of inclusive interventions for abusive partners in Lesbian, Gay, Bisexual, and/or Transgender (LGB and/or T) relationships. Drawing on their findings from their empirical research undertaken on Coral Project, they present an analysis of LGB and/or T experiences of abuse, with a primary focus on practitioner perspectives on the viability of developing interventions for perpetrators from LGB and/or T background.

References

Burke, L., & Collet, S. (2015). *Delivering rehabilitation. The politics, governance and control of probation*. London: Routledge.
Council of Europe. (2011). *Council of Europe Convention on Preventing and Combating Violence against Women and Domestic Violence*. Strasbourg: Council of Europe.
Dobash, R. E., & Dobash, R. P. (Eds.) (1998). *Rethinking violence against women*. London: SAGE.
FitzGibbons, W., & Lea, J. (2014). Defending probation. Beyond privatisation and security. *European Journal of Probation, 6*(1), 24–41.
Hester, M. (2009). *Who does what to whom? Gender and domestic violence perpetrators*. Bristol: University of Bristol and Newcastle, Northern Rock Foundation.
Nash, M. (2010). Singing from the same MAPPA hymn sheet-but can we hear all the voices? In A. Pycroft & D. Gough (Eds.), *Multi-agency working in criminal justice. Control and care in contemporary correctional practice* (pp. 111–122). Bristol: Policy Press.

Part I

Protection

2

Domestic Violence: Applying a Human Rights Discourse

Ronagh McQuigg

Introduction

Arguably one of the inherent failings of societies in addressing the issue of domestic violence effectively is a common reticence to view the commission of such behaviours as a basic violation of a person's human rights. An individual's rights to life, to be free from torture and inhuman or degrading treatment and to respect for private and family life[1] are clearly contravened in the commission of domestic violence. However, it is only relatively recently that domestic violence has been recognised as an issue falling within the ambit of human rights law. Adopting a primarily legal perspective, this chapter will consider why it has taken so long for domestic violence to be recognised as a human rights issue and the

---

[1] From a UK perspective, these rights are afforded by the *Human Rights Act* 1998, which incorporates the majority of the rights found in the European Convention on Human Rights into domestic law.

R. McQuigg (✉)
School of Law, Queen's University of Belfast, Belfast, N. Ireland

© The Editor(s) (if applicable) and The Author(s) 2016
S. Hilder, V. Bettinson (eds.), *Domestic Violence*,
DOI 10.1057/978-1-137-52452-2_2

benefits and challenges of considering it in this vein. An overview of key guidance at the United Nations (UN) level as well as a discussion of developments within regional human rights systems, such as the Council of Europe, is provided.[2] Whilst the European Court of Human Rights (ECtHR) has issued judgments in cases involving domestic violence on a regular basis since 2007, the impact of such a discourse has, at times, been slow to permeate more broadly, as will be highlighted here. The new approach adopted by the Council of Europe (2011) Convention on Preventing and Combating Violence against Women and Domestic Violence (the Istanbul Convention) offers a different legal strategy, with implications for the 18 member states of the Council of Europe that have ratified the Convention so far, at the time of writing. This new provision will also be explored and, in particular, the extent to which a gendered approach has been integrated into a human rights based dialogue at UN and regional levels.

Of course, a human rights framework is not a panacea for addressing the issue of domestic violence, and substantial challenges in the implementation and enforcement of a human rights perspective remain. However, this chapter builds on prior arguments (see Choudhry & Herring, 2006a, 2006b; McQuigg, 2011a, 2012a) that the conceptualisation of domestic violence as a human rights violation has the potential to make an important contribution to the movement to combat domestic violence, albeit its application remains problematic. 'To couch a claim in terms of rights is a major step towards a recognition of a social wrong' (Smart, 1989, p. 143). A human rights discourse provides a level of formality to the claim and to the status of the petitioning victims, or those petitioning on their behalf, recognising them as persons with dignity, demanding fairness. It carries significant symbolic importance, identifying the unjust suffering incurred, as well as occasions when there has been a lack of state recognition of the need to intervene and protect. Addressing the violation of another person's rights by an individual perpetrator is important, but so also is the process of holding to account those responsible for citizen

---

[2] In this chapter, the term 'regional' is used to refer to the three primary regional human rights systems. These are the Council of Europe, the Inter-American system and the African system. Regional human rights systems are relatively independent regimes of human rights protection, which exist alongside international (UN) human rights law.

safety, for their failures to intervene appropriately in domestic violence cases. Human rights cases can, therefore, also place additional pressure on governments to take appropriate further steps in the development of national strategies to combat domestic violence, as well as addressing specific victim experiences.

Recognising Domestic Violence as a Human Rights Issue

The Universal Declaration of Human Rights, which is generally viewed as being the foundation of modern human rights law, was adopted by the UN General Assembly on 10 December 1948. The rights contained in this Declaration were then translated into binding legal obligations in 1966 by the formulation of two treaties, the International Covenant on Civil and Political Rights (ICCPR) and the International Covenant on Economic, Social and Cultural Rights (ICESCR). The European Convention on Human Rights (ECHR) entered into force in 1950. However, it was not until the 1990s that substantive steps were taken towards the recognition of domestic violence as an issue falling within the scope of international human rights law. Most notably, the UN Convention on the Elimination of All Forms of Discrimination against Women (CEDAW), which was adopted in 1979, contained no express mention of domestic violence, or indeed of violence against women more generally. This is unsurprising perhaps, considering the low public profile of domestic violence issues during this time, with any positive actions being driven primarily by feminist activist campaigners and with limited governmental recognition and support. At this time, domestic violence was barely recognised as a relevant issue for any branch of law, let alone human rights law (see Burton, 2008, p. 2).

In addition to the delay in the establishment of domestic violence as a serious harm and potentially criminal matter, the application of a human rights discourse was hindered further by the inherent structure of international human rights law itself. This body of law was constructed to protect individuals from interference by the state. Historically, for example, the ECHR was intended largely to act as a defence against totalitarianism in the wake of the Second World War. In its original formulation, therefore, human rights law contained no obligations on the state to protect one individual from the activities of another individual. Indeed, in situations such as domestic violence, which primarily take place in private, human rights instruments simply had no application. This led to what is commonly known as the public/private dichotomy in international human rights law.[3] The application of human rights law has, however, developed significantly from this early inception. As issues of state oppression have become gradually of less concern, the concept of state responsibility has emerged and with it a duty to exercise 'due diligence' to protect individuals from human rights abuses occurring in the private sphere (see Cook, 1994a). In the context of the Council of Europe, the ECtHR has developed a substantial body of case law on the 'positive obligations' to which state parties to the ECHR are subject (see Mowbray, 2004). These developments have, thus, paved the way for domestic violence to be encompassed within a human rights framework. The relationship, therefore, is one of mutual advantage. Establishing domestic violence as a public matter can lead to an application of human rights arguments to address deficits in a state response and conversely the adoption of a human rights discourse serves to reinforce the acknowledgement of domestic violence as a serious public concern.

Developments within the UN System

The approaches adopted by international human rights instruments to the issue of domestic violence are primarily based on a gendered perspective and are situated essentially in frameworks for addressing violence or discrimination against women. Whilst CEDAW contains no express mention of domestic violence, in 1992, the CEDAW Committee[4] issued General Recommendation 19, which officially interpreted CEDAW

---

[3] For further discussion of the public/private dichotomy in international human rights law, see Romany, 1993, 1994; Cook, 1994b; and Charlesworth & Chinkin, 2000.
[4] The CEDAW Committee is the monitoring body for CEDAW. For further information on the work of the CEDAW Committee, see http://www.ohchr.org/en/hrbodies/cedaw/pages/cedawindex.aspx (accessed 1 July 2015).

2 Domestic Violence: Applying a Human Rights Discourse

as prohibiting violence against women, in both the public and private spheres. The General Recommendation states that, 'The full implementation of the Convention require(s) States to take positive measures to eliminate all forms of violence against women' (CEDAW, 1992, para. 4) and asserts that,

> The definition of discrimination includes gender-based violence, that is, violence that is directed against a woman because she is a woman or that affects women disproportionately.... Gender-based violence may breach specific provisions of the Convention, regardless of whether those provisions expressly mention violence. (para. 6)

The General Recommendation states that gender-based violence may breach, *inter alia*,[5] the right to life; the right not to be subject to torture or to cruel, inhuman or degrading treatment or punishment; and the right to liberty and security of person (para. 7). It also asserts that,

> Under general international law and specific human rights covenants, States may be responsible for private acts if they fail to act with due diligence to prevent violations of rights or to investigate and punish acts of violence, and for providing compensation. (para. 9)

General Recommendation 19 certainly constituted a crucial development in that it served to bring domestic violence and indeed other types of violence against women, within the scope of CEDAW, as a form of discrimination and human rights violation. However, in technical terms, General Recommendations are seen as 'soft law', meaning that they are not legally binding. Manjoo (2014, para. 59), the current UN Special Rapporteur on violence against women, its causes and consequences, has commented that, 'the lack of a legally binding instrument on violence against women precludes the articulation of the issue as a human rights violation in and of itself' and makes it difficult to hold states to account (UN Women, 2012). Regional treaties such as the Istanbul Convention, however, go some way to addressing this and have been developed to

---

[5] *Inter Alia* – Amongst other things.

address explicitly the issue of violence against women, including domestic violence, as discussed later in this chapter.

Notwithstanding the lack of any legally binding treaty, a substantial number of recommendations have now been issued by various UN bodies in relation to domestic violence, such as those found in the 1993 UN General Assembly Declaration on the Elimination of Violence against Women (UN General Assembly, 1993). In addition, the first Special Rapporteur on violence against women (appointed by the UN Commission on Human Rights in 1994) produced a model framework for legislation on domestic violence in 1996, which included recommendations for appropriate state responses, encompassing criminal justice and civil law measures, and the provision of social support measures to victims (Coomaraswamy, 1996).

The Fourth World Conference on Women held in Beijing in 1995 also resulted in detailed recommendations on the measures that states should adopt in response to violence against women, with the Beijing Platform for Action asserting that states should:

> exercise due diligence to prevent, investigate and, in accordance with national legislation, punish acts of violence against women, whether those acts are perpetrated by the State or by private persons. (UN, 1995, para. 124(b))

The CEDAW Committee has also now considered a number of complaints relating to poor state responses to issues of domestic violence[6] under the Optional Protocol procedure that came into force in December 2000, which allows individuals or groups to submit claims of breaches. A strategic response to address issues of domestic violence continues to be intertwined, therefore, with wider issues of violence against women and girls, discrimination and gender equality. A sustained commitment to reducing the prevalence and harm caused by domestic violence is also

---

[6] *AT v Hungary* Communication No.: 2/2003, views adopted 26 January 2005; *Goekce v Austria* Communication No.: 5/2005, views adopted 6 August 2007; *Yildirim v Austria* Communication No.: 6/2005, views adopted 6 August 2007; *VK v Bulgaria* Communication No.: 20/2008, views adopted 25 July 2011; and *Jallow v Bulgaria* Communication No.: 32/2011, views adopted 23 July 2012. Violations of CEDAW were found in all five of these instances.

clearly reliant on proactive correlations between national, regional and international developments.

Regional Developments: The Convention of Belem do Para and the Maputo Protocol

The UN endorsement of domestic violence as an issue that engages fundamental human rights remains immensely significant. However, with no legally binding treaty at the UN level, regional human rights systems, which expressly address violence against women, including domestic violence, are also of great value. The earliest of these instruments, the Inter-American Convention on the Prevention, Punishment and Eradication of Violence against Women (also known as 'the Convention of Belem do Para'), was adopted by the General Assembly of the Organization of American States on 9 June 1994. Although the actual term 'domestic violence' is not to be found in this Convention, it is nevertheless approached as an integral facet of violence against women more generally as stipulated in article 1.[7] Elsewhere across the globe, the Protocol to the African Charter on Human and Peoples' Rights on the Rights of Women in Africa (also known as 'the Maputo Protocol') was adopted by the African Union in 2003, and entered into force in 2005. Again, the term 'domestic violence' is not used in this instrument; however, under article 1(b) of the Protocol, 'violence against women' is defined as encompassing 'all acts perpetrated against women which cause or could cause them physical, sexual, psychological, and economic harm, including the threat to take such acts'. Albeit that the issue of domestic violence is subsumed within more general terminology to end all violence against women, both instruments place a range of duties on state parties as regards to their responses to such issues.

---

[7] Article 1 of the Convention of Belem do Para states that 'For the purposes of this Convention, violence against women shall be understood as any act or conduct, based on gender, which causes death or physical, sexual or psychological harm or suffering to women, whether in the public or the private sphere.'

Regional Developments: Council of Europe Responses

Use of the ECHR

The strategic response of the Council of Europe to domestic violence currently consists primarily of two elements, firstly the results of litigation and the developing case law of the ECtHR, based on the relevant provisions of the ECHR, and secondly the Convention on Preventing and Combating Violence against Women and Domestic Violence (the Istanbul Convention).[8] In relation to the first of these elements, the ECtHR has built up a substantial body of case law on domestic violence in a relatively short space of time.[9] Violations of the right to life under article 2, the right to be free from torture and from inhuman or degrading treatment under article 3, the right to respect for private and family life under article 8 and the prohibition of discrimination under article 14 have all been found in cases involving domestic violence. In the UK context, the rights contained in the ECHR have largely been incorporated into domestic law through the *Human Rights Act* 1998. Section 6(1) of this Act states that, 'It is unlawful for a public authority to act in a way which is incompatible with a Convention right', and under section 7, an individual may bring proceedings against a public authority that has not complied with this duty. The *Human Rights Act* 1998, therefore, requires public authorities such as the government, police, prosecution authorities and courts to take positive steps to protect victims of violence.

There is some evidence that the courts in the UK have recognised domestic violence as a human rights issue, and one example is *McPherson v Secretary of State for the Home Department*.[10] In this case, the appellant and her two children had come to the UK from Jamaica. However, fol-

---

[8] In addition, the Committee of Ministers of the Council of Europe has adopted Resolutions relevant to the issue of domestic violence, most notably Recommendation Rec(2002)5 on the protection of women against violence. Also in 2002, the Parliamentary Assembly of the Council of Europe adopted Resolution 1582 on domestic violence against women.

[9] For a summary of the case law of the European Court of Human Rights on domestic violence, see European Court of Human Rights Press Unit, 2015.

[10] [2001] EWCA Civ 1955 (England and Wales Court of Appeal, Civil Division).

lowing a conviction for an offence of supplying drugs, the appellant and her children were facing deportation. Arguing that a return to Jamaica would place her at a risk of violence from a former partner, the appellant maintained that deportation would be a breach of her rights under articles 3 and 8 of the ECHR. The article 8 claim related to any period of separation and its impact on her relationship with the two children, while the article 3 claim related to her fear of violence from her ex-partner. The Court of Appeal remitted the claims to another adjudicator, as the original adjudicator had made no decision on the article 8 point; however, in doing so Arden L.J. commented that,

> if the appellant were able to show to the requisite standard of proof that the remedies provided under the law of Jamaica against domestic violence were unlikely to be an effective deterrent… she would have shown that her removal from the UK to Jamaica would violate her rights under art 3 of the European Convention on Human Rights. ([2001] EWCA Civ 1955. At para.38)

Whilst the recognition of domestic violence as a serious violation of the appellant's human rights is noted, some of the challenges of a human rights law discourse on domestic violence are immediately apparent, with a burden of proof on the appellant to demonstrate that she would not be adequately protected should she return to her country of origin (see Bishop, Chap. 4, for further discussion of the limitations of legal responses). Realistically, many victims will be unlikely to be able to satisfy such legal requirements, or will be reluctant to pursue such a course of action for fear of reprisals, re-victimisation and the personal intrusions it will incur.

Despite the ongoing challenges of legal redresses, however, the production of a substantial body of ECHR case law on domestic violence remains a noteworthy achievement. The very existence of this case law strengthens the conceptualisation of domestic violence as constituting a human rights issue, and the jurisprudence of the European Court is legally binding on the 47 states that make up the Council of Europe. However, to date, this body of case law has focused almost exclusively on the responses of national criminal justice agencies. The Court has not yet been seen to place duties on states in relation to other aspects of domestic violence intervention, such as, for example, the provision of social support measures for victims. Indeed, courts tend to be somewhat reluctant to enter into the arena of resource allocation. Again, in the UK context, this point is well illustrated by the case of *Oxfordshire County Council v R (on the application of Khan) and another.*[11] In this case, the applicant was a national of Pakistan who was granted leave to enter the UK to join her husband. However, the relationship proved to be a violent one, resulting in the applicant moving into an Oxfordshire refuge. Oxfordshire County Council undertook an assessment of the applicant's needs, pursuant to section 47 of the *National Health Service and Community Care Act* 1990, and recognised that she needed safe and secure accommodation, legal advice and financial support. Her solicitors requested accommodation under section 21 of the *National Assistance Act* 1948, and the provision of financial support under section 2 of the *Local Government Act* 2000. The applicant had no immediate recourse to social funds in the UK and the council responded that she did not meet the criteria for such social support, as she was not suffering from a physical disability, learning disability or mental health condition. In reply to the argument that she was at risk of physical harm from her husband, the council stated that the applicant could take steps to prevent such violence by going to the police or taking out an injunction. Arguments were made that the Council had failed to observe the applicant's rights under articles 3 and 8 of the ECHR (the right to be free from torture and from inhuman or degrading treatment; and the right to respect for private and family life). It was considered whether section 3 of the *Human Rights Act* 1998 required the national assistance and financial support legislation to be interpreted in such a way that a violation of the Convention rights was avoided.[12]

However, the Court of Appeal emphasised 'the extremely limited scope for the operation of articles 3 and 8 in this area' and stated that, 'while Strasbourg has recognised the possibility that article 8 may oblige a State to provide positive welfare support in special circumstances, it has made

---

[11] [2004] EWCA Civ 309.
[12] Article 3(1) of the Human Rights Act states that, 'So far as it is possible to do so, primary legislation and subordinate legislation must be read and given effect in a way which is compatible with the Convention rights'

it plain that neither article 3 nor article 8 imposes such a requirement as a matter of course' (at para. 52). It was held that section 3 of the Human Rights Act did not require the relevant legislation to be interpreted in any special manner (see also McQuigg, 2011a, Chaps. 4 and 5). This case serves to illustrate the difficulties involved in seeking to use a litigation approach to apply human rights discourses to prevention and intervention strategies, as opposed to failures to protect. It also highlights a lack of insight as regards the Council response in relation to the general difficulties that many victims may encounter when seeking to secure criminal or civil measures of protection, such as issues of disempowerment and potential re-victimisation.

Under section 7 of the *Human Rights Act* 1998, an individual who claims that a public authority has not complied with the section 6(1) duty may only bring proceedings against the authority in question if he or she is 'a victim of the unlawful act'. Under both the ECHR and the *Human Rights Act* 1998, the test of standing is very limited, and essentially a party wishing to bring a case under either of these instruments must clearly adhere to a 'victim' status. A high percentage of victims simply may not wish to engage in litigation (see McQuigg, 2011b), and taking a case under the Human Rights Act or to the ECtHR constitutes a daunting prospect. It is unlikely that many individual victims would be willing to adopt this course of action without substantial support being afforded by a specialist domestic violence agency.

There are also wider difficulties relating to the effectiveness of litigation as a method of promoting change. In general, judges can only address the precise issue presented in the case that is before them and they are not able to generalise more broadly on societal matters. The judicial process is costly and slow and only produces changes in the law in very small increments (Epp, 1998, p. 3). An overreliance on adversarial litigation and judicial process to address and promote durable social change, therefore, has profound limitations (Van Schaack, 2004, p. 2307) and such an approach can 'grossly exaggerate the role that lawyers and litigation can play in a strategy for change' (Scheingold, 2004, p. 5; see also McQuigg, 2011a, pp. 16–18). However, it must be remembered that litigation is not the only way of using human rights law, which is a subject to which this discussion now turns.

The Istanbul Convention

Where states are not fulfilling their obligations under human rights law, non-governmental organisations have utilised a human rights discourse to campaign and apply pressure on the state to make greater efforts to address the issues in question.[13] Utilising human rights law without relying on litigation is recognised as a strategy by the Council of Europe. In 2006, a report entitled *Combating Violence against Women: Stocktaking study on the measures and actions taken in Council of Europe member states* (Council of Europe, 2006) was published, which highlighted a number of shortcomings as regards the responses of states to violence against women. A Council of Europe Task Force to Combat Violence against Women, including domestic violence, had also been established and based on the blueprint developed by this task force; a campaign to combat violence against women was launched in November 2006. At the same time, a separate body, the European Committee on Crime Problems (CDPC), carried out a feasibility study regarding a convention on domestic violence, and recommended in June 2007 that such an instrument be adopted (European Committee on Crime Problems (CDPC), 2007). Following the 2006 Task Force's assessment of national measures across Europe, the need for harmonised legal standards was identified to ensure that all European domestic violence victims were afforded the same levels of protection.

In its Final Activity Report, issued in 2008 (Council of Europe Task Force, 2008), it was recommended that the Council of Europe develop a convention on violence against women. In December 2008, the Committee of Ministers of the Council of Europe established an Ad Hoc Committee on Preventing and Combating Violence against Women and Domestic Violence, with the mandate of drafting such an instrument. The resulting draft Convention was adopted by the Committee of Ministers on 7 April 2011 and was opened for signature in Istanbul on 11 May 2011. The Convention on Preventing and Combating Violence against Women and Domestic Violence (or Istanbul Convention) sub-

---

[13] For further discussion of such a strategy, see McQuigg, 2011a, pp. 121–123.

sequently entered into force on 1 August 2014 and has currently been ratified by 18 member states.

Domestic violence is repeatedly separated out as a term within the Convention from violence against women more generally. This relates to a broader issue as to whether a gender-neutral approach should be adopted towards domestic violence or whether a gendered approach is appropriate, a matter which has already raised substantial debate (see Dobash & Dobash, 2004; Kimmel, 2002; Johnson, 2006). It is recognised in the Istanbul Convention that men may be victims of domestic violence and the definition of domestic violence provided in article 3(b)[14] is not gender-specific. Experiences of domestic violence are not, therefore, fully encompassed by the term 'violence against women' alone. Nevertheless, whilst article 2(2) states that, 'Parties are encouraged to apply this Convention to all victims of domestic violence', it is also clarified that 'Parties shall pay particular attention to women victims of gender-based violence in implementing the provisions of this Convention.' In addition, it is stated that, 'This Convention shall apply to all forms of violence against women, including domestic violence, which affect women disproportionately' (article 2(1)). The language of the Convention, therefore, satisfies to some extent the comments made by the CDPC report in 2007, which advised that,

> Even though the majority of victims are women, a convention (on domestic violence) would preferably use gender-neutral terminology. That would not preclude a gender-based analysis of the underlying problem, nor a gender-sensitive implementation of the convention. Furthermore, it would provide the tools to address male victimisation in domestic violence when necessary. (2007, p. 13)

However, the Istanbul Convention's language also recognises that women are more often the victims of such abuse and are likely to experience more disparate economic and social consequences (Chinkin, 2014).

---

[14] 'Domestic violence' is defined as meaning 'all acts of physical, sexual, psychological or economic violence that occur within the family or domestic unit or between former or current spouses or partners, whether or not the perpetrator shares or has shared the same residence with the victim'. Istanbul Convention Article 3b.

The Convention arguably seeks a compromise between a gender-neutral approach, which may be seen as more palatable to a legal and criminal justice audience (for examples within the UK, see Bishop, Chap. 4, this volume) and an approach that conceptualises domestic violence as a form of violence against women only. Nevertheless, violence against women taken as a whole, in all of its forms, constitutes one of the most widespread human rights violations taking place at a global level. It is, therefore, improbable and arguably inappropriate that the adoption of two entirely separate instruments, a gender-neutral convention on domestic violence and a convention on forms of violence against women other than domestic violence, would have constituted a viable approach.

The Istanbul Convention marks a crucial advancement as an instrument that places detailed duties on state parties in terms of developing their responses to domestic violence. For example, articles 12–17 focus specifically on raising public awareness, with the aim of eradicating prejudices and practices that are based on the idea of the inferiority of women. Under article 15, state parties are required to provide training for those professionals working with victims, or those working with the perpetrators of such violence, covering issues such as the detection of violence and the rights and needs of victims. The Convention also addresses the range of support services that should be made available to victims, including legal advice, counselling, financial assistance, housing, education, employment and training (article 20(1)). The need for accessible emergency refuge accommodation is stipulated (article 23), as is the necessity for proactive outreach work to secure victim engagement. Under article 53, there is a requirement that civil law measures, such as restraining orders or protection orders,[15] should be made available to victims.

Detailed consideration is also afforded to how the various national criminal justice systems should respond to the issue of violence against women; for example, the role of law enforcement agencies in securing immediate and adequate protection for victims is specified in article 50. Overall, the responsibilities addressed under the Convention are extremely comprehensive, with monitoring systems for their implementation to be

---

[15] In the UK such measures are referred to as non-molestation orders and occupation orders.

led by a group of experts, provided for under articles 66–70. The primary monitoring mechanism is a reporting procedure, similar in style to those adopted for UN human rights treaties such as CEDAW. Initial and then periodic review reports will be undertaken by states on national measures giving effect to the Convention's provisions.

The adoption of the Istanbul Convention by the Council of Europe constitutes a positive landmark in affirming the magnitude of the problem of violence against women in its various forms. However, the importance of the Convention reaches beyond a purely symbolic role. Although most of the measures referred to in the Convention as regards domestic violence have been previously articulated in documents produced by UN bodies such as the CEDAW Committee, such documents are not legally binding. They, therefore, present a rather insecure foundation upon which to build and sustain progress in reducing the harm caused by domestic violence. Many organisations require more than a moral obligation for action and will not proactively address social issues until legally compelled to do so. Whilst the decisions of the ECtHR are indeed legally binding on all states within the Council of Europe, case law on domestic violence, as illustrated previously, is often limited to an examination of state duties applied in the criminal justice arena, with an onus on the victim to demonstrate that a threat to their safety has been incurred and a duty to protect has been neglected. Other crucial matters, such as the provision of social support measures to victims, have not been addressed. The ECtHR must also restrict itself to considering the specific issue in the case in question. A monitoring body, such as that which is established by the Istanbul Convention, however, is at liberty to adopt a much broader approach, which may be more productive in facilitating positive change and is free to comment on any aspect of state compliance with the Convention. The monitoring mechanisms to be adopted do not rely upon a litigation approach and therefore there is no reliance on the willingness of individual victims to take cases to court. The difficulties surrounding the application of a litigation approach to an 'unseen crime' such as domestic violence are thereby avoided.

Nevertheless, there are a number of potential difficulties, which may serve to hinder the Istanbul Convention's effectiveness. For example, to date, this instrument has been ratified by only 18 of the 47 member states of the Council of Europe. The reluctance to ratify the Convention may be due to the high level of obligations that it places on state parties, requiring significant expenditure and ongoing resourcing. This may be particularly challenging to sustain in the current economic climate. The UK became a signatory to the Convention on 8 June 2012, but it had yet to ratify this instrument at the time of writing this article, despite a commitment to work towards doing so, which was made in the 2014 Action Plan, *A Call to End Violence Against Women and Girls* (Home Office, 2014, p. 36). This delay is seen in part to be due to the need for domestic legislation to be enacted in the UK in order to comply with article 44 of the Convention. This requires state parties to apply the criminal offences encompassed by this instrument to conduct by nationals of the state party when they are abroad. The position is further complicated by the fact that any necessary changes to the criminal law in Scotland and Northern Ireland are matters for the devolved administrations (Joint Committee on Human Rights, 2015, paras. 227–228). Nevertheless, in a report published in February 2015, the Joint Committee on Human Rights[16] highlighted its concern that the delay in ratifying the Istanbul Convention could harm the international reputation of the UK (Joint Committee on Human Rights, 2015, para. 230) for progress in this arena.

The monitoring and enforcement processes of the Convention are also not without their challenges. Operating in a manner similar to monitoring processes for UN human rights treaties, some particular issues might be anticipated relating to the transference of the provisions into national frameworks. For example, commenting on CEDAW, Schopp-Schilling observes that:

> many State Parties have often not addressed issues of legal reform or programmes to improve the material situation of women to enable and empower them to claim, exercise and enjoy their human rights, even if they ratified the CEDAW 15 or 20 years ago. (2007, p. 201)

---

[16] The Joint Committee on Human Rights is appointed by the House of Lords and the House of Commons to consider matters relating to human rights in the UK.

The implementation of human rights standards has been very inconsistent. Even though a state ratifies a human rights treaty, this by no means guarantees that the state in question will comply with the obligations contained therein. The UN has no effective method of forcing states to comply with their duties under international human rights law. Instead, the treaty-monitoring bodies must attempt to persuade states to comply with their duties (Ulrich, 2000, pp. 638–639). However, the majority of states are concerned about their reputations internationally and therefore if a treaty-monitoring body highlights a persistent problem with a state's response to a particular issue, the state in question may be 'shamed' into complying. Nevertheless, if there is no political will to implement human rights standards, there is in reality little that can be done by a treaty-monitoring body to rectify the situation. Reporting procedures are usually the primary method of monitoring state compliance, and such procedures rely on governments to subject their implementation programmes to an objective and critical analysis before compiling their assessments. The absence of any independent supervision can lead to reports being overly optimistic, or complacent in their view of governmental achievements (Fortin, 2003, p. 16). The Istanbul Convention's monitoring mechanisms are likely to encounter similar challenges (see McQuigg, 2012a, 2012b). In addition, unlike the majority of the UN human rights treaties, the Istanbul Convention does not incorporate an individual complaints mechanism. Thus, there is no direct route of access, whereby a single victim of domestic violence may take a complaint alleging that a state is failing to comply with its obligations under the Convention.

Conclusion

It is only relatively recently that domestic violence has been recognised as falling within the scope of human rights law; however, there are now a sizeable number of instruments that address this issue at both international and regional levels. This chapter has focused, in particular, on the response of the Council of Europe to domestic violence. Although the jurisprudence of the ECtHR on this issue is immensely important, it nevertheless suffers from drawbacks that are inherent to the use of a litigation strategy, particularly when addressing an 'unseen crime' such as domestic violence. The adoption of the Istanbul Convention is, therefore, much to be welcomed. In addition, it is notable that this instrument demonstrates a move away from the previous treatment of domestic violence in human rights law as being purely a form of violence against women, although the Convention is still far from gender-neutral in its approach to this issue. As noted earlier in the chapter, although the Convention acknowledges that men may be victims of domestic violence, it also recognises that women are more frequently the victims of such abuse.

A human rights approach is by no means a complete solution to the issue of domestic violence. Indeed, as this chapter has explored, the discourse of human rights faces major challenges, particularly in relation to implementation and enforcement. However, it is nevertheless argued that a rights-based discourse can be used in an effective manner by those seeking to advance the campaign to provide better services and protection for victims and address the risk posed by perpetrators. A human rights discourse recognises victims as being persons with dignity who are seeking justice and it can be used to place additional pressure on governments to adopt further measures and advance national strategies. The evocation of human rights frameworks by campaigners serves to transpose the claims and arguments in question into the language of the law, which can constitute a powerful tool to promote change and influence those in power. Framing claims in legal language may serve in particular to increase support from those working within the legal profession, where understandings of the nature and prevalence of domestic violence remain problematic (see Bishop, Chap. 4). From a UK perspective, the future of the *Human Rights Act* 1998 is currently uncertain, with proposals to replace the Act with a 'UK Bill of Rights' or 'British Bill of Rights'. However, it is notable that the debate centres not on the importance of fundamental human rights law standards, but on how these standards should be interpreted. The majority of those who object to the current human rights system in the UK object to the ways in which the ECtHR interprets and applies the ECHR as regards certain matters, as opposed to objecting to the provisions of the ECHR itself.[17] As Smart (1989, p. 143) correctly

---

[17] The Conservative government's proposals are available online at: https://www.conservatives.com/~/media/files/downloadable%20Files/human_rights.pdf (accessed 20 June 2015).

remarks, 'It is almost as hard to be against rights as it is to be against virtue'. For this reason, the discourse of human rights constitutes a tool of substantial importance, which should not be overlooked in seeking to address victims' rights and reduce the harm caused by domestic violence.

References

Burton, M. (2008). *Legal responses to domestic violence*. Abingdon: Routledge-Cavendish.

Charlesworth, H., & Chinkin, C. (2000). *The boundaries of international law – A feminist analysis*. Manchester: Manchester University Press.

Chinkin, C. (2014). Addressing violence against women in the Commonwealth within states' obligations under international law. *Commonwealth Law Bulletin, 40*, 471—4501.

Choudhry, S., & Herring, J. (2006a). Domestic violence and the Human Rights Act 1998: A new means of legal intervention. *Public Law, 2006*, 752–784.

Choudhry, S., & Herring, J. (2006b). Righting domestic violence. *International Journal of Law, Policy and the Family, 20*, 95–119.

Committee on the Elimination All Forms of of Discrimination Against Women. (1992). General Recommendation No.19, U.N. Doc. A/47/38.

Cook, R. J. (1994a). State responsibility for violations of women's human rights. *Harvard Human Rights Journal, 7*, 125–175.

Cook, R. J. (1994b). Women's international human rights law: The way forward. In R. J. Cook (Ed.), *Human rights of women – National and international perspectives*. Philadelphia: University of Pennsylvania Press.

Coomaraswamy, R. (1996). *A framework for model legislation on domestic violence*. E/CN.4/1996/53/Add.2.

Council of Europe. (2006). *Combating Violence against Women: Stocktaking study on the measures and actions taken in Council of Europe member states*. Strasbourg: Directorate of Human Rights.

Council of Europe. (2008). Council of Europe Task Force to Combat Violence against Women, including domestic violence EG-TFV 6. Retrieved July 1, 2015, from http://www.coe.int/t/dg2/equality/domesticviolencecampaign/Source/Final_Activity_Report.pdf

Council of Europe. (2011). *Council of Europe Convention on Preventing and Combating Violence against Women and Domestic Violence*. Strasbourg: Council of Europe.

Dobash, R. P., & Dobash, R. E. (2004). Women's violence to men in intimate relationships: Working on a puzzle. *British Journal of Criminology, 44,* 324–349.
Epp, C. R. (1998). *The rights revolution.* Chicago and London: University of Chicago Press.
European Committee on Crime Problems. (2007). *Feasibility study for a convention against domestic violence.* Strasbourg: Council of Europe.
European Court of Human Rights Press Unit. (2015). *Factsheet – Domestic violence.* Retrieved June 20, 2015, from http://www.echr.coe.int/Documents/FS_Domestic_violence_ENG.pdf
Fortin, J. (2003). *Children's rights and the developing law.* London: Butterworths.
Home Office. (2014). *A call to end violence against women and girls: Action Plan 2014.* Retrieved July 2, 2015, from https://www.gov.uk/government/uploads/system/uploads/attachment_data/file/287758/VAWG_Action_Plan.pdf
Human Rights Act 1998 C42. Retrieved October 12, 2015, from http://www.legislation.gov.uk/ukpga/1998/42/contents
Johnson, M. P. (2006). Conflict and control: Gender symmetry and asymmetry in domestic violence. *Violence Against Women, 12,* 1003–1018.
Joint Committee on Human Rights. (2015). *Violence against women and girls, sixth report of session 2014–2015.* London: The Stationery Office Limited. Retrieved July 2, 2015, from http://www.publications.parliament.uk/pa/jt201415/jtselect/jtrights/106/106.pdf
Kimmel, M. S. (2002). "Gender symmetry" in domestic violence: A substantive and methodological research review. *Violence Against Women, 6,* 1332–1363.
Local Government Act 2000 C22. Retrieved October 12, 2015, from http://www.legislation.gov.uk/ukpga/2000/22/contents
Manjoo, R. (2014). *Report of the Special Rapporteur on violence against women, its causes and consequences to the UN General Assembly.* U.N. Doc. A/69/368.
McQuigg, R. (2011a). *International human rights law and domestic violence.* Abingdon: Routledge.
McQuigg, R. (2011b). The victim test under the Human Rights Act 1998 and its implications for domestic violence cases. *European Human Rights Law Review, 3,* 294–303.
McQuigg, R. (2012a). What potential does the Council of Europe convention on violence against women hold as regards domestic violence? *International Journal of Human Rights, 16,* 947–962.
McQuigg, R. (2012b). A contextual analysis of the Council of Europe's convention on preventing and combating violence against women. *International Human Rights Law Review, 1,* 367–381.

Mowbray, A. R. (2004). *The development of positive obligations under the European Convention on Human Rights by the European court of human rights.* Oxford: Hart Publishing.
National Assistance Act 1948 c29. Retrieved from October 12, 2015, from http://www.legislation.gov.uk/ukpga/Geo6/11-12/29/contents
National Health Service and Community Care Act 1990 C19. Retrieved from October 12, 2015, from http://www.legislation.gov.uk/ukpga/1990/19/contents
Romany, C. (1993). Women as aliens: A feminist critique of the public/private distinction in international human rights law. *Harvard Human Rights Journal,* 6, 87–125.
Romany, C. (1994). State responsibility goes private: A feminist critique of the public/private distinction in international human rights law. In R. J. Cook (Ed.), *Human rights of women – National and international perspectives.* Philadelphia: University of Pennsylvania Press.
Scheingold, S. A. (2004). *The politics of rights: Lawyers, public policy, and political change.* Ann Arbor: University of Michigan Press.
Schopp-Schilling, H. B. (2007). Treaty body reform: The case of the committee on the elimination of discrimination against women. *Human Rights Law Review,* 7, 201–224.
Smart, C. (1989). *Feminism and the power of law.* London: Routledge.
Ulrich, J. L. (2000). Confronting gender-based violence with international instruments: Is a solution to the pandemic within reach? *Indiana Journal of Global Legal Studies,* 7, 629–654.
UN General Assembly. (1993). *Declaration on the Elimination of Violence against Women.* A/RES/48/104.
UN (1995) Platform for Action and the Beijing Declaration. Fourth world Conference on Women: Beijing, China 4–15 September 1995. New York: department of Public Information. United Nations.
UN Women. (2012). *Needed: Specific international legally binding instrument on violence against women,* November 1, 2012. Retrieved July 3, 2015, from http://www.unwomen.org/en/news/stories/2012/11/needed-specific-international-legally-binding-instrument-on-violence-against-women
Van Schaack, B. (2004). With all deliberate speed: Civil human rights litigation as a tool for social change. *Vanderbilt Law Review,* 57, 2305–2348.

3

A Fresh Approach to Policing Domestic Violence

Mandy Burton

Introduction

This chapter will examine the policing of domestic violence in England and Wales over the past three decades, with a particular focus on Her Majesty's Inspectorate of Constabulary (HMIC) report 2014 and the introduction of the Domestic Violence Protection Notice and Orders (DVPN/Os). It will highlight the ongoing challenges of establishing domestic violence as core police work despite the shift towards police-led, multi-agency responses to domestic violence from the 1990s onwards. Despite these improvements, there are still concerns about the adequacy of police interventions in domestic violence cases and attitudes and responses within the organisation, particularly at a frontline officer level. HMIC (2014) reported that the police are still failing victims in too many cases, for example, by missing opportunities to gather evidence to support a prosecution. The dynamics of domestic violence remain

---

M. Burton (✉)
Leicester Law School, University of Leicester, Leicester, UK

© The Editor(s) (if applicable) and The Author(s) 2016
S. Hilder, V. Bettinson (eds.), *Domestic Violence*,
DOI 10.1057/978-1-137-52452-2_3

poorly understood and a persistence of certain cultural attitudes within the police service continues to underplay its seriousness. This chapter will examine the continuing obstacles to effective police interventions and consider whether the police can do more to improve the situation of victims of domestic violence and abuse. The new tools of the policing armoury to tackle domestic violence, the DVPN/O emergency protection orders, are civil in nature. The question arises as to whether these new powers constitute a positive innovation in the policing of domestic violence and abuse, or a retrograde step to treating the issue as a non-criminal matter. This chapter will review the limited evidence to date.

Historical Weaknesses in the Policing of Domestic Violence

The relationship between policing and the political and social structures of the time is a complex one. However, it can certainly be argued that the lack of police commitment to addressing domestic violence in the early and mid-twentieth century was a reflection of the broader dismissal of the issue across society as a whole. However, as issues of gender equality and the incidence of women experiencing violence in the domestic sphere started to permeate the social consciousness, the police reaction has remained somewhat lethargic and has often failed to keep pace. Historically, the police did not consider tackling domestic violence to be 'real' police work and remained largely indifferent to the problem throughout the 1980s (Dobash & Dobash, 1979; Groves & Thomas, 2014). In cases where the police did attend the scene of a domestic violence incident and if the perpetrator was present, they might attempt mediation, which essentially sought to encourage reconciliation. The removal of the perpetrator through arrest was not a priority; rather, the emphasis was on trying to preserve the family unit. As domestic violence was not viewed as a crime, but as a civil or private matter, it is, perhaps, not surprising that the police did not perceive arrest and prosecution to be appropriate responses (Edwards, 1989). In Edwards' study of the policing of domestic violence in the 1980s, one of the main reasons that the police gave for refusing to make arrests was the anticipation of the victim's withdrawal. The police emphasised that the victim needed to support an arrest and prosecution in order for it to be successful. Edwards observed that the police appeared to have little understanding of why victims might find it difficult to continue with a prosecution (Edwards, 1989, p. 104). Unfortunately, she found that the negative stereotyping of victims and victim-blaming attitudes contributed to a poor police response. Edwards was not alone in documenting such failings. For example, Bourlet (1990), a former police officer turned academic, described similar attitudes and barriers to effective police interventions.

The issues emerging in the 1980s and the impact of the growing body of feminist research and campaigns highlighting violence against women as a substantial social and legal problem (Schneider, 2000)[1] resulted in significant policy developments in policing from the 1990s onwards. Notably, they aimed at encouraging the police to use their powers under the criminal law to arrest perpetrators of domestic violence (Home Office, 1990). In policy terms, the message was unequivocally conveyed that domestic violence was a crime to be treated like any other in the way it was to be recorded and investigated. For the first time, specialisation in domestic violence was recommended, and domestic violence training was implemented to ensure police officers were aware of their powers and responded sympathetically and with an understanding of the situations victims faced. However, the translation of policy into practice proved to be difficult (Grace, 1995).

Although in the 1990s some police forces began to introduce specialist units to deal with domestic violence, the trend to specialisation was 'slow to take off' (Burton, 2008, p. 91). It also proved to be a double-edged sword in that whilst many victims reported positive experiences when being dealt with by specialists, the mainstream frontline response of non-specialist officers continued to be poor (Grace, 1995). On many occasions, it was reported that frontline police officers still sought to deal with domestic violence as a breach of the peace matter at most, seeking to simply try and calm the situation, but with no arrest being made

---

[1] It has been suggested that victims' rights became a guise for crime control initiatives (Roach, 1999) and changes to law and practice were not, in reality, focused on better support or outcomes for victims.

(Grace, 1995). The development of a comprehensive training strategy for all police officers was recommended (Plotinikoff & Woolfson, 1998), as were more clearly defined priorities for domestic violence specialists and more effective lines of accountability to ensure that policies were implemented in practice.

A controversial issue emerging from the literature on the policing of domestic violence is the extent to which a patriarchal police culture, with negative stereotyping of 'undeserving' victims, has played a role in explaining low arrest rates. Whilst Edwards (1989) had described a culture that was hostile to victims who might be perceived to have provoked their own demise, by 'nagging' or poor housekeeping, for example, Hoyle (1998) challenged this interpretation. Hoyle argued that negative stereotyping was not the key to understanding inaction, but rather that it occurred as a result of a gap between the expectations of the police and the expectations and wishes of victims. Hoyle (1998) argued that many victims did not want prosecution to follow an arrest and thus it should not be assumed that non-enforcement of the criminal law was a police failing in domestic violence cases. However, there was much more that needed to be achieved to ensure that the police recognised the significance of frequent call-outs: in terms of risk and escalation, the causes of any victim reluctance to engage and the impact of domestic violence on children.

In 2000, the Home Office revised the domestic violence circular to police, strengthening the pro-arrest policy (Home Office, 2000). The policy emphasised the need for effective evidence gathering, so that the police did not just rely on the victim's statement but gathered all available evidence. Gathering supportive evidence can be useful not just in cases where the victim withdraws his or her support for the prosecution, but to enhance cases where the victim wants the prosecution to proceed (Ellison, 2003). As such, 'effective' or 'enhanced' evidence gathering is not necessarily inconsistent with the idea of allowing the victim to express a view on the case proceeding, which may, subject to the wider public interest, be determinative. Pursuing a prosecution against a victim's wishes has been the subject of some controversy and the impact of any public interest decision to prosecute must always have fully considered the implications of proceeding on the victim's safety.

Her Majesty's Crown Prosecution Service Inspectorate (HMCPSI) and HMIC (2004) inspection, however, found that in the years immediately following Home Office Circular 1999/2000, the message about effective evidence gathering was not fully understood and translated into practice (HMCPSI and HMIC, 2004). Evidence such as the recordings of the initial emergency call, medical evidence of injuries, statements from neighbours and other independent witnesses, photos of injuries and CCTV footage are all potentially valuable to the prosecution. However, the inspectors found that these types of evidence were not being routinely gathered and the quality of evidence supporting the victim's statement was generally inadequate. Further examination revealed that these concerns were not limited to the evidence-gathering stage and the inspectors identified problems from the outset with the police response, starting with the way in which call handlers graded incidents (HMCPSI and HMIC, 2004).

The initial response by the call handler is one of the most crucial decision-making points for the police. In a dangerous, potentially life-threatening situation, the victim requires an immediate response. However, in 2004, the inspectors found that, in some of the police services examined, call handlers were regularly undergrading the importance of the call and victims had to call again and/or wait several hours for police attendance (HMCPSI and HMIC, 2004). The tragic consequences of this in more recent years can be seen in the case of Joanna Michael who was killed by her former partner. Ms. Michael had initially called the police when her former partner attended her home and threatened to kill her. If the police had responded immediately to this emergency call, her life might have been saved; however, due to failings by two police services, there was a delay in the police attending. When they finally sent officers to her address in response to Ms. Michael's second emergency call, they found her dead. A recent Supreme Court decision determined that there should be no liability in negligence for the police failure to act in this case (Michael and others v Chief Constable of South Wales and another [2015] UKSC2).[2] This result was, perhaps, predictable given the

---

[2] Michael and others v Chief Constable of South Wales and another [2015] UKSC2, judgement available online at: https://www.supremecourt.uk/decided-cases/docs/UKSC_2013_0043_Judgment.pdf accessed on October 25, 2015.

earlier decisions in *Hill and Van Colle* and *Smith* (Burton, 2009).[3] Yet, as Lady Hale in the minority suggests, this outcome is open to challenge. The police could be held liable in cases where proximity[4] is established, where they knew or ought to have known of an imminent threat of death or injury to a particular individual, which they could have prevented. Lady Hale observes 'It is difficult indeed to see how recognising the possibility of such claims could make the task of policing any more difficult than it already is. It might conceivably, however, lead to some much needed improvements in their response to threats of serious domestic abuse' (Michael and others [2015] at para 198). Lady Hale supports this statement with reference to the recent HMIC report (2014) to reinforce that further advancements in police practice are still required.

Contemporary Weaknesses in the Policing of Domestic Violence: All Too Familiar

The HMIC (2014) inspection reveals very little progress from the previous HMCPSI and HMIC (2004) inspection a decade earlier. The central theme of both the inspections is the gap between policy and practice. On paper what the police say they are going to do is often good, but far too frequently what they actually do is inadequate. The HMIC (2014) reviewed the effectiveness of the police approach to domestic violence to ascertain, in particular, whether victims deemed at future risk are appropriately managed and whether the police have learnt from past experiences. Had they been proactive in adapting their approach or were further changes still needed (HMIC, 2014)? The inspectors, who comprised a multi-disciplinary team including specialist non-government organisations (NGOs), reviewed data from all 43 police services across

---

[3] In *Hill* v Chief Constable of West Yorkshire (1989) AC 53, the family of the last victim of Peter Sutcliffe (the 'Yorkshire ripper') sought unsuccessfully to establish police negligence in failing to prevent her murder. In *Van Colle* and *Smith* (2008) UKHL 50, a claim for negligence was rejected, where a man was seriously assaulted by his former partner in circumstances where the police had failed to act on previous complaints of threatened violence.

[4] 'Proximity' requires the police to be aware of a specific threat to a particular victim, but even in cases where this might be established, claims for negligence have failed on policy grounds (Burton, 2009).

England and Wales, analysing a sample of case files, surveying the views of specialist domestic abuse partner agencies and gathering the views of victims through surveys and focus groups. They concluded that whilst there were pockets of good practice and partnership initiatives, 'the overall police response to victims of domestic abuse is not good enough' (HMIC, 2014, p. 6). The inspectorate found that 'in too many forces there are weaknesses in the service provided to victims; some of these are serious and this means that victims are put at unnecessary risk' (HMIC, 2014, p. 6).

Some of the more specific findings from the 2014 study were also disturbingly familiar. The inspectorate stated that there are still 'alarming' weaknesses in the collection of police evidence. The case file analysis revealed missed opportunities in the golden hour immediately following the incident, with, for example, less than half of all cases surveyed including photographs of the victim or crime scene (HMIC, 2014, p. 58). The inspectors also commented on the underuse or ineffective use of body cameras and insufficient consideration being given to the value of house-to-house inquiries. Ironically, the cases where victim withdrawal was anticipated and therefore most likely to require additional evidence if a prosecution was to be pursued were those less likely to be thoroughly investigated (HMIC, 2014, p. 60).

According to the inspectorate, whilst the initial call handling in domestic violence cases has improved over the past decade, problems remain in that some police services do not have adequate systems and processes in place for identifying repeat victims and giving adequate information about the case to police officers attending the scene (HMIC, 2014, p. 46). This finding demonstrates that the problems present in the Michael case are still apparent and are not isolated to the two police services involved, but can be found across all police services in varying degrees. The inspectorate also found that 'significant improvements are required in the initial response' of frontline police officers attending the scene (HMIC, 2014, pp. 47–48). Whilst there were many victims who said that they had been dealt with in a supportive and sympathetic way, other observations echoed Edward's research of three decades ago (Edwards, 1987, 1989), in that the inspectorate received reports of unacceptable attitudes being displayed by officers. This included appearing not to take the incident seriously, a lack of empathy and being judgemental about the victim (HMIC, 2014, pp. 49–51). Whilst the inspectorate concludes that some of these issues may stem from police officers' frustration about their ability to have any significant impact in domestic abuse cases (HMIC, 2014, p. 52), the report also observes that the poor management and supervision of officers means that the 'right behaviours, attitudes and actions' are not being reinforced across all professional levels. Frontline officers in particular often lack the skills and knowledge to deal 'confidently and competently' with victims and the senior management practices across the organisation do not serve to address this. The profile of domestic violence work within police services continues to imply that many officers view it less seriously than other areas of policing and the inspectorate concluded that policing domestic abuse was still the 'poor relation' to other types of crime, with 'little kudos' or recognition of the achievements of domestic abuse specialists (HMIC, 2014, p. 67).

HMIC (2014) made 11 recommendations for changes that would improve the handling of domestic violence by police services. Progress will be charted by a national oversight and monitoring group set up to review the implementation of the inspectorate's recommendations over a 12-month period (HMIC, 2014, p. 19). Every police service has been encouraged to publish a detailed action plan that stipulates how it will improve performance in line with the examples of best practice identified by the HMIC. Senior managers within the police services were also recommended to review how they will ensure that policy is reflected in practice. This is to include an assessment of their service's organisational culture and attitudes towards domestic violence, recognising and rewarding good police practice in this area to make certain that the police response to domestic abuse is prioritised and valued (HMIC, 2014, p. 20). Improvements to data collection were also recommended, including the application of evaluation methods to capture victims' views of their experience with the police as part of a monitoring and development process. HMIC (2014) recommended that the College of Policing should take into account the findings of the inspection whilst updating its practice standards for the policing of domestic abuse and reiterate the protocols for matters, such as effective evidence gathering, positive action and arrest and risk assessment. It was also advised that the College of Policing undertake a comprehensive review of domestic violence training available to officers of all grades. Training should be face-to-face, rather than facilitated by an online training pack and should provide an informed professional with a detailed understanding of the complex dynamics of domestic abuse, which challenges poor attitudes, commonly held myths and stereotypes. The inspectorate recognises, however, that 'training alone will not address this vitally important issue of officers' negative attitudes, insensitivity and lack of understanding and a call is made for "robust supervision" to "reinforce the attitudes and behaviours expected of officers"' (HMIC, 2014, p. 3). Further recommendations relate to best practice with serial offenders, the approach to be taken to homicide reviews and the need for a further examination of how police services work together with other agencies to tackle domestic abuse (HMIC, 2014, pp. 24–25).

Whilst partnership forums and strategies may lead to the police becoming involved in prevention measures, their primary role remains one of protection. In this respect, a key challenge for the police has been to identify those victims who are at greatest risk of serious harm and ensure that their policies and practices are effective in protecting 'high-risk' victims, by mobilising resources promptly and effectively. In recent years, considerable efforts have gone into developing multi-agency arrangements, such as Multi-Agency Risk Assessment Conferences (MARACs), to improve risk assessment and victim safety strategies. The information that the police hold and their powers to intervene are vital to such a process and the MARAC system could not function effectively without police cooperation (Brookman & Robinson, 2012; also see Robinson and Payton, Chap. 12, this volume). In the 2014 HMIC review, there is surprisingly little focus on other innovative approaches to the policing of domestic violence. There have, however, been pockets of innovation and development by the police in this area. Earlier initiatives, for example, have aimed at reducing repeat victimisation through a graded police response. The Killingbeck model used by Yorkshire police in the 1990s aimed to reduce repeat victimisation by a three-tier graded response dependent on the history of interventions in a domestic violence case (Hamner, Griffiths, & Jerwood, 1999). In cases where a situation of domestic violence had a known history with the police and other intervening agencies, it would be allocated to a higher tier where further additional strategies to ensure the victim's safety might be pursued. Where appropriate and with the victim's consent, this might include the instigation of a neighbourhood 'cocoon watch' to enlist the help of neighbours, family and other agencies in contacting the police if further incidents occurred. In a review of the policing of domestic violence by Westmarland, Thornby, Wistow, and Gadd (2014), it has been argued that graded response interventions have shown some benefits and it is advocated that the Killingbeck model should be 're-examined in a contemporary context' (Westmarland et al., 2014, p. 4).

There are undoubtedly some pockets of good practice in criminal justice interventions, which could be developed further if there were resources and the will to do so. Yet, certain questions remain: Why 25 years after Home Office Circular 1990 does HMIC find that the police response to domestic violence is still unacceptably poor? Placing the issues of knowledge, attitudes and understandings of domestic violence to one side momentarily, the police approach is also driven by the application of legal procedure. One argument may be, therefore, that the inadequacies of the police response also stem from the criminal law itself, which is largely a lost cause or blunt instrument in domestic violence cases (see Bishop, Chap. 4, this volume). If so, can the use of civil law remedies offer the police more effective opportunities to ensure victim safety? The police in England and Wales now have powers to issue short-term protection orders, or DVPNs, which can exclude the perpetrator of domestic violence from a home shared with a victim for a period of 48 hours. The idea behind these notices is to give the police time to apply to the magistrates' court for a longer barring order, or DVPOs, by which the magistrates can exclude the perpetrator from the family home for up to 28 days. DVPOs are civil orders, granted on the balance of probabilities and with civil sanctions for breach. As a departure from the traditional criminal justice approach, to what extent do these new orders provide the police with a fresh opportunity to improve their response to domestic violence?

Domestic Violence Prevention Orders: A New Approach to Policing Domestic Violence?

The Crime and Security Act 2010 introduced DVPNs and DVPOs. Initially, the orders were piloted in three areas of England and Wales and subject to an evaluation commissioned by the Home Office. The pilot evaluation suggested that the new orders were beneficial and, in particular, that, in some cases, they may help to reduce repeat victimisation (Kelly Kelly, Alder, Howarth, Lovett, Coulson, Kernohan and Gray, 2013). Consequently, the decision was taken to roll out the orders nationally, and since 2014, the police have been able to issue and apply for DVPNs and DVPOs across England and Wales.

The legislative framework for the orders makes it clear that they can be made without the consent of the victim, although the guidance accompanying the legislation says that the victim's wishes should be taken into account (Home Office, 2011). To issue a DVPN, the authorising police officer, who must be of the rank of superintendant, must have reasonable grounds for believing that violence has been used, or threatened by the perpetrator against an 'associated person', and that the making of the order is 'necessary' to protect the victim from violence, or the threat of violence. Once the police have issued a DVPN, they can apply to the magistrates' court for a DVPO and the DVPN will continue until such time as the application is determined. The grounds for the courts making a DVPO are the same as the DVPN and if the magistrates make the order, it can be for the duration of 14–28 days.

When the orders were first introduced, some commentators speculated that they might be used as an inappropriate substitute for the criminal law (Crompton, 2014; see Bettinson, Chap. 5, this volume). In most instances, what could be achieved by a DVPN could probably also be achieved by arresting and bailing the perpetrator. Bail conditions can be imposed to exclude the perpetrator from an area where the victim lives and additionally can order no contact with the victim (subject to the requirements of the *Bail Act 1976* being met). Such conditions, in theory, might be more effective than a DVPN in keeping the perpetrator away from the victim in that a breach of bail conditions is a criminal offence. There are no criminal sanctions for breach of DVPNs and DVPOs. Assuming that effective sanctions are a prerequisite for orders to be effective, the lack of criminal sanctions for breach might be regarded as problematic. In fact, some of the participants in Kelly et al.'s (2013) evaluation study remarked on the desirability of stronger sanctions for breach, and the authors recommended that consideration should be given to criminalisation of breaches of DVPOs. However, there are practical and theoretical objections to using the criminal law as an enforcement mechanism for civil orders (Burton, 2003). It is also useful to remember that DVPNs and DVPOs may have been issued without the consent of the victim and as such the victim's autonomy has already potentially been undermined in the issuing of the order. Enforcing a civil order through criminal sanctions without the agreement of the victim could put the victim at greater risk of reprisals or, if the sanction is a fine, might result in the victim and perhaps children of the family suffering to pay a penalty for the breach of an order designed for their own protection. Civil sanctions also include fines and imprisonment for contempt but, in theory, are under the greater control of the victim. Ultimately, the practical obstacles to using the criminal law to enforce a DVPO against the victim's wishes would probably mean that in most cases criminal sanctions would not be applied to breaches even if those powers existed. The prosecution of such a breach would often rely on the victim reporting and giving evidence, which may not be forthcoming (Burton, 2015).

Thus, as civil orders with civil sanctions for breach, the police are arguably being diverted down a very different route in this approach to domestic violence cases. One of the most enduring complaints about the police approach, to date, has been that they have treated domestic violence as a civil rather than a criminal matter, advising victims to see a solicitor and secure a civil remedy rather than pursuing a legal redress via the criminal law (Edwards, 1989). The message to the police for the past 25 years, therefore, has been to arrest and prosecute domestic violence perpetrators and the application for an emergency civil protection order to facilitate a "breathing space" in a scenario of domestic abuse might be seen as a retrograde step. Alternatively, however, in view of the failings of the criminal justice system to respond effectively in many cases of domestic violence, the idea of creating some space for the victim to consider longer term safety planning may be a more realistic and attractive proposal for many. The Home Office guidance actually suggests a hybrid approach, where emergency protection orders supplement the criminal law rather than replace it, stipulating that it is 'essential' that criminal offences be 'thoroughly investigated and actively pursued' (Home Office, 2011, para 3.3.2). The potential added value of the DVPO, therefore, is likely to occur for cases where no criminal prosecution can be brought, or where the high threshold applied to assessing risk under the *Bail Act 1976* has resulted in the defendant being arrested but then being bailed without any conditions, enabling a further layer of protection to be applied.

The extent to which DVPOs were being used as a replacement measure by the police as an alternative to the pursuit of an arrest and possible criminal prosecution was not addressed by the pilot evaluation. It would be extremely difficult to assess, but arguably is very important. If DVPOs are being sought in cases where the police should be prosecuting for a criminal offence, the protection offered to victims by the law may be undermined. Whilst the effectiveness of the criminal law as an effective protective measure is disputed, as has already been highlighted here, the pursuit of criminal proceedings also serves an important symbolic function. Pro-arrest and pro-prosecution policies are often advocated on the basis that they send out a message that domestic violence is serious and a matter of public interest. As such, perpetrators must be held to account for their actions via criminal proceedings. The symbolic power of the DVPO is much weaker. It might be argued, therefore, that they are effectively a sophisticated step towards the decriminalisation of domestic violence. However, such concerns are counterbalanced, to an extent, by the practical value of the measures, as demonstrated by the empirical research that supported their implementation.

The effectiveness of barring orders has been the subject of empirical research in other jurisdictions, albeit somewhat limited, for example, in Austria and Germany (Burton, 2015). The barring orders of other European Countries are similar to DVPOs in some respects and served as a catalyst for their introduction in England and Wales. However, at the time of writing this chapter, the empirical research on DVPOs in England and Wales is restricted to the pilot study alone. Kelly et al. (2013) examined the implementation of the DVPNs and DVPOs across the three pilot areas in England and Wales over a 15-month period. During that time, 487 DVPNs were authorised by the police and 414 DVPOs were issued by the courts. It is difficult to ascertain whether this reflects an appropriate use of the orders; however, the researchers identified a number of obstacles that may have prevented the orders from being more fully utilised, which are discussed more fully later in the text. In addition, there was a wide variation in the use of the orders across the three sites in the study, suggesting that the criteria for the orders may have been variably interpreted, with some areas using them more effectively than others. The authors report that the explanation of the variation is unclear (Kelly et al., 2013, p. 11).

There were three main factors attributed to the possible underutilisation of DVPNs and DVPOs: firstly, the level of authorisation required for a DVPN, secondly, the short duration of the DVPN and, thirdly, the cultural attitudes of the police. It has already been observed previously here that authorisation for a DVPN must be by a police officer of the rank of superintendant. Kelly et al. note that this 'was an issue of contention throughout the pilot' (Kelly et al., 2013. p. 21). The problem with this high level of authorisation is that senior officers might not always be available and some junior officers may feel inhibited about asking them to authorise a DVPN. This is not an insurmountable obstacle to the more effective use of DVPNs, as the level of authorisation could be reduced or, if junior officers do not want to approach superintendants, an intermediate layer of authorisation could be introduced (Kelly et al., 2013, pp. 43–44). The short duration of the DVPN, just 48 hours, also meant that officers did not have long to prepare an application for a DVPO and in some cases, the application could not be heard by specialist magistrates in a specialist domestic violence court (SDVC), because the courts did not sit frequently enough (see Bettinson, Chap. 5, this volume). The original plan was that specialist magistrates would hear applications because they are best placed, given their training, to understand the context of domestic violence. Some of respondents in the study stated that non-specialist magistrates appeared to apply a higher criminal standard of proof to the making of a DVPO than the civil balance of probabilities test, which should apply in civil proceedings.

Kelly et al. (2013) observe that there are two ways of trying to overcome the range of problems caused by the short duration of the DVPN. Firstly, in the short-term, emphasis could be given to training all magistrates so that it is, perhaps, less important for applications for DVPOs to be dealt with in the SDVC. In fact, very few applications for DVPOs were refused by magistrates during the pilot period. The problem of non-specialist magistrates hearing applications does not, therefore, appear to be as significant as making sure that the police have adequate time to prepare their applications. In the medium term, the authors suggest that the duration of the DVPN might be extended to 4 or even up to 7 days (Kelly et al., 2013, p. 11).

Changing the process for gaining authorisation for DVPNs and extending the duration of notices will only have an impact, however, if there is a culture amongst the police, which is supportive of DVPNs and DVPOs. Kelly et al., (2013). found that majority, 64 % of the police officer respondents in their study, were positive about DVPNs and DVPOs in principle and were generally supportive of their use. This is a significant finding, as the provision of new practice directives and the granting of additional police powers does not always guarantee that they will be implemented, as the earlier inspection reports discovered. For any new measure to be successful, there needs to be support for the approach at a practical, frontline decision-making level. It was anticipated that DVPNs and DVPOs might be particularly useful in cases where the police had significant concerns about an individual's safety, but were unable to make an arrest because a criminal offence had not been committed; or where there was no reasonable suspicion that an offence was about to be committed under the grounds of *s 24 PACE ACT 1984*. This might, for example, relate to psychological abuse, where the victim is experiencing severe distress, but where, traditionally, the criminal law has struggled to accommodate coercive control that may not include the use of physical violence. However, whether DVPNs and DVPOs can plug a gap in the protection offered to victims remains doubtful, given the negative cultural attitudes illustrated by some of the other police officers in Kelly et al.'s (2013) study, together with the more generalised issues of frontline police officers' lack of understanding of domestic violence illustrated in the HMIC reports cited previously.

A minority of officers in the study viewed DVPNs and DVPOs as 'disproportionate', especially for low-level violence and the researchers observed that there is a need for further training to address police officers' mind sets in relation to domestic violence and, in particular, tendencies to minimise the seriousness of non-physical violence (Kelly et al., 2013, p. 20). However, as the comparative analysis of the HMIC in 2004 and the HMIC of 2014 demonstrates, police culture is notoriously difficult to change. It is also worth reflecting that there may be a gap between what police officers say and what they do (Waddington, 1999). Negative banter about domestic violence does not always mean inaction in practice, with police officers behaving more responsibly to individual cases, whilst they may continue to collude with negative stereotypes informally with colleagues at other times. Nevertheless, it is discouraging to find that only just over two-thirds of the police respondents in the DVPO pilot felt that domestic violence 'was a 'public matter' (69 %) and that positive action should be taken (63 %) (Kelly et al., 2013, p. 20).

Despite the concerns regarding the police implementation of the DVPNs and DVPOs, the findings of Kelly et al.'s (2013) study are supportive of the measures overall. Although the researchers were only able to directly access a small number of perpetrators in their study, victims also reported that perpetrators were accepting of the DVPNs and DVPOs and that there was little opposition to their introduction in this respect. The data from the victim interviews, although again quite small as a sample size (16 victims/survivors were interviewed), also indicated that victims were generally quite positive about the DVPO process. A few of the victims interviewed were critical about decisions being made without their participation, and this is an obvious point of contention for an order that can be made non-consensually. It should be noted that most of the victims interviewed by Kelly et al. (2013) were recruited by support services and therefore, already receiving additional support, which is envisaged to be an essential part of the DVPO package. However, about a third of the victims in the DVPO pilot did not receive any referral to support services and it may be that, had they also been interviewed, they would have been less positive about the process (Kelly et al., 2013, p. 13). The referral of victims to support services is not a mandatory aspect of the DVPO in England and Wales, as it is, for example, in Austria and some other European countries and evaluations elsewhere have shown the availability of adequately funded support services to be crucial to the success of the barring order from the victim's perspective (Burton, 2015).

Amongst the victim group interviewed by Kelly et al., (2013) very few had pursued any longer term protection orders under the *Family Law Act* 1996. Whilst the DVPO scheme was specifically designed to give victims time and space to receive legal advice and apply for longer term protection orders if appropriate, only two of the victims in the study had successfully done so (Kelly et al., 2013, p 26). Given the small size of the victim sample, it may have been that a larger group of victims would have seen more applications for long-term remedies stemming from the imposition of a DVPO. However, Legal Services Commission data accessed by the researchers showed that approximately only 7% of all DVPOs resulted in applications for injunctions supported by legal aid (Kelly et al., 2003, p. 26). This may be related to the recent restrictions on securing legal aid for domestic violence cases, which have been subject to an unsuccessful challenge in judicial review.[5] There may be many victims who would want to pursue a longer term order but are unable to do so, because they cannot afford it and are unable to satisfy the legal aid rules. However, this low take-up of longer term injunctions following on from DVPOs does not mean that the emergency orders themselves should be judged as a failure in trying to increase the protection of domestic violence victims.

Kelly et al. (2013) found that the DVPO appears to have an impact on recidivism amongst perpetrators and may be an effective measure for protecting victims of domestic violence in the medium term. Although it is methodologically challenging to measure the impact of barring orders on repeat victimisation, Kelly et al. (2013) compared repeat call-outs in DVPO cases to a control sample of matched non-DVPO cases (Kelly et al., 2013, p. 29). Comparing cases where a barring order was issued, to those where the police took no further action, the researchers found that where an order had been issued, there was, on average, one less repeat call to the police in the 9–19-month follow-up period (Kelly et al., 2013, p. 29). Furthermore, in cases where there was a longer history of police

---

[5] Legal Aid judgement (R) (on the application of Rights of Women v Secretary of State for Justice (2015) EWHC 35 (Admin)), available online at: http://www.familylaw.co.uk/system/redactor_assets/documents/2603/R__Rights_of_Women__v_Lord_Chancellor___Anor__2015__EWHC_35__Admin_.rtf

call-outs and attendance for domestic violence prior to the DVPO, the DVPO appeared to have a more marked effect on recidivism. In the so-called chronic cases where the police had attended three or more times before issuing a DVPO, there was a reduction, on average, of approximately two attendances following the imposition of the DVPO, compared with cases where the police did not issue an order. Kelly et al., (2013) conclude that DVPOs are a potentially useful tool in reducing repeat victimisation, particularly in cases where there is a more established history of police attendance. However, it must be remembered that a reduction in police call-outs alone is an imperfect measure of a cessation or reduction in domestic violence. It may well be the case that the impact of a DVPO on a perpetrator causes the perpetrator to reflect and for the dynamics of a relationship to change, resulting in positive changes in behaviour, but also potentially via the empowerment of the victim to end the relationship. However, the repercussions for the victim may also be more negative, particularly if the DVPO was imposed without their consent, resulting in an increased reluctance to engage further with the authorities again in the future. The latter explanation may also reduce the number of times a call to the police is made.

Insofar as there is evidence that DVPOs are effective, a key factor in their success seems to be their application as part of an effective multi-agency response, rather than being applied in isolation. As stated previously, in England and Wales, an automatic referral to specialist support services was not built into the legislative framework for DVPOs and, in turn, domestic violence support service providers were not given any extra funding to deal with the potential increased demand for their services that DVPOs might produce. Doing more for less in times of austerity has become a significant challenge. Arguably, the police need to work hard to ensure that victims who have DVPNs and DVPOs in place are engaging with specialist support services during the period of emergency protection, although this, of course, does not negate their own responsibilities to victims to improve their own organisational response. Measuring the success of DVPOs should not simply be about looking at the recidivism rate in terms of police call-outs, but how well the police work with other agencies to ensure the victims get longer term protection and support that they need.

Conclusion

It can be argued, as Bishop (Chap. 4) suggests elsewhere in this volume, that the criminal law is an inadequate instrument for dealing with the complexities of victim and perpetrator issues inherent in the commission of domestic violence. There are undoubtedly significant limitations with a reliance on the criminal law in domestic violence cases and recent developments in police powers, such as the introduction of DVPNs and DVPOs, suggest that policymakers, at least implicitly, recognise these prior limitations. DVPOs represent a significant shift from the criminal law paradigm as they are civil orders with civil sanctions for breach, but are applied for by a criminal justice agency. Placing the practical issues of their application, such as timescales aside, both Kelly et al. (2013) and the HMIC (2014) found that for the implementation of any policing tool and wider improvements in the police response to domestic violence to be achieved, much more work needs to be done to change the cultural attitudes of the police. In particular, better understanding of non-physical, coercive behaviours is required. Any measures of protection for domestic violence victims will only succeed if the professionals applying them recognise the importance and value of the work. However, if the willingness and commitment to improve the response to domestic violence is achieved across all levels of policing, the research examined in this chapter suggests that the introduction of the DVPOs could be a positive development. However, such orders ultimately are only likely to be successful if they are supported by multi-agency work and they should not be restricted in this sense to high-risk, MARAC referral cases only. There are also issues highlighted here in relation to the dangers of an overreliance on reductions in police call-outs in the short to medium term as evidence of a reduction in recidivism. The lack of access for victims to legal aid to secure longer term injunctions is also of concern. These factors suggest that DVPNs and DVPOs should be seen as a starting point, from which victims might be empowered to access a longer term strategy to ensure their safety, rather than an end in themselves. The police cannot operate effectively in domestic violence cases if they work in isolation from other agencies and the success of DVPOs is highly dependent on this realisation.

References

Bourlet, A. (1990). *Police interventions in marital violence*. Milton Keynes: Open University Press.
Brookman, F., & Robinson, A. (2012). Violent crime. In M. Maguire, R. M. Morgan, & R. Reiner (Eds.), *The Oxford handbook of criminology* (5th ed.). Oxford: Oxford University Press.
Burton, M. (2003). Criminalising civil orders for protection from domestic violence. *Criminal Law Review, 301*–313.
Burton, M. (2008). *Legal responses to domestic violence*. Abingdon: Routledge.
Burton, M. (2009). Failing to protect: Victims' rights and police liability. *Modern Law Review, 72*(2), 283–295.
Burton, M. (2015). Emergency barring orders in domestic violence cases: What can England and Wales learn from other European countries? *Child and Family Law Quarterly, 21*(1), 25–42.
Crime and Security Act 2010 c17. Retrieved October 25, 2015, from http://www.legislation.gov.uk/ukpga/2010/17/contents
Crompton, L. (2014). DVP notices and orders: Protecting victims or the public purse? *Family Law, 44*, 62–68.
Dobash, R. E., & Dobash, R. P. (1979). *Violence against women: The case against patriarchy*. London: Open Books.
Edwards, S. (1987). Provoking her own demise: From common assault to homicide. In J. Hamner & M. Maynard (Eds.), *Women, violence and social control*. London: Macmillan.
Edwards, S. (1989). *Policing "domestic" violence: Women, the law and the state*. London: SAGE.
Ellison, L. (2003). Responding to victim withdrawal in domestic violence prosecutions. *Criminal Law Review, 67*–72.
Family Law Act 1996 c27. Retrieved October 25, 2015, from http://www.legislation.gov.uk/ukpga/1996/27/contents
Grace, S. (1995). *Policing domestic violence in the 1990s, Home Office Research Study 139*. London: Home Office.
Groves, N., & Thomas, T. (2014). *Domestic violence and criminal justice*. London: Routledge.
Hamner, J., Griffiths, S., & Jerwood, D. (1999). *Arresting evidence: Domestic violence and repeat victimisation, Police Research Series Paper 104*. London: Home Office.

Her Majesty's Crown Prosecution Service Inspectorate (HMCPSI) and Her Majesty's Inspectorate of Constabulary (HMIC). (2004). *Violence at home: Joint inspection of the investigation and prosecution of cases involving domestic violence.* London: HMCPSI and HMIC.

Her Majesty's Inspectorate of Constabulary (HMIC). (2014). *Everyone's business: Improving the police response to domestic abuse.* London: HMIC.

Home Office. (1990). *Domestic Violence Home Office Circular 60/1990.* London: Home Office.

Home Office. (2000). *Domestic Violence Home Office Circular 19/2000.* London: Home Office.

Home Office. (2011). *Domestic Violence Prevention Notices (DVPNs) and Domestic Violence Prevention Orders (DVPOs)-Sections 24–33 Crime and Security Act 2010: Interim Guidance Document for Police Regional Pilot Schemes, June 2011–June 2012.* London: Home Office.

Hoyle, C. (1998). *Negotiating domestic violence: Police, criminal justice and victims.* Oxford: Clarendon Press.

Kelly, L., Alder, J., Howarth, M., Lovett, J., Coulson, M., Kernohan, D., et al. (2013). *Evaluation of the pilot of domestic violence protection orders, Home Office Research Report 76.* London: Home Office.

Plotinikoff, J., & Woolfson, R. (1998). *Policing domestic violence: Effective organisational structures, Police Research Series Report 100.* London: Home Office.

Police and Criminal Evidence Act 1984 c60. Retrieved October 25, 2015, from http://www.legislation.gov.uk/ukpga/1984/60/contents

Roach, K. (1999). *Due process and victims' rights: The new law and politics of criminal justice.* Toronto: Toronto University Press.

Schneider, E. (2000). *Battered women and feminist law making.* New Haven and London: Yale University Press.

Waddington, P. (1999). Police (canteen) subculture: An appreciation. *British Journal of Criminology, 39*(2), 286–309.

Westmarland, N., Thornby, K., Wistow, J., & Gadd, D. (2014). *Domestic violence: Evidence review.* N8 Policing Research Partnership.

4

Domestic Violence: The Limitations of a Legal Response

Charlotte Bishop

Introduction

This chapter examines the benefits and limitations of the main legislative remedies currently available to address domestic violence in England and Wales. Whilst the author writes from a legal perspective, the critique offered is grounded in two key arguments, which are well supported by socio-legal and social science literature (Anderson, 2009; Dutton & Goodman, 2005; Hanna, 2009; Stark, 2007, 2009; Tadros, 2005; Williamson, 2010). The first is that rather than resulting from the deviancy of particular individuals or dysfunctional relationship dynamics alone, the commission of domestic violence often has its roots in broader social and cultural conditions of gender inequality. The second argument is that domestic violence frequently manifests as a systematic process of controlling behaviours aimed at disempowering the victim, with physical violence being just one of the tools mobilised by the perpetrator to achieve this. That these considerations have yet to fully permeate legal

---

C. Bishop (✉)
Law School, University of Exeter, Exeter, UK

© The Editor(s) (if applicable) and The Author(s) 2016
S. Hilder, V. Bettinson (eds.), *Domestic Violence*,
DOI 10.1057/978-1-137-52452-2_4

understandings of domestic violence will be shown to have detrimental and far reaching consequences when seeking to utilise legal provisions to protect, prevent and intervene in domestic violence cases. In particular, the legal system will be seen to create and sustain a 'hierarchy of harm', whereby physical violence still dominates in the assessment of both the existence and severity of domestic violence, even in light of broader recognitions that many abusive behaviours do not include physical contact. In the absence of direct physical violence, legal interpretative tendencies remain, which view the impact of the abuse on the victim as less serious, or not 'high-risk' enough to warrant intervention. This then leads to a legal response inherently limited in its ability to comprehend and provide redress for all victims of domestic violence. As a result, some victims and certain aspects of victims' experiences continue to fall outside of the law's protection.

Rather than continuing to perpetuate the enduring reliance on physical injury as evidence of domestic violence, it is argued here that the legal system would more effectively encapsulate the harm caused by domestic violence by conceptualising it as a 'liberty crime' (Stark, 2007; Williamson, 2010). It is further suggested, based on the current accumulation of knowledge from academic research and the non-governmental, specialist domestic violence sector, that this deprivation of liberty is often 'gendered' in its commission. The majority of domestic violence perpetrators are heterosexual males and reports of abuse frequently involve behaviours that demonstrate attitudes of male dominance and proprietary. The current legal response in England and Wales, however, assumes a gender neutrality, thus appearing to resist a more nuanced approach based on an understanding of the gendered nature of the issue. One explanation for this resistance is that the legal system itself remains one of the most heavily male-dominated and patriarchal institutions within society, where gendered assumptions are still clearly evident and often go unchallenged. The legal system is, therefore, one of the overarching macro-level institutions, which can serve to foster the inequalities and gendered societal expectations, values and beliefs that enable the commission of domestic violence to fester at familial and individual levels (Brownridge, 2009). Whilst purporting to address domestic violence by providing protection for victims, the legal approach may largely dismiss the impact of gendered relations in the commission of domestic violence and indeed appears to ignore some of its own inherent reinforcement of gendered roles and stereotypes.

A Gendered Phenomenon

It is recognised here and discussed elsewhere in this volume (see Martin, Chap. 9), that males can be victims of domestic violence and that domestic violence can occur in all forms of intimate partner relationships. However, there is evidence that highlights that women are more likely to experience abuse and be subjected to incidents of repeat victimisation.[1] The vast majority of domestic violence perpetrators are heterosexual males and therefore investigating the role that gendered power inequalities play in a vast number of domestic violence cases is clearly an important and legitimate pursuit. Whilst far more complex and sophisticated understandings of domestic violence are emerging, a two-dimensional approach to any analysis of perpetrator behaviours often still occurs. This retreats either into descriptions of coercive controlling violence (Kelly & Johnson, 2008), based on the systematic oppression of the victim through a range of behaviours and violent actions applied over time (see also Hilder and Freeman, Chap. 13, this volume), or situational couple violence (Kelly & Johnson, 2008), where both partners may use expressive violence at different times. However, the situational couple violence model has tended to dominate in large survey samples assessing the rate of domestic violence.

A common application of the Conflict Tactic Scale[2] (CTS) (Straus, 1979; Straus, Hamby, Boney-McCoy, & Sugarman, 1996) often does not differentiate the level of severity or context of the violent acts committed by each partner, or by focusing on discrete acts of physical violence, fails to represent the dynamics apparent in between each isolated incident.

---

[1] According to the Office for National Statistics (2014) in 2012/13, a total of 7.1 % of women and 4.4 % of men reported having experienced domestic abuse in the last year, equivalent to an estimated 1.2 million female victims of domestic abuse and 700,000 male victims.
[2] The Conflict Tactic Scale is a self-completion scoring method used to assess levels of physical violence and conflict in a domestic setting. Created by Murray Straus in 1979.

Research that has focused on discrete and de-contextualised acts can, therefore, be seen to equate 'a woman who has committed one trivial act' with 'a man who has committed several serious acts of a different nature' (Reece, 2006). However, for example, 'throwing a lamp at a partner is very different from throwing a pillow … [yet] both are recorded as throwing an object at one's partner' (Dobash & Dobash, 2004, p. 329). This conflation is concerning because it can lead to misinformed policies and practice. For example, concepts of coercive controlling violence are far less apparent in any legal analysis, which prefers to adopt an approach based on this assumed symmetry between violence inflicted by male and female partners as individual, physically aggressive responses to a relationship dispute. In doing so, it lacks full comprehension of the harm caused by the systematic process of oppressive behaviours highlighted by Stark (2007), the long-term psychological damage caused to victims and their children and, most importantly, key indicators that risks may be escalating and indeed may be exacerbated by the legal response adopted.

Legal Constructions of Gender Role Expectations

The significant lack of any constructive gendered analysis of perpetrator and victim conduct within the legal system can also be attributed to the nature of the institution itself. The construction and reinforcement of familial norms and gender-specific roles are clearly illustrated in the practices of the legal system and it remains a key site for the creation of patriarchal and stereotypical gendered expectations. Whilst significant strides have been made, a pervading preference for heterosexuality, marriage and two-parent families, with specifically assigned gendered roles, remains apparent. This is evidenced in parliamentary debates concerning in vitro fertilisation (see McCandless & Sheldon, 2010), and high court decisions over child contact and residency.[3] A number of commentators

---

[3] Members of the senior judiciary have stated that it is 'axiomatic that the ideal environment for the upbringing of a child [is] the home of loving, caring and sensible parents: the mother and father' and 'undesirable' for a child to 'learn or understand at any age the nature of [their] mother's [lesbian] relationship' (*C v C* (*Custody of Child*) [1991] FCR 254).

have also examined the way in which judicial decisions and sentencing patterns have been seen to reinforce assumptions about familial roles and 'appropriate' male and female behaviours (Campbell, 2008; Walklate, 2004; Worrall, 2008).

Legal institutions also offer a powerful discourse as the regulators of social roles and behaviours (Smart, 1995). Despite developments in training, such as those provided by the Judicial Studies Board (2013), which now warn explicitly against the use of sexual stereotypes (*Equal Treatment Bench Book on Gender*), there are still enduring examples of senior judges in England and Wales employing 'crude and problematic sexual stereotypes in their judgements or overlook[ing] the use of such stereotypes by trials judges' (Elvin, 2010, p. 277). Senior members of the judiciary and parliament have been known to make sweeping generalisations pertaining to 'differences' in male and female behaviours (Elvin, 2010) and numerous judicial statements perpetuating stereotypical views of men and women, based on the existence of supposed biological differences, can be found within civil and criminal case law. The assumptions that prevail include the idea that women provoke male violence, thereby reducing the perpetrator's level of responsibility for their actions,[4] and that women are less likely to be provoked to use violence themselves[5] and are more prone to psychological disorders.[6] The overt use and continuing acceptance of these viewpoints, devoid of any evidential substantiation, may indicate that they are 'seen as unproblematic at a wider level within at least certain leading elements of the legal profession in England and Wales' (Elvin, 2010, pp. 276–277). A stereotype 'does not need to be widespread in order for it to be important if the person wielding it is in a position of power over others, and appellate judges are clearly in this position' (Elvin, 2010, p. 277).

Whilst Stark (2007, 2009) and Anderson (2009) highlight that the exact nature of gendered role expectations changes over time and varies within different cultural and community contexts, they frequently continue to

---

[4] See, for example, *Re H (A Child) (Contact: Domestic Violence)* [2006] 1 FCR 102.
[5] See for example *R v Smith (Morgan)* [2001] 1 AC 146 and *Attorney General for Jersey v Holley* [2006] UKPC 23.
[6] See *Bonser v UK Coal Mining Ltd.* [2003] EWCA Civ 1296.

prescribe a state of male privilege. An acceptance that male aggression is an inherent characteristic extends beyond any domestic violence discourse, with constructions of masculinity that view certain types of inter-male violence as inevitable, particularly amongst young men, being evident within the courts. Two key cases (R v Jones and R v Aitken[7]) assert, quite explicitly, that when males are injured, even quite seriously, in the context of 'rough and undisciplined horseplay', they have consented to such behaviours simply as a result of their presence in a male-dominated environment. This effectively sets a permissive context that allows men to be violent in some circumstances. The criminal law, thus, replicates and reinforces social constructions of male violence as normal and natural (Bibbings, 2000).

Anderson (2009) develops the work of Stark (2007) through her examination of Connell's work (1995) on masculinities and argues that it is not gendered socialisation that causes men's violence, but the 'vulnerability and instability of masculine identities [that] may lead some men to use violence to temporarily shore up or restore their sense of selves as "real men"' (Anderson, 2009, p. 1445). For Stark, there is a cultural link between masculine identity and being in control, which has been shown to be the central purpose in a range of tactics found in abusive relationships. Thus, some men will use coercive control to bolster their threatened sense of masculine identity (Anderson, 2009, p. 1446). In contrast female violence, Anderson argues, is frequently viewed as an abnormality. The societal expectations of femininity mean that if women try and use the same abusive tactics, they are often seen as ineffective because they do not carry the same meaning (Anderson, 2009), or they are viewed as a manifestation of temporary or permanent mental impairment that causes the transgression of accepted gendered 'norms'. Interview responses in a study by Dobash and Dobash (2004) highlighted that a female partner's violence is often viewed as insignificant, comical or ludicrous. This clearly also has implications for the experiences of male victims or victims in lesbian relationships where the impact of the female perpetrator's actions are likely to be viewed less seriously (see Martin, Chap. 9 and Barnes and Donovan, Chap. 14, this volume).

---

[7] *R v Jones; R v Campbell; R v Smith; R v Nicholas, R v Blackwood and R v Muir* (1986) 83 Cr App R 375 and *R v Aitken; R v Bennett and R v Barson* [1992] 1 WLR 1006.

Walker (2009) conducted research that indicated that women in marriages where there was a rigid approach to the assignment of gender-specific roles were at a higher risk of experiencing domestic violence. Coercive control strategies utilised by the perpetrator are likely to reinforce a specific construction of feminine identity via the micro-regulation of everyday activities, such as how the victim dresses, cooks, cleans, looks after her children and performs sexually (Anderson, 2009, p. 1447). Victims comply because they recognise they are held accountable for this performance and because resistance frequently leads to punishment. It is important, however, that this compliance is not seen by the courts as being truly voluntary, otherwise there is the danger that the strategies engaged in by the victim in an attempt to reduce the likelihood of threatened consequences being imposed may be misinterpreted as consent. Evidence suggests that abused women tend to have very rigid ideas about what constitutes an achievement for a woman and base feelings of self-worth on how they view their capacity to be a good wife and homemaker (Walker, 2009). Similar reflections have been found in studies with adolescents identifying how early gendered role expectations may be established (Chung, 2005; see Crowther Dowey, Gillespie and Hopkins, Chap. 8, this volume). Stark's finding that coercive control is gendered and focuses on 'imposing sex stereotypes in everyday life' (Stark, 2009, p. 205), also enables a link with broader structural issues of sexism and discrimination. Understanding this link is integral to the creation of legal and other measures that can respond effectively to domestic violence.

Legal Tools for Addressing Domestic Violence

The primary legislation used to prosecute domestic violence perpetrators[8] was introduced more than 150 years ago to deal with problems of stranger violence and public order and is based on physical violence that is typically committed in public by one man against another. It

---

[8] The offences consist of assault occasioning actual bodily harm, malicious wounding and grievous bodily harm under sections 18, 20 and 47 of the *Offences Against the Person Act* 1861.

originates from a time when violence occurring in the domestic sphere was not considered to be a social problem, let alone a criminal matter. Thus, the protection offered by the criminal justice system in situations of domestic violence often relies on the application of criminal law provisions, which are often ill-suited and fail to take into account the unique dynamics and type of harm caused. The legislation befits occasions where a physical injury has occurred in the presence of witnesses. Such legal instruments, therefore, often fall short in adequately addressing domestic violence cases that rely on victim testimony, or where there may be minor physical injuries, but much longer term severe psychological distress. As a result, sentences may not reflect the severity of the harm inflicted, or the level of ongoing protection required. It might be affirmed, therefore, that the mechanics involved in the violent and abusive acts committed by an intimate partner cannot be adequately equated to legal provisions intended to address bar brawls and street fights (Mill, 2003, p. 51).

The *Domestic Violence Crime and Victims Act* 2004 aimed to improve the protection available for victims by harmonising the civil and criminal justice system responses to domestic violence, but it did not depart from established understandings of harm caused. The new offence of coercive and controlling behaviour under section 76 *Serious Crime Act* 2015 may change this situation to a certain extent. The implementation of this new provision remains in its infancy and is revisited later in this chapter. However, the inherent procedural difficulties in determining an evidence of harm within the more established available legal protection tools also remain and are further analysed in the discussion that follows.

Domestic Violence and Evidence of Harm

In the legal field, the harm caused by domestic violence continues to be predominantly conceptualised as the infliction of a physical injury, albeit with some increasing recognition that other types of violence and abuse may also occur. However, a clear body of knowledge now exists, which reveals this primary conceptualisation as inaccurate, with victim accounts of the profound psychological impact of abuse, which may never actually include violent physical contact. Coercive and controlling forms of domestic violence are not one-off incidents and may include a series of strategies, rules and demands made by the perpetrator that dictate how the victim must respond in all aspects of everyday life (Stark, 2009). These may be reinforced by credible threats of physical violence or other threatened negative consequences (Dutton & Goodman, 2005). In instances where the physical threat is then enacted upon, or is supported as 'being real' by prior incidents of assault, the legal system is able to respond with appropriate charges (assault, battery, actual bodily harm, grievous bodily harm and malicious wounding). However, other 'punishments' may be threatened by the perpetrator, such as taking the children away from their mother, embarrassing a woman in front of her family or applying pressure on her to accept infidelities if she is unwilling to engage in unwanted sexual behaviours (Dutton & Goodman, 2005). These types of intimidation do not constitute an illegal act in themselves and do not afford the victim any form of legal intervention or protection, whether they are enacted upon or not. Yet, the use of such threats to ensure compliance from the victim can be extremely powerful and psychologically damaging. The victim is subjected to a continuing 'stage of siege' (Dutton, 1993, p. 1208), with the constant awareness that any failure to abide by the perpetrator's demands and rules will result in these threatened consequences being instigated.

Surveillance is another common method whereby perpetrators maintain power and control over the victim by making it clear that all of their actions are being monitored. By creating a perpetual state of fear, again often reinforced by past experiences, the victim is kept in a constant state of disempowerment. This often does not require any further actual act of physical aggression, just the promise that it could erupt again at any point (Fischer, Vidmar, & Ellis, 1992). This analysis clearly highlights that the impact of domestic violence may not have any visible physical form, but can operate at such an alarmingly distressing level psychologically that it hinders the victim's everyday functioning and the capacity to make and exercise meaningful decisions. Legal provisions again struggle to effectively address this. Even the criminal offence based on the 'fear of violence' (s 2 *Protection from Harassment Act* 1997) is unable to respond to this aspect of psychological harm due to its requirement for fear to be evidenced, on at least two occasions, by a tangible threat that physical violence will be used against the victim. It is unrealistic to envisage that charges would be brought under this act to deal with a situation where a victim lives in a permanent state of fear brought about via the use of credible threats of other negative and harmful consequences. Thus, this type of harm is largely excluded from the legal discourse on domestic violence and is viewed implicitly as being less serious than a fear of direct physical violence, supported by prior evidence of assaults.

The primary focus on physically violent acts means a single incident or violent episode is frequently abstracted from the rest of the perpetrator's abusive behaviour and actions. This incident-based approach is often in contrast to the lived experience of a victim for whom the abuse is a process of everyday life (Robinson, 2014). Whilst preceding patterns of behaviour, threats and coercion in the context of an intimate relationship may be recognised as aggravating features at the point of sentencing, they will very rarely be considered for the purposes of proving a criminal offence. Thus, if a perpetrator is charged, the index offence is unlikely to reflect the full severity and impact of the victim's experience. Efforts have been made to address this. *The Protection from Harassment Act* 1997 has been utilised in the context of abusive relationships, and its provision to address a 'course of conduct' suggests that it would be well suited to accommodating the patterns of behaviour experienced by victims, outlined above. However, judicial decisions interpreting the Act have confounded such an analysis by lapsing back into an examination of individual incidents of assault and battery, to ascertain whether or not these, in combination, amount to a course of conduct that constitutes harassment (Bettinson & Bishop, 2015).

The cross-government definition of domestic violence (Home Office, 2013) also seems promising at first due to the inclusion of coercive and controlling behaviour and its reference to a 'pattern' of acts. However, this is not a legal definition and again retains a focus on individual incidents or acts rather than on the impact of the pattern of abusive behaviour taken as a whole. When viewed out of context, acts can appear small and trivial. Only when set in the context of an ongoing situation of abuse is their weight and significance fully appreciated and their impact on the victim fully understood. Therefore, the harm of domestic violence needs to be reconceptualised in a way that comprehends the impact of the behaviours on the victim's autonomy and liberty and not from the infliction of physical injury per se.

Harm Caused by the Erosion of Autonomy and Liberty

Williamson (2010) found that decision making itself can become frightening for a victim of domestic violence, as whatever choice is made will be wrong and will lead to abuse that they then consider themselves to have 'caused' (Williamson, 2010, p. 1415). For a victim subject to coercive and controlling behaviours, everything they do needs to be considered in terms of their partner's response and thus they can no longer be viewed as autonomous individuals (Williamson, 2010, p. 1418). Tadros (2005) also suggests that the harm caused by domestic violence does not result simply from a reduction in liberty and the capacity to make personal choices, but also because the choices that remain are subject to the arbitrary control of another (Tadros, 2005, p. 998). The victim can make decisions only within a framework controlled by the perpetrator, and, thus, this element of freedom is not really a 'free' choice at all. The undermining of the autonomy and decision-making ability of the victim that occurs within the dynamics of many domestic violence cases has led to social science definitions of domestic violence as a 'liberty crime' (Williamson, 2010, p. 1412). The central harm is the deprivation of liberty, not the infliction of physical injury. However, legal and broader societal understandings of domestic violence continue to identify victims of abuse under the more outdated conceptual auspices of the 'battered woman' (Walker, 1979, 2009). A hierarchy of harms, with extreme physical violence at its peak, therefore, remains in existence and arguably hampers the application of legal measures. This focus is particularly evident within the criminal justice system's definition of 'bodily harm' when considering charges for non-fatal offences.

Criminal Justice System: Bodily Harm

Psychiatric injury[9] is no longer completely excluded from the ambit of 'bodily harm' for the purposes of the non-fatal offences, but harm to the mind must amount to a 'recognisable psychiatric injury', with a clear clarification that 'it does not include mere emotions such as fear or distress nor panic'. Non-physical harm is, therefore, 'either psychiatric' or 'merely' emotional, with only the infliction of the former 'meriting criminalisation' (Munro & Shah, 2010, p. 264). This legal guidance emphasises the problematic nature of attempts to apply existing offences against the person in the context of domestic violence, with limited capacity within existing legal frameworks to accommodate the harm caused by coercive and controlling non-physical examples of abuse, unless the impact on the victim results in a diagnosed psychiatric condition.

The challenges presented by such a medically defined threshold were evident in the 2006 case of Dhaliwal[10] where the Court of Appeal affirmed the requirement for a recognised psychiatric injury, thus effectively dismissing the impact of domestic abuse on a victim where there was no formal diagnosis of battered woman's syndrome or post-traumatic stress disorder (Burton, 2010). Despite finding 'some features of depression' that would have affected the victim's psychological functioning, the psychiatric experts in the case did not find any evidence of a recognisable psychiatric injury, and the prosecution failed. Burton notes the 'privileging of medical knowledge over a large body of social science research relating to the effects of domestic abuse' (2010, p. 258), although medical opinion in itself is subjective and not an exact science (Burton, 2010). The implications of a formal diagnosis of a significant psychiatric disorder may also clearly be something that a victim may wish to avoid, because although it may meet court requirements, there may be serious ramifications elsewhere. For example, family courts and social services are likely to have concerns regarding a victim's capacity to care for their children if there are serious mental health concerns (Hester, 2006).

---

[9] Within the legal arena, 'psychiatric injury' means non-physical injury arising from nervous shock or a mental condition that is found with the DSM (Diagnostic and Statistical Manual of Mental Disorders).

[10] *R v Dhaliwal* [2006] 2 Cr App R 24.

The case of Dhaliwal provided the Court of Appeal with the opportunity to reconceptualise bodily harm in line with the lived experiences of domestic violence victims by recognising that significant psychological symptoms might, in cases where a minimum level of severity is attained, amount to bodily harm despite the lack of a medical diagnosis. In declining to take this approach, however, the court can be seen to be reluctant to amend current legal understandings of harm in a way that would recognise the impact of emotional suffering, which, 'where it is severe in its effects and sustained in its duration, can have serious, harmful consequences' (Munro & Shah, 2010, p. 263).

Legal Recognition of Coercion and Control

The new offence of coercive and controlling behaviour, highlighted previously, has been introduced via section 76 *Serious Crime Act* 2015. The offence is committed when the perpetrator 'repeatedly or continuously engages in behaviour that is controlling or coercive' and that has a 'serious effect' on the victim either because the victim fears, on at least two occasions, that violence will be used against them, or because it causes them serious alarm or distress, which has a significant adverse effect on their usual day-to-day activities (for a full discussion see Bettinson & Bishop, 2015). Initially, this new legislation appears encouraging due to its encapsulation of the harm of domestic violence discussed previously; the new offence recognises the effect that a stream of continuous abusive behaviours can have on the daily life of a victim. However, whilst this can be seen as a positive move that sends the message, at a legal and societal level, that such behaviours constitute domestic abuse and are criminal, there are concerns that the new offence does not go far enough in terms of challenging existing preconceptions that serious physical violence is central to the commission of severe abuse.

The new offence co-exists alongside the established criminal law framework for dealing with domestic violence, thus perpetuating the view that coercive and controlling behaviour is a new and distinct form of domestic violence, which again falls prey to an isolated pursuit of any tangible evidence of its existence. The argument that domestic violence is best conceptualised as a programme of coercive and controlling behaviours, which will manifest differently over time and which may or may not include physical violence, has still not been fully comprehended by this legal approach. It is suggested, therefore, that this new offence is likely to reproduce the hierarchy of harm response discussed previously. As it carries a maximum sentence of only five years imprisonment, there is also an inference that it is less serious in nature than direct physical violence. However the psychological harm resulting from an ongoing programme of coercive control can be extreme, with known cases of victims taking their own lives.[11] Therefore, if coercion and control were viewed along the same lines as the spectrum of criminal offences against the person, arguably at its very highest peak, it is as serious as an offence of grievous bodily harm with intent and thus should carry the same maximum sentence of life imprisonment.

Civil Law

A hierarchical emphasis on the commission of physical harm is also evident within the interpretation and application of the available civil law remedies to protect domestic violence victims. It also occurs within housing provision and legal aid assessments prohibiting many victims from securing a safe pathway out of an abusive situation (see Burnet, Chap. 11, this volume). Civil law remedies consist of non-molestation orders that prohibit a person from 'molesting' another (S. 42 *Family Law Act* 1996) and occupation orders (Ss. 33–36 *Family Law Act* 1996) that may be used to exclude the perpetrator of violence from the shared home, provided certain criteria are met. Whilst the definition of molestation is wide and extends beyond physical violence to conduct that would make it 'impossible or intolerable … for the other partner, or the children, to remain at home', occupation orders may be harder to obtain, particularly where there is no evidence of physical violence. In an example case from 2000, the friction between two parties was attributed to their 'incompatible personalities' and as the wife had 'not suffered any violence at the

---

[11] Research cited by Refuge indicates that almost 30 women attempt suicide every day, and three women a week succeed in taking their own lives as a result of experiencing domestic violence. See www.refuge.org.uk/what-we-do/campaigns/takinglives/

hands of the husband' (at para 30), an order excluding her husband from the family home was held to be inappropriate.[12] Whilst this narrow interpretation of a domestic violence scenario might now be strongly refuted, orders excluding the perpetrator of violence from the family home are still deemed draconian and only to be granted as 'a last resort' in exceptional circumstances. It is likely they will remain difficult to obtain in the absence of serious physical violence, as there has been no recent case law indicating a change in precedent from this position.

Legal Aid Criteria

In principle, civil legal aid is still available to enable victims to pursue non-molestation orders and some areas of family law, following the changes implemented by the *Legal Aid, Sentencing and Punishment of Offenders Act* 2012 (LASPO), provided the victims are financially eligible. For example, ancillary relief, private law family and child contact and residence cases will be covered. However, legal advice on issues such as housing, employment, debt, welfare benefits and immigration will not be funded, suggesting a failure to appreciate some of the most serious problems victims face when they leave a violent relationship (see section 33 of *The Civil Legal Aid (Procedure) Regulations* 2012).

Under the new criteria, however, legal aid is available to applicants only in the areas of family law identified earlier on the provision of specific documental evidence of domestic violence. This includes proof of the granting of a civil protection order, a criminal conviction for a domestic violence offence by the other party towards the applicant, a referral to a Multi Agency Risk Assessment Conference (MARAC) as a high-risk victim of domestic violence or a letter from a health professional. These forms of evidence are unlikely to be available in the absence of an officially recorded act of serious physical violence (Hunter, 2014). A victim of abuse may not formally disclose the experience to the police and seek legal redress because they believe that the criminal justice system will be ineffective and may exacerbate the risk posed to them. There is also the

---

[12] See *G v G (Occupation Order: Conduct)* [2000] WL 416.

fear of revictimisation through cross-examination. Even where a criminal law approach is pursued, as has been discussed previously, certain types of abuse, particularly those of a non-physical nature, may not reach the burden of proof required to secure a conviction (Hester, 2006). Referrals to MARACs and interventions from General Practitioners also require the victim to be engaging with these other agencies and for the professional assessments to conclude that the risk of further serious harm being inflicted on the victim is high. A study conducted in 2013 found that approximately half of the women who experienced domestic violence did not have any of the prescribed forms of evidence to access legal aid (Rights of Women, 2013). The reasons included being too frightened to go to the police, being unable to obtain a refuge place, which was also seen as proof of the abuse, not having a copy of the necessary written evidence, not knowing who to ask to obtain it, unable to pay the charges incurred for acquiring copies of the evidence from the police and health professionals, cultural reasons for not wanting to disclose to a General Practitioner and the difficulty of establishing the impact of non-physical abuse (Rights of Women, 2013; Blacklaws, 2014; Hunter, 2014).

Housing Law Provision

Developments in housing sector responses to domestic violence are covered extensively in this volume by Burnet, Chap. 11. Significantly, however, recent case law[13] suggests that in the context of housing provision appeals, the courts are beginning to interpret domestic violence in a less restrictive way, which is no longer limited to the commission of violent acts of physical contact. Nevertheless, the determination that it 'must reach some level of seriousness' to warrant appropriate interventions and access to housing resources may prove problematic, dependent on the understandings of seriousness that are utilised as a benchmark for such judgements. If this looks to criminal law interpretations, the threshold of seriousness is unlikely to be reached without evidence of serious bodily harm or a medically recognised psychiatric condition.

---

[13] *Yemshaw v London Borough of Hounslow* [2011] UKSC 3.

These issues are highlighted in the recent case of Yemshaw, relating to an appeal over a local council decision that had concluded that there was no obligation to house a domestic violence victim because she had not suffered physical violence at the hands of her husband. The original council decision was overturned once the case reached the House of Lords, but even so, one of the judges, whilst not dissenting, stated that he did not believe that at any point the 'domestic violence' provisions at issue in the case were intended to extend beyond the limits of physical violence and nor did Parliament contemplate or intend for psychological abuse to be 'violence'.[14] This viewpoint is clearly of concern, as is the fact that the case had to be decided on appeal and it reveals, perhaps, that the requirement for evidence of physical violence also presides in interpretations of protections which can be mobilised under current housing law.

The emphasis given to physical injury in the various forms of legal analysis determining the impact and seriousness of domestic violence means that the legal focus is drawn away from the space in between violent incidents, Dutton's (1993) 'state of siege'. The incident-based approach of the legal system, therefore, dismisses the accumulative processes of abuse that may occur over time within an intimate relationship. The focus on isolated incidents of physical violence also suggests a series of individual triggers and antecedents for each physical act, thus ignoring the functional role of domestic violence in sustaining unequal power relations between the two intimate partners. The tactics employed by many perpetrators to ensure the reduction of the autonomy and liberty of the victim frequently remain overlooked or trivialised.

Conclusion

This chapter has shown that not only is a gendered analysis missing from much of the legal discourse surrounding domestic violence, but that the institutions of the legal system itself remain central sites for the perpetu-

---

[14] Lord Brown allowed the appeal despite his 'very real doubts' (para 60) because he did not 'feel sufficiently strongly as to the proper outcome of the appeal to carry these doubts to the point of dissent'.

ation of unequal gendered power relations, with a continuing reliance on gendered stereotypes clearly in evidence. These discriminatory gendered perspectives are known to be exploited in the context of an abusive relationship. Therefore, seeking to eradicate their existence and increasing understandings of the role gender plays in the commission of many scenarios of domestic violence are vital in order to address domestic violence effectively.

Despite an increased awareness of the need to incorporate the non-physical aspects of domestic violence into legal definitions and remedies, an analysis of the legal responses also reveals a continuing focus on serious physical violence as evidence of abuse, with non-physical aspects of abuse, where recognised, being deemed to be less serious (the 'hierarchy of harm'). With ongoing tendencies to situate explanations of domestic violence within individual deviant offender pathologies or particular relationship dynamics, rather than fully considering the ways in which wider social and structural inequalities feed into the functional and systematic nature of many experiences of abuse, a legal approach continues to treat domestic violence as isolated incidents, where the reliance on physical violence is reinforced. This focus results in the exclusion, or trivialisation, of the serious psychological harm that can be caused by the coercive and controlling features of victims' experiences. A dangerous assumption follows on from this that once physical violence has ceased, the harm caused has also subsided. However, physical aggression may simply be used to establish an atmosphere of intimidation and coercion. Once this is established and the victim is conforming to the perpetrator's demands, the threat of a further range of negative consequences may be enough to sustain the situation of power and control. The legal system's comprehension of victim behaviours remains limited in this respect.

The responses of key legal agencies will improve if they begin to operate with an understanding that many situations of domestic violence extend beyond a conceptualisation of it as a crime of violence and move towards an understanding of its central harm as being the deprivation of freedom and autonomy. However, this transformation can only be fully achieved if the key institutions within the legal system also consider their own organisational values and practice. Whilst the adoption of a gender-neutral approach to the treatment of domestic violence is purported to be a strategy that supports equality and anti-discriminatory practice, it actually misses the point. Many domestic violence relationships are not gender-neutral; they are fuelled by distorted expectations of gender roles, which are utilised as tools of status and control. To ignore this will mean that many of the lived experiences of victims will continue to fail to secure any effective form of legal redress.

References

Anderson, K. (2009). Gendering coercive control. *Violence Against Women, 15*(12), 1444–1457.
Bettinson, V., & Bishop, C. (2015). Is the creation of a discrete offence of coercive control necessary to combat domestic violence? *Northern Ireland Legal Quarterly, 66*(2), 179–197.
Bibbings, L. (2000). Boys will be boys: Masculinity and offences against the person. In D. Nicolson & L. Bibbings (Eds.), *Feminist perspectives on criminal law*. London: Cavendish Publishing.
Blacklaws, C. (2014). The impact of the LASPO changes to date in private family law and mediation. *Family Law, 44*, 626–628.
Brownridge, D. A. (2009). *Violence against women: Vulnerable populations*. London: Routledge.
Burton, M. (2010). Commentary on R v Dhaliwal. In R. Hunter, C. McGlynn, & E. Rackley (Eds.), *Feminist judgments: From theory to practice*. Oxford: Hart Publishing.
Campbell, B. (2008). Boys will be boys. In K. Evans & J. Jamieson (Eds.), *Gender and crime a reader*. Maidenhead: Open University Press.
Chung, D. (2005). Violence, control, romance and gender equality: Young women and heterosexual relationships. *Women's Studies International Forum, 28*, 445–455.
(The) *Civil Legal Aid (Procedure) Regulations 2012* 3098. Retrieved October 13, 2015, from http://www.legislation.gov.uk/uksi/2012/3098/contents/made
Connell, R. W. (1995). *Masculinities*. Berkeley: University of California Press.
Dobash, R. P., & Dobash, R. E. (2004). Women's violence to men in intimate relationships: Working on a puzzle. *British Journal of Criminology, 44*(3), 324–349.
Domestic Violence Victims of Crime Act 2004 c28. Retrieved October 12, 2015, from http://www.legislation.gov.uk/ukpga/2004/28/contents

Dutton, M. (1993). Understanding women's responses to domestic violence: A redefinition of battered woman syndrome. *Hofstra Law Review, 21*(4), 1191–1242.

Dutton, M. A., & Goodman, L. A. (2005). Coercion in intimate partner violence: Toward a new conceptualization. *Sex Roles, 52,* 743–744.

Elvin, J. (2010). The continuing use of problematic sexual stereotypes in judicial decision-making. *Feminist Legal Studies, 18*(3), 275–297.

Family Law Act 1996 c 27. Retrieved October 29, 2015, from http://www.legislation.gov.uk/ukpga/1996/27/contents

Fischer, K., Vidmar, N., & Ellis, R. (1992). The culture of battering and the roles of mediation in domestic violence cases. *SMU Law Review, 46,* 2117–2174.

Hanna, C. (2009). The paradox of progress: Translating E. Stark's coercive control into legal doctrine for abused women. *Violence Against Women, 15*(12), 1458–1476.

Hester, M. (2006). Making it through the criminal justice system: Attrition and domestic violence. *Social Policy and Society, 5*(1), 79–90.

Home Office. (2013). *Home Office Circular 003/2013: New government domestic violence and abuse definition.* Retrieved October 13, 2015, from https://www.gov.uk/government/publications/new-government-domestic-violence-and-abuse-definition

Hunter, R. (2014). Exploring the "LASPO Gap". *Family Law, 44* (5) 660–663.

Judicial Studies Board. (2013). *Equal treatment bench book.* London: Judicial Studies Board.

Kelly, J. B., & Johnson, M. P. (2008). Differentiation among types of intimate partner violence: Research update and implications for interventions. *Family Court Review, 46*(3), 476–499.

Legal Aid, Sentencing and Punishment of Offenders Act 2012 c10. Retrieved October 13, 2015, from http://www.legislation.gov.uk/ukpga/2012/10/contents/enacted

McCandless, J., & Sheldon, S. (2010). "No Father Required"? The welfare assessment in the Human Fertilisation and Embryology Act 2008. *Feminist Legal Studies, 18*(3), 201–225.

Mills, L. (2003). *Insult to Injury: Rethinking our Responses to Intimate Abuse.* Princeton and Oxford: Princeton University Press.

Munro, V., & Shah, S. (2010). R v Dhaliwal Judgment. In R. Hunter, C. McGlynn, & E. Rackley (Eds.), *Feminist judgments: From theory to practice.* Oxford: Hart.

Offences Against the Person Act 1861 c100. Retrieved October 12, 2015, from http://www.legislation.gov.uk/ukpga/Vict/24-25/100/contents

Protection of Harassment Act 1997 c40. Retrieved October 13, 2015, from http://www.legislation.gov.uk/ukpga/1997/40/contents

Reece, H. (2006). The End of Domestic Violence. *Modern Law Review* (5) 770–791.

Rights of Women. (2013). *Evidencing domestic violence: A barrier to family law legal aid*. Retrieved October 25, 2015, from http://rightsofwomen.org.uk/wp-content/uploads/2014/10/Evidencing-DV-a-barrier-2013.pdf

Robinson, A. (2014). Pie in the sky? The use of criminal justice policies and practices for intimate partner violence. In H. Johnson, B. S. Fisher, & V. Jaquier (Eds.), *Critical issues on violence against women: International perspectives and promising strategies*. London: Routledge.

Serious Crime Act 2015 C9. Retrieved October 12, 2015, from http://www.legislation.gov.uk/ukpga/2015/9/contents/enacted

Smart, C. (1995). *Law, crime and sexuality: Essays in feminism*. London: SAGE.

Stark, E. (2007). *Coercive control: How men entrap women in personal life*. Oxford: Oxford University Press.

Stark, E. (2009). Rethinking coercive control. *Violence Against Women, 16*(12), 1509–1525.

Straus, A. (1979). Measuring intrafamily conflict and violence: The Conflict Tactics (CT) Scales. *Journal of Marriage and Family, 41*(1), 75–88.

Straus, A., Hamby, S., Boney-McCoy, S., & Sugarman, D. (1996). The revised Conflict Tactic Scales (CTS2): Development and preliminary psychometric data. *Journal of Family Issues, 17*(3), 283–316.

Tadros, V. (2005). The distinctiveness of domestic abuse: A freedom-based account. *Louisiana Law Review, 65*, 989–1014.

Walker, L. (1979). *The battered woman*. New York: Harper and Row.

Walker, L. (2009). *The battered woman syndrome* (3rd ed.). New York: Springer Publishing Company.

Walklate, S. (2004). *Gender crime and justice* (2nd ed.). Cullompton: Willan Publishing.

Williamson, E. (2010). Living in the world of the domestic violence perpetrator: Negotiating the unreality of coercive control. *Violence Against Women, 16*(12), 1412–1423.

Worrall, A. (2008). Twisted sister, ladette and the new penology; the social construction of "violent girls". In K. Evans & J. Jamieson (Eds.), *Gender and crime a reader*. Maidenhead: Open University Press.

5

Surviving Times of Austerity: Preserving the Specialist Domestic Violence Court Provision

Vanessa Bettinson

Introduction

The importance of the criminal justice system's role in providing effective responses to domestic violence and abuse (DVA) has been acknowledged by successive governments and is contained in the *National Strategy to End Violence Against Women and Girls* in England and Wales (Home Office, 2011). The criminal justice system has long been criticised for its failure to provide adequate protection or preventative measures in DVA cases. Recently, the police drew further negative attention following Her Majesty's Inspectorate of Constabulary (HMIC, 2014) report that found the police response to DVA remained unsatisfactory in many areas, with many frontline officers lacking in an understanding of DVA issues. Developments in policing powers are discussed elsewhere in this volume, see Burton, Chap. 3, whilst Bishop, Chap. 4, discusses the limitations of a legal response and some of the underpinning issues that

V. Bettinson (✉)
De Montfort Business and Law, De Montfort University, Leicester, UK

© The Editor(s) (if applicable) and The Author(s) 2016
S. Hilder, V. Bettinson (eds.), *Domestic Violence*,
DOI 10.1057/978-1-137-52452-2_5

contribute to it. This chapter examines the criminal court system and the introduction of Specialist Domestic Violence Court (SDVC) provision in England and Wales, with some comparative discussion of variances in its implementation in other jurisdictions. The creation of these courts came from the necessity to address several inadequacies with the court process itself, including the apparent reluctance of victims/survivors to engage with the prosecution authorities, concerns regarding victim safety and the lack of training in domestic violence issues for key court practitioners. However, whilst the number of SDVCs has risen since their original inception as a result of their success, with additional government support since 2005, their continued existence is more tenuous during the current political period of austerity. There have been a number of studies regarding the early SDVCs (Cook, Burton, Robinson, & Vallely, 2004; Vallely, Robinson, Burton, & Tregidga, 2005) and the development of SDVC provision has been well documented (Burton, 2008; Robinson, 2010). Bowen, Qasim, and Tetenbaum (2014) note that there is continued practitioner support for the SDVC; however, budgetary cuts have seen the enforcement of a Courts Closure Programme (MoJ, 2015), reduced access to legal aid and a lack of funding for services providing independent victim advocates at court.

This chapter provides an overview that outlines the objectives and developments of the SDVC in England and Wales. Drawing upon a small-scale observational study conducted by the author, it will highlight some of the key challenges faced by the SDVC provision in terms of case identification and budgetary pressures. The importance of increasing the presence of court-based victim advocates and maintaining a victim-centred approach is discussed. Comparisons are made with the development and progress of specialist Domestic Abuse Courts in Scotland, which emphasises the significance of strong working relationships between the police, prosecuting authorities and DVA services. The chapter considers the impact of police diversion from courts in DVA cases and argues that SDVCs could provide welcome oversight of police cautions and out-of-court disposals. Finally, the chapter reflects on issues of sentencing, noting that the use of a victim surcharge may not be in the best interests of victims/survivors.

An overview of Specialist Domestic Violence Court

SDVCs first began in England and Wales in 1999 in Leeds. They introduced a multi-agency working approach within the criminal justice system by providing an independent victim advocate in the court and the appropriate specialist training of court personnel to achieve a more victim-centred environment. The advocate is able to connect victims/survivors with specialist agency support and liaise between agencies, the statutory sector and the court on the victim's/survivor's behalf. Low levels of victim/survivor confidence were previously evidenced by high levels of retraction or non-attendance at court compared to other crimes (Cretney & Davies, 1997; Robinson & Cook, 2006). The reasons for this lack of engagement with the criminal court process are complex and personal, with research indicating a variety of factors. They include views of the criminal courts as overly or insufficiently punitive, the fear of future harm and retaliation by the perpetrator or their friends and family members (Dawson & Dinovitzer, 2001) and being ill-informed about court procedures and processes (Robinson & Cook, 2006). The introduction of SDVCs sought to address these concerns. Early evaluations found that even where conviction rates were not significantly higher in the SDVCs compared to their non-specialist counterparts, victims'/survivors' experiences of the court process were comparatively more positive (Cook, Burton, Robinson, & Vallely, 2004; Vallely et al., 2005). A significant reason for this finding was the supportive role provided by a domestic violence victims' advocate throughout the court process. This role grew and came to be known as the Independent Domestic Violence Advocate (Advisor) (IDVA) whose evolution and wider multi-agency role are discussed by Robinson and Payton, see Chap. 12, this volume.

Policymakers were influenced by the specialist court provision that had grown in the USA, which included a variety of models, with some sitting as criminal courts only and others combining civil and criminal hearings. Regardless of the format, all US courts had the united objectives of improving victim safety and increasing the accountability of perpetrators. Examples of how these objectives were to be realised included providing access to independent advocacy support for victims/survivors, securing higher conviction rates and appropriate referrals to treatment programmes for perpetrators (Burton, 2008). Much of this ethos is shared by SDVCs in England and Wales, the success of which is based on the close coordination of agencies (Bowen et al., 2014; Taylor-Dunn, 2015). However, multi-agency working is not such a familiar component to legal professionals and the operation of the courts and the SDVCs in England and Wales tend to be limited in focus to criminal matters.

Case Identification

The means of identifying cases for SDVCs vary across different courts. Often, the police or Crown Prosecution Service (CPS) are required to flag up cases suitable for the SDVC, although the level of their involvement in doing so differs. In some courts, custody officers have been assisted in this task by a specialist SDVC coordinator, with an early example illustrated at the Wolverhampton court (Cook et al., 2004). A further small-scale observational study conducted by the author examined 24 SDVC hearings at a court over a three day period in 2012. Whilst such an exercise has some clear limitations as a research tool (see Watkins & Burton, 2013) and as such cannot be relied on for providing any accurate broader generalisations on the SDVC process, it provides some insight into further areas of investigation.

One emerging theme pertained to the process of case identification and the loss of an experienced SDVC coordinator, as a result of budgetary cuts. In a sample of 24 hearings, six involved cases where the conduct alleged was between non-intimate partners. Although, three of these six offences occurred within the home, the remaining cases were incorrectly listed as traffic offences. The remaining 18 hearings concerned intimate partner violence (IPV) involving varying degrees of gravity. Although the anomalous cases were also handled by the SDVC, serving also as a 'normal' Magistrates' Court, this did not make good use of the SDVC facility and the specialised training involved. These findings suggest that the role and the function of the SDVC are not fully understood by the police and the CPS. Whilst Burton's (2008) analysis does not outline any similar difficulties, she does observe that good case identification is viewed as essential to the specialisation process. Where court IDVAs have become embedded within an SDVC, this has assisted the identification of cases as found by Taylor-Dunn (2015). IDVAs are able to bring the knowledge gained through their experiences with victims/survivors to the SDVC, thereby improving its running and efficiency.

Definitional Challenges

The difficulties of case identification may also be explained in part by the varied definitions of DVA. The non-statutory definition adopted by agencies since 2013 has not, until recently, been reflected in the criminal law (Home Office, 2013). The scope of the non-statutory definition for DVA is wide; it captures controlling and coercive behaviours and also extends to family relationships. Alongside its usage, however, the terms 'domestic violence' and 'domestic abuse' are used differently by agencies; for some, the terms act as distinctive concepts, whilst for others they embody the same range and types of behaviour (Bettinson & Bishop, 2015). For the process to be effective at the SDVC, a shared understanding of what amounts to DVA is needed between the police, prosecution, magistrates and other representatives. In England and Wales, the extent to which non-intimate domestic relationships fall within the ambit of DVA has also increased with the introduction of a new offence of coercive and controlling behaviour introduced by section 76 Serious Crime Act 2015. This offence (as outlined in Bishop's Chap. 4) applies in cases where the victim/survivor and perpetrator are personally connected (section 76(1)(b)) and includes 'members of the same family' as well as immediate partners (section 76(2)(b)). The need to improve understandings of DVA within the criminal justice system is, therefore, essential to effectively incorporate the Home Office definition and this new offence into practice.

The HMIC (2014) report revealed that some police officers felt that the Home Office definition had become too inclusive as a term, prompting a response on occasion where it was inappropriate, for example, where the conduct concerned siblings. The police officers' concern was that the definition now reached too far into non-intimate domestic relationships. There is some academic support for this view and Youngs (2015) notes that the harm is qualitatively different when it occurs between intimate or formerly intimate partners, compared to other forms of relationships and this should be reflected in legal provisions. However, the HMIC (2014) report took the overview that the current definition should stand, albeit with the more effective training of officers so that they are able to better understand the risks to the victim/survivor of DVA. As with other agencies, it is thought that a greater understanding of the nature of DVA will improve the police response.

There has also been a variation in definitions of DVA adopted by SDVCs, and future evaluations need to take this into account. The author's observations reveal that the identified cases at the particular SDVC studied were not limited to IPV. In contrast, in Cook et al.'s (2004) study, West London Magistrates' Court had undertaken a dedicated approach to IPV cases only. Definitional alignment would be a useful tool for monitoring SDVCs' performance; however, it may not be realistic, now that the language of, and approach to, DVA has become so varied. However, if achieved, it would provide greater opportunity for researchers to gather comparable data and address the current significant limitations in evaluating SDVC court performance (Bowen et al., 2014).

Integration and Multi-Agency Working

In England and Wales, the court system is divided between a civil jurisdiction and a separate criminal court system. Solicitors train in specific fields and it is unusual for a solicitor to work across both civil and criminal law. on a wider variety of work that spans both legal jurisdictions. However, the additional expense of a barrister means that solicitors are more common to the Magistrates' Court. Robinson's study (Robinson, 2007) highlights the current lack of coordination between the criminal and civil legal jurisdictions despite the fact that a victim/survivor of DVA may seek remedies or redress from both of them. The study revealed that generally there was no interface between the criminal and civil courts unless a solicitor experienced in DVA legal matters in both, or a specialist advocate from a women's support agency was involved. Unless the advocate provides information of criminal proceedings to the civil court, there is no information sharing between the two courts. This has ramifications when making important decisions relating in particular to child contact cases. There are also cost and time efficiency implications. If one court is able to deal with all of the legal issues arising from a DVA case, clear cost reductions can be made.

Examples of an integrated specialist domestic violence court in the USA found a key benefit of this approach to be the avoidance of inconsistent orders that tended to frustrate victims/survivors (Burton, 2008). Integrating the two jurisdictions for DVA cases was piloted in the UK in Croydon, but an early evaluation showed the result to be disappointing (Hester, Pearce, & Westmarland, 2008). The integrated court at Croydon sought to follow the principle of 'one family, one court' used in the examples from USA, to address cases that involved overlapping criminal and family law matters. The reasons suggested for its limited success, however, included difficulties in identifying suitable cases, a lack of funding leading to low levels of advocacy support and solicitors' lack of expertise in both civil and criminal law. As stated previously, within the legal context, information sharing and collaborative working between the civil and criminal systems are not commonplace, which stands at odds with the multi-agency practices established amongst other DVA services. SDVCs in England and Wales have continued, therefore, to deal only with criminal cases of DVA within the Magistrates' Court jurisdiction. Bowen et al. (2014) note that the work of SDVCs remains subject to wide regional variation, with many being combined with other matters and dealing with criminal bail hearings, pre-trial hearings, pleas and sentencing hearings for summary offences. Some courts also host trials within the summary jurisdiction. The listing for an SDVC can also be as limited as one day/week. There is, therefore, only a very small amount of court time dedicated to DVA specialisation.

Victim-Centred Courts and the IDVA

Following on from the challenges of bringing different legal jurisdictions and agency functions together, a core principle of the SDVCs is the creation of a more victim-centred legal process, providing support via victims' advocates and leading to efficient, swifter justice and better informed legal decisions (Eley, 2005). Both independent and government research demonstrates that SDVCs lead to a higher rate of convictions. From the CPS's position, this is evidence that SDVCs have improved criminal justice outcomes in DVA cases. This is further supported by the upward trend of successful prosecutions of violence against women, which have increased from 60 % to 74 % from 2005–2012 (CPS, 2012). Such was the success of the SDVCs that following recommendations from early evaluations, an expansion programme was launched, with numbers reaching a peak of 143 courts in 2010; this number fell short of the forecasted number of approximately 200 by 2011, suggested under the Government's 2008 Action Plan (Home Office, 2008).

The IDVA is central to the SDVC's success. A system of fast tracking or clustering of DVA cases identified for the court enables the IDVA to be present at court to support a victim/survivor, or their interests, when requested to do so. This can lead to the IDVA handling many cases in one court sitting. The IDVA can support the victim/survivor with their needs both in terms of the court case and in a holistic manner. The early evaluations of the SDVCs showed the presence of an IDVA helped to improve victim confidence in the criminal justice system. This finding prompted Cook et al. (2004) to recommend that SDVCs should have victims' advocates dedicated to the specialist court environment. However, Taylor-Dunn (2015) states that this has not materialised into practice and there is limited government attention placed on the role of the IDVA in the court setting. Given the pivotal position of the IDVA to the successful operation of the SDVC, greater government funding arrangements for this role should be considered. Taylor-Dunn (2015) provides a contemporary analysis of victim advocacy, looking at a single SDVC case study, where the court clearly benefited from court-based IDVAs. She found that where IDVAs were involved, a higher proportion of victims/survivors provided evidence to support the prosecution's case and/or attended court compared to the national profile. Views expressed by the IDVAs in the case study suggested that the reasons for this were the comprehensive support and dedicated focus on the victim that they provided. For example, the IDVA was able to assist the victim/survivor in accessing other agencies that they might need outside the ambit of the criminal law.

IDVAs are independent and non-judgemental in their approach, which also includes the attitude towards the victim's decision regarding whether or not to support the prosecution's case. The IDVAs use their ability to reassure the victims/survivors about the actual court process and using the knowledge that they have gained through their increasing experience of the court's procedures, the possible consequences of the court hearings. This helps to establish trust between the IDVA and the victim, which is further strengthened by their efforts and organisational liaison to ensure the safety of the victim in the court environment. They can provide a means of voicing the victim's wishes to the prosecution and the court, for example, by checking that special measures are applied for and put in place and by collecting the victim impact statement. The DVA witness is thereby supported and given greater confidence of their safety whilst cooperating with the court process. It is essential that austerity cuts do not remove the IDVA's presence from the legal process and that the court room remains an area of access for victims/survivors and their advocates.

In Taylor-Dunn's (2015) study, the IDVAs who were interviewed noticed that in cases where a victim attended court, the perpetrators were more likely to enter a guilty plea. They believed this was based on the advice of defence solicitors as a means of preventing the victim from giving their evidence, with the possibility that a more severe sentence would be imposed if the defendant was found guilty on a full hearing of that evidence. Taylor-Dunn notes that the IDVAs in her study commented that they had used their knowledge of how defence solicitors tend to advise their clients to better inform the victim. The victim's attendance was found to be 'regularly used by prosecutors as a bargaining tool, irrespective of whether or not the victim is willing to give evidence' (2015, p. 7). This is an important observation, although this experience did not alter the focus of the IDVAs, who were clear that their role was not to increase the level of successful prosecutions, but to focus on the needs of the victim. Where prosecution rates did increase, this was deemed to be a positive by-product of their service. Taylor-Dunn's study builds on the recommendations made by Cook et al. (2004) to embed a court-based IDVA service within all SDVCs. The experience gained by IDVAs based at courts can be used to encourage victim participation and may have an impact on the approaches taken by defence solicitors. With the greater encouragement of victim attendance at court, the SDVCs become more visibly balanced between the needs of the victim and the fair trial of the defendant within the court room.

Scottish Domestic Abuse Courts

The implementation of the SDVC has varied, and some subtle differences are apparent in the approach taken to meeting some of the challenges rehearsed previously in this chapter. In Scotland, with its own unique judicial system, Domestic Abuse Courts were first piloted in 2004 in Glasgow (Reid Howie Associates, 2007), then rolled out as a model to other areas, including Edinburgh. One of the key differences of the Scottish approach to that adopted in England and Wales is the reported strength of the relationship between the police and prosecution authorities in Scotland on matters of domestic violence (Connelly, 2011). Conversely, Bowen et al. (2014) found that in England and Wales, there was poor evidence gathering and information sharing between the police and the CPS, who were often inadequately prepared for the SDVC. Connelly explains that the Scottish criminal justice agencies 'have worked together to develop specialist responses to domestic [violence and/or] abuse that reflect the national commitment and strategy to both aid victims and respond to perpetrators' (Connelly, 2011, p. 110). The strong joint working practices of the Scottish police and Scotland's prosecuting authority, the Crown Office and Procurator Fiscal Service are reflected in a Joint Protocol, the focus of which is exclusively centred on a definition of IPV, offering an alternative approach that could be adopted in England and Wales. The definition of the term 'domestic abuse' used by the police in Scotland and the prosecuting authorities is also found in the Joint Protocol and refers to:

> any form of physical, sexual or mental and emotional abuse which might amount to criminal conduct and which takes place within the context of a relationship. The relationship will be between partners (married, cohabiting, civil partnership or otherwise) or ex-partners. The abuse can be committed in the home or elsewhere. (Police Scotland and Crown Office Procurator Fiscal Service, 2013, p. 2)

The police work closely with the prosecuting authorities, reflecting, perhaps, lower levels of cynicism on the issue of DVA than their English and Welsh counterparts. The focus placed on IPV by the support agencies involved also specifically addresses DVA between current and former partners. Clarity as to the nature of DVA cases at police and prosecution levels enables smoother working relationships between the two criminal justice agencies. The Joint Protocol does adopt a gender-neutral definition, but acknowledges that evidence shows that most cases involve male abuse towards women. An understanding of DVA as a gender-based crime is also embedded within Scotland's National Strategy to Address Domestic Abuse in Scotland (Scottish Government, 2015).

The daily running of Scotland's Specialist Domestic Abuse Courts ensures that cases are processed promptly, with the additional benefits of a professional judge (sheriff) presiding who is trained in DVA issues (Lynch, 2011). IDVAs also attend the Scottish Specialist Domestic Abuse Courts, provided by independent third-sector agencies such as ASSIST (Advocacy, Support, Safety, Information and Services Together) in Glasgow and Women's Aid in Edinburgh. The frequency of the Scottish Specialist Courts enables the IDVAs' working relationships with the procurator fiscal and the police to become better established for the benefit of the victim/survivor. Therefore, locating DVA cases daily in the same courtroom aids these relationships and encourages an efficient process. The capacity of the SDVCs in England and Wales to replicate these benefits is again severely limited by the Courts Closure Programme (MoJ, 2015), resulting in many local Magistrates' Courts being closed, affecting the availability and distribution of SDVCs in local areas.

The Defence at the SDVC

In Scotland, the Scottish Legal Aid Board worked to ensure that a dedicated duty solicitor is available for all domestic abuse cases at the Domestic Abuse Court. Alternatively, the accused is entitled to have their own regular solicitor represent them, with legal aid granted automatically on a 'time in line' basis (Connelly, 2011). There are unique legal aid arrangements for this court with designated procurator fiscal-deputes available to discuss cases with defence solicitors (Lynch, 2011). In comparison, legal aid in England and Wales does not provide a specialist domestic violence duty solicitor, although a general criminal law duty solicitor is present in the court house. To receive representation at court, the accused can either rely on the free advice and representation of the duty solicitor or their own solicitor if legal aid is granted, or they are able to use personal funds. Many defence solicitors are unlikely to have received training on DVA issues. Where the alleged perpetrator has not approached a solicitor, the legal clerk at the SDVC will assist where possible.

The Rise in Police Diversion

In Scotland, the police must arrest the alleged perpetrator and inform the procurator fiscal (the prosecutor) who will consider whether there is sufficient evidence to pursue a prosecution. This can occur whether the victim/survivor decides to make a complaint or not. Even when a case does not proceed to court, follow-on contact with the victim/survivor is made by a police officer from the Domestic Abuse Investigation Unit. This framework ensures that all DVA cases reported to the police will be subject to input from trained specialist police officers or procurator fiscals. The focus is on victim safety and avoids the diversion of perpetrators from the courts by main grade, non-specialist police officers. In England and Wales, there are concerns that the police are employing out-of-court disposals to divert criminal cases, including DVA, from the courts (Donoghue, 2014). The overall number of criminal cases that come before the magistrates has decreased by 14 % over the past four years

(Gibbs, 2014). That this may have impacted SDVC output is suggested by figures showing an increase of police reporting of DVA, alongside a decline in the conviction rate, although this still remains higher than before the introduction of SDVC provision. Bowen et al. (2014) chart a 13 % decrease in the number of DVA cases referred to the CPS by the police since 2010–2013. As Donoghue (2014) reveals, the use of out-of-court police disposals have included more serious forms of offending and persistent offenders, both of which are prevalent features of DVA cases.

In light of the HMIC report on the responses of the police to DVA, this is a particularly disturbing development (HMIC, 2014). Diverting cases away from the court undermines the role of the SDVC as a court of first response to DVA and results in a displacement of business by the police. Considering the long time it takes for many victims/survivors to report the violence and/or abuse they are experiencing and pursue a criminal justice response, diversion is an inappropriate outcome. It is accepted that the necessity for the pursuit of a criminal sanction is not a universally held perspective (Mills, 1998). However, as the Scottish model illustrates, with good working relationships between the police, prosecuting authorities and DVA agencies, focusing on victim safety, criminal justice responses to acts of DVA may further improve. Whilst some police practices in England and Wales have seen positive developments and have moved beyond the stereotypical image of their past indifference to DVA (Musgrove & Groves, 2008), further scrutiny of police decision-making in the use of summary penalties is required. If the use of police discretion is resulting in a significant shift of DVA cases away from the courts, the criminal justice response to DVA cannot be well judged.

Similar concerns arise regarding the use of cautions for matters of assault. These do not contribute to official crime statistics and such diversion skews the data of DVA and consequently the perception of the volume of this offence. Many DVA cases are charged as assaults and will not be officially counted in recorded crime figures (Burton, 2008). As commented previously, the concern is that the use of this and other police diversion tactics have impacted the disparity between the increase in reporting rates of DVA and the decrease in conviction rates (Bowen et al., 2014; HMIC, 2014). Although not without its own challenges, further reflection on the Scottish approach outlined in the Joint Protocol, developing a stronger relationship between the police and prosecution authorities may assist, as may the Scottish requirement that the police contact specialist support services in all DVA situations. The connection to the holistic support approach provided by the SDVC encourages victims/survivors to engage with the court process, or if they withdraw from it, they do so following an improved experience, which may encourage them to re-engage at a later stage. To weaken the role of the SDVC as the result of diversionary strategies is arguably a false economy, which does not utilise the expertise of specialist personnel and does not lead to improved protection from DVA.

The Impact of Courthouse Closures

The Court Estate Closure Programme (CERP) was implemented by the Coalition Government and ran from 2010 to 2014. It resulted in the closure of 140 court buildings (MoJ, 2015). The continuation of a policy to reduce the number of court houses was announced in March 2014 by the Lord Chancellor, Lord Chief Justice of England and Wales and Senior President of Tribunals. A consultation document released in July 2015 outlines the proposed reforms that are intended to facilitate quicker and fairer access to justice and to establish a justice system that reflects the way people use services (MoJ, 2015). Amongst these reforms, it is proposed that 57 more Magistrates' Courts will be closed, which amounts to 257 court rooms. The rationale for this action is based on the HM Court and Tribunal Services figures that reveal only a 47 % utilisation level of Magistrates' Courts in 2014–2015, a decrease from 55 % in 2013–2014 (MoJ, 2015).

Fears that these closures would include courts running SDVCs have been voiced. For example, Hyde (2011) noted that the Ministry of Justice plans to close 142 courts between 2010 and 2014, including 23 SDVCs. However, this figure is not visible in the official view of the number of specialist courts affected. As highlighted at the beginning of this chapter, at the height of its expansion in 2009 there were 143 accredited SDVCs operating in England and Wales. By 2011, this had decreased to 135. Bowen et al. (2014) recorded a slight increase to 138 SDVCs in operation during 2013. Areas that have lost their Magistrates' Court have had their SDVC provision moved to another one of the accredited courts within their Local Justice Area, as confirmed by responses to a recent Freedom of Information request. The impact of these closures is being monitored by a National Steering Group, although DVA specialist agencies are not involved in that evaluation. The Ministry of Justice terminology has notably changed from one of individual SDVCs to SDVC 'systems', arguing that closure of a court is not the closure of the SDVC 'system' and that adequate provision will continue. The relocation of SDVC courts to other locations accounts for the much lower than feared volume of SDVC closures overall. However, the issue of SDVC relocation is clearly a very real concern to DVA services and the victims/survivors they work with, who may be more reluctant to attend court if they have a long distance to travel (Hyde, 2011).

Current proposals for further reductions in court house facilities do acknowledge matters of victim safety and the consequences for accessing justice. It is proposed that where courts are closed, leaving an area without a local, accessible Magistrates' Court, other civic buildings could be used as alternative locations, although the necessary levels of security personnel may not be available. Alternative venues must be carefully vetted to ensure that victim safety is preserved with, for example, different entrances and waiting room areas for victims/survivors and perpetrators (Bowen et al., 2014). Special measures, such as video links, must also be made available. The proposals openly reflect that a key aim of the policy is to reduce the current and future cost of running the estate. Acknowledging that further court house reductions will dilute local justice, the proposal suggests that more than 95 % of the population could travel to a court within an hour by car after the introduction of these reforms (MoJ, 2015). There is no specific reference to the preservation of SDVC provision in the new proposals, implying that systems will continue to be maintained. However, ensuring access for victims/survivors, the availability of appropriate safety measures and the need to support IDVAs where their workload increases across a wider geographical area, perhaps, warrants more particular attention.

Donoghue (2014) observes that the unique nature of Magistrates' Courts in England and Wales with its employment of 'lay' justices is also now threatened by these trends of administrative efficiency. Court closures have also inevitably resulted in a decline in the number of magistrates, which decreased by 8000 from 2010, with a further reduction of almost 2000 magistrates in 2013. There are now 19,634 magistrates (Judicial Office, 2015) across England and Wales, amounting to a 20 % decrease since the start of the Court Closure Programme. This general trend must invariably have an impact on the operation of the SDVCs, which are all located within the Magistrates' Court system. In the previous Coalition Government's (2012) White Paper *Swift and Sure Justice*, core themes of efficiency and the reliable delivery of justice to enhance public confidence were apparent (MoJ, 2012a) and changes to the role of the magistracy was part of that vision (Donoghue, 2014). For SDVCs, however, it is vital that enough magistrates continue to be trained in DVA matters to fulfil the vision of efficiency for this specialist provision and the associated improvements in public levels of confidence in the criminal justice system. One way to satisfy these objectives could be to extend the scope of the work undertaken by the SDVC.

Extending the Scope of SDVCs

To ensure that perceptions of their 'value' increases during times of economic shortages, it is worthwhile to reflect on possible extensions to the SDVC function. For example, Donoghue (2014) advocates that police diversionary decisions should be scrutinised by magistrates. Whilst budgetary cuts to the criminal justice system may make out-of-court disposals more attractive, variations in the application of diversionary disposals need to be addressed (Ashworth, 2013). The examination of out-of-court disposals is currently limited to judicial review or by complaint via the Independent Police Complaints Commission. Padfield, Morgan, and Maguire (2012) argue that such decision-making should be subject to judicial scrutiny, rather than giving the responsibility of oversight and accountability to politicians, civil servants or the police, the latter of whom may be prone to bias as a result of police performance-related targets (Donoghue, 2014; Patrick, 2011). Extending the magistrates' powers of scrutiny over police cautions has received judicial approval in *R (on the application of Stratton) v Chief Constable of Thames Valley Police* [2013] EWHC 1561 (Admin) where the court agreed that magisterial review 'may well be the more efficacious and cost effective way of ensuring that the use of cautions is in accordance with law and the public interest is protected'. This review procedure could be introduced within the work of SDVCs as a useful additional way to monitor the appropriateness of repeat cautions in DVA cases. There is currently no formal framework for these reviews, and scrutiny panels have grown only on an ad hoc basis. Those that have emerged are not ports for appeals, but work closely with the police 'to obtain further clarity about the circumstances in which particular cases have not been brought to court, to provide greater consistency in the use of disposals and to monitor any departures from statutory guidance' (Donoghue, 2014, p. 950). These observations have particular resonance with the HMIC (2014) report on the unsatisfactory approach taken to DVA cases by the police, with an overuse of out-of-court disposals. Donoghue (2014) argues that running panels more frequently would enable magistrates to communicate more routinely with the police about the appropriateness of summary penalties in particular cases, as well as general patterns that may cause concern. In this sense, magistrates are well placed to ensure the 'accountability, consistency and compliance with sentencing guidelines' (Donoghue, 2014, p. 962), with those trained for the SDVC having a greater understanding of DVA.

A further possible extension to the SDVC remit could include a dedicated function relating to the issue and oversight of Domestic Violence Protection Orders (DVPO) introduced by the *Crime and Security Act 2010* (see Burton, Chap. 3). A police officer (27(1)(2)) applies to the Magistrates' Court who can make a DVPO where it is satisfied 'on the balance of probabilities that P[the alleged perpetrator] has been violent towards, or has threatened violence towards, an associated person' and the court thinks it is 'necessary to protect that person from violence or a threat of violence by P' (section 28(2) and (3)). Kelly, Alder, Howarth, Lovett, Coulson, Kernohan and Gray (2013) recommended, following a pilot evaluation of the scheme, 'greater tailoring' of the orders. With its specialist knowledge, the SDVC could achieve this by ensuring that orders were an appropriate length in each case and by providing a channel whereby IDVAs can ensure that there is some engagement with victims/survivors to assist and provide access to other services, regardless of whether or not a criminal prosecution is ultimately pursued.

Sentencing

Sentencers in the SDVC, as with any criminal sentencing court, are required by section 142(1) *Criminal Justice Act 2003* to have regard to a number of aims of sentencing, which include the punishment of offenders, deterrence, public protection, rehabilitation and reparation. Whilst some commentators have reflected that this sentencing framework can be generally problematic, Bettinson and Dingwall (2012) have argued that a well-judged use of discretion allows sentencers to balance the prescribed aims to maximise the potential for a successful outcome in DVA cases. The Sentencing Guidelines Council (2006) unequivocally states that courts must regard offences taking place within the domestic setting as seriously as those that occur elsewhere. With the creation of the SDVCs, it was envisaged that specialism would give rise to greater effectiveness and consistency in sentencing practice. This, however, has not been easy to establish and further work is needed to improve the data pertaining to sentencing outcomes (Bowen et al., 2014). A problematic use of financial penalties by SDVCs has been raised by Robinson (2008) who found that these, along with discharges, were the most common form of penalty utilised by SDVCs. Financial penalties may bring little victim satisfaction, potentially placing further strain on a household rather than increasing victim safety. More positively, Cook et al. (2004) found that a third of sentences issued by SDVCs involved a referral to a domestic violence perpetrator programme (see Hilder and Freeman, Chap. 13). Whilst the evidence base is not extensive, several studies have shown that court-sanctioned specialist rehabilitation programmes can serve to reduce recidivism (Lewis, 2004). However, it has been found that there is greater success in cases where such sanctions are also subject to continued court monitoring (Gondolf, 2002; Mazur & Aldrich, 2003). Bowen et al. (2014) suggest that SDVCs would be improved by issuing more tailored protection orders and introducing a post-sentence review to strengthen the monitoring of perpetrators.

Returning to the author's own small-scale SDVC study, three of nine sentencing cases were adjourned for the preparation of a Pre-Sentence Report (PSR) and a further case was adjourned following a non-appearance by the defendant. All cases where a PSR was ordered involved instances of physical assaults and/or threats of physical violence. In addition, each case demonstrated a history of similar behaviour. The prospect of rehabilitation and the need to prevent further offending were reflected in the penalties applied for the five remaining cases with the use of community supervision and suspended custodial sentences. Restraining orders were also used in cases where the victim and the defendant were no longer in a relationship, with conditions prohibiting contact.

Evident in all of the completed sentencing hearings observed was the implementation of a victim surcharge. Offenders were ordered to pay a victim surcharge generally amounting to 60 pounds to the court. This surcharge was first implemented in April 2007 through the *Criminal Justice Act 2003 (Surcharge No. 2) Order* 2007; however, it has since been extended in terms of the value and the number of offences it can be applied to. Following the *Criminal Justice Act (Surcharge) Order 2012*, a court must order the Victim Surcharge for offences committed after 1 October 2012.[1] Where a community order is made, the charge is 60 pounds for an offender aged more than 18 and increases up a scale thereafter where a custodial sentence is made. Revenue raised from the surcharge 'is used to fund emotional and practical support for victims of crime' (Ministry of Justice, 2012b). This surcharge, therefore, differs from compensation, as it is not payable to the victim directly. It is not difficult to imagine that DVA victims/survivors may view the surcharge in an equally negative manner to financial penalties. If the funds raised were used directly to support the work of court IDVAs, they might be better justified.

---

[1] *Criminal Justice Act (Surcharge) Order 2012*, *Criminal Justice Act 2003 (Surcharge No. 2) Order 2007*. For details of surcharge provisions and scale see https://www.sentencingcouncil.org.uk/explanatory-material/item/fines-and-financial-orders/victim-surcharge/ accessed on October 25, 2015.

Conclusion

This chapter has illustrated how good working relationships between the police, prosecuting authorities and DVA services are vital to the successful operation of SDVCs. Comparisons with Scotland's criminal justice response to DVA reveal that there are some aspects of good practice that could be used to inform progress in England and Wales. The pivotal point of the system currently is the IDVA, resulting in better communication between the prosecution authorities, support services, the victim/survivor and the magistrates. With changes occurring as a result of reduced costs, such as the closure of courthouses, a reduction in magistrate numbers and less focused funding on court-located IDVAs, it is imperative that the position of the SDVC as a key aspect of the criminal justice system's effective response to DVA is noted and that it survives current austerity measures. The justification for the SDVC remains intact, although the ability to monitor and address issues of impact is hindered by different definitional interpretations and the disparate nature of recording outcomes, such as victim satisfaction, safety and recidivism levels (Bowen et al., 2014). On the contrary, this chapter has argued that with there is an opportunity to increase the work of SDVCs. SDVCs offer a means to monitor police decisions, deal with DVPOs and provide post-sentence reviews to increase the monitoring of rehabilitative progress made by perpetrators. They can achieve this on account of their specialist knowledge, offering a more formal space to connect agencies, both statutory and non-statutory and hold them to account in their protection of the victim/survivor. In this way, the SDVC should not only be preserved in times of austerity, but also improved.

References

Ashworth, A. (2013). Penalty notices for disorder and summary justice. *Criminal Law Review, 11*, 869–870.

Bettinson, V., & Bishop, C. (2015). Is the creation of a discrete offence of coercive control necessary to combat domestic violence? *Northern Ireland Legal Quarterly, 66*(2), 179–197.

Bettinson, V., & Dingwall, G. (2012). Applying generic sentencing aims in domestic violence cases in England and Wales. *International Journal of Law, Crime and Justice, 40*(3), 242–254.

Bowen, P., Qasim, A., & Tetenbaum, L. (2014). Better courts: A snapshot of domestic violence courts in 2013. London: Centre for Justice Innovation. Retrieved from http://b.3cdn.net/nefoundation/667bd380bdc5bac599_e4m6b0z7o.pdf

Burton, M. (2008). *Legal responses to domestic violence.* Abingdon: Routledge.

Connelly, C. (2011). Specialist responses to domestic abuse. In H. Hughes (Ed.), *Domestic Abuse and Scots Law*. Edinburgh: W Green/Thomson Reuters.

Cook, D., Burton, M., Robinson, A., & Vallely, C. (2004). *Evaluation of specialist domestic violence courts/fast track systems*. London: Crown Prosecution Service and Department of Constitutional Affairs.

Cretney, A., & Davies, G. (1997). Prosecuting domestic assault: Victims failing courts, or courts failing victims? *Howard Journal of Criminal Justice, 36*(2), 146–157.

Crown Prosecution Service (CPS). (2012). *Violence Against Women Crime Report 2011–2012*. London: CPS Management Information Branch.

Dawson, M., & Dinovitzer, R. (2001). Victim cooperation and the prosecution of domestic violence in a specialized court. *Justice Quarterly, 18*(3), 593–622.

Donoghue, J. C. (2014). Reforming the role of magistrates: Implications for summary justice in England and Wales. *Modern Law Review, 77*(6), 928–963.

Eley, S. (2005). Changing practices: The specialised domestic violence court process. *The Howard Journal, 44*(2), 113–124.

Gibbs, P. (2014). *Why has the magistracy shrunk?* London: Transform Justice.

Gondolf, E. (2002). *Batterer intervention systems*. London: SAGE.

Her Majesty's Inspectorate of Constabulary (HMIC). (2014). *Everyone's business: Improving the police response to domestic violence*. London: HMIC.

Hester, M., Pearce, P., & Westmarland, N. (2008). *Early evaluation of the Integrated Domestic Violence Court, Croydon*. Ministry of Justice Series 18/08. Retrieved October 25, 2015, from http://www.bristol.ac.uk/media-library/sites/sps/migrated/documents/rk6668reportpart2.pdf

Home Office. (2008). *Call to End Violence against Women and Girls: Action Plan.* London: HM Government.

Home Office. (2011). *A Call to End Violence against Women and Girls: Action Plan*. London: HM Government.

Home Office. (2013). *Home Office Circular 003/2013: New government domestic violence and abuse definition*. Retrieved October 24, 2015, from https://www.

gov.uk/government/publications/new-government-domestic-violence-and-abuse-definition

Hyde, J. (2011). Domestic violence courts to close. *Law Gazette*, 6 May.

Judicial Office. (2015). *Serving magistrates report for July 2015*. London: Courts and Tribunals Judiciary.

Kelly, L., Alder, J., Howarth, M., Lovett, J., Coulson, M., Kernohan, D., et al. (2013). *Evaluation of the pilot of domestic violence protection orders*. Research Report 76. London: Home Office.

Lewis, R. (2004). Making justice work effective legal interventions for domestic violence. *British Journal of Criminology, 44*, 204–224.

Lynch, P. (2011). The criminal justice system. In H. Hughes (Ed.), *Domestic Abuse and Scots Law*. Edinburgh: W. Green/Thomson Reuters.

Mazur, R., & Aldrich, L. (2003). What makes a domestic violence court work – Lessons from New York. *Judges Journal, 42*(2), 5–10.

Mills, L. G. (1998). Mandatory arrest and prosecution policies for domestic violence a critical literature review and the case for more research to test victim empowerment approaches. *Criminal Justice and Behavior, 25*(3), 306–318.

Ministry of Justice. (2012a). *Swift and sure justice: The government's plans for reform of the criminal justice system*. Cm 8388. London: Ministry of Justice.

Ministry of Justice. (2012b). *Circular 2012/05: Increase and extension of the Victim Surcharge*. London: Justice Reform, Justice Policy Group, Ministry of Justice.

Ministry of Justice. (2015). *Proposal on the provision of court and tribunal services in England and Wales*. London: HM Court and Tribunal Services, Ministry of Justice.

Musgrove, A., & Groves, N. (2008). The Domestic Violence, Crime and Victims Act 2004: Relevant or "removed" legislation? *The Journal of Social Welfare and Family Law, 29*(3–4), 233–244.

Padfield, N., Morgan, R., & Maguire, M. (2012). Out of court, out of sight? Criminal sanctions and non-judicial decision-making. In M. Maguire, R. Morgan, & R. Reiner (Eds.), *The Oxford handbook of criminology*. Oxford: Oxford University Press.

Patrick, R. (2011). Reading tea leaves: An assessment of the reliability of the police recorded crime statistics. *Police Journal, 84*, 47–67.

Police Scotland and Crown Office and Procurator Fiscal Service. (2013). *Joint protocol between Police Scotland and Crown Office and Procurator Fiscal Service: In partnership challenging domestic abuse*. Retrieved October 25, 2015, from http://www.scotland.police.uk/assets/pdf/keep_safe/175573?view=Standard

Reid Howie Associates. (2007). *Evaluation of the pilot domestic abuse court*. Edinburgh: Scottish Executive Justice Department.

Robinson, A. (2007). Improving the civil-criminal interface for victims of domestic violence. *The Howard Journal, 46*(4), 356–371.

Robinson, A. (2010). Domestic violence. In F. Brookman, M. Maguire, H. Pierpoint, & T. Bennet (Eds.), *Handbook on crime*. Devon: Willan Publishing.

Robinson, A. L. (2008). *Measuring what matters in specialist domestic violence courts (No. 102)*. Cardiff: Cardiff School of Social Sciences, Cardiff University.

Robinson, A., & Cook, D. (2006). Understanding victim retraction in cases of domestic violence: Specialist courts, government policy, and victim-centred justice. *Contemporary Justice Review, 9*(2), 189–213.

Scottish Government. (2015). *Preventing domestic abuse. A national strategy*. Retrieved October 25, 2015, from http://www.gov.scot/Publications/2003/09/18185/26440

Sentencing Guidelines Council. (2006). *Overarching principles: Domestic violence*. London: SGC.

Serious Crime Act 2015 c9. Retrieved October 25, 2015, from http://www.legislation.gov.uk/ukpga/2015/9/contents/enacted

Taylor-Dunn, H. (2015). The impact of victim advocacy on the prosecution of domestic violence offences: Lessons from a realistic evaluation. *Criminology and Criminal Justice*, 1–19.

Vallely, C., Robinson, A. L., Burton, M., & Tregidga, J. (2005). *Evaluation of domestic violence pilot sites at Caerphilly (Gwent) and Croydon*. London: Crown Prosecution Service.

Watkins, D., & Burton, M. (2013). *Research methods in law*. London: Routledge.

Youngs, J. (2015). Domestic violence and the criminal law: Reconceptualising reform. *Journal of Criminal Law, 79*(1), 55–70.

Part II

Prevention and Intervention

6

Victim Support Services and the World of Commissioning

Di Turgoose

Introduction

In 2012–2013, a total of 1.2 million women experienced domestic violence and abuse (DVA) and a domestic violence 'incident' was reported every minute to the police (Office of National Statistics, 2015). In 2012–2013, a total of 82,517 women and 14,000 children accessed non-refuge, specialist DVA support services and 19,684 women and children accessed a safe house or specialist refuge provision (Women's Aid, 2013a). These figures are an increase on the previous year's recorded statistics. The fact that more victims appear to be accessing services can be attributed to a range of factors and in particular, to the positive progress that has been achieved in raising the profile of DVA issues and securing government commitment in the form of the Ending Violence Against Women and Girls Strategy (Home Office, 2011, 2014, 2015). However, these positive steps are now being systematically undermined by the impact of austerity

D. Turgoose (✉)
Community and Criminal Justice Division,
De Montfort University, Leicester, UK

cuts. A myriad of commissioning and funding processes has emerged, which sees DVA service providers struggling to maintain satisfactory levels of support and intervention for victims, with very little scope for development and expansion.

The discourse as to whether an exploration of gender is relevant to an examination of DVA issues is covered effectively elsewhere in this volume in relation to legal proceedings (see Bishop, Chap. 4), the shaping of victim experiences (see Martin, Chap. 9) and explanations of and responses to perpetrator behaviours (see Hilder and Freeman, Chap. 13). Its relevancy here, however, pertains to resourcing. Although statistics are disputed, it is broadly accepted that women are far more likely to become victims of domestic abuse than men and are most likely to be subject to repeat acts of victimisation (Walby, 2009). It is also recognised by academics such as Dempsey (2013) that the nature of the support pursued by male victims may not be adequately provided for by simply extending the services available to female victims. This calls for new pathways of research, practice development and resourcing for male victim support and the diverse groups of males that this may encompass. However, what has occurred in reality is a quick- fix solution, which professes gender neutrality as a cover for strategies that seek to further devolve the already dwindling financial resources available for victims of DVA. The origins of the DVA sector discussed in this chapter are intertwined with issues of gender inequality and concerns about the violence and harm caused, primarily to women, within the domestic sphere. These issues arguably would not have become a public concern had it not been for the feminist campaigns, which sought to address gender discrimination and oppression in all its many forms. However, a fast-forward to the modern day finds that whilst the moral obligation to act may now be much clearer, the funds acquired to support female victims of DVA are already proving insufficient and simply cannot be divided and diluted any further.

This chapter commences by providing a broad overview of DVA service development in the UK, from the early inception of the DVA sector to the present day. The primary focus of the discussion is on the victim support role within the specialist DVA non-government sector. It is also the case that DVA organisations deliver perpetrator work and that this is part of the commissioning process. However, the development of perpetrator interventions can be read about in more detail elsewhere in this volume (see Hilder and Freeman, Chap. 13; Barnes and Donovan, Chap. 14). This chapter explores the expansion of service provision as influenced by feminist campaigners from the 1970s onwards and the challenges made in the post-feminist era regarding assumptions of the 'commonality of female experience'. The impact of the emerging partnership, multi-agency and risk assessment agendas of the 1990s is then highlighted. This leads to the contemporary challenges of the economic downturn of the past 5 years and the introduction of commissioning processes. The discussion examines how the move towards a 'mainstreaming' of DVA service provision has left it vulnerable to competitive, market force ideologies. These applications have undermined areas of quality in service provision and hindered opportunities to address complex needs and increase victim engagement. As a result, providers are left floundering with the complex interplay of issues such as class, faith, age, race, sexuality, mental health and disability that may shape the commission of DVA and are left in a position where knowledge and expectation far exceeds service delivery capacity. The chapter concludes by supporting the call for a re-think (All Party Parliamentary Group, 2015) to ensure increased prevention, protection and intervention for all DVA victims in the future.

The Grass Root Beginnings of the DVA Sector

An understanding of the dynamics of DVA and the provision of specialist support services is embedded in a history of self-determination and the empowerment of survivors, who have themselves then metamorphosed into 'activists' to champion the pursuit of legal, policy and practice developments in primary, secondary and tertiary interventions for victims. The rise of the Women's Liberation Movement in the 1970s highlights an era of radicalisation for women's rights and is commonly attributed as the starting point of the DVA sector in the UK. The development of DVA services occurred in an environment where women were achieving other advancements across a broad range of equality issues, such as the legal steps taken towards addressing equal pay, sexual discrimination and reproduction rights. Issues of DVA and violence against women were highlighted by feminist media campaigns[1] and the first Rape Crisis Centre was opened in 1973. However, other challenges remained relatively impassable. For example, concepts of the nuclear family and the stability of the marital home continued to prevail, with women unable to obtain a mortgage in their own right without a guarantor. The impact of all this was extremely significant when it came to women seeking to leave situations of DVA.

The 1970s saw a small number of consciousness-raising groups of women meeting informally to look at issues relating to women's societal oppression (Hague & Malos, 1993). The political ideology of the DVA sector emerged from these small beginnings as the urgent need to provide safe housing for women experiencing violence in the domestic sphere was identified. Many of these early campaigners had links with other parts of the civil rights counter culture that was building at the time, such as the Black Liberation Movement[2] (Hague & Malos, 1993; Mama, 1996). The 1960s witnessed a severe UK housing crisis. Activists responded and the 'family squatting' movement was established, where groups of people took possession of empty housing for their own use. This opportunity was utilised by volunteer DVA campaigners and the first women's refuge for victims of DVA was opened in Chiswick,[3] London, in 1971, exploiting the legal framework for squatter's rights. Media coverage highlighted the mobilisation of empty houses as safe places for women fleeing violence at the hands of their husbands in the absence of any state provision. This, in turn, served to increase public awareness of the nature of the plight of victims, which would render them willing to live in such poor conditions.

---

[1] *Spare Rib*, a feminist collective magazine, was first published in 1972. The *Reclaim The Night* marches started in the UK on November 12, 1977, when torch-lit marches were held across England in Leeds, York, Bristol, Manchester, Newcastle, Brighton and London. They were called by the Leeds Revolutionary Feminist Group as part of coordinated action to address sexual harassment and sexual violence against women.

[2] The Black Liberation movement was also known as the Black Panther Movement.

The Chiswick refuge was founded by Ms. Pizzen. Refuge later left the Women's Aid network to become Refuge UK.

[3] Such as the Brixton riot(s). A confrontation between the Metropolitan Police and protesters in Brixton in the London Borough of Lambeth in April 1981and again in 1985 and 1995. Brixton was an area with social and economic problems and issues of inappropriate and oppressive policing tactics targeting the African Caribbean community.

6 Victim Support Services and the World of Commissioning 111

The refuge movement was, therefore, founded via this process of women coming together to enable others to escape violence in the marital home, thus challenging the wider patriarchal structures and gendered role expectations that reinforced such behaviours. It assumed a female commonality of experience, characterised at its most radical perimeters by a separatist agenda. Whilst this common voice was useful politically, it was later critiqued for assuming that patriarchy manifested itself in the same way across all heterosexual relationships. Typically, the Women's Liberation Movement at that stage was dominated by feminists from white, middle-class, educated backgrounds who presumed that the movement spoke for all women (Hague & Malos, 1993; Mama, 1996).

By 1974, the exponential take up of refuge resulted in the establishment of two refuge Federations, Scottish Women's Aid and the National Women's Aid Federation (NWAF), which coalesced refuge and safe house services across England, Wales and Northern Ireland. The Federations maintained the premise of women's self-help, whilst simultaneously seeking state recognition of the issue of men's violence against women. By 1975, the demand for refuge places had increased to such an extent that the Government Select Committee on Violence in Marriage recommended funding for one family refuge place per 10,000 families in the UK, a figure not met to date. Women's Aid continued lobbying to highlight the predicament of women and children experiencing homelessness as a result of DVA. The barriers to accessing alternative safe housing often included perceptions that victims had made themselves 'intentionally homeless' (see Burnet, Chap. 11). Lobbyists' efforts were met with some success, and the *Housing (Homeless Persons) Act* 1977 recognised that women and children fleeing domestic violence were entitled to state-funded, temporary accommodation. By the late 1970s, Women's Aid Federations were established in England, Wales, Scotland and Northern Ireland as both political campaigning bodies and DVA service providers. It remains a challenging balancing act, often requiring an engagement with state-funded services in order to support victims, whilst also seeking to challenge some of the dominant government orthodoxy in this arena.

As services for women and children continued to develop throughout the late 1970s and early 1980s, the majority of the funding was coming from official government bodies, local authority housing and social services committees, joint funding schemes and special housing association projects (Hague & Malos, 1993).

An Expansion of Service Provision

As previously highlighted, the activist era of the 1970s and 1980s was not restricted to the pursuit of gender politics alone and saw a wave of anti-establishment, anti-oppressive discourses, highlighting the experiences of a variety of marginalised social groups. Attention was paid initially to issues of race and ethnicity, largely due to the high profile of the inner-city riots of this era and the concerns raised regarding the oppressive policing tactics within black and minority ethnic (BME) communities.[4] Unsurprisingly, therefore, it was also initially the experiences of BME DVA victims that resulted in calls for more diverse understandings of the issue and a wider variety of specialist services to be made available. Black feminists insisted that they should not be 'grafted onto feminism in a tokenistic manner'(Carby, 1997, p. 54) and sought to re-define feminism for BME women. One of the consequences of this shift in thinking was the recognition that DVA services needed to evolve to address the differentiated experiences of black and Asian women (Carby, 1997; Davis, 1981; Parmar, 1982), where structural issues of both racism and patriarchy interplayed. The London inner-city feminist group *Southall Black Sisters* was formed in 1979, and since that time has provided legal advice, refuges and individual support for black and Asian DVA victims and has campaigned nationally for black and Asian DVA victim rights. The extension of such provisions nationally, however, remains piecemeal, with particular issues of isolation for BME women in rural communities.

It has been gradually acknowledged that other issues of identity, community and culture shape experiences of DVA and victims' access to appropriate support. However, the exploration of religion, mental health, disability, sexuality, age and class has arguably been slower to permeate. Early definitions of disability, for example, took a very one-dimensional,

---

[4] More information on the *Southall Black Sisters* is retrieved October 25, 2015, from http://www.southallblacksisters.org.uk/

medical-model approach, which focused on only practical issues such as the victim's physical access to buildings (Oliver, 1990), rather than on any broader understanding of an individual's complex needs. That said, the expansion of services during the 1980s was primarily a victim-led movement, marked by a significant level of autonomy and stability within the voluntary sector. However, the period was not without significant challenges. The 'right to buy' scheme initiated by the Conservative Government generated the need to encourage more private landlords, to compensate for reduced local authority housing stock. However, the deregulation of rent thresholds saw sharp increases in private renting costs, making it harder for DVA victims to find permanent affordable accommodation (Carlen, 1988). By 1987, a national domestic violence helpline had been established to cope with the increasing demand for refuge provision and it also served as a national referral point and advice line for both victims and professionals. Initiatives in outreach work were supported and there was also an emerging recognition that leaving the family home was simply not an option for many women. This resulted in the pursuit of more diverse approaches to support and safety, including further campaigns for increased legal protection and improved responses from the police. It was also increasingly recognised that ending violence and abuse was simply not enough and that victims needed longer term practical and emotional support to empower their recovery from DVA (Abrahams, 2007, 2010).

The Move Towards Partnership

The first formal state recognition of victims' statutory rights was established in the form of the *Victim's Charter* in 1990. The charter applied to all victims of crime, and although it was not legally binding, it embraced the emerging human rights agenda of the time. Subsequent revised charters and national victim strategies have followed, with government rhetoric placing victim concerns as a priority across a broad range of public sector functions. For statutory children services, however, the focus was child protection, with the *Children's Act 1989* highlighting that the safety of any child in a DVA scenario was paramount. The tensions that this created with the DVA sector and the impact on victims who were threatened with the removal of their children have been highlighted (Hester, 2013). However, despite this child focus, the actual development of specialist services to support children witnessing DVA were chronically underfunded (Hague, Kelly, Malos, & Mullender, 1996), with almost no form of outreach services whatsoever. Until the 1990s, the Criminal Justice System had also paid little attention to the impact of DVA on women and children, with many women feeling unprotected and unable to report their experiences (Morley & Mullender, 1994).

Symbolic milestones events occurred such as the criminalisation of rape within marriage in 1991. However, calls to bridge the gap between voluntary and statutory sector understandings of and approaches to DVA continued, although they were also now influenced by broader political, policy debates on multi-agency working, victims' rights and public protection. That methods of working should have an evidence base that supported a rationale for their adoption was also starting to prevail and a 'plan and do' approach to service provision was increasingly being seen as unacceptable. The principles of partnership and joint working responsibilities for organisations were presented in the landmark Morgan report (Home Office, 1991). Whilst its recommendations were never fully implemented, the report, commissioned by the government, promoted an approach built on the premise that no single agency can be 'responsible' for dealing with complex issues such as community safety and the problem of crime. *The Crime and Disorder Act 1998* placed a duty on the police and the local authorities to work together with other organisations to tackle crimes such as DVA; thus, the local Crime and Disorder Reduction Partnership (CDRP) network was established. The Home Office was also designated as the lead government ministry for DVA. Domestic violence forums often formed part of the local CDRP strategies set up to develop shared working practices across agencies to improve women's and children's safety. However, Domestic Violence Forums remained unfunded; hence, they struggled to realise significant levels of practical change in the longer term (Hague, 1998).

An increasing preoccupation with the assessment and management of high-risk offenders in the statutory sector led to a formalisation of joint working between the police, probation and social services, with the introduction of Multi-Agency Public Protection Arrangements (MAPPA) via the *Criminal Justice and Court Services Act 2000*. The adoption of the risk, need and responsivity model[5] in offending behaviour work saw risk assessment aligned with the allocation and intensity of the supervision and resources applied (Chapman & Hough, 1998). Although, perhaps, not known at the time, the implications of this for the DVA sector would be significant. The MAPPA framework was influential in the development of the Multi-Agency Risk Assessment Conference (MARAC) process for DVA victims, which began in Cardiff in 2004 and rolled out nationally in 2006. This, in turn, led to the provision of Independent Domestic Violence Advisers (IDVAs) to assist DVA victims in navigating the complex array of interventions and services involved (see Robinson and Payton Chap. 12, this volume). Specialist Domestic Violence Courts (SDVCs) were also introduced from 1999 onwards in an attempt to address civil and legal issues holistically (see Bettinson, Chap. 5). Whilst the MARAC process is victim-centred, it again primarily targets high-risk cases, often where victims are already engaged with either the Criminal Justice System (CJS) or statutory agencies. DVA providers often take on a specialist assessment role in this context and may supervise the IDVA working with the victim. Concerns have been raised, however, that the focus on high-risk rationalises resources away from other lower level cases and fails to appreciate the fluid nature of DVA and the importance of early intervention (Robinson, 2010). However, as financial concerns started to impinge more acutely on the statutory and voluntary sector, tendencies to divert monies to those seen to be at the highest point of crisis are evident.

The coordinated community response model (Home Office, 2015), which originated in the voluntary sector, predicated joint DVA work on the basis of need rather than risk. Its adoption, however, was also linked to the increasing struggle experienced by DVA providers to meet

---

[5] The Risk, Need and Responsivity Principles, or model, became the core theoretical framework used in correctional systems around the world that use 'science' as a basis for offender rehabilitation. The risk principle states that the most intensive and extensive supervision should be targeted at those who present the highest risk. Criminogenic needs are factors that have a direct link to offending. The Responsivity principle states interventions should be delivered in ways which will maximise active participation.

the expanding demand for services and the challenges of competitive tendering processes, which were being introduced into funding pathways. The 'mainstream' establishment and expansion of voluntary DVA services rendered them vulnerable to a need for core funding and placed them at the receiving end of the introduction of market forces, which have been very apparent in the public sector. That this introduction of competitive financial valuations of service delivery actually raises standards and improves practice arguably is 'an ideological position not a self-evident truth' (Canton, 2011, p. 188). Whilst an ability to evidence quality and effectiveness is clearly important, competitive tendering can actually serve to undermine a partnership ideology by pitting providers against each other. The economic downturn offered a further dimension as organisations sought to combine forces, expand and diversify to ensure they were 'the provider of choice' for funders and commissioners, but arguably losing the benefits of a smaller, unique style of DVA service delivery. The 2000s also saw a move towards more generic provisions for DVA, including a step towards gender neutrality and the assumption that many services were easily able to support male as well as female victims.

Commissioning and the DVA Sector

A barrage of funding and commissioning guidance, co-commissioning models and social return on investment (SROI) methodologies have emerged in the UK. Current commissioning frameworks for domestic violence include Health-NHS England, Clinical Commissioning Groups, Police Service areas, Police and Crime Commissioners and local authorities. Unsurprisingly, integrated and co-commissioning models, which establish regional and local partnerships between these funding bodies, have also been advocated (NICE, 2014) and training to establish Primary Care and third-sector safety partnership approaches has been undertaken (IRIS, 2014). However, the pursuit of the formal adoption of these measures has advanced in some areas more than in others and gaps in Joint Strategic Needs Assessments and 'Joined up' funding streams remain (Cutland, 2014).

With more reductions in spending occurring following the general election of 2015, the pattern of health funding, in particular, is now subject to further significant changes. As a result, providers of DVA services are compelled to continue to engage in a valuation analysis of their resourcing, practice, outcomes and impact in an ever changing funding landscape (Refuge and NEF consulting, 2013). Measured outcomes frequently include the achievement of victim expectations stated at the point of entry to a service, often citing factors such as increased safety, health, social well-being and economic independence (Refuge and NEF consulting, 2013). The impact of other services, however, may be harder to evidence, especially in the shorter term. For example, outreach work to widen the accessibility of DVA service support often includes awareness raising and educational activities, the impact of which is more difficult to measure. Service user and stakeholder demand, throughput and the completion of interventions also feature significantly in other indicators of agency 'value'.

There is evidence that the commissioning practices and austerity cuts imposed by the UK Government since 2011 have had a disproportionate impact on smaller DVA services, resulting in a geographical lottery of service provision and interventions for victims (Imkaan, 2014; Women's Aid, 2013b, 2014). Retrograde steps have arguably occurred with the issues that Coy, Kelly and Foord highlighted in 2009, with just two thirds of all local authorities having specialised provisions for DVA, being likely to re-materialise. Smaller specialist support services receive, on average, a 70 % cut compared to 29 % for larger non-specialist or mainstream services (Walby & Towers, 2012). As a result, specialist DVA services are finding that they need to access money from an increasing number of other sources. Some have invested in their own fund raising strategies as a core element of their business, whilst others tender to as many as 40 different places for very 'small scraps' of money (Howard, 2010). This is time-consuming, demotivating and detracts from possibilities for improvements and expansion in frontline services, due to a hand-to-mouth, short-term cycle of existence. Often, providers have endeavoured to continue to maintain a service without any dedicated funding, running either on reserve capital or on a voluntary basis, with others being forced to close.

Nash (2010) highlights that in order to be able to respond effectively to commissioning processes, an infrastructure needs to be in place within an organisation or network of partnership agencies to enable the collection of the necessary data. To be able to clearly evidence a rationale for funding, some service providers have undertaken systematic economic valuations across their organisational activities, and Social Return on Investment methodologies have been applied to their core functions and outcomes. However, they tend to be utilised by larger organisations such as Safe Lives and Refuge (Wood & Leighton, 2010) and are often not seen as practical or affordable by smaller providers. The open nature of commissioning frameworks has also enabled non-specialist providers to tender for contracts, often resulting in significant changes to the ethos underpinning the shelter, counselling or other support service available.

The closure of safe houses across the UK, or the loss of their funding to non-specialist providers, has had a profound impact (Eddo-Lodge, 2015). Owing to issues of safety and protection, it has been commonplace for women and children to be forced to re-locate outside of their local authority area as a result of their experience of DVA. Quilgars and Pleace (2010) revealed that 70 % of all refuge referrals come from outside the local authority areas in which the service is located and the national network of refuges have worked together under this premise (Bowstead, 2013) However, some local authority commissioning tenders for the provision of refuges have recently included a 'local connection' specification, with some stipulating that as high as 80 % of all refuge spaces should be reserved for local women and children (Women's Aid, 2015). The 'localism' of this strategy fails to comprehend the realities of a DVA victim's experience and puts women and children at risk (Women's Aid, 2014). More than one-third of referrals to specialist refuges had to be turned away in 2013 due to lack of capacity (Women's Aid, 2014). Although further emergency funds have been immobilised nationally by the government in 2015 to support refuges, a longer term sustainable strategy is required.

Whilst the policy rhetoric on commissioning focuses on establishing services on the basis of service user need, short-term crisis interventions for high-risk situations are often prioritised, with the longer terms issues of addressing trauma, loss and recovery being frequently neglected

(Abrahams, 2010). SafeLives (2015) have reported an increase in the demand for IDVA services. A number of factors such as an overall rise in reporting rates of DVA and victims' engagement with services may have contributed to this increase. However it may also be the case that earlier stage interventions are not readily accessible to victims and the DVA scenario reaches a high risk crisis point before any agency support is activated. If a refuge is needed, then outreach support or sanctuary measures are unlikely to keep a victim safe (Jones, Bretherton, Bowles, & Croucher, 2010).The provision of services must be appropriate to the identified need. The victim is best placed to know the nature of the risks they face and consultation with service users is essential both to the provision of individual support (Hague, 2005) and the wider commissioning process (Women's Aid, 2015).

The DVA sector has responded to calls for joint working, innovation, capacity building and evaluation and as a result, has radically changed some of its practices. The UK Refuge 'on track' referral system, for example, has radically changed the way that referrals are made (Women's Aid, 2014). The system enables staff to routinely collect data on the service user's needs, the type and amount of support provided and the service exit outcomes, all as an integral part of the daily practice of the organisation. Thus, the provider is seeking to comply with expectations of valuation, whilst striving to maintain a good quality of frontline service delivery. The extended use of volunteers has also been evident. Whilst volunteers have always made a critical and valued contribution to service provision in the DVA sector, decreases in funding for paid frontline staff have resulted in more than half of all services reporting an increase in the use of volunteers (Women's Aid, 2014). Concerns are, however, that the changing balance of expertise between professionally trained and support staff is affecting service models and delivery (Women's Aid, 2015).

Whilst the professional autonomy of the DVA sector is clearly affected by the economic frameworks it has been subjected to, the commitment of those working within the sector to speak out about it has not been thwarted, supported also by the endeavours of academic researchers. The activist origins of the DVA sector continue to effervesce to some positive effect and the All Party Parliamentary Group (APPG) on Domestic and

Sexual Violence (2015) has called for sustainable funding that enables DVA providers to innovate, rather than simply battle for survival. It states that the current system of commissioning does not address the specific needs of victims and that a diversity of provision, in particular, has been stifled. The request to policymakers and funders is not simply for more money, or a return to the relatively more relaxed approach to expenditure experienced in the earlier days of the DVA movement of the 1980s. It is, however, a call for realism, rather than further rationalisation.

Commissioning, Diversity and Complex Needs

It is increasingly recognised that those requiring DVA interventions are likely to have many complex needs (Against Violence and Abuse (AVA), 2015) and that agencies may already 'share' many clients. There are also multiple entry points by which service users access support and intervention across specialist DVA, health, local authority, legal and criminal justice sector agencies, which will again shape experiences, expectations, impact and outcomes. Integrated services and joint training initiatives have emerged to try and ensure a more effective approach across a range of both specialist and non-specialist agencies who are likely to have contact with, or be the point of first disclosure, for a DVA victim. Nevertheless, the opportunities to innovate and expand provision to meet diverse needs remain hindered by financial restraints. The impact is significant across a range of different areas. The calls for the increased recognition of the experiences of Black and Minority Ethnic and Refugee (BAMER) women, for example, first heralded in the 1980s, remain as poignant today. Barriers to BAMER women's access to DVA services are still prevalent. They are more likely to remain in an abusive situation for longer before seeking help and experience higher levels of isolation and marginalisation (Goldhill 2010; Fawcett, 2005; SafeLives, 2015), with a higher incidence of self-harm and self-inflicted death than their white UK counterparts across all age groups (Imkaan, 2008, 2014; McManus, 2001). Those with insecure immigration status and/or no recourse to public funds experience additional barriers to seeking help and so may be coerced into remaining in abusive relationships or face stark destitution.

Refuges for BAMER women have been seen by some commissioning bodies as not offering good value for money, with some being defunded and taken over by larger generic providers (Eddo-Lodge, 2015). BAMER services have also been seen as an 'add on' to generic service provision in other areas, which has been viewed as a regressive step by many service users. (Imkaan, 2014; Walby & Towers, 2012).

Other areas of DVA practice have seen even less development. Barnes and Donovan (see Chap. 14) found in their recent study of DVA within Lesbian Gay Bisexual and/or Transgender relationships that victims were more likely to access private counselling than any other form of health, social care, criminal justice or specialist intervention. The DVA sector has much to do to improve awareness of DVA and access to appropriate support in this field (Donovan, Barnes, & Nixon, 2014). However, existing agencies again currently find it hard to justify any significant investment in the specialist outreach and educational work that this may entail and often are left resigned to an approach that simply professes an 'open access to all', which is often not the reality. Meanwhile, the specific issues of engagement and need for different groups are left unattended. This argument may equally be applied to the experiences of male victims, as highlighted earlier, where demands are made for existing DVA services to accommodate men, with very limited, if any, additional resource. There appears to be very little thought given as to whether this is appropriate and whether male victims' needs are indeed the same as their female counterparts (see Martin, Chap. 9, this volume).

The first national UK study of the needs and service provision for disabled women experiencing DVA commissioned by Women's Aid and funded by lottery aid (Hague, Thiara, & McGowan, 2007)) found that disabled women were twice as likely to be victims of DVA, less likely to escape their abuse and more likely to be isolated (Hague et al., 2007; Ravi, Hague, Bashall, Ellis, & Mullender, 2012). In cases where a DVA victim has other significant care and support needs, there may be heightened dependency on their perpetrator, which, in turn, may limit opportunities for disclosure. Clearly, all of those involved in health and social care require appropriate training to be sensitive to the possibility that abuse is occurring and facilities to support a disabled victim should also be able to provide a realistic route towards empowerment and change.

Whilst healthcare professionals are well placed to identify DVA, it is often overlooked, especially for older women (McGarry, 2008; SafeLives, 2015); however, steps are being taken to try and address this (IRIS, 2014; NICE, 2014). When it is recognised, DVA relating to disabled or elderly victims tends to be encompassed under wider safeguarding policies relating to vulnerable adults. This suggests a core focus on the victim's capacity and safety, rather than the relationship dynamics or the perpetrator's actions and may, therefore, limit the exploration of DVA interventions that are available. Ultimately, this area of DVA experience currently remains a very hidden, covert experience and is unlikely to feature significantly as an area of investment and development in many commissioning assessments.

Women experiencing DVA are more likely to misuse alcohol and drugs as a coping mechanism (Stark & Flitcraft, 1996). Barron (2004) asserts that many women accessing drug and alcohol services are experiencing DVA, but this is often masked by the primary presenting need of their substance use. A similar experience has been evident in the access of mental health services (AVA 2015, Stella Project). This is not a new revelation and has been previously addressed in the 1990s (Department of Health, 2002). However, health services, in particular, have tended to work in silos, with limited understandings of the ways in which the issues of substance use, mental health and DVA inter-relate and impact on service user engagement. Whilst these complex points of intersectionality are beginning to be investigated by frontline services, the overlap also needs to be fully understood by funding and commissioning bodies. Second-tier national DVA organisations, in particular, have expanded their remit to provide key training and development in some of these areas.

It is smaller organisations, however, often by their very nature, that are uniquely community-based and user-focused and can be perceived as being more accessible by some DVA victims, for whom the thought of being part of a wider network of professionals can be intimidating. Integrated services may also be seen as an opportunity by funders and commissioners to rationalise provision where there is a perceived duplication rather than an opportunity to innovate and expand. Therefore, despite the increasing profile and work of activists in the areas discussed here and others which are not, the needs of many victims of DVA are simply not being met.

Conclusion

Three Steps Backwards, The Next Step Forward

Since the emergence of the DVA sector from its activist beginnings in the 1970s, significant strides have been made in addressing violence against women and girls, with advances in victim-led service development and knowledge of DVA across a wide range of experiences and contexts. National campaigns driven by the DVA sector have also called for fundamental changes in culture and practice across the statutory sector with the development of partnerships and multi-agency working. DVA work has been integral to statutory safeguarding frameworks and stronger relationships with family courts, children and families and child protection teams have been established, although key challenges also remain (Wills, Jacobs, Montique, & Croom, 2011). A recognition that DVA is indeed 'Everyone's Business' (HMIC, 2014) is now far more apparent across health, social care and criminal justice sectors. However, although this moral obligation is perhaps more broadly accepted, the last five years have seen alarming trends in DVA specialist provision. The impact of austerity cuts has been severe, and the devolvement of core funding to local commissioning bodies has opened up tendering processes resulting in 'anyone applying for DVA business' and the specialist expertise of the DVA sector potentially diminishing (APPG, 2015). The government commitment to the VAWG strategy (Home Office, 2015) is, therefore, undermined by its approach to funding and as the 'demand' for specialist sexual violence and domestic violence services has been increasing, the 'supply' has been decreasing (Women's Aid, 2013a, 32013b, 2014). Whilst the 'SOS' campaign (Women's Aid, 2015) to prevent the closure of further refuges resulted in the provision of an additional £10 million from the now Conservative Government, with further bidding funds made available in August 2015, these impulsive reactions to high-profile issues that attract significant media attention are insufficient. They do not serve to maintain quality in the services that do exist, or develop the much needed outreach and accessible provision required, some of which has been highlighted here. Concern that standards in DVA service provision should be established and maintained has become a matter of European significance and is formally addressed with the establishment of the Istanbul Convention (Council of Europe, 2011). Whilst at the time of writing this chapter, the UK had yet to ratify the Istanbul convention that came into force in August 2014, its principles are strongly aligned and encompassed in the Women's Aid National Quality Standards (revised 2015). It is recommended that these standards are used as a benchmark by commissioners in determining the most appropriate service providers, including seven core areas, namely, safety security and dignity; rights and access; physical and emotional health; stability, resilience and autonomy; children and young people; prevention; accountability and leadership, which must be considered in the organisational approach to victim-centred DVA practice. . Whilst quality marks are awarded by Women's Aid, such an endorsement is not currently required by commissioners. This needs to change.

The introduction of the risk model into DVA work has also been a matter of mixed fortune. It has enabled a stronger connection with the statutory sector via multi-agency working on high-risk cases, mobilising resources promptly at identified points of crisis. However, DVA victims are not well served by a system that allocates resources on the basis of risk levels rather than need (Home Office, 2013; Regan, 2007; Women's Aid, 2015). Commissioners need to be encouraged to adopt a holistic approach to funding, which also recognises the significant value of prevention, early intervention and longer term issues of recovery. Commissioning practices also need to be victim-driven. The victim's voice is integral to determining value and impact in the provision of DVA services (Hague, 2005) and this is embedded, in principle at least, in the majority of the existing frameworks. However, the broader discourse, for those whose voice may not yet be fully heard on the fringes of current DVA practice, also needs to be considered. An approach that simply stipulates that everyone is welcome here, does not mean that victims of all ages, genders, sexualities, race, faith, backgrounds, those in isolated rural areas, those with a disability and those with complex needs will suddenly feel able to walk through the door. The Public Sector Equality Duty, which came into force in 2011, has been misinterpreted (APPG, 2015)—all victims do not need access to the same service; they are, however, legally entitled to the same level of opportunity to access the same quality of service as appropriate to their needs.

Short-term commissioning practices have exacerbated feelings of uncertainty in the specialist DVA sector. The costs of frequent re-tendering means resources have to be re-directed away from frontline provision and long-term planning. The impact of change fatigue on morale and the retention of frontline staff has also been substantial. It is time for a sea change. At the time of writing this chapter, the APPG on sexual violence and domestic violence inquiry 2015 has advocated key areas of policy transformation for commissioning in this area. They include the collection of data on DVA, sustainable funding that enables agencies to develop their practice and capacity in the longer term, a ministerial lead to ensure the better coordination of domestic violence and sexual violence services, a need-led approach to commissioning decisions and joint guidance that reaches across all existing commissioning frameworks. The latter would include the Department of Communities and Local Government, the Ministry of Justice, the Department of Health and local government authorities. The DVA sector has recognised the value of a joined-up approach and has been a forerunner, leading to a wider recognition of statutory sector responsibilities in this area. However, the fragmented approach to funding has undermined many of these efforts and it is now time for government bodies to 'join up' their thinking too.

References

Abrahams, H. (2007). *Supporting women after domestic violence: Loss trauma and recovery*. London: Jessica Kingsley.
Abrahams, H. (2010). *Rebuilding lives after domestic violence: Understanding long-term outcomes*. London: Jessica Kingsley.
Against Violence and Abuse (AVA). (2015). *The Stella Project*. Retrieved October 25, 2015, from http://www.avaproject.org.uk/our-projects/stella-project.aspx

All Party Parliamentary Group (APPG). (2015). *The changing landscape of domestic and sexual violence services: Domestic and sexual violence inquiry*. Bristol: Women's Aid.
Barron, J. (2004). *Struggle to survive: Challenges for delivering services on mental health, substance misuse and domestic violence*. Bristol: Women's Aid Federation of England.
Bowstead, J. (2013). What if anything is local about domestic violence? *Safe, 47*, 10.
Canton, R. (2011). *Probation working with offenders*. Abingdon: Routledge.
Carby, H. (1997). White woman listen! Black feminism and the boundaries of sisterhood. In H. S. Mirza (Ed.), *Black British feminism*. London: Routledge.
Carlen, P. (1988). *Women, crime and poverty*. London: Open University Press.
Chapman, T., & Hough, M. (1998). *Evidence based practice: A guide to effective practice*. London: HM Inspectorate of Probation.
Children's Act 1989 c41. Retrieved October 25, 2015, from http://www.legislation.gov.uk/ukpga/1989/41/contents
Council of Europe. (2011). *Council of Europe convention on preventing and combating violence against women and domestic violence*. Strasbourg: Council of Europe.
Coy, M., Kelly, L., & Foord, J. (2009). *Map of gaps 2: The postcode lottery of violence against women support services in Britain*. Retrieved October 25, 2015, from http://www.endviolenceagainstwomen.org.uk/resources/27/map-of-gaps-ii-january-2009
Criminal Justice and Court Services Act 2000 c43. Retrieved October 25, 2015, from http://www.legislation.gov.uk/ukpga/2000/43/contents
Crime and Disorder Act 1998 c37. Retrieved October 25, 2015, from http://www.legislation.gov.uk/ukpga/1998/37/contents
Cutland, C. (2014). *Nottinghamshire domestic abuse review. Funding and commissioning arrangements*. Nottingham: Nottinghamshire Police Crime Commissioner's Office.
Davis, A. Y. (1981). *Women, race and class*. London: The Women's Press.
Dempsey, B. (2013). *Men's experience of domestic abuse in Scotland. What we know and how we can know more*. Edinburgh: AMIS.
Department of Health. (2002). *Women's mental health: Into the mainstream*. London: Department Of Health.
Donovan, C., Barnes, R., & Nixon, C. (2014) *The Coral Project: Exploring abusive behaviours in lesbian, gay, bisexual and/or transgender relationships*. Interim Report. Sunderland/Leicester: University of Sunderland/University of Leicester.

Eddo-Lodge, R. (2015). Latin American women in the UK need this domestic violence refuge. Why are we facing closure. *The Telegraph*, 26 August 2015. Retrieved October 25, 2015, from http://www.telegraph.co.uk/women/womens-life/11418045/Latin-American-women-in-UK-need-this-domestic-violence-refuge.-Badly.html

Fawcett Society. (2005). *Black and minority ethnic women in the UK*. London: The Fawcett Society.

Goldhill, R. (2010). From pillar to post; multi agency working with women offenders. In A. Pycroft & D. Gough (Eds.), *Multi agency working in criminal justice: Control and care in contemporary correctional practice*. Bristol: Policy Press.

Hague, G. (2005). Domestic violence survivors forums in the UK: An experiment in involving abused women in the development of domestic violence services and policy making. *Journal of Gender Studies, 14*(3), 191–203.

Hague, G., Thiara, R. K., & McGowan, P. (2007). *Making the links: Disabled women and domestic violence*. Retrieved October 25, 2015.

Hague, G., Kelly, L., Malos, E., & Mullender, A. (1996). *Children, domestic violence and refuges*. Bristol: WAFE.

Hague, G., & Malos, E. (1993). *Domestic violence: Action for change*. Cheltenham: New Clarion Press.

Her Majesty's Inspectorate of Constabulary (HMIC). (2014). *Everyone's business: Improving the police response to domestic abuse*. London: HMIC.

Hester, M. (2013). The "Three Plant Model": Towards an understanding of contradictions in approaches to women and children's safety in contexts of domestic violence. In N. Lombard & L. McMillan (Eds.), *Violence against women: Current theory and practice in domestic abuse, sexual violence and exploitation*. London: Jessica Kingsley.

Home Office. (1991). *Safer communities: The local delivery of crime prevention through the partnership approach*. Report of the Standing Conference on Crime Prevention (The Morgan Report). London: Home Office.

Home Office. (2011). *A call to end violence against women and girls*. London: Home Office.

Home Office. (2013). *Domestic homicide reviews: Common themes identified as lessons to be learnt*. London: Home Office.

Home Office. (2014). *A call to end violence against women and girls: Action Plan 2014*. London: Home Office.

Home Office. (2015). *A call to end violence against women and girls: Progress report*. London: Home Office.

Housing (Homeless Persons) Act 1977 c48. Retrieved October 25, 2015, from http://www.legislation.gov.uk/ukpga/1977/48/contents/enacted

Howard, J. E. (2010). The beauty of reflection and the beast of multi-agency cooperation. In A. Pycroft & D. Gough (Eds.), *Multi agency working in criminal justice: Control and care in contemporary correctional practice*. Bristol: Policy Press.

Imkaan. (2008). *A matter of life and death: A right to exist – The eradication of specialist services to BAMER women and children fleeing violence*. London: Imkaan.

Imkaan. (2014). Supporting black and minority ethnic women and girls. London: Imkaan.

IRIS (Identification and Referral to Improve Safety). (2014). *Commissioning guidance the IRIS solution – Responding to domestic violence and abuse in general practice*. Retrieved October 25, 2015, from http://www.irisdomesticviolence.org.uk/holding/IRIS_Commissioning_Guidance.pdf

Jones, A., Bretherton, A., Bowles, A., & Croucher, K. (2010). *Sanctuary schemes for households at risk of domestic violence*. York: Centre for Housing Policy, Department for Communities and Local Government, University of York.

Mama, A. (1996). *The hidden struggle: Statutory and voluntary sector responses to violence against black women in the home*. Nottingham: Russell Press.

McGarry, J. (2008). Exploring relationships between older people and nurses at home. *Nursing Times, 104*(28), 32–33.

McManus, J. (2001). *Friends or strangers? Faith communities and community safety*. London: NACRO.

Morley, R., & Mullender, A. (1994) *Preventing domestic violence to women*. Police Research Group Crime Prevention Unit Series 48. London: Home Office.

Nash, M. (2010). Singing from the same MAPP hymn sheet – But can we hear all the voices? In A. Pycroft & D. Gough (Eds.), *Multi agency working in criminal justice: Control and care in contemporary correctional practice*. Bristol: Policy Press.

NICE (National Institute for Health and Care Excellence). (2014). *Public health guideline on 'Domestic violence and abuse: How services can respond effectively' (PH50)*. Retrieved October 25, 2015, from https://www.nice.org.uk/guidance/ph50

Office of National Statistics. (2015). *Crime statistics. Focus on violent crime and sexual offences 2012/13 release*. Retrieved October 24, 2015, from http://www.ons.gov.uk/ons/rel/crime-stats/crime-statistics/focus-on-violent-crime-

and-sexual-offences–2012-13/rpt---chapter-4---intimate-personal-violence-and-partner-abuse.html#tab-conclusions

Oliver, M. (1990). *The politics of disablement: A sociological approach*. Basingstoke: Palgrave Macmillan.

Parmar, P. (1982). Gender race and class: Asian women in resistance. In H. Carby (Ed.), *The empire strikes back: Race and racism in the 70s*. Abingdon: Routledge.

Quilgars, D., & Pleace, N. (2010). *Meeting the needs of households at risk of domestic violence in England*. York: University of York, CLG.

Ravi, T. K., Hague, G., Bashall, R., Ellis, B., & Mullender, A. (2012). *Disabled women and domestic violence responding to experiences of survivors*. London: Jessica Kingsley Press.

Refuge and NEF consulting. (2013). *Social valuation of Refuge services for survivors of domestic violence*. Retrieved October 25, 2015, from http://www.refuge.org.uk/files/Refuge-SROI-report-25-09-13-NCV2.pdf

Regan, L. (2007). *"If only we'd known": An explanatory study of seven intimate partner homicides in England and Wales*. London: Child and Women Abuse Studies Unit, Metropolitan University.

Robinson, A. L. (2010). Risk and intimate partner violence. In H. Kemshall & B. Wilkinson (Eds.), *Good practice in risk assessment and risk management* (3rd ed.). London: Jessica Kingsley Publishers.

SafeLives. (2015). *Getting it right first time*. Retrieved October 25, 2015, from, http://www.safelives.org.uk/policy-evidence/getting-it-right-first-time

Stark, E., & Flitcraft, A. (1996). *Women at risk: Domestic violence and women's health*. Thousand Oaks, CA: SAGE.

Walby, S. (2009). *The cost of domestic violence*. Lancaster: University of Lancaster.

Walby, S., & Towers, J. (2012). *Measuring the impact of cuts in public expenditure on the provision of services to prevent violence against women and girls*. Lancaster: University of Lancaster.

Wills, A., Jacobs, N., Montique, B., & Croom, L. (2011). *Standing together against domestic violence: In search of excellence: A guide to effective partnership*. Retrieved October 25, 2015, from www.standingtogether.org.uk

Women's Aid. (2015). *SOS: Save refuges, save lives – Data report on specialist domestic violence services in England*. Bristol: Women's Aid.

Women's Aid. (2014). *Annual survey; domestic violence services*. Bristol: Women's Aid.

Women's Aid. (2013a). *Annual survey; Domestic violence services*. Bristol: Women's Aid.

Women's Aid. (2013b). *A growing crisis of unmet need; What the figures alone don't show you.* Bristol: Women's Aid.

Wood, C., & Leighton, D. (2010). *Measuring social value – The gap between policy and practice.* London: Demos.

7

Children and Domestic Violence: What Do Family Intervention Workers Have to Offer?

Jo Little and Fae Garland

Introduction

Recent research on domestic violence in the UK and other western jurisdictions has increasingly focused on the wider household and family context. Studies have recognised that the causes, experiences and outcomes of domestic violence go beyond the individual victim and perpetrator, and frequently include other family members (Pain, 2013). Particular concern has surrounded the effects of close contact with domestic violence on children, with considerable evidence now existing to suggest that domestic violence has a direct and lasting impact on children in terms of present and future well-being in a variety of ways (see Kitzman, Gaylord, Holt, & Kenny, 2003; Mullender et al., 2002). This wider family context has also emerged in law, policy and practitioner responses to domestic violence, with a recent

---

J. Little (✉)
Department of Geography, University of Exeter, Exeter, UK

F. Garland
University of Exeter, Exeter, UK

© The Editor(s) (if applicable) and The Author(s) 2016
S. Hilder, V. Bettinson (eds.), *Domestic Violence*,
DOI 10.1057/978-1-137-52452-2_7

131

emphasis on addressing domestic violence as part of a comprehensive approach to family welfare evident in social policy in the UK and elsewhere (Laing, Humphreys, & Cavanagh, 2013). While such developments are considered positive in terms of their appreciation of the scale and impact of domestic violence, they clearly involve challenges for policymakers in both the conceptualisation of domestic violence and the formulation and implementation of practical responses. Such challenges must be carefully identified and understood if broader family-based responses are to be successful.

This chapter critically explores the wider focus of domestic violence intervention through a study of work with children. The study examines the practices employed in supporting children and the adults (mothers) who care for them, following the reporting of domestic violence and the subsequent break-up of the family. It considers how effectively such early interventions can prevent, or at least limit, the impact of domestic violence on children and prevent families from reaching crisis points in the future. Underpinning our study is a recognition of the ways in which domestic violence spreads beyond the intimate partners to affect children and other household members. Additionally, it appreciates how support for children is a necessary part of the victim's ability to respond to and cope with the violence they have encountered. The empirical research referred to here is, at this stage, preliminary in nature and limited in scale. It examines the activities of one particular organisation working to support children and mothers in addressing domestic violence and in so doing asserts the importance of an in-depth and highly focused study. The limitations of the research are recognised, but arguments made, nevertheless, that it serves to highlight some important issues. The research stresses the value of first-hand reports from victims and professionals that illustrate the individual nature of both the problems encountered by families and their appropriate solution. Such reports may not include large data sets that enable direct comparison and extrapolation, but they do provide some of the detail essential to understanding the nature and benefit of specific approaches and targeted responses.[1]

---

[1] Research methodologies involving a small number of in-depth conversations with women who had experienced domestic abuse have been used in studies such as Pain (2013). See also Baker and Edwards (2012).

The discussion is organised into three main parts. Firstly, we situate the study in a brief conceptualisation of domestic violence, law and policy that locates family-based approaches within a wider understanding of the impact of violence, primarily on children. The second section outlines the research methodology and the nature and context of policy and practitioner responses, as illustrated largely through the post of the Domestic Violence Family Intervention Worker (FIW) within our study area. The third section presents some of the findings in a discussion of the work of the FIW and child-centred responses to domestic violence. The chapter's conclusion reflects on the efficacy of the FIWs in preventing and reducing the impact of domestic violence, as well as their contribution to improving other services' understandings and management of the needs of individuals and families. Finally, this chapter concludes with some suggested lessons for future domestic violence law and policy development.

Conceptualising Domestic Violence in Families

Before examining the law, policy and practitioner responses to domestic violence to see how different individuals and agencies intersect, it is important to consider the conceptualisation of domestic violence itself and to examine how social and legal understandings of domestic violence effect and incorporate an appreciation of its wider significance within the family and household. As research has developed, social and legal depictions of domestic violence have moved from the idea of it being a private affair limited to married or cohabiting relationships (Groves & Thomas, 2014). Instead, understandings have broadened and crucially, domestic violence has begun to be acknowledged as a public issue, affecting a diverse range of intimate partners and their families, both within and outside the home (Pain, 2013). Now, rather than 'drawing the curtains' on domestic violence, an array of civil and criminal law remedies exist, including occupation and non-molestation orders under the *Family Law Act* 1996 *Part IV* and exclusion orders under the *Children's Act* 1989.[2] These orders are designed to stop threatening, violent and abusive behaviour directed towards the vic-

---

[2] Section 38A *Children Act* 1989 as amended by *Family Law Act* 1996.

tim and children. Moreover, both law and policy have widened the reach of domestic violence to include a greater number of primary victims, with, most recently, the Home Office (2013) expanding its definition of domestic violence beyond intimate partners to also include family members.

While the socio-legal scope of domestic violence has significantly widened, so too has the understanding of harm. Research has demonstrated that the nature of domestic violence must be seen as more than physical attack or injury. Stark (2007, 2009) particularly focuses on the broader notion of 'coercive control' that recognises that the isolation and control that many victims experience can be as abusive as physical violence. Stark and others (Pain, 2013) have looked at the ways in which victims (predominantly women) are frequently subjected to severe control through restrictions on their finances, restrictions on access to leisure time and friends and comments about dress and appearance. Such control may restrict their capacity for independent decision-making, reinforcing their dependency on their partners and making it impossible for them to leave. The Home Office's (2013) definition now also includes this concept of coercive control, alongside controlling behaviour and abuse, which is psychological, physical, sexual, financial and emotional. Coercive control has now also been translated into law as a criminal offence through *section 76 Serious Crime Act* 2015. Clearly then, work on the conceptualisation of domestic violence has helped to broaden its meaning and show how it incorporates many methods of control. However, the understanding of domestic violence within both law and policy is arguably limited to the original site of the violence, namely, the dynamics between perpetrators and primary victims. Although the explanatory notes for the Home Office's definition (2013) recognise the impact of children witnessing and living with domestic violence, the definition's wording makes no reference to secondary victims and thus, it is unclear whether they are included within 'family members'; provision for such children is, therefore, at best, extremely weak.

Whilst these children appear somewhat absent from law and policy definitions, academics and practitioners have paid particular attention to the implications for child witnesses. As violence spreads beyond the immediate victim and perpetrator and is seen as more than specific physical acts, its effects on children within the household have been recognised as profound and very often, long-lasting. Research has shown, therefore, how domestic violence has been linked to behavioural problems in children, learning difficulties and their ability to socialise (Rivett, Howarth, & Harold, 2006). This impact varies according to the child's developmental stage. Younger children and infants often exhibit difficulties with toilet training, sleep disturbances and emotional distress, including separation anxiety and also aggression (Lundy & Grossman, 2005). Older children are more likely to exhibit disruptive behaviour at school, from withdrawal to aggression (Byrne & Taylor, 2007; Mullender et al., 2002), and may underperform academically (Barron, 2007; Bream & Buchanan, 2003). Moreover, recent figures suggest that children growing up in households where domestic violence takes place rarely escape exposure to such violence and many are direct witnesses to domestic violence incidents (Stanley, Miller, Foster, & Thomson, 2011). It is also acknowledged that children are often used as part of the controlling behaviour by perpetrators and may also experience violence themselves (Rivett et al., 2006). There is also research, which has, importantly, sought evidence of the lasting effects of witnessing domestic violence as a child, showing how growing up in a household where there is domestic abuse can dramatically increase a child's propensity to become violent themselves in later life (Edleson, 1999; Indermaur, 2001; Murrell, Christoff, & Henning, 2007). Exposure to domestic violence can, therefore, have profound and extensive effects on children, heightened also by the current lack of legal provision for them as child witnesses. In 2012, approximately 130,000 children and young persons were living in households where there was a high risk of domestic abuse (CAADA, 2012). There is clearly, therefore, a very real need at both individual and societal levels for child-focused interventions to limit the impact of domestic violence. This arguably may reduce the need for other societal resources and expenditure to deal with the aftermath of the abuse, both now and in the future.

Background to the Family Intervention Worker Role

The examination of the law, policy and practitioner responses to these wider family implications of domestic violence has generally focused on practice issues and on the application of specific measures. Hester (2013), however, sought to look more conceptually at the formation and implementation of law and policy in attempting to understand approaches to the wider issues around safeguarding children, parents and in particular, mothers, in cases of domestic violence. Her framework is a *Three planets model*, employed to 'conceptualise what is happening on the ground' and explain the difficulties and frustrations experienced by victims and practitioners in specialist domestic violence services, as they attempt to navigate across different agencies and legal structures to access support for women and children in finding safety (Hester, 2013, p. 36). Hester (2013, p. 37) cites and draws upon the work of Bourdieu (2000), arguing that conceptualising different areas of work as 'planets' helps to demonstrate the ways in which those working in separate areas of authority and practice internalise the structures of their 'world' and as a result create divisions between areas of professional responsibility. Crucially, these different areas of responsibility all possess distinct cultural/organisational histories that shape the way they work and respond to problems.

Hester develops her *Three planets model* by examining the relationship between the areas of domestic violence intervention, child safety and postseparation child contact. She argues that legal and practitioner responses to domestic violence are adult-centric, with specialist domestic violence agencies tending to focus on individual (female) victims, whilst often having only a limited understanding of how their work relates to that of children's services. The Multi-Agency Risk Assessment Conferences (MARACs) designed to support high-risk victims of domestic violence may involve children's services (see Robinson, 2003; Robinson and Payton Chap. 12, this volume). However, Hester argues that little is known about further interventions by children's services resulting from this involvement due to lack of research. Comparatively, the agencies and courts involved in both child protection and child contact cases have been critiqued for their apparent lack of understanding about the nature of domestic violence. The focus on protecting children has often involved very poor links with specialist domestic violence agencies. The father's abuse of the mother is also rarely prosecuted in this context, because, as Hester argues, a predominately welfare, rather than criminalising, approach prevails within the work of child support agencies. Consequently, the female victim is frequently identified as the main problem, as gender stereotyping places primary responsibility for child welfare with the mother.

A similar approach can be seen in child contact disputes where the family courts have established a strong precedent that maintains that contact with the father is almost always in the child's best interest.[3] Even with significant attempts in policy and practice to change this approach, the pro-contact standard is still dominant (Hester, 2013). Mothers, therefore, unsurprisingly, believe that the court sees contact as inevitable, which renders their safety and consequently the safety of their child to be a secondary consideration (Robinson, 2003). As Hester (2013, p. 49) concludes:

> On the 'child contact planet' [the mother] is ordered to allow contact between her violent ex-partner and the children, leaving her not only bewildered and confused but left to manage her ex-partner's violence, and yet again scared for the safety of her children, let alone herself.

Thus, the legal understanding of what is in the 'best interests' of the child, in practice, can serve to disempower the primary victim of the domestic violence. Rather than considering the mother to be a victim, the courts and associated children's agencies often construe her to be the main problem. She has either failed to protect her children by not leaving an abusive partner or is being implacably hostile to contact (Hester, 2013).

As has been noted by Hester and others (see Stanley et al., 2011), specific measures have been taken by some agencies to develop multi-agency approaches and to integrate different areas of law and policymaking. Notwithstanding the concerns about the continued influence in some cases of historic organisational cultures, some of these initiatives have been seen as highly positive (Hester, 2013). Attempts to encourage interagency working and coordination across different areas of responsibility have also been enshrined in some broader policy directions. For example, the UK government's 2010–2015 'Troubled Families' policy (HM Government, 2015) targets families encountering multiple forms of disadvantage and aims to address issues such as poverty and child neglect through a raft of measures applied to specific families. This initiative aimed to support

---

[3] See Re O (A Minor) (Contact: Imposition of Conditions) [1995] 2 FLR 124.

120,000 families across the country who were identified as having a range of complex and diverse problems; it was thought that doing so would not only raise such families out of poverty, but would also reduce the longer term cost to society incurred as the result of a decrease in anti-social behaviour. As claimed at the policy's launch:

> [The] National Centre for Social Research shows that intensive intervention to support and challenge troubled families is effective in turning round their lives-a family getting intensive support and challenge is twice as likely to stop anti-social behaviour as one not getting the intervention. (Casey, 2012)

These kinds of policy directives have also been criticised, however, not only for focusing more on anti-social behaviour rather than social disadvantage (Hayden & Jenkins, 2014), but also for diverting funds from elsewhere. Whilst the 'Troubled Families' initiative has attracted significant government funding, it has been argued that this is not 'new money' but rather represents a top slicing of other budgets (Hayden & Jenkins, 2014). Thus, overall domestic violence support services have been strongly affected by the reduction in the welfare budget, despite this 'new' contribution (see Turgoose, Chap. 6, this volume).

Initiatives such as 'Troubled Families' have also been challenged for the ways in which they construct domestic violence as something that happens largely within dysfunctional families and make automatic links to a wider set of problems, including women's mental health (Hayden & Jenkins, 2014). Whilst it may be the case that those suffering multiple forms of deprivation may be particularly vulnerable to family breakdown and violence, research has long indicated that domestic violence happens across all sections of society, class and background (Levitas, 2012). In linking domestic violence to multiple forms of disadvantage, there is a danger that certain families, and particularly women as mothers, will be seen as failing on a number of levels. Those escaping and recovering from domestic violence often live through further chaotic periods as they attempt to manage the complex and often profound changes needed in their lives to leave a violent partner. As Hester (2013) makes clear in her 'three planets' approach, the different and at times, contradictory laws, cultures and priorities of the various agencies involved in supporting domestic violence victims can magnify this sense of chaos. However, this can serve to reinforce a misconception that domestic violence happens only within dysfunctional families who lack the ability to change patterns of behaviour and to cope with day to day life. Within this context then, perhaps, the FIW can offer a 'cross-planetary' response that helps to challenge this perspective by assisting families in effectively and positively navigating these worlds.

This chapter now examines the work of a domestic violence organisation operating within this multi-agency context to offer support to families. The support is delivered through the work of a specialist practitioner, the FIW and is focused on the wider needs of children *and* parents (mothers) in cases of high-risk domestic violence. As aforementioned, this is an in-depth, but limited, piece of research. We recognise that these findings need to be followed up by further research, but they are arguably important not only in providing detailed observations about a particular service, but also in contributing to the general development of specialist domestic violence support. The discussion that follows provides an overview of the FIW post, a summary of the study's methodology and a report of key findings.

Domestic Violence Family Intervention Worker: An Overview

The FIW activity studied here is as a result of a post established in a local authority in the South of England. Although not unique,[4] it is unusual because FIW posts are not typically employed in the domestic violence sphere. However, there were other FIW models operating across the local authority, providing a template for defining the scope and duties of this particular role. The post was initiated in August 2013, initially for a one year period, and subsequently extended on a part-time basis. The FIW reported, in terms of line management, to the project leader of the domes-

---

[4] Similar posts operate in neighbouring authorities where there is the same domestic violence service.

tic violence support service and worked as part of a team involving the Independent Domestic Violence Advisors (IDVAs) (see Robinson and Payton, Chap. 12, this volume). The responsibilities of the post stretch across all five districts in its county, covering a large geographical area and a diverse range of partner organisations and professionals.

The FIW's overall responsibility is to support families who have experienced, or are possibly still experiencing, domestic violence and are recognised by MARAC as high risk. The post is designed to focus on children and to work with them in understanding and rebuilding relationships and pursuing more positive behaviours at home and at school. The FIW delivers a package of support to the family, tailored to their specific needs and works with both children and parents to implement the measures. The FIW, operating through the MARAC framework, co-coordinates the involvement of relevant professionals and attends child protection conferences as appropriate. The emphasis is on meeting the needs of children in a way that integrates different elements of support and maximises the impact of the intervention. Within this broad approach, the FIW performs a variety of tasks. In the early stages of the commencement of the role, each client was referred to the FIW by their IDVA, where the IDVA believed the family would need and benefit from more comprehensive support. However, this practice subsequently changed so that *all* clients with children were automatically referred to the FIW. The referred clients were then offered different levels of intervention, depending on their identified needs and response. The services offered included the following:

> Bronze—clients receive a leaflet with information about domestic abuse, strategies to support children plus telephone numbers of relevant agencies and the FIW's contact details.
>
> Silver—clients are offered pre-school support groups which operate from children's centres across the county. These groups provide peer-support and advice about parenting strategies and play. They also offer information on other services and support.
>
> Gold—for clients who have specific needs that cannot be met through the group sessions. These clients receive individual support including family, parent and children's sessions. The support spans a 4–8 week period and provides parenting guidance, art and play therapy sessions. It also includes

meeting and liaison with various other professionals and the creation of local support networks.

Platinum—for those clients who have the highest levels of need, receiving intensive levels of ongoing individual support and group work.

Whilst these different levels of support indicate how the FIW engages with different families, the FIW is also an important point of contact for all families beyond the immediate point of crisis. This is continuous, regardless of the stage reached, or the level of support being pursued.

During our research study, the FIW had worked with 47 families, involving 95 children, but with no contact with any fathers of the children. Of these 47 families, 15 families (27 children) were receiving or had received the Bronze level of support; 5 families (10 children) were receiving or had received the Silver level of support; 25 families (53 children) were receiving or had received the Gold level of support; and 2 families (5 children) were receiving or had received the Platinum level of support. Whilst these numbers were smaller than initially envisaged, they are comparable with those found in other literature on other types of FIW programmes, which indicate that full-time case workers who deliver family interventions tend to work with between 5 and 15 families at any one time (Casey, 2012). The size of the FIW's caseload was also restricted by the part-time hours allocation, the vast amount of time and resources demanded for such a highly intensive role, the geography covered and the time taken for travel.

Research Methodology

The project took place over a three month period in the summer of 2013. It involved intensive liaison with the third-sector organisation commissioned to run specialist domestic violence support services throughout the county that was managing the FIW. The research and data gathered and reported here was commissioned by the service provider as part of an internal evaluation of the FIW post and was fully supported by the organisation and its workers. Data was gathered through three distinct methods: interviews; participant observation and an analysis of case records. In-depth, semi-structured interviews were held with five professionals including the FIW, two IDVAS, the manager of the managing organisation and a representative of another external partner agency. Interviews lasted between 45 and 90 minutes. They were recorded and fully transcribed. Three interviews were conducted with the FIW over the course of the research.

In addition, the researchers shadowed the FIW for a day to gain further insight into the role. Two observations session occurred. The first was a group session and the second was an initial assessment meeting between the FIW and a newly referred mother. Three other mothers who had engaged with the FIW service were also interviewed. Each mother was at a different stage of the FIW process and they were receiving various levels of support. Mother 1 was receiving one-to-one sessions with the FIW, identified as Gold level support, and was interviewed before her second meeting with the FIW. Mother 2 was receiving a mixture of group sessions and one-to-one support, identified as Platinum level support and had already had a number of sessions with the FIW. Mother 3 had received one-to-one support, identified as Gold level support and had finished working with the service. The age range of the children included in the data spanned from preschool to teenage years. Each interview with the FIW clients lasted up to 30 minutes. They were asked a series of questions related to the referral process, the interventions received, the impact of the FIW's input with their families and the clients' overall views on the service. Again, these interviews were fully transcribed and analysed. The research also included a review of case files, accessed via discussion with the FIW. Whilst this was a small, qualitative study, the range of data collected at various points of the FIW intervention process is one of its strengths.

Families' Needs and the Family intervention Worker

All of the professionals and the mothers interviewed strongly expressed the need for a service, or individual, that would focus on families and in particular, pick up on the needs of children who had lived in the context of a violent relationship. The professional respondents all recognised the value of having a specific member of the team dedicated to the needs of the child. The IDVAs spoke of being too busy and too focused on the victim's immediate safety to be able to give enough attention to the children. One respondent felt that in the work of other agencies such as social services, 'everything pointed *down* to the child', whereas the FIW could be child-centred and give them the time and attention they required. This need for a specific focus was exacerbated, it was felt, by the complexity of the problems facing the children and the need to spend time with them to fully understand and support them. As one IDVA reported:

> I see [the] role more of an extra, you know, we couldn't do it before, we just haven't got the capacity to do the touchy, feely, friendly. (IDVA)

Similarly, the children's services manager from an external agency who was interviewed, who coordinated a series of projects very similar to that supplied by the FIW in the study, thought there was a more general gap in addressing children's psychological well-being.

> Well, there is a gap, I mean there's a massive gap. I think it's … the support for children who, kind of, fall into that bracket, children with mental health issues is the biggest gap that I can see out there at the moment. (interviewee from outside agency)

A particular benefit of the role which was expressed related to ideas that it may address the longer term effects of domestic violence and that the FIW might help shape the future behaviour of children. In this respect, concern was voiced regarding the future of children who had witnessed domestic violence and the possibility that they would repeat violent behaviour if they were not supported promptly from the point of referral. The professionals interviewed also spoke of children from abusive backgrounds learning behaviours that may result in them becoming vulnerable to becoming perpetrators or victims themselves in the future:

> In one case it was the son who was 15 who was being violent and abusive to Mum. So that's how it was presented but actually on work with that cli-

ent it came about that the husband had been violent and abusive to her for many, many, many years. (Project Manager)

The respondents articulated the fear that, where unsupported, children's behaviour would get worse until it reached a crisis point. During this time, it was likely that the effects would be felt at home and at school, leading to truancy and other behavioural problems mirroring the findings of other research in this area, as discussed previously. The FIW strongly advocated that one of the most important aspects of the role was limiting the long-term impact of domestic violence. They also believed that children's behavioural difficulties often stemmed from experiences of domestic violence.

> I've found that a lot of these young people, who then exhibit risky behaviours and chaotic behaviours in the classroom and refusing to go to school … a lot of those families … would have a history of domestic violence…. (FIW)

The mothers interviewed confirmed their need for this type of support as they indicated that domestic violence had an impact on their child in a way that they felt unable to deal with, or they needed further support to manage. In particular, there were concerns expressed by mothers that the behaviour of their children was becoming increasingly aggressive and there were fears that the domestic violence witnessed would contribute to the cycle of abuse later on:

> … his behaviour is becoming quite aggressive as well…. (Mother's Interview)
> … well I was most concerned that children that have been part of abusive relationships … will have problems with abuse, or be abusive later in their life, and being boys, I was just really concerned that somehow, you know that sort of theory that, the cycle of abuse somehow continues into older life …. (Mother's Interview)

The ability to identify children in need before they reached a critical point was also seen as vital to the role's success. The IDVAs suggested that, because child social care services only worked with children who needed to be made safe, another group of less visible children, who were being affected by domestic violence, were falling through the gaps in service provision. Such children often appeared to be coping, but were likely to demonstrate problems later. Through the work of the FIW, needs could be recognised and addressed that were not necessarily about crisis work, but about the ongoing problems and issues facing children in families where domestic violence had occurred. So, as one respondent explained:

> I understand how busy they [Child Social Care] are and how they need to deal fast, especially in crisis situations, they always will send somebody out to do an initial assessment… and when they can see that mummy is looking after that child and its clean and the bedrooms look nice and you know, there's no injuries on the child then they'll just walk away … and that's covering the immediate safety element but it's not covering the mental issues to me at all as regards the child. (IDVA)

The fact that the FIW works independently was seen as highly important in terms of their ability to focus specifically on the family. One benefit of working separately from other services, including IDVAs and social services, was the ability to be flexible, as explained by the FIW in an interview:

> Because I am independent I can just work with the families which actually is a real bonus because some of these families don't need me to liaise with other people, they are down the line. They've gone through that process and they want someone they can talk to and they gain support from and who will empower them. (FIW)

The independence of the FIW role enabled them to work with families and other professionals to devise a tailored package of support and safety plan for as long as the family needed, although this was usually for a period of eight weeks. The plan incorporated techniques for providing support and promoting change in children's behaviour, for example, using one-to-one discussions and art therapy and outcome stars, to promote goals and achievements. Whilst the focus was on the children, a lot of work was also undertaken with parents to sustain positive changes made and establish and implement routines.

Building Trust

Beyond the general importance of the FIW role in supporting families and children where domestic violence had taken place, the research identified some additional qualities of the post, illustrating the value of providing an interagency role and the prioritisation of wider family needs. Our research revealed that the FIW built close and trusting working relationships with the clients whom we interviewed and this was in due, in part, to the family-focused approach that was used. All of the mothers we spoke to felt that they had been able to effectively talk through their experiences in a positive and constructive manner without feeling judged:

> It's just having someone to talk to that knows your situation, that's not prying, that's not one-sided or, you know, negative, which is always useful…. (Mother 2)

The skills and expertise of the individual in the FIW role are the keys to success, making suggestions and offering practical advice in a sensitive and tactful way. Consequently, the mothers in the study not only felt listened to, but were also very much involved in the decision-making processes and had a real choice over service delivery:

> … even what we're working on has been, like, my decision … it's only a suggestion. We didn't have to do anything [unless] I was comfortable. (Mother's Interview)

The importance placed on communication and choice strengthened the trust between the FIW and the family. Mothers often described these interactions as like 'talking to a friend' and this close working relationship meant that the mothers positively engaged with the programme. The FIW clearly set out the limits of the role to clients at the start of the programmes, emphasising that the sessions were not totally confidential, particularly if safeguarding issues were raised. However, the independence of the FIW meant that mothers felt FIW represented the family's interests rather than any particular agency, perceiving the FIW as a 'professional friend'. Accordingly, the mothers actually confided a great deal in the FIW, which helped to identify specific needs and potential risks and allowed the FIW to successfully navigate difficult conversations with other agencies on the mother's behalf. It was recognised by the FIW and service provider that work should also be undertaken with fathers where appropriate; however, there were no cases where that was currently happening.

Managing Communication with Children and Services

One of the FIW's key responsibilities was to initiate and manage conversations, both within the family and between the family and the support services. In explaining this, the FIW talked of the difficulties this created and also the broader benefits accruing from such conversations. They talked about initiating conversations with children and providing them with the opportunity to discuss their experiences and make sense of their often unsettled lifestyles. As the FIW told us:

> My job ... is just to, very sensitively, go in and just to offer an ear, really. Because a lot of the time what these children have had, lots of professionals come in sometimes, and lots of strategies and ... [they have] had to move away from all their friends, different locations, settling in to schools, things that are difficult for young people anyway, with a parent, potentially, who is quite chaotic and who is suffering emotionally themselves and often quite depressed, and maybe there's other issues and they're having to cope with all these things. It's just a listening ear, sometimes, is really important because they haven't had the chance to sit down and talk about their experiences. Because, you know, professionals and parents are so careful about what they say to children and are quite protective. A lot of what I do is about managing those conversations, that things can be quite difficult. (FIW)

This function gave the children a voice, where other services may not have done so and where parents and carers felt that they could not engage in such a conversation on their own with the child without it reaching a crisis point.

> It made them [the children] feel more important I think. Made their situation more important that they could actually analyse what had happened and not sweep things under the carpet ... each situation seemed to give the big boys extra confidence of knowing what was right and wrong really (Mother's Interview).

The mothers noted improvements in their children's behaviour after these interventions and felt that their children were able to process and understand what had happened in a much more positive way. This had a number of related benefits in terms of their school performance and relationships with friends, their relationship with the perpetrator where contact continued and their general outlook (see Crowther-Dowey, Gillespie and Hopkins Chap. 8 this volume). It, therefore, served both to improve the child's ability to communicate effectively and increase their self-confidence.

Whilst the long-term impact of this role is hard to determine and requires further research, its immediate success in managing conversations with other service providers was evident. As previously mentioned, the FIW is required to work closely with a diverse range of agencies, organisations and professionals across the whole county, liaising with, amongst others, schools, Child and Adolescent Mental Health Service (CAMHS) and general practitioners. The FIW can provide an overview to other professionals, set up multi-agency meetings and help build better relationships between the family and other services and in particular, with social services, which can often be the site of some tension. The FIW represents the family's interests at meetings with agencies and because of the trusting relationship built with the mothers, they are able to talk frankly with the carers and provide another perspective on what might have been perceived as a hostile situation. As the FIW noted:

> I can be the bridge between Social Services and the family, where they need Social Service's support ... I can help them make the right choices about

making safe decisions for their families so that actually you can build a better relationship with Social Care. (FIW)

Often this improves, or at least neutralises, the relationship between the client and the other service. In the observation of an initial assessment meeting with a mother, for example, the mother expressed her view that she thought social services staff were not listening to her side of the story. The FIW listened carefully and suggested an alternative perspective and offered to talk to the service on the mother's behalf, which the mother agreed to. The mother trusted the FIW's judgement and the FIW was able to maximise the level of support, which could be gained from other service providers by encouraging further engagement.

Importantly, the FIW can navigate difficult conversations between the families and the legal system. The FIW often helped explain complex language and the meaning of court proceeding decisions, helping to deal with the impact that this had on the family. Whilst the IDVAs were predominantly responsible for disseminating the legal information, the FIW helped the children make sense of what was happening, as well as assisting parents and carers to come to terms with changing dynamics and family situations, to move forward emotionally following developments in legal proceedings. As one mother explained:

> For the elder boys they did a lot of talking about who was in their family and who was in court…. (Mother's interview)

Our interviews with the IDVAs also highlighted the importance of the FIW's assessment when dealing with contact proceedings between the domestic violence perpetrator and the child. The IDVA would put together a report to highlight the concerns from an adult point of view about the impact contact was having on the family as a whole. However, the FIW could provide further insight into the impact that this was having on the child's psychological well-being. The belief was that this would lead to a fairer hearing and help empower the mother to feel that both her and her children's best interests had been adequately represented.

Another integral aspect of the FIW's role is signposting. For some families, the process of moving forward with their lives is relatively straightforward and clear, but for others that process is far more complicated.

The FIW not only draws together different professionals to keep them informed of the 'whole picture' from the family's perspective, but it also has oversight of the range of different services that the family can utilise. Therefore, the FIW is able to promptly identify the most appropriate service to help the family further, particularly the children.

> ... if there's an identified need, say, in mental health, I would make a referral to the CAMHS team and try and actually call a meeting so that, actually, something physical happens, and we can see some progress there. (FIW)

This applies to both professional services and community services. Often, the families had relocated to unfamiliar areas and felt isolated and frightened. An integral part of the FIW role was to signpost families to local resources and activities in the area, ensuring that they were settled in their local area as well as receiving any necessary professional support. This was often as simple as helping children pursue hobbies, for example, finding somewhere where a child could learn to play the drums.

Conclusion

In this chapter we have focused on the importance of working with the wider family in cases of domestic violence and in particular, supporting children through the process of recovery to prevent, or at least reduce the impact of the abusive experience. Although the limitations of this small-scale study are clear and have been discussed, our research has identified some of what can be achieved through an intensive focus on the family. Much is written about the need for and benefits of supporting children following exposure to domestic violence, yet relatively little is known about the 'on the ground' work that is done and how this is received by children and parents. This research, therefore, provides some insight into the day-to-day working of service providers and the daily lives of families that might otherwise not be captured in the evaluation of broader-based developments in domestic violence interventions. Whilst more work is needed, these preliminary results suggest that such interventions can have a significant effect on children who witness domestic violence. Thus, in the absence of any coherent policy or legal response towards secondary victims at this time, these interventions are becoming increasingly important to support child witnesses.

This study has also started to explore the detail of children's recovery in the context of the broader process of victims rebuilding their lives. In doing so, the FIW role offers a 'cross-planetary' approach that helps families to navigate the 'planetary problems' that arise from the different and often contradictory cultures, laws and priorities that exist in Hester's (2013) three planets of domestic violence work. However, with the FIW role, the coordination and communication is primarily child-focused, something which has not occurred before, complemented by the support provided to the parent by the IDVA. The FIW not only made children more prominent on the domestic violence planet by strengthening the links between IDVAs and various children's services, but also assisted in the negotiation of other legal and social services, supporting families in moving forward. Consequently, the FIW helped mothers improve their relationships with agencies concerned with child protection priorities and was also able to professionally represent the wider impact of the domestic violence on the child to the Family Courts, liaising between 'the planets'. Our research indicated that having an independent professional that families trust to provide intensive support was greatly valued by those accessing the service. FIWs assisted families through the complex process of rebuilding their lives and managing the various stages and 'planets' they are likely to encounter. These observations would suggest that a further investment and more extensive evaluation of this intervention model could potentially offer a more unified and holistic approach to effectively safeguard women and children in domestic violence cases. However, regrettably, the intensity of time and level of resources required for this form of intervention may question any likelihood of any further expansion and review for the foreseeable future.

References

Baker, S., & Edwards, R. (2012). *How many qualitative interviews is enough? Expert voices and early career reflections on sampling and cases in qualitative.* Research National Centre for Research Methods Review Paper NCRM;

ESRC. Retrieved October 29, 2015, from http://eprints.ncrm.ac.uk/2273/4/how_many_interviews.pdf

Barron, J. (2007). *Kidspeak. Giving children and young people a voice on domestic violence*. Bristol: Women's Aid Federation of England.

Bream, V., & Buchanan, A. (2003). Distress among children whose separated or divorced parents cannot agree arrangements for them. *British Journal of Social Work, 33*(2), 227–238.

Byrne, D., & Taylor, B. (2007). Children at risk from domestic violence and their educational attainment: Perspectives of education welfare officers, social workers and teachers. *Child Care in Practice, 3*(3), 185–201.

Casey, L. (2012). *Listening to troubled families*. London: Department for Communities and Local Government.

Children's Act 1989 c41. Retrieved October 29, 2015, from http://www.legislation.gov.uk/ukpga/1989/41/contents

Coordinated Action Against Domestic Abuse (CAADA). (2012). *CAADA Insights 1: A place of greater safety*. Bristol: CAADA.

Edleson, J. (1999). Children's witnessing of adult domestic violence. *Journal of Interpersonal Violence, 14*(8), 839–870.

Family Law Act 1996 c 27. Retrieved October 29, 2015, from http://www.legislation.gov.uk/ukpga/1996/27/contents

Groves, N., & Thomas, T. (2014). *Domestic violence and criminal justice*. Abingdon: Routledge.

Hayden, C., & Jenkins, C. (2014). "Troubled Families" Programme in England: "Wicked problems" and policy based evidence. *Policy Studies, 35*, 631–649.

Hester, M. (2013). The "Three Plant Model": Towards an understanding of contradictions in approaches to women and children's safety in contexts of domestic violence. In N. Lombard & L. McMillan (Eds.), *Violence against women: Current theory and practice in domestic abuse, sexual violence and exploitation*. London: Jessica Kingsley.

HM Government. (2015). *2010 to 2015 government policy: Support for families*. Retrieved October 29, 2015, from https://www.gov.uk/government/publications/2010-to-2015-government-policy-support-for-families/2010-to-2015-government-policy-support-for-families#appendix-2-how-the-troubled-families-programme-will-work

Home Office. (2013). *Home Office Circular 003/2013: New government domestic violence and abuse definition*. Retrieved October 29, 2015, from https://www.gov.uk/government/publications/new-government-domestic-violence-and-abuse-definition

Indermaur, D. (2001). Young Australians and domestic violence. *Trends and Issues in Crime and Criminal Justice, 195*, 1–6.

Kitzman, K., Gaylord, N., Holt, A., & Kenny, E. (2003). Child witnesses to domestic violence: A meta-analytic review. *Journal of Consulting Clinical Psychology, 71*, 339–352.

Laing, L., Humphreys, C., & Cavanagh, K. (2013). *Social work and domestic violence: Developing critical and reflexive practice*. London: SAGE.

Levitas, R. (2012). *There may be 'trouble' ahead: What we know about those 120,000 'troubled' families. Report (3) to the Policy Exclusion Unit*. ESRC Policy and Social Exclusion.

Lundy, M., & Grossman, S. F. (2005). The mental health and service needs of young children exposed to domestic violence: Supportive data. *Families in Society, 86*(1), 17–29.

Mullender, A., Hague, G., Imam, U., Kelly, L., Malos, E., & Regan, L. (2002). *Children's perspectives on domestic violence*. London: SAGE.

Murrell, A., Christoff, K., & Henning, K. (2007). Characteristics of domestic violence offenders: Associations with childhood exposure to violence. *Journal of Family Violence, 22*(7), 523–532.

Pain, R. (2013). *Everyday terrorism: How fear works in domestic abuse*. Durham: Durham University.

Rivett, M., Howarth, E., & Harold, G. (2006). "Watching from the stairs": Towards an evidence-based practice in work with child witnesses of domestic violence. *Clinical Child Psychology and Psychiatry, 11*(2), 103–125.

Robinson, A. L. (2003). *The Cardiff Women's Safety Unit: A multi-agency approach to domestic violence*. Cardiff: Cardiff School of Social Sciences, Cardiff University.

Serious Crime Act 2015 c9. Retrieved October 29, 2015, from http://www.legislation.gov.uk/ukpga/2015/9/contents/enacted

Stanley, N., Miller, P., Foster, R. H., & Thomson, G. (2011). Children's experiences of domestic violence: Developing an integrated response from police and child protection services. *Journal of Interpersonal Violence, 26*(12), 2372–2391.

Stark, E. (2007). *Coercive control: How men entrap women in personal life*. New York: Oxford University Press.

Stark, E. (2009). Rethinking coercive control. *Violence Against Women, 15*(12), 1509–1525.

# 8

Building Healthy Relationships for Young People and the Prevention of Domestic Abuse

Christopher Crowther-Dowey, Terry Gillespie, and Kristan Hopkins

Introduction

This chapter focuses on debates surrounding healthy relationships and the prevention of domestic abuse with reference to children and young people. The discussion examines the view that abusive behaviour is observed and potentially learnt by children and young people within the family environment and amongst their peers as they mature into adults. This recognises that this group is not just harmed physically and emotionally as a result of being witness to domestic abuse between adults, but that violence also occurs in young people's own relationships posing a threat to their safety and well-being. This discourse signifies a reconfiguration of current thinking and responses to domestic abuse.

C. Crowther-Dowey (✉)
Division of Sociology, Nottingham Trent University, Nottingham, UK

T. Gillespie • K. Hopkins
School of Social Sciences, Nottingham Trent University, Nottingham, UK

© The Editor(s) (if applicable) and The Author(s) 2016
S. Hilder, V. Bettinson (eds.), *Domestic Violence*,
DOI 10.1057/978-1-137-52452-2_8

With reference to our own empirical research,[1] this chapter examines how academic and policy discourses on these issues at a national level impact on developments within an urban housing estate in the Midlands region. The project undertaken examined the concept of a 'Firebreak', which seeks to disrupt and prevent the transmission of unhealthy and abusive attitudes towards intimate partner relationships from the older to younger generation (Crowther-Dowey, Gillespie, Hopkins Burke, & Kumarage, 2014). One of our central contentions is that a consideration of the 'local' is essential to any proposed intervention, taking into account the relevance of the conditions and circumstances in which the abusive behaviours occur.

The chapter is divided into four main sections. Firstly, we provide some brief context to the main discussion in terms of current policies, which have seen a greater emphasis on domestic abuse work with young people. We then seek to situate the notion of healthy relationships in the context of research about domestic abuse in general and young people in particular. At this juncture, the discussion briefly touches on the importance of recognising intersectional identities and the interaction of gender, age, sexuality, race and ethnicity (Henne & Troshynski, 2013), thus acknowledging that service provision must be sufficiently sensitised to the needs of a diverse society. Accordingly, more research on young people and their perceptions of healthy, 'good' relationships and abusive, 'bad' relationships is needed (Barter, McCarry, Berridge, & Evans, 2009; Gadd, Fox, & Corr, 2012). In addition, an understanding of the interplay between individual, relationship, community and institutional factors and how they mutually influence the formation of abusive attitudes and conduct for both perpetrators and survivors is key to the identification of successful policy and interventions (Flood, 2011). This leads to the third section of the discussion, which outlines some of the current myriad of interventions created to prevent and respond to domestic abuse. In this section, we consider the view that domestic abuse should not be treated solely as an issue of individual responsibility but also as a social and collective

---

[1] Firebreak Project: a study of an intergenerational 'Firebreak' to aid the prevention of domestic abuse. Empirical research undertaken by the authors as employees of Nottingham Trent University. Commissioned by City Council and partners in the Midlands region. 2013–2014. For a full copy of the report, see Crowther-Dowey et al. (2014).

responsibility that is shaped by the diverse identities of people inhabiting particular communities, what we term as a 'whole community approach'.

In the final section of the chapter, we refer to some of our 'Firebreak' research findings to further explore the issues covered previously. This provides a context for a discussion of the potential development of community-based interventions that seek to prevent the formation or reinforcement of abusive attitudes and behaviour. This, it is argued, requires an analysis of the factors influencing the lived realities of young people and their understandings of appropriate relationship interactions and boundaries and what constitutes abuse within intimate partner relationships.

Policy Background

The discourse on domestic abuse and young people is set in the wider context of a changing social and political landscape, with successive governments in the UK, pledging to take violence against women and girls (VAWG) seriously (Home Office, 2011). There has also been anxiety expressed in policy and governmental circles about the rise of domestic abuse amongst young people, with the revision of the Home Office (2013) definition of domestic abuse, which now includes behaviours exhibited by 16–17-year-olds (Starmer, 2011). Running parallel to this are steps to strengthen criminal justice responses to domestic abuse, which raises concerns about the potential reach this may have across teenage relationships (Home Office, 2014) and with a clear need for policymakers to be more conscious of the specific needs of children and young people in the planning of domestic abuse services. The VAWG Strategy Action Plan (Home Office, 2011) highlighted how young women and girls in particular (Kelly & Westmarland, 2015) can be subjected to sexually abusive and violent relationships (Home Office, 2015). This signalled a 'preventative turn' in this field (Peeters, 2015), a leitmotif articulated explicitly by the Home Office in 2015, who 'put prevention at the heart of' its 'approach to tackle VAWG' (2015, p. 13). The 'preventative turn' is not without its challenges, particularly if it is realised through the anticipation and prediction of future conduct as a means of identifying 'pre-delinquents' who require intervention.

The development of new innovations and interventions is also currently situated within a period of restricted growth, where the economic downturn has resulted in demands for effectiveness and efficiency to substantiate future investment. Austerity measures have an uneven impact on the capacity of the statutory, commercial, voluntary and community sectors to respond to complex social problems (Walby & Towers, 2012; see Turgoose, Chap. 6, this volume). It can be concluded, therefore, that within the domain of interventions for abusive relationships, as with all social problems, there is currently intense competition for scarce resources. As a result, addressing the diverse needs of survivors, perpetrators and those vulnerable to entering into abusive relationships are subject to difficult yet inevitable choices to be made pertaining to 'who gets what?'

Healthy Relationships, Domestic Abuse and Young People

In this section we review the literature to consider definitional issues of domestic abuse relating to age and gender. This is followed by some deliberation of the attitudinal (behavioural) and institutional (societal and structural) factors shaping domestic abuse amongst young people. The pattern of victimisation characterising these relationships is outlined, together with a consideration of an intersectionality that stretches beyond gender, recognising the 'multiple axes of oppression', such as class, sexuality and ethnicity, which interact to shape relations (Barbaret, 2014; Thiara & Breslin, 2006; see also Martin, Chap. 9; Barnes and Donovan, Chap. 13, this volume).

Definitional issues

There are clear societal views about healthy relationships, emphasising trust, love, care, humour and safety; unhealthy relationships are characterised as physically and verbally violent, abusive and controlling (Wills, 2013). The Home Office definition of domestic violence and abuse, which is in use across governmental departments, refers to:

> any incident or pattern of incidents of controlling, coercive, threatening behaviour, violence or abuse between those aged 16 or over who are, or have been, intimate partners or family members regardless of gender or sexuality. (Home Office, 2013, p. 29)

The addition of 16- and 17-year-olds to this definition in March 2013 is an acknowledgement that domestic abuse can occur between young people, although the mechanisms of the abuse tend to be slightly different from those found in adult relationships. For example, in the context of emotional abuse, it has been found that young people employ a relatively high level of surveillance through 'mobile phones, specifically the use of text messages' (Barter et al., 2009, p. 113). The lowering of the age range of the definition, therefore, reflects the reality of this problem for this age group as relative to their day-to-day experiences. It is important, however, that by dropping the age-inclusion criteria, the policymakers prioritise welfare-orientated and preventative measures over and above enforcement-led and punitive approaches. If this proves to be the case, then this is a welcome change, which we would suggest ought to be extended to young people under the age of 16 years, as supported by our research.

Factors Influencing Abusive Behaviour

There is a wealth of research concerned with attitudes and perceptions that influence the infliction of VAWG, which underpins the work of the Convention on the Elimination of All Forms of Discrimination Against Women (CEDAW) Committee (see the Women's Resource Centre's, 2013; Barbaret, 2014). However, in the UK, there has been little research on abusive relationships among younger people compared to that among adults (Barter et al., 2009). The research that does exist recognises specific areas that require further exploration, including patterns of behaviour between different age groups and the development of appropriate age-specific interventions (Barter, 2011; Fox, Corr, Gadd and Butler, 2012; Fox, Corr, & Gadd, 2013; Gadd et al., 2012; Walby & Towers, 2012). There is some evidence to suggest that gender-based violence starts to manifest at 16 years or below and that the 16–19-year-old age group remains at a higher risk than others (Walby & Allen, 2004). Currently little is known about what influences young people to become perpetrators at a young age, or about victim vulnerability, thus making solutions to the problem difficult to determine.

The inclusion of emotional abuse and coercive behaviour in current definitions of domestic abuse is, however, very important, as it exposes the elusive nature of many forms of abuse that can be applied to experiences across all age groups (Home Office, 2014). This was evidenced in our own study where two female participants, aged below 18, believed that the reason their partner wanted to know where they were all the time was 'because they loved them', displaying a blurred line between 'concern' and 'control' (Barter et al., 2009).

Despite targeted government responses to dealing with VAWG (Home Office, 2015), domestic abuse is vastly under-reported amongst young people, with evidence to suggest that the scale of under-reporting might also be under-estimated (Barter et al., 2009). However, more recent figures suggest that there is a greater willingness to report sexual violence occurring outside of a relationship (Office of National Statistics, 2015). Burton, Kitzinger, Kelly, and Regan (1998) studied the tolerance and acceptability of violence against girls, informing a later study by Burman and Cartmel (2005), which explored young peoples' attitudes towards gendered violence. Burman and Cartmel sought the views of young people aged 14–18 on domestic abuse, which revealed that young women were more likely to suffer emotional and violent abuse at the hands of their partner than men (Burman & Cartmel, 2005).

The relationship between domestic abuse, social class and social and economic deprivation has been seen as somewhat more contentious. Domestic abuse is not confined to poor and socio-economically marginalised areas and occurs in all communities, affluent and poor alike (Ray, 2011). There is, however, an association between domestic abuse and socio-economic forms of exclusion, as there is for violent crime in general and acquisitive crime. Finney (2006) found that *British Crime Survey* data shows that:

> Indicators of socio-economic status such as household income, vehicle ownership, tenure type and council/non-council areas [which] suggest fairly consistently that higher prevalence rates of intimate abuse are associated with relatively lower levels of socio-economic status … it is more vulnerable groups that are more likely to experience intimate violence or abuse. (Finney, 2006, p. 9)

More up-to-date research regarding this issue is clearly required; however, the point is of theoretical significance for our study and the unpublished statistical data we were provided with by the research commissioners also confirmed this pattern. That said, the relationship between socio-economic status and reporting is complex and the focus of our study is primarily concerned with observations at a micro level on one housing estate. Poverty is certainly not contended here as a 'cause' of domestic abuse; however, the stresses and strains of unemployment, low income, residential instability and other forms of disadvantage can be indicators of risk in abusive situations and can pose challenges to vulnerable gendered identities.

Victimisation, Male and Female Victims

Criminologists have debated for some time whether abusive intimate partner relationships are either 'gender symmetrical', in the sense that men and women are equally culpable of violence, or 'gender asymmetrical', meaning that male and female perpetrators behave differently (Dobash & Dobash, 2012; Hester, 2013). Our own observations concur with Hester (2013), that in heterosexual relationships domestic abuse is asymmetrical with males more likely to be more controlling, coercive and violent than their female counterparts, something that is sustained by a hypermasculine culture (Crowther-Dowey et al., 2014). Whilst another study found that 10 % of young women and 8 % of young men participating in a survey reported that their partner had tried to force them to have sex (Burman & Cartmel, 2005), the onus generally is placed on female victims, who are often blamed for being abused and with a 'widespread acceptance of forced sex and physical violence against women' (Burton et al., 1998, p. 1).

Attitudes of Young People Towards Abusive Relationships

Although underlying attitudes can encourage people to behave in a certain way, the extent to which they may influence acts of abuse is contested, and 'research findings into the influence of attitudinal factors on the perpetration of domestic abuse are not consistent' (Burman &

Cartmel, 2005, p. 11). Maxwell and Aggleton (2009) state that young men are often socialised to believe that if they are not interested in taking a leading role in initiating sexual behaviours, or if they do not have several sexual partners, they will be subject to humiliation by their peer groups. Young males experience pressure from peers to behave in a promiscuous manner, influenced by other factors such as status and self-worth, resulting in them condoning aggressive sexual behaviour towards young females. There is a sense of a 'normalisation' and a tolerance of sexual abuse against girls and young women (Burman & Cartmel, 2005, p. 43). This unhealthy cycle continues to drive the acceptance of abuse in young people's relationships, with peer group influences playing a significant role in shaping young people's perceptions. There is also a set of expectations imposed on young women to be compliant with such aggressive behaviour. It has been observed that young females may be led to believe that if a male spends a lot of money on them, they are then expected to engage in sexual relations with them (Home Office, 2012). Questions are raised regarding the experiences of young people and what has led to them holding such unhealthy attitudes and believing such behaviours to be acceptable. The overwhelming influence of peer pressure enables such attitudes to be 'normalised', but where do they originate from?

One apparent justification for physical violence, which has been provided by young people, is female infidelity, that is, a young female sleeping with someone else (Bell, 2008). More boys than girls thought that a physical retaliation in this type of situation was acceptable, which shows a gendered disparity of beliefs. When evaluating young people's attitudes towards abusive relationships, Bell's study suggests that young males are seemingly the driving force behind these demeaning and destructive attitudes. However, many girls held the same view, which suggests that young females can assist in maintaining the oppressive culture, internalising it and accepting responsibility for any form of violence committed against them. Whilst they may consider the actual act of violence to be inappropriate, the perceived provocation leads them to consider it to be an understandable response, as it is accepted that males are more likely to react aggressively in such circumstances. There is a general consensus that the education of young people, both male and female, who may be vulnerable to forming such attitudes, can help in increasing their awareness that they do not have to inhabit unacceptably abusive relationships (Home Office, 2015). Arguably, this is a realistic aspiration, as most young people, of all age groups, articulate a clear disapproval of all forms of violence, stating that it is 'pointless, stupid, disgusting' and 'never worth it, a last resort, or a sign of immaturity' (Burman & Cartmel, 2005, p. 44). However, this has been qualified by others who refer to the situational context and type of relationship, with more pessimistic observations and an almost tacit agreement that violence is acceptable against girls in certain relationships, on certain occasions (Burton et al., 1998).

Intersectionality

The growing body of work examining VAWG, and young people in particular, clearly highlights issues of gender, but there is a limited exploration of a wider intersectional approach to young people's experience of abuse in intimate relationships. Our own research adds to this body of work by exploring the extent to which the attitudes of young people towards relationships are shaped principally by age and gender on a single housing estate with residents from a low socio-economic background. We also explore the feasibility of changing negative attitudes at the level of the individual and wider community. The more diverse explanations of VAWG often draw upon psychology and the social sciences in general, but our stance is explicitly sociological in terms of its concern with cultural and structural influences on behaviour. The discourse we present to explain male violence and its impact recognises that there is a complex relationship between male on female violence, age and social class and that there are multiple forms of oppression shaping rather than determining the connections between these factors. There are other axes of subordination, resulting in complex relationships, such as the intertwining of gender with sexual orientation, race and ethnicity and immigration status (Gill & Anitha, 2011). Overall, there is a paucity of research in terms of children and young people and their experiences of domestic abuse within same-sex relationships and in relation to different race, ethnicity, culture and faith backgrounds. The specific experiences and needs of these groups lead to inequalities, which are not experienced by white, heterosexual females (Murray & Mobley, 2009) and whilst patterns will emerge, too many assumptions regarding 'commonalities' of experience pertaining to a single identity factor should be avoided.

Interventions Targeting Abusive Relationships

Efforts to address domestic abuse have seen initiatives more widely in areas of law enforcement, education and welfare, including partnership working (Barter, 2011; Ellis & Thiara, 2014; Home Office, 2015). The importance of such responses to domestic abuse is undeniable; however, many perpetrators of abusive behaviours can be resistant to change and ensuring they desist from future offending is challenging (see Hilder and Freeman, Chap. 13, this volume). With the current limitations of research on interventions promoting healthy and unhealthy relationships and the links with domestic abuse amongst young people, our research also drew upon recommendations relating to interventions designed for adults. However, it should not be assumed that they are automatically transferable to work with young people.

In 2000, under the government's Crime Reduction Programme, a number of pilot prevention strategy projects were implemented to reduce interpersonal violence. Work was undertaken in primary and secondary schools to prevent the formation of abusive attitudes and beliefs by increasing knowledge and understanding of domestic abuse (Hester & Westmarland, 2005). The delivery of lessons about abusive and healthy relationships was included in the Personal, Social Health and Citizenship Education (PSHCE) curriculum (Department of Education and Employment, 1999), although it was recommended that this material should be cross-curricular and school-wide (Hester & Westmarland, 2005). This student-centred work focused on safety, self-esteem, feelings and family and often adopted visual input approach and the use of drama. Bell and Stanley (2006) argue that drama can be a useful medium for developing positive ideas about relationships, although some young people were still unclear about the gendered nature of domestic violence after completing the programme. Nevertheless, lessons in school on domestic abuse appeal to young people because they are 'social actors' in their own right and want to be listened to (Mullender et al., 2002). Schewe (2002) suggests that providing prevention programmes as part of school-based work would be more effective if the focus was on increasing desired behaviours rather than decreasing unwanted behaviours. Hester and Westmarland (2005) continued to advocate for primary prevention strategies to raise awareness and challenge the attitudes of young people in relation to issues of domestic abuse. However, insufficient attention and resourcing was directed towards this group, a situation that persisted until the more recent Home Office Strategy to end VAWG highlighted previously (Home Office, 2011).

Anthony Wills, Chief Executive for Standing Together Against Domestic Violence, reiterates the need for 'healthy relationships' to be part of PSHCE programme. To supplement traditional approaches to reaching children, he advocates the use of alternative methods such as social media. Achievement of this depends on building effective partnerships, which, in turn, require raised awareness of the issue amongst professionals, including not only teachers and police officers, but also general practitioners and school nurses (Wills, 2013). This can be difficult as Gadd, Fox, and Hale (2013) demonstrate in their critique of social marketing approaches. Owing to a 'boomerang effect', media campaigns can trigger the exact opposite of what is intended by the creators. For example, in one anti-domestic abuse campaign, young men were only temporarily influenced by a media message to stop using violence, but, in the longer term, interpreted the message to reinforce their own negative views about female victims. Wider social media initiatives are also very limited in being able to take into account the different social and cultural contexts where children and young people grow up, with interventions potentially being misinterpreted and undermined by what goes on within the family and wider community settings.

The role of education and schools is taken up elsewhere by Gadd et al. (2013) who have designed an Attitudes towards Domestic Violence (ADV) questionnaire, which can be used by teachers. This is part of the READAPT (Relationship Education and Domestic Abuse Prevention Tuition) project, which uses a quasi-experimental design to measure changes in children's attitudes to domestic abuse following exposure to programmes across three regions, namely, England, Spain and France. The findings from the three sites are complex and in some cases, contradictory; however, following the completion of all three programmes, it appears that boys remain more accepting of domestic abuse than girls, to varying degrees.

The 'This is Abuse' campaign in the UK, which focuses on 13–18-year-olds (Home Office, 2015), aspires to tackle abusive attitudes before they result in actions that come to the attention of the police, youth offending teams and courts. This is also discernible in the Aggression Project of the National Society for the Prevention of Cruelty to Children (NSPCC), a programme designed to disrupt the habits and social context of 11–18-year-olds to reduce their aggressive behaviour in a way that is sustained into adulthood (Miller, 2013). There is a cautionary note to be had, however, in relation to the limitations of more formal and legal interventions. There is insufficient evidence to show that they work unless they are reinforced by sources of informal control in the home and neighbourhoods (Fagan, 1995). Internalised negative beliefs and unhelpful social bonds at an individual level must be challenged and healthy attitudes to relationships must be reinforced through positive normative behaviours in local communities.

The Firebreak Project: Key Findings

Context

Data provided by the City Council highlighted that the place where this this study was conducted was subject to high rates of unemployment and welfare dependency, along with lone-parent families and in particular, female-headed households. Owing to high levels of social deprivation and exclusion, a significant number of people were dependent on welfare, which, as already discussed, has been shown to have some influence on the dynamics of family and intimate relationships (Barter, 2011; Barter et al., 2009; Finney, 2006). The community in this study was relatively distinctive across the city as a whole for its homogeneity, particularly in terms of ethnicity; the inhabitants of the estate were predominantly white, working class, with a so-called hyper-masculine culture. It was thought that this culture was enabling young males to sustain controlling, aggressive and domineering attitudes towards girls and women. The purpose of the research study was to consider the nature of potential interventions to address this culture on the estate at different levels, ranging from the individual to the social structures, as part of a 'spectrum of prevention' (Flood, 2011). This is consistent with Heise's (1998) ecological model,[2] which was utilised to inform our analysis.

Here, we tease out some of the key findings relating to the participants' perceptions about age and gender with regard to relationships. Focus groups with different ages and gender of participants were undertaken, as were a series of semi-structured interviews. The topics for discussion focused on young people's understandings of appropriate relationships, relationship boundaries and what constitutes abusive behaviour in a relationship. There were 74 participants: 23 (8–11 years, 'young children'), 15 (12–14 years, 'older children'), 19 (15–18 years, 'young teenagers') and 17 (19 plus, 'older teenagers and adults'). The study was primarily qualitative, although some statistical data were made available to the researchers, with the majority of it being confidential. The research was time-limited and cross-sectional in design. The interview and focus group data were interpreted using a thematic analysis (Braun & Clarke, 2006). The research has prompted some critical reflections of the policy implications that emerge from the data, rather than the evolution of a specific intervention, which is yet to be fully determined (for a full discussion of the methodology and analysis applied, see Crowther-Dowey et al., 2014).

Participant Response: Healthy or Abusive Relationships?

The different age groups of young people were essentially asked the same range of questions, with the only deviation being the replacement of the words healthy/unhealthy with the words good/bad for the younger chil-

---

[2] Heise describes four levels where interventions can be implemented: *personal history* and *the microsystem*, the family and the immediate context, where decisions can be taken to control behaviour; *the exosystem*, the immediate socio-economic position and the ways in which aggressive and abusive behaviour might be held in high esteem; *the macrosystem*, where broader cultural values around masculinities and violence may manifest.

dren. The first question concerned the participants' understanding of the word relationship, revealing a clear gender divide. Males perceived relationships in narrow dyadic terms, such as boyfriend and girlfriend, whereas females were more likely to see relationships as complex and extended to female family members and friends. What follows is an analysis of responses to some of the other questions of particular interest.

What Does a Healthy Relationship Look Like?

Key features of a healthy relationship were described by the participants as trust, communication, respect, loyalty, a lack of deception and love, with trust seen as the most important. Females focused more on feeling safe and secure in relationships, with some, especially the older teenage female participants, referring directly to domestic or sexual abuse within unhealthy relationships. Young and older teenage males focused more on deceit, lying and cheating regarding financial issues as a feature of unhealthy relationships, an issue not mentioned at all by any females. These risk factors, including jealousy and the controlling behaviour it engenders, are evident in adult male perpetrator populations, suggesting here that they manifest and need to be addressed at an early age.

Is aggression and Violence Acceptable in Relationships?

Physical violence and overt aggression were tacitly recognised as a fact of life in the community, yet they were not explicitly condoned. None of the female participants understood arguments, aggression or violence as positive attributes. One 10-year-old girl said:

> a relationship can't be violent; gonna have to trust the person and erm, other people have to agree that person is nice.

Some of the male participants made an explicit distinction between arguments and violence, such as a 15-year-old male participant who stated that:

some arguments can make a relationship healthy.

Crucially, arguments were treated as something different from violence, and there was no recognition from the participants that arguing could also lead to the escalation of coercive and controlling behaviours.

Have You Ever Seen a Bad Relationship? If So, How Did You Feel and What Did You Do?

The child participants aged 8–14 saw unhealthy or 'bad' relationships in terms of fear, worry, anxiety and sadness. Many, across the age groups, had witnessed violence that had upset them, including bullying and domestic abuse. Despite this, all of the young participants did not generally discuss domestic abuse and tended to see it as a sensitive and private matter that is 'not anybody's business', demonstrated by the relative absence of disclosures. There were gender differences regarding experiences of witnessing domestic violence and the construction of abusive relationships. Male participants stated that they did not want to become abusers in adulthood and female participants stated that they did not want to become victims:

> It didn't make me feel too good 'cos you could come out like that. (15-year-old male)
> I just wouldn't want to get in one. (15-year-old female)

This lends some support to the view that abusive relationships are asymmetrical (Dobash, 2012), in the sense that male participants might recognise themselves as potential abusers, whereas female participants identified themselves as potential victims. In light of the next question, however, the findings were more ambiguous.

Who Behaves Worse in Relationships, Boys Or Girls?

Views about whether males or females were 'worse' in terms of abuse within relationships were mixed; while granting that males were more forceful and argumentative, there was a consensus amongst the younger participants that 'both are as bad as each other'. In contrast, some older female children, drawing on their experience, thought that males were more abusive. A female focus group of 12–15-year-olds, for example, said the following:

> 'The men', 'the boys', 'That's not true', 'You can't say that though', 'It could be the girls as well 'cos I'm more violent than my boyfriend…I'm more aggressive', 'It's not always men, that's just stereotyping.'

In a male focus group of 15–16-year-olds, the following responses were elicited:

> 'Could be either at times', 'Most people say it's only like boys but sometimes it's like girls who are aggressive in the relationship.'

What Causes Problems in Relationships?

Domesticity and gendered roles can generate tensions. Expectations about gendered roles are apparent and influence the normalisation of conflict at an early age. A 9-year-old girl identified 'washing the pots' as helping to define a good relationship. She also referred to 'not washing the pots' as characterising a bad relationship, adding that boys not cleaning up after themselves can cause arguments. This reveals an implicit recognition of the gendered nature of domestic abuse and issues of power and control within the domestic sphere. For example, as one young male participant stated:

> I've got a few friends and they're always like fighting with their missus, arguing. It's like you go round there to their place and that, sometimes it's their place and that, well sometimes it's the missus' place and you go round and there's loads of people round all the time and she comes back from work and then starts swearing saying "ah, you ain't done this, you ain't done that" and then they're like arguing in front of ya [laughter from group] so you just get up and go.

What Can Be Done to Resolve a Bad/Unhealthy Relationship?

The children participating in the study, although some of them had seen their parents engage in violence, were generally more positive, creative and hopeful about fostering good relationships, perhaps a reflection of their limited life experience. For instance, some of the younger children referred to the relatively positive impact professionals and counsellors had in their lives, especially youth workers and peer support workers. They enjoyed, for example, role-play sessions on healthy relationships. A 10-year-old girl also talked about involving social workers more in educational activities based in schools:

> Other people, like social workers, could be more at school and ask pupils what they've been through and if there's been violence in the house or on the streets and what their life's been like.

One 13-year-old boy suggested that a good way to get the message across to people about healthy relationships would be to:

> Put it on a banner or like on a sign on the roads where like every time you go past in a car or walk you can see it...on a banner and, erm, on gates and on lamp posts and bus stops where people can go everyday.

Teenage and young adult participants were more cynical, expressing, at times, an almost fatalistic attitude, that nothing could be done to prevent bad relationships. They were inclined to express negative views about the possibility of changing societal attitudes towards abusive relationships, and they were not optimistic about stopping abusive behaviour.

> Sometimes there's nothing you can do really, if anything, it's best not to get involved 'cos it's their business not yours. (15-year-old female)

An older male, aged 19, stated:

> There's nothing you can do, it's always gonna happen no matter what, it always has happened ... when a relationship starts to go bad you just get

out of it rather than staying in an unhealthy relationship … rather than waiting and hoping that it blows over.

A 17-year-old male participant in a one-to-one interview replied:

Can't do anything if it is a bad relationship.

A female in a 13–19-year-olds focus group suggested that it would be:

Better to keep it between themselves and not let everyone know.

A 15-year-old girl also seemed resigned to such bad relationships:

You can't tell them, it's their choice. You try to help, but it is their choice.

Some older teenage and young adult females talked about running away and 'getting away from them [men]', and speaking out, or seeking help rather than expecting men to change. For some in this group, there was a sense that abuse and violence are normal and something to be tolerated. An 18-year-old female participant captured this when asked to think about change in the context of abusive relationships:

That's a hard one, I don't know. I don't think society can help, it's like all inwards like in people. Obviously there's gonna be support groups, like for abuse and for women who have been abused and things like that, but nothing's gonna stop the person from doing it.

The findings in this section suggest that to prevent abusive attitudes and behaviour, it is essential to focus on children's early perceptions and explore positive views about identities and relationships with them, ascertaining and negating the influences that appear to cause this to change as they get older. This was seen as key to the work and interventions, which may emerge in relation to an intergenerational 'Firebreak'.

Potential Interventions for Preventing Abusive Attitudes and Behaviour

There is arguably a requirement for age-differentiated responses to working with young people on issues of domestic abuse that reflect some of the subtle transitions occurring between the ages of 8 and 18 years and beyond. However, there is a lack of any consensus across international research about the most appropriate age for work with children and young people to take place. The earlier an intervention occurs, the sooner a child can engage with alternative views and learn to make healthy choices in relationships. However, educational programmes may also need to be repeated frequently in response to different types of abuse and the personal and social issues that arise at different ages.

The NSPCC's Aggression Project has a long-term ambition to reduce aggressive behaviours through the disruption of habits and the social context of 11–18-year-olds (Miller, 2013). Any change is likely to be gradual, while preventative interventions of this sort are required at different levels of social reality, ranging from the individual to society as a whole. This is why we draw on a multi-dimensional approach that addresses the 'interplay of individual, relationship, community, institutional and societal factors' highlighted at the start of this chapter (Flood, 2011, p. 361). This is consistent with the four levels of intervention identified by Heise (1998).

The *personal history* of the individual is very important and although it is not feasible to create bespoke responses for each person, their own stories, such as those revealed in the interviews and focus groups, should be heard. This suggests that personal narrative, including disclosures, are key ingredients for any intervention. It is imperative that individual attitudes are acknowledged in order to understand the different expectations males and females have of relationships, with recognition of the emotional maturity and literacy of different age groups. In doing this, a number of patterns can be discerned relating to age and gender. It appears that young children are quite optimistic about the potential for change and improving unhealthy relationships, whereas older children are more fatalistic and sceptical about their ability to influence and transform relationships.

The *microsystem* refers to the nature of relationships in the community. The research participants tended to view relationships exclusively in terms of familial and intimate relationships. However, there needs to be some consideration of the extent to which these relationships are shaped by cultural norms in the wider community, with learned behaviours reinforced by peer contact, sustaining stereotypical gendered roles and hyper-masculinities. By no means were all intimate relationships abusive or violent, but many were, and almost all the participants were aware of such behaviour. Although participants recognised that both genders across all age groups could be abusive, males were widely viewed as more problematic, not only for their abuse, but for their behaviour more generally. This was also demonstrated, in part, by crime statistics for the geographical area studied. Familial ideologies and the prescription of gender roles are also influential and complex gender relationships require further consideration.

The *exosystem* covers issues at the level of the community, such as poverty, socio-economic status and levels of social cohesion. Any interventions such as educational and awareness packages should not neglect these factors and the need for a 'whole community approach'. The presence of strong social ties in relatively homogenous communities can lead to the continuance of pro-violent attitudes and behaviour, which pose challenges for statutory and voluntary community sector agencies that are required to bring about attitudinal change at individual and community levels. The estate in the study had the third highest rate of recorded violent crime in the city, which was also characterised by some evidence of a hyper-masculine culture. Owing to the nature of labour markets in the area, some males would appear to be marginalised on the estate because of their unemployment status and lack of regular income. These men were, in some respects, economically dependent on women, which, in some cases, manifested in the form of subordinated masculinities and the infantilisation of some men. An aggressive hyper-masculine culture otherwise remained very influential, a legacy of 'traditional' forms of masculinity, enabling males to control and dominate females through the use of violence and other forms of coercive behaviour. The nature of changing forms of masculinity and their influence on children's and adolescents' perceptions was less clear.

Finally, the *macrosystem* consists of wider influences on the community, such as norms that support the view that women and girls should be controlled and that violence is accepted as a method of resolving conflict and establishing control, thereby normalising abusive attitudes and behaviours. Whilst this was beyond the remit of our own study, these considerations are vital in the design of interventions, which may ensue.

Conclusion

In this chapter, we have identified the need for location-relevant interventions when addressing young people's experiences of domestic abuse. Whilst it is important to situate policies within the wider context of national and international policy on violence against women and girls, it is vital that work on interventions is targeted to meet the needs of young people within their own social networks and communities. By focusing on young people talking about their respective experiences of familial and intimate relationships on one estate, our understanding of relationships can be enriched. Beyond the accounts of the individual participants, evidence suggests that community-based norms and wider influences, such as hyper-masculine cultures and stereotypical notions of gender-based roles, have an impact on children, young people and adults, constraining their choices and actions. This is compounded by central government under-investment in the resources, if not the rhetoric, needed to reach and change young people's perspectives in the context of their families, peer groups and the wider community.

It is clear that difficult choices need to be made when developing interventions that may inadvertently exclude certain groups and their interests. This is particularly relevant for those working with young people on healthy relationships. There is a gap in the literature on intersectionality, young people and domestic abuse that warrants further research and investigation.

Our study also revealed another particular challenge in that there appears to be a particular form of subordinated masculinity amongst young males, which was evident in the interplay of interpersonal and gendered relations and the wider socio-economic context of the estate and which is manifest in domestic abuse against female partners. In addition, of significant concern is the young people's sense of fatalism about abuse, the view that it is normal or a stubborn problem that is essentially unchangeable. A more optimistic reading of our account is that there is potential for children to follow a different pathway before they enter their teenage years, although it is not clear if they will have the capacity to make these positive changes in the context of a hyper-masculine subculture, where older teenagers and adults appear to have relinquished hope.

It is understood that policymakers at national and local levels are faced with the difficulties arising from finite resources and the diversity of groups in need and it is not yet known how the full impact of austerity policies will affect intervention work around young people and domestic abuse. What is clear is that while work with young people on healthy relationships has resource implications for already hard-pressed authorities, it is vital for long-term reductions in the incidence of domestic abuse. Finally, this chapter has identified a need for further work on a multi-dimensional approach (Flood, 2011; Heise, 1998), noting the opportunities and risks associated with the 'preventative turn' (Home Office, 2015; Peeters, 2015). We see this as a fruitful area for further research on domestic abuse interventions targeting young people.

References

Barbaret, R. (2014). *Women, crime and criminal justice: A global inquiry*. London: Routledge.
Barter, C. (2011). Domestic violence: Not just an adult problem. *Criminal Justice Matters, 85*, 22–23.
Barter, C., McCarry, M., Berridge, D., & Evans, K. (2009). *Partner exploitation and violence in teenage intimate relationships*. Retrieved August 6, 2015, from http://www.nspcc.org.uk/inform/research/findings/partner_exploitation_and_violence_wdomestic_abuse68092.html
Bell, J. (2008). *Attitudes of young people towards domestic violence*. Northern Ireland: Northern Ireland Statistics and Research Agency.

Bell, J., & Stanley, N. (2006). Learning about domestic violence: Young people's responses to a healthy relationships programme. *Sex Education, 6*(3), 237–250.

Braun, V., & Clarke, V. (2006). Using thematic analysis in psychology. *Qualitative Research in Psychology, 3*(2), 77–101.

Burman, B., & Cartmel, F. (2005). *Young people's attitudes towards gendered violence*. Edinburgh: NHS Scotland.

Burton, S., Kitzinger, J., Kelly, L., & Regan, L. (1998). *Young people's attitudes towards violence, sex and relationships*. Edinburgh: Zero Tolerance Charitable Trust.

Crowther-Dowey, C., Gillespie, T., Hopkins Burke, K., & Kumarage, C. (2014). *Firebreak project report: Young people's views on healthy and unhealthy relationships*. Nottingham: Nottingham Trent University.

Department of Education and Employment. (1999). *National Healthy Schools standard guidance*. London: NHSS

Dobash, R. P., & Dobash, R. E. (2012). Women's violence to men in intimate relationships: Working on a puzzle. *British Journal of Criminology, 44*, 324–349.

Ellis, J., & Thiara, R. K. (Eds.) (2014). *Preventing violence against women and girls: Educational work with children and young people*. Bristol: Policy Press.

Fagan, J. (1995). *The criminalisation of domestic violence: Promises and limits*. Washington, DC: US Department of Justice Office of Justice Programs, National Institute of Justice.

Finney, A. (2006). *Domestic violence, sexual assault and stalking: Findings from the British Crime Survey*. Home Office Online Report 12/06. London: Home Office.

Flood, M. (2011). Involving men in efforts to end violence against women. *Men and Masculinities, 14*(3), 358–377.

Fox, C., Corr, M. L., & Gadd, D. (2013). Young teenagers' experiences of domestic abuse. *Journal of Youth Studies, 17*(4), 510–526.

Fox, C., Corr, M. L., Gadd, D., & Butler, I. (2012). *From boys to men: Phase one key findings*. Retrieved October 25, 2015, from http://pure.qub.ac.uk/portal/en/publications/from-boys-to-men-phase-one-key-findings(7c3167d1-7482-4b24-9f3b-0daf94e9062b).html

Gadd, D., Fox, C., & Corr, M.-L. (2012). Young people's attitudes towards and experiences of domestic abuse: How are they connected? In *Early Career Academic Networks Bulletin* (pp. 9–11). London: Howard League for Penal Reform.

Gadd, D., Fox, C., & Hale, B. (2013). Young people and violence against women. *Criminal Justice Matters, 92*(June), 36–37.

Gill, A. K., & Anitha, S. (2011). Introduction: Forced marriage as a form of violence against women. In A. K. Gill & S. Anitha (Eds.), *Forced marriage: In a social justice and human rights perspective*. London: Zed Books.

Heise, L. L. (1998). Violence against women: An integrated ecological framework. *Violence Against Women, 4*, 262–290.

Henne, K., & Troshynski, E. (2013). Mapping the margins of intersectionality: Criminological possibilities in a transnational world. *Theoretical Criminology, 17*(4), 455–473.

Hester, M. (2013). Who does what to whom? Gender and domestic violence perpetrators in English police records. *European Journal of Criminology, 10*(5), 623–637.

Hester, M., & Westmarland, N. (2005) *Tackling domestic violence: Effective interventions and approaches*. HORS 290. London: Home Office.

Home Office. (2011). *A call to end violence against women and girls*. London: HMSO.

Home Office. (2012). *Do you know if your teenager is in an abusive relationship?* Retrieved August 6, 2015, from https://www.gov.uk/government/uploads/system/uploads/attachment_domestic abuseta/file/97768/parents-leaflet.pdf

Home Office. (2013). *Home Office Circular 003/2013: New government domestic violence and abuse definition*. Retrieved April 26, 2015, from https://www.gov.uk/government/publications/new-government-domestic-violence-and-abuse-definition

Home Office. (2014). *Strengthening the law on domestic abuse: A consultation*. London: Home Office.

Home Office. (2015). *A call to end violence against women and girls: Progress Report 2010–2015*. London: Home Office.

Kelly, L., & Westmarland, N. (2015). *Domestic violence perpetrator programmes: Steps towards change. Project Mirabal final report*. Durham: Durham University.

Maxwell, C., & Aggleton, P. (2009). *Young women and their relationships – Power and pleasure*. Institute of Education. Retrieved August 6, 2015, from http://www.ioe.ac.uk/young_womens_feedback_document_final_221009.pdf

Miller, P. (2013). *NSPCC: Addressing domestic abuse in young people's relationship*. Paper presented at Domestic Violence and Young People: Tackling Teenage Relationship Abuse. A Public Policy Exchange Symposium. October 23, 2013.

Mullender, A., Hague, G., Imam, U., Kelly, L., Malos, E., & Regan, L. (2002). *Children's perspectives on domestic violence*. London: SAGE.

Murray, C., & Mobley, K. (2009). Empirical research about same-sex intimate partner violence: A methodological review. *Journal of Homosexuality, 56*(3), 361–386.
Office for National Statistics. (2015). *Crime statistics, focus on violent crime and sexual offences, 2013/2014.* London: ONS.
Peeters, R. (2015). The price of prevention: The preventative turn in crime policy and its consequences for the role of the state. *Punishment and Society, 17*(2), 163–183.
Ray, L. (2011). *Violence and society.* London: SAGE.
Schewe, P. (2002). Guidelines for developing rape prevention and rape reduction interventions. In P. Schewe (Ed.), *Preventing violence in relationships. Interventions across the life span.* Washington, DC: American Psychological Association.
Starmer, K. (2011). *Domestic violence: The facts, the issues, the future.* Crown Prosecution Service. Retrieved October 25, 2015, from www.cps.gov.uk/news/articles/domestic_violence_-_the_facts_the_issues_the_future/
Thiara, R. K., & Breslin, R. (2006). Black and minority ethnic children and domestic violence. *Community Care, November*, 32–33.
Walby, S., & Allen, J. (2004). *Domestic violence, sexual assault and stalking.* HORS 276. London: Home Office.
Walby, S., & Towers, J. (2012). *Measuring the impact of cuts in public expenditure on the provision of services to prevent violence against women and girls.* Lancaster University. Retrieved October 25, 2015, from http://www.trustforlondon.org.uk/research/publication/professor-sylvia-walby-reports-on-the-impact-of-cuts-on-violence-against-women-services/
Wills, A. (2013). *Domestic violence and young people: Tackling teenage relationship abuse*, Paper presented at Domestic Violence and Young People: Tackling Teenage Relationship Abuse. A Public Policy Exchange Symposium. October 23, 2013.
Women's Resource Centre. (2013). *Women's equality in the UK – A health check.* Shadow Report from the UK CEDAW Working Group Assessing the United Kingdom Government's Progress in Implementing the United Nations Convention on the Elimination of All Forms of Discrimination Against Women (CEDAW). London: Women's Resource Centre.

9

Debates of Difference: Male Victims of Domestic Violence and Abuse

Luke Martin

Introduction

The historical campaign to raise the profile of violence within the domestic sphere has primarily conceptualised the issue as a heterosexual concern, with men as the perpetrators and women as the victims (Dobash & Dobash, 2004). However, the past two decades have seen an increase in research that examines the experience of male victims (Brogden & Harkin, 2000; Dempsey, 2013; Gadd, Farrall, Dallimore, & Lombard, 2002), with national campaigns for the improvement of specialist support services for men (Mankind, 2015). The response has, however, remained predominantly heteronormative, with violence perpetrated by women against men receiving more attention (Johnson, 1995, 2006), and with very little regard at this time to the experiences of lesbian, gay, bisexual and/or transgender (LGB and/or T) communities (see Donavon and Barnes, Chap. 12).

L. Martin (✉)
Martin Training and Consultancy, Brighton, UK

This chapter is informed by the author's experience for seven years as an Independent Domestic Violence Advisor (IDVA) for male victims. It seeks to explore the experiences of men who are victims of domestic abuse from a number of different theoretical, policy and practice-based angles. The discussion starts with an examination of some of the debates and data utilised to examine the prevalence of male victimisation, the scale of the issue and how it equates with female experiences. This leads to a consideration of the feminist analysis of domestic abuse, which has dominated debates so far and the extent to which concepts of patriarchy and hegemonic masculinity assist an understanding of male victim experiences. Some broader observations are then offered on the main similarities and differences that male victims of domestic abuse have reported, both in terms of a comparison with the experiences of female victims, across heterosexual and same-sex relationships and for those of transgender identity. The chapter concludes with an examination of responses to the abuse of male victims and key challenges pertaining to the reporting of abuse, measures of protection, the identification of needs and access to support services.

The Prevalence of Male Victimisation

The prevalence of domestic abuse perpetrated against male victims has been a somewhat contentious matter, with varying approaches to the collection and analysis of data, which both amplify and diminish its occurrence. For example, in the USA, figures for the prevalence of male victimisation have been estimated between 100,000 to 6 million, dependent on the form of survey and the study accessed (Rennison & Welchans, 2000). Researchers such as Hamel (2007) have suggested that the number of men experiencing domestic abuse is approximately equivalent to that of female victims. Other studies have refuted this (Berk, Berk, Loseke, & Rauma, 1983; Dobash & Dobash, 2004; Mirrlees-Black, 1999), highlighting, in addition, the different types of experience occurring across genders, with male perpetrators more likely to use coercive and controlling forms of abuse and with female victims more likely to experience repeat victimisation over a prolonged period (Hester, 2009). In 2012–2013, the Crime Survey of England and Wales stated that 30 % of women and 16.3 % of men had experienced some form of domestic abuse since the age of 16 years, equivalent to an estimated 4.9 million female victims of domestic abuse and 2.7 million male victims (Office of National Statistics, 2015). However, these data cover a range of possible family scenarios and do not identify the sexuality of the perpetrator and the victim.

Whilst all forms of domestic abuse are likely to be under-reported, Brown (2004) found that women were four times more likely than men to report their experiences of partner violence to the police. However, Hester (2009) found that only one in ten police call-outs to a domestic abuse incident ever resulted in the actual arrest of a male perpetrator, whereas one in three call-outs resulted in an arrest where the perpetrator was female. It is likely that assumptions about relationship dynamics and gender roles in situations of abuse are one of many factors that influence the response from the police and other agencies. Maybe the most honest answer at this stage is that the real figures of crime for the incidence of domestic violence against men and women are simply not known, but there are some clear indications that the rate and nature of the experience across genders are worthy of further exploration. It might also be safely assumed that both men and women are reluctant to report abuse, for a whole variety of reasons, some of which will be related to gendered role expectations.

Feminism, Hegemonic Masculinity and Domestic Abuse

Dempsey (2013) and Hester, Radford, and Kelly (1995), amongst others, discuss the feminist paradigm that has shaped domestic violence policies and responses across England and Wales over the past four decades. For many, this is an essential framework that reflects the societal issues that serve to perpetuate conditions conducive to the commission of domestic abuse, whereas for others, it is an unsubstantiated ideology. At its most radical extremes, the paradigm, a product of feminist sociopolitical theory, postulates that the root cause of domestic abuse is found in patriarchal structures of male dominance and has focused on the systemic oppression of women and gender inequalities as the backdrop to the commission of abuse. More latterly, this feminist analysis has extended to consider how other forms of marginalisation interplay with gender to contribute to a victim's experiences and their access to, or lack of, resources for support. Elsewhere, those who advocate a more 'gender-neutral' approach have pursued theoretical explanations centred more on psychological issues, personality traits, family systems and relationship dynamics (Dixon, Archer, & Graham-Kevan, 2012).

More broadly, feminist criminology and victimology has also encouraged an analysis of gender in relation to male offending and the construction of criminality as way of 'doing gender' (Connell, 2005; Messerschmitt, 1997). Hegemonic masculinity is a term coined to explain the interactive societal processes that lead to a dominant expression of maleness and manhood, subordinating other forms of masculinity. Whilst masculinity may be expressed differently in varying cultural and social contexts, it is most commonly associated with heterosexuality, strength, power, restraint of emotional expression, aggression and risk-taking. Various social mechanisms such as the mass media and popular culture perpetuate a hierarchy of masculinities that influence male-gendered relations not only with women, but also with other men. This conceptualisation has been seen useful when seeking to explore male violence including domestic abuse, which is underpinned by an intrinsic 'normalisation' of aggressive and dominant male behaviours (see Crowther-Dowey, Gillespie and Hopkins, Chap. 8, this volume). However, gender–power relations are not fixed, and are subject to challenge and restructuring through social practices. Conversely, therefore, some experiences of male 'victimisation' within personal relationships have also been attributed to men's sense of displacement, as patriarchal structures and dominant concepts of masculinity start to change (Messner, 1993). From this form of analysis, it is suggested that the male victim's 'abuse' is more a manifestation of the male partner's struggle to accept changing relationship dynamics and gendered roles, rather than any oppressive intentions from the other party. Following this through, the male presenting as a 'victim' may, therefore, be asked to reflect on issues of personal identity and his own values and beliefs about status and roles within intimate partner relationships and couple counselling may be recommended. Whilst for some men, responding to shifting boundaries in gendered relations may be challenging, this approach also clearly has the potential for male victim experiences of actual abuse to be denied more generally.

Hegemonic masculinity is also useful when examining male victims' reports of abuse, which are often elucidated by a sense of emasculation, either in terms of the actual experience of the abuse itself, or the subsequent reaction from others at the point of disclosur, or both. Becoming a male victim of domestic abuse challenges perceptions of personal identity and 'what it is to be a man' across heterosexual, gay, bisexual and/or trans male identities. For gay, bisexual and/or trans men, this can be further compounded by an already entrenched internalisation that their expression of maleness is marginalised and dismissed by a large section of society. Chan, 2006; Cochran, 2005 and Courtenay, 2000 highlight men's reluctance to access any form of emotional support following their abuse, because of the concern that disclosures are perceived as a weakness, with tendencies to minimise the extent and impact of the abuse as a way of retaining some semblance of male strength and power. George (2002) continues that men who have been classified as 'victims', particularly as a result of the behaviours of female perpetrators, have often been publicly humiliated and chastised. Whilst guilt and shame are common features of many victims' experiences, both male and female, for men this underpinning sense of shame and stigma can be connected to broader issues of gendered conditioning, which views men as the aggressor, belittling and ridiculing those who 'allow' themselves to be victimised (Cook, 1997; Hamel, 2007; Hines, Brown, & Dunning, 2007).

Whilst fears of not being believed are also commonplace for female victims, Hogan, Hegarty, Ward, and Dodd (2012) suggest that the reasons for this fear differ slightly for male victims and they may often be treated with suspicion when seeking help, with the motivation for their disclosure doubted. To this extent, advancing the cause of male victims has been perceived by some as an attempt to undermine the seriousness of domestic violence and abuse against women and girls, by professing a notion of gender neutrality both in terms of the frequency and the impact of the harm caused by violence to both men and women, which has yet to be substantiated. Thus, when men make disclosures of abuse perpetrated against them, they may be screened[1] and assessed to ascertain if they are, in fact, the primary perpetrator and if they are making counter-allegations to detract attention away from their own actions (Hearn, 1998; Wolf-Light, 1999). Whilst knowledge of heterosexual male perpetrators' strategies of coercion and manipulation may, on some levels, lead to an understanding of such a response, it is unlikely that female victims would receive the same level of scrutiny. Arguably, therefore, the professed victim-centred ethos of the domestic violence sector is variably applied.

Following Johnson's (2008) typologies, there may be other prevailing dynamics, such as violent resistance and situational couple violence, where the use of expressive and instrumental violence within a relationship follows a more complex pattern. In the author's experience, some men may present as victims of abuse, but on further investigation, it may be revealed that they are unhappy with a volatile relationship that is characterised by expressive outbursts, but where patterns of coercive and controlling abusive behaviour are not otherwise apparent. In cases where reports of arguments with partners are not underpinned by fears of violence, or by details of other measures that systematically seek to undermine the individual, the pursuit of 'victim' support may be inappropriate and unhelpful and other forms of practical and legal advice, anger management or, again, couple counselling may be more suitable. However, a further note of caution must occur at this juncture, as assumptions based on the aforementioned experiences can also clearly continue to perpetuate an incredulous reaction to a situation where a male victim is indeed systematically abused by a female or same-sex partner. As a result, the male victim experiencing the intimate terrorism described by Johnson (2008) may continue to struggle to be taken seriously.

---

[1] Screening Assessment tools have been developed by some domestic violence victim support services across England and Wales. These tools were created to assess the validity of victim disclosures. Where these tools are utilised, it becomes apparent that 'genuine' male victims of domestic abuse may experience some very significant challenges in being believed.

The Experiences of Male Victims

Heterosexual Male Victims

The fact that so many female victims have endured abuse for incredibly long periods before seeking any support and that many may decide to remain in an abusive relationship, even if the abuse should continue, has left them vulnerable to judgemental responses from those lacking a full understanding of the complicated nature of domestic abuse. Male victims are also subjected to some profound expressions of negative disbelief, either that they tolerate such behaviours from a female heterosexual partner, or again a degree of scepticism that they are not at least a co-instigator of the abuse and that their own actions must have, in some way, triggered their partner's emotional instability.

Hines and Douglas (2010) found that many of the heterosexual men who sustained very serious forms of intimate partner violence advised that they remained in the relationship because of a psychological investment to their family and children and an emotional commitment to their relationship. However, Hogan et al. (2012) discuss a number of various other social realities that serve to silence the male victim and render him more likely to stay in an abusive relationship. They emphasise the societal expectation that men should be able to look after themselves and not fall foul to victimisation of any kind, resulting in disclosure becoming even less likely for males than it is for females. In fact, the gendered role expectation that a man should be in control physically, financially and emotionally, which may be attributed to the distorted behaviours of many male domestic abuse perpetrators, can equally be the gendered role expectation that inhibits male victims from coming forward (Tsui, Cheung, & Leung, 2010). Men are also less likely to identify themselves with a victim status or classify the behaviours occurring within the relationship as abuse. Research conducted by Gadd et al. (2002) reported that only one-third of the abused men surveyed identified as victim, as opposed to nearly four-fifths of the abused women. The researchers also found that men were less likely to state that they felt fearful in their own home, with just 2 % of the male participants expressing this fear in comparison with 15 % of the women. However, this lower rate for males may again be due, in part, to a greater reluctance to be publicly associated with characteristics of emotional distress and may not reflect many of the men's true experiences. Dempsey (2013) found that male victims reported less issues of financial dependency, but many had concerns for their children's welfare. An anxiety that they would not be able to see their children following a separation also prevailed in male victims' decisions to stay with their abusive female partners.

In the study by Drijber, Reijnders, and Celeen (2012), 23 % of heterosexual men reporting their experience of domestic abuse advised that the use of alcohol and/or drugs featured in the commission of the abuse. In 60 % of these cases, substance use was seen only in perpetrators and not in the victims. Research suggests, however, that men are far less likely to be seriously injured by a female perpetrator (Gadd, Farrall, Dallimore, & Lombard, 2003) and this is also reflected in the comparative figures for the number of men and women killed by their current or previous heterosexual partner, with 76 % of intimate partner violence murder victims being female and 24 % being male (Fox & Zawitz, 2004). However, female perpetrators are more likely to use a weapon (Hester, 2009), in 54 % of cases (Drijber et al., 2012).

It could be suggested that society finds it far more acceptable for an angry, indignant woman to respond 'emotionally' with physical violence against a male, whereas male violence against a female is more widely condoned. Hamel (2007) has previously contended that women initiate physical aggression in relationships as often as men and that this is rarely in self-defence. However, he makes a 'physical strength' argument that females are unlikely to be able to inflict as much physical damage as males, resulting in more minor injuries, although the reported use of weapons may contradict this. In 2010–2011, only 4 % of the heterosexual men who reported abuse to the Men's Advice Line in England and Wales advised that they had experienced sexual abuse from a female perpetrator (Debbonaire & Panteloudakis, 2012). However, psychological abuse aimed at undermining a victim's sense of masculine identity is relatively common. Hamel (2007) suggests that female perpetrators utilise psychologically abusive strategies at frequencies similar to male perpetrators, although other studies have indicated that rates of reporting for this form of abuse are much lower for males (Pimlott-Kubiak & Cortina, 2003). Johnson (2008) argues that coercive, controlling forms of domestic violence feature less in female perpetrator behaviours, whereas violent resistance, where a victim is responding to the oppressive abuse of their partner, is almost exclusively used by women. Nowinski and Bowen (2012) argue that these different patterns of motivation for violence in intimate relationships account for the varying levels of reported abuse across male and female genders.

Gay and Bisexual Male Victims

Although there is some previous research, mainly in the USA, that examines violence within gay male relationships, it is limited. The Coral Project (2015), therefore, represents a significant development in the exploration of perpetrators' behaviours within the LGB and/or T community, and is discussed elsewhere in this volume (see Barnes and Donovan, Chap. 13). Soothill, Francis, Ackerley, and Collett (1999) have highlighted previously that gay men are at an increased risk of partner homicide compared to heterosexual men and women, with lesbian women far less likely to be killed by their same-sex partner. For male victims in same-sex relationships, issues of masculine identity and sexual orientation can be used as a tool of abuse by the perpetrator, most commonly in the form of threats of disclosure for a victim whose family, friends, children or work colleagues may not be aware of their sexuality. Trans male and female victims may also experience similar issues in relation to their gender identity. Gay and bisexual male victims who are members of faith-based and cultural communities where their sexuality is not openly accepted may also have little, if any, option for the disclosure of abuse committed by their partner, as the relationship itself may not be publicly acknowledged. Bourne, Reid, Hickson, Torres Rueda, and Weatherburn (2014) highlighted that social environments where recreational drugs such as ketamine, methadrone and GHB (gamma hydroxybutrate) and GBL (gamma-butyrolactone) were being used, have also been exploited as opportunities by some gay male perpetrators to force their partners into unsafe and unwanted sexual behaviours. Male victims in same-sex relationships reported their experiences of abuse at a higher rate than heterosexual males, as evidenced by reports from the Men's Advice Line in England and Wales (Debbonaire & Panteloudakis, 2012).

Concepts of masculinity and gendered stereotypes also feature in the commission of domestic abuse in gay male relationships, with some perpetrators justifying their actions as an expression of their masculinity rather than perceiving their actions as a strategy of domination and control (Elliott, 1996). Other perpetrators and victims may not have recognised behaviours as abuse, as they have viewed domestic violence as something that inhabits heterosexual domains only, as a result of gender inequalities, which are not apparent in gay male relationships. Perpetrators may further reinforce this by convincing victims that specialist services will not support a male victim who identifies as gay, bisexual and/or trans gender. There is very little recognition of gay male experiences within mainstream support service provisions, with even those minority services that do offer support to male victims often retaining a heteronormative bias.

There are indications that there is a heightened risk of domestic abuse occurring in a person's first experience of a lesbian, gay or bisexual relationship. One possible explanation for this is the lack of any significant mainstream promotion and positive role modelling of healthy adult gay and bisexual relationships (Hidden Hurt, 2015). Closely related to this are experiences of isolation. A gay or bisexual male victim may not only experience a disconnection from family members who are not aware of their sexuality and therefore are unaware of the intimate relationship, but may also be isolated within a LGB and/or T community, which has yet to develop any significant awareness and sensitivity towards issues of domestic abuse. Some gay male victims may remain in abusive relationships because they fear that a separation would also lead to their rejection by their immediate circle of LGB and/or T friends, who may be the only ones who are aware of their sexual orientation.

Trans Male Victims

There is very little research available on domestic abuse experienced by trans males, who are biologically assigned female status at birth, but who gender identify as male. However, in one of the few studies that does exist, Roch, Morton, and Ritchie (2010) highlight dramatically high figures of trans people experiencing abuse, with 80 % of those surveyed stating that they had experienced emotional, sexual or physical abuse from a partner or ex-partner. Whilst this research highlights many of the same patterns of abusive and controlling behaviours that are prevalent in heterosexual, lesbian, gay and bisexual cisgender studies, there were additional forms of abuse noted for trans people, which centred around being made to feel ashamed of their identity and being labelled as an incomplete man or woman. Suicide rates are high across trans people populations, primarily attributed to issues of social rejection and non-acceptance (Whittle, Turner, Combs, & Rhodes, 2008) and this vulnerability may be exploited by a perpetrator of abuse. Extreme cases of abuse have included experiences where the victims have been forced to undertake unwanted surgeries to further alter their appearance. Discrimination in the workplace and problems in securing stable employment also often result in trans male victims relying significantly on partners financially (Grant, Mottet, & Tanis, 2009). Roch et al. (2010) found that 47 % of trans people taking part in their survey had experienced one or more forms of sexually abusive behaviours, including the victim being forced to engage in sexual activity with the perpetrator and/or others. Only 7 % of the trans people participants stated that they had been in contact with a domestic abuse support service, with just 13 % reporting their abuse to the police.

Male victims' Experiences of Reporting Abuse and Accessing Services

The Policy Approach

The Home Office (2013a) definition of Domestic Violence and Abuse, although not legally binding, has been broadly adopted across statutory and voluntary sectors in England and Wales. It stipulates that Domestic Violence and Abuse is:

Any incident or pattern of incidents of controlling, coercive or threatening behaviour, violence or abuse between those aged 16 or over who are or have been intimate partners or family members regardless of gender or sexuality. (Home Office, 2013a).

The phrasing of this statement, however, whilst endeavouring to be inclusive across male and female, LGB and/or T experiences of abuse, arguably is actually achieving the reverse. By adopting a neutrality approach, which focuses on the intimate relationship 'regardless' of gender or sexuality, the definition actually dismisses the significance of gender and sexuality in terms of both the nature of the abusive experience and access to appropriate resources for protection and support. Whist it may be appealing to those more resistant to any specific form of gender analysis of domestic abuse, it can be seen to encourage a response that concludes that generic service provisions, which are simply open to both men and women and people of all sexualities, are 'good enough'. It fails to highlight that much more than that is needed and that further work needs to be undertaken with both male and female victims across all types of intimate partner relationships to explore how support needs may differ and how they might best be accommodated.

The integration of commissioner funding strategies for domestic violence and sexual violence has also resulted in the resourcing and development of services for 'male victims', encompassing a broad remit that includes all forms of sexual violence against men and male rape. This terminology covers a vast range of experiences of male victimisation, not all of which are related to abuse by an intimate partner and with very few concerned with the actions of female perpetrators in heterosexual relationships. Therefore, whilst in December 2011, the Home Office launched a 2-year funding programme of support for male victims with 12 organisations receiving up to £10,000 to develop services for men who had experienced violence and abuse (Home Office, 2013b), the approach has been piecemeal, difficult to sustain in the longer term and has not focused specifically on male experiences of domestic abuse.

Similarly, following the 2012 Ministry of Justice, Victims and Witnesses Consultation, a further commitment was made to provide specialist services for victims of domestic and sexual violence, including a £500,000 to support male victims of sexual violence. A further balance of £2 million in 2014–2015 was to be divided; with £200,000 for the national commissioning of training to build capacity in the voluntary sector for advocacy services for victims of sexual violence and £1.3 million to be devolved to Police and Crime Commissioners (PCCs) as part of their 2014–2015 victims' services grant (Ministry of Justice, 2012). Once again, the profile of male experiences of domestic abuse was receding from policy and funding rhetoric, due to its merger with other issues of sexual violence against males. The charity, RESPECT, which runs the National Men's Helpline for men who are victims of domestic violence, has seen a large increase in calls made to them, from 2732 in 2012 to approximately 4500 in 2013. However, specialist domestic abuse support services for men are rarely highlighted as a service provision gap in funding commissioners' assessments of need at a local level (Cooper, 2015).

The Police and Judicial Response to Male Victims

Her Majesty Inspectorate of Constabulary (HMIC) (2014) report found that the national police response to issue of domestic violence and abuse was unsatisfactory overall. A comprehensive strategy of data collection had included focus groups with male victims and the value of developing specialist services in this area was recognised, although not otherwise addressed specifically in the police training and action plan developments that ensued from the inspection. In their earlier study in Northern Ireland, Brogden and Nijhar (2000) had also found that strategies for improving the police response to domestic violence and abuse were very much centred on a heterosexual model, which constructed the male as the perpetrator. Scenarios where the male was the victim were described as problematic and confusing for police personnel. Douglas and Hines (2011) also discovered, in their survey of male victims in the USA, that family and friends were rated as the most reliable form of support for male victims, followed by mental health counsellors and with the police and specialist domestic violence agencies being rated as the most unreceptive and poorly equipped to assist men seeking to escape situations of abuse.

Drijber et al. (2012), again in the USA, found that less than 32 % of the men surveyed who had experienced abuse had spoken to the police about their situation, with only 15 % officially reporting the matter. The use of a weapon as an escalation in the level of severity of the abuse was often the trigger for an official report being made. The male victims who had filed an official police statement stated that they wanted the police to stop the violence (42 %) and needed help (40 %). However, the vast majority of male victims who had not involved the police said that they feared they would not be taken seriously, they felt ashamed of their experience and they believed there would be nothing the police could do to stop the abuse occurring. In the author's own anecdotal experience, male victims may also perceive the police service to a have very dominant 'macho' archetypal culture, which leads to assumptions that there will be a lack of sensitivity towards a male victim's experience.

Whilst there has been very little formal investigation of the judicial response to male victims of domestic abuse, American studies of male victims' experiences of legal processes highlighted that men were less likely to be granted restraining orders against their (ex) partners, with judges being approximately 13 times more likely to grant an order requested by a female than a male (Muller, Desmarais, & Hamel, 2009). However, this discrimination was more common to cases that involved low-level violence, whereas high-risk cases of severe violence and abuse resulted in some increased parity of decision making across genders. Brogden and Nijhar (2000) found that social services and family courts tended to favour a female perpetrator's account of the domestic situation, with the approach from health being slightly more ambiguous, mainly dependent on the attitude and insights of the individual attending practitioner. Agency tendencies to hold a perception of the male as the aggressor and other heteronormative assumptions of the vulnerability of the female continue. Gadd et al.'s (2002) Scottish research study found that male assailants in same-sex relationships were far less likely to be referred to the Scottish public prosecutor (Procurator Fiscal) than assailants in heterosexual relationships.

Access to Specialist Domestic Violence and Abuse Support Services

Male victims' experiences of domestic violence and abuse support services centre around issues of suitability and accessibility. Changes to the nature of service funding and commissioning frameworks now require local authorities and specialist agencies to provide access to support for male victims. However, as previously stated in many cases, this has simply resulted in an extension of the provisions already available for female victims in a generic, 'open-to-all' style of response. This approach, as with other diverse experiences of abuse, often does not serve to encourage engagement from victims who cannot recognise their own experiences in the mission statements and organisational structures of the service providers originating from the women's sector.

As highlighted in the earlier discussion, male victims, particularly those experiencing abuse from a female perpetrator, are more likely to seek support with practical issues rather than emotional concerns, although they may open up further to the emotional impact of their experience once an empathetic response is provided. More generally, however, they will be looking for legal advice on issues such as non-molestation orders, child contact and parental rights, immigration and housing. Gadd et al. (2003) found that very few men seek refuge accommodation, and for those who do require such support, the provision of safe accommodation for male victims is minimal across the UK. Men would, therefore, have to travel extreme distances to access a refuge. This would make it virtually impossible for any male victim to access a 'safe house' locally to sustain geographical links and enable ongoing child contact or employment commitments to be maintained. Male victims are, however, far more likely to continue in full-time employment following their separation from an abusive partner, resulting in them often having to pay full rent on any new, temporary accommodation.

Trying to sustain full-time employment presents other significant barriers for male victims seeking support. Specialist support agencies often have concerns that any evidence of an under-utilisation of the resources they have employed for male victims may result in more general cuts to their funding. In order to try and prevent this occurring, support for male victims is often only offered on a part-time basis (Drijber et al., 2012). The National Helpline for Male Victims, for example, is only available during office hours, Monday to Friday, which clearly is problematic for men in full-time employment. Equally, the provision of IDVAs for male victims is often only resourced for 1–2 days a week, if at all, across many local authority boroughs. High-risk cases of male victimisation may, therefore, experience significant delays in any appropriate coordination of safety planning work occurring between agencies. Whilst SafeLives (2015) data for 2014–2015 highlighted that only 4.5 % of high-risk cases presented at the Multi-Agency Risk Assessment Conferences concerned male victims, again this figure may benefit from further reflection. Firstly, there are clear issues of support service accessibility, which may result in a male victim case not coming to the attention of the organisations that would undertake a formal risk assessment of his case. It is also quite possible that assumptions of 'male resilience' influence the risk assessments that are made with male victims, which may lead to an under-estimate of the risk posed, particularly in relation to the impact of psychological abuse. Specialist practitioners are trained and experienced in recognising minimisation and denial as a coping strategy for female victims and the need to build trust and engagement to build a full picture of the abusive scenario. An examination as to whether the same principles and approach are consistently applied to male victims of abuse would certainly be of further interest.

The community-based domestic violence and abuse sector is also now a key player in the provision of perpetrator programmes, but similarly, knowledge, expertise and a provision of appropriate interventions for heterosexual female perpetrators and male and female perpetrators in same-sex relationships are only just starting to emerge. The victim liaison work, which is considered to be vital to such work, has also yet to fully recognise the needs of male victims and both the statutory and voluntary sectors have little familiarity with this type of victim support to date. Again there is a danger that an assumption is made that the approach adopted for female victims can simply be transferred across to male victims without a fuller understanding of the differing needs and experiences across genders. Several well-established organisations offer specific support for LGB and/or T victims of abuse, with a majority of these being London-based, including Galop, Stonewall Housing and PACE Health. There are very limited services outside of London, with some exceptions such as *Broken Rainbow* (2015), which offers an LGB and/or T IDVA in Manchester and a national domestic abuse helpline for LGB and/or T victims.

Conclusion

The discussion of male victims' experiences of domestic violence and abuse has become embroiled in contentious disputes of its comparable worth in relation to female victim experiences. These arguments are variably motivated and perceived as attempts to undermine the seriousness of issues of violence against women and girls committed primarily by males, as a direct threat to the resourcing of specialist support for women, which is already under considerable strain or as a blatant dismissal by society of men's very real experiences of victimisation and their subsequent support needs. This chapter has endeavoured to offer some insights into the relevance of gender and in particular, gender roles stereotypes, which inhibit men's willingness to discuss experiences of abuse and the discriminatory reactions they may experience when they do. The pattern and frequency of men's victimisation in the domestic sphere is different from that of female victims and is likely to vary further across heterosexual, gay and bisexual relationships. Trans gender identity may also result in particular manifestations of abuse occurring. It is currently difficult to know exactly how these experiences differ. However, regardless of the extent to which male victims are actually in a minority when it comes to experiences of domestic abuse, their status as such does not justify simply placing support for men as an 'add on' to current specialist service provisions. The battle for recognition and competition for already scarce resources detracts from the development of effective support strategies. All of the diverse ways in which intimate relationships may end up becoming oppressive and harmful need to be more fully understood, so those at the receiving end of the abuse can be offered more realistic options for change.

References

Berk, R., Berk, S. F., Loseke, D., & Rauma, D. (1983). Mutual combat and other family violence myths. In D. Finkelhor, G. J. Gelles, J. T. Hotaling, & M. A. Straus (Eds.), *The dark side of families: Current family violence research*. Beverly Hills, CA: SAGE.

Bourne, A., Reid, D., Hickson, F., Torres Rueda, S., & Weatherburn, P. (2014). *The chemsex study: Drug use in sexual settings among gay and bisexual men in Lambeth, Southwark and Lewisham*. London: Sigma Research, London School of Hygiene and Tropical Medicine.

Brogden, M., & Harkin, S. (2000). *Male victims of domestic violence: Report to the Northern Ireland Domestic Violence Forum*. Belfast: Institute of Criminology, Queen's University.

Brogden, M., & Nijhar, S. K. (2000). *Abuse of adult males in intimate partner relationships in Northern Ireland*. Belfast: Northern Ireland assembly on behalf of the Northern Ireland Domestic Violence Forum.

Broken Rainbow. (2015). Retrieved October 24, 2015, from http://www.brokenrainbow.org.uk (home page).

Brown, G. A. (2004). Gender as a factor in the response of the law-enforcement system to violence against partners. *Sexuality and Culture, 8*(3–4), 3–139.

Chan, K. L. (2006). The Chinese concept of face and violence against women. *International Social Work, 49*(1), 65–73.

Cochran, S. V. (2005). Evidence-based assessment with men. *Journal of Clinical Psychology, 61*, 649–660.

Connell, R. W. (2005). *Masculinities* (2nd ed.). Cambridge, MA: Polity Press.

Cook, P. W. (1997). *Abused men: The hidden side of domestic violence*. London: Praeger.

Cooper, K. (2015). Breaking the Taboo: Male victims of domestic violence. *Inside Housing*. Retrieved May 15, 2015, from http://www.insidehousing.co.uk/breaking-the-taboo-male-victims-of-domestic-violence/7008409.article

Courtenay, W. H. (2000). Constructions of masculinity and their influence on men's well-being: A theory of gender and health. *Social Science and Medicine, 50*, 1385–1401.

Debbonaire, T., & Panteloudakis, I. (2012). *Working with male victims of domestic violence*. London: RESPECT.

Dempsey, B. (2013). *Men's experience of domestic abuse in Scotland. What we know and how we can know more*. Edinburgh: AMIS.

Dixon, L., Archer, J., & Graham-Kevan, N. (2012). Perpetrator programmes for partner violence: Are they based on ideology or evidence. *Legal and Criminological Psychology, 17*, 196–215.

Dobash, R. P., & Dobash, R. E. (2004). Women's violence to men in intimate relationships: Working on a puzzle. *British Journal of Criminology, 44*(3), 324–349.

Douglas, E., & Hines, D. (2011). The helpseeking experiences of men who sustain intimate partner violence: An overlooked population and implications for practice. *Journal of Family Violence, 26*(6), 473–485.
Drijber, B. C., Reijnders, U. J. L., & Celeen, M. (2012). Male victims of domestic violence. *Journal of Family Violence, 28*(1), 173–178.
Elliott, P. (1996). Shattering illusions: Same-sex domestic violence. In C. M. Renzetti & C. H. Miley (Eds.), *Violence in gay and lesbian domestic partnerships*. New York, NY: Harrington Park Press.
Fox, J., & Zawitz, M. (2004). *Homicide trends in the United States*. Washington, DC: US Department of Justice.
Gadd, D., Farrall, S., Dallimore, D., & Lombard, N. (2002). *Domestic abuse against men in Scotland*. Edinburgh: Scottish Executive Central Research Unit.
Gadd, D., Farrall, S., Dallimore, D., & Lombard, N. (2003). Male victims of domestic violence. *Criminal Justice Matters, 53*(1), 16–17.
George, M. J. (2002). Skimmington revisited. *The Journal of Men's Studies, 10*(2), 111–127.
Grant, J. M., Mottet, L. A., & Tanis, J. (2009). *Injustice at every turn. A report of the National Transgender Discrimination Survey*. Washington, DC: National Center for Transgender Equality/National Gay and Lesbian Task Force.
Hamel, J. (2007). Toward a gender-inclusive conception of intimate partner violence research and theory: Traditional perspectives. *International Journal of Men's Health, 6*, 36–53.
Hearn, J. (1998). *The violence of men: How men talk about and how agencies respond to men's violence to women*. London: SAGE.
Her Majesty's Inspectorate of Constabulary (HMIC). (2014). *Everyone's business: Improving the police response to domestic abuse*. London: HMIC.
Hester, M. (2009). *Who does what to whom? Gender and domestic violence perpetrators*. Bristol: University of Bristol and Newcastle: Northern Rock Foundation.
Hester, M., Radford, J., & Kelly, L. (1995). *Women, violence and male power: Feminist activism research and practice*. Buckingham: Oxford University Press.
Hidden Hurt. (2015). *Male victims of domestic violence*. Retrieved October 13, 2015, from http://www.hiddenhurt.co.uk/male_victims_of_domestic_violence.html
Hines, D. A., & Douglas, E. M. (2010). A closer look at men who sustain intimate terrorism by women. *Partner Abuse, 1*(3), 286–313.
Hines, D., Brown, J., & Dunning, E. (2007). Characteristics of callers to domestic abuse helpline for men. *Journal of Family Violence, 22*(2), 63–72.

Hogan, K. F., Hegarty, J. R., Ward, T., & Dodd, L. J. (2012). Counsellors' experiences of working with male victims of female-perpetrated domestic abuse. *Counselling and Psychology Research, 12*(1), 44–52.

Home Office. (2013a). *Home Office Circular 003/2013: New government domestic violence and abuse definition.* Retrieved August 26, 2015, from https://www.gov.uk/government/publications/new-government-domestic-violence-and-abuse-definition

Home Office. (2013b). *Domestic violence and abuse.* London: Home Office. Retrieved October 13, 2015, from https://www.gov.uk/guidance/domestic-violence-and-abuse

Johnson, M. (1995). Patriarchal terrorism and common couple violence: Two forms of violence against women. *Journal of Marriage and the Family, 57*, 283–294.

Johnson, M. (2006). *Conflict and control: Gender symmetry and asymmetry in domestic violence.* Paper presented at the National Institute of Justice Gender Symmetry Workshop, Arlington, VA.

Johnson, M. (2008). *A typology of domestic violence. Intimate terrorism, violent resistance and situational couple violence.* New England: Northeastern University Press.

Mankind. (2015). *Types of abuse.* Retrieved October 23, 2015, from http://www.mankind.org.uk/

Messerschmitt, J. W. (1997). *Crime as structured action: Gender, race, class and crime in the making.* London: SAGE.

Messner, M. (1993). "Changing Men" and feminist politics in the United States. *Theory and Society, 22*(5), 723–737.

Ministry of Justice. (2012). *Getting it right for victims and witnesses: The Government response.* Retrieved August 26, 2015, from https://consult.justice.gov.uk/digital-communications/victims-witnesses/results/a-gov-response-getting-right-victims-witnesses.pdf

Mirrlees-Black, C. (1999) *Domestic violence: Findings from a new British Crime Survey self-completion questionnaire.* Home Office Research Study 91. London: Home Office.

Muller, H. J., Desmarais, S. L., & Hamel, J. M. (2009). Do judicial responses to restraining order requests discriminate against male victims of domestic violence? *Journal of Family Violence, 24*, 625–637.

Nowinski, S. N., & Bowen, E. (2012). Partner violence against heterosexual and gay men: Prevalence and correlates. *Aggression and Violent Behavior, 12*, 36–52.

Office of National Statistics. (2015). *Crime statistics. Focus on violent crime and sexual offences 2012/13 release*. London: ONS. Retrieved from http://www.ons.gov.uk/ons/rel/crime-stats/crime-statistics/focus-on-violent-crime-and-sexual-offences--2012-13/rpt---chapter-4---intimate-personal-violence-and-partner-abuse.html#tab-conclusions

Pimlott-Kubiak, S., & Cortina, L. M. (2003). Gender, victimization, and outcomes: Reconceptualizing risk. *Journal of Consulting and Clinical Psychology, 71*(3), 528–539.

Rennison, C. M., & Welchans, S. (2000). Intimate partner violence: Special report. *Bureau of Justice Statistics*. Washington, DC: US Department of Justice. Retrieved August 15, 2015, from www.ojp.usdoj.gov/bjs/

Roch, A., Morton, J., & Ritchie, G. (2010). *Out of sight, out of mind? – Transgender people's experience of domestic abuse*. Edinburgh: LGBT Youth Scotland, Scottish Trans Alliance and Equality Network.

SafeLives. (2015). *Latest MARAC data*. Retrieved October 12, 2015, from http://safelives.org.uk/practice-support/resources-marac-meetings/latest-marac-data

Soothill, K., Francis, B., Ackerley, E., & Collett, S. (1999). *Homicide in Britain: A comparative study of rates in Scotland and England & Wales*. Edinburgh: Scottish Executive Central Research Unit.

Tsui, V., Cheung, M., & Leung, P. (2010). Help-seeking among male victims of partner abuse: Men's hard times. *Journal of Community Psychology, 38*(6), 769–780.

Whittle, S., Turner, L., Combs, R., & Rhodes, S. (2008). *Transgender EuroStudy. Legal survey and focus on the transgender experience of health care*. Brussels: Press for Change, Transgender Europe.

Wolf-Light, P. (1999). Men, violence and love. In J. Wild (Ed.), *Working with men for change*. London: UCL Press.

10

The Relationship Between Spiritual Abuse and Domestic Violence and Abuse in Faith-Based Communities

Lisa Oakley and Kathryn Kinmond

Introduction

The recent focus on domestic violence and abuse (DVA) in the UK has led to a number of new laws and initiatives.[1] There has also been an increase in awareness of the existence and impact of spiritual abuse (Oakley & Kinmond, 2013a; Ward, 2011). However, the link between DVA and spiritual abuse remains under-researched and rarely considered. This chapter will discuss the links between DVA and spiritual abuse, arguing the importance of reviewing the two forms of abuse as interconnected and co-constructed in both their active compounds and their personal impact. The chapter will widen current debates via a discussion of the intersectionality of faith and experiences of DVA, which may

---

[1] For example, see ACPO (2012) *Clare's Law—The Domestic Abuse Disclosure Scheme*.

L. Oakley (✉) • K. Kinmond
Department of Interdisciplinary Studies, Manchester Metropolitan University, Crewe, UK

© The Editor(s) (if applicable) and The Author(s) 2016
S. Hilder, V. Bettinson (eds.), *Domestic Violence*,
DOI 10.1057/978-1-137-52452-2_10

serve to inform the development of more effective multi-agency working. However, the discussion centres primarily on understandings of the victim experience and faith community responsibilities rather than on perpetrator interventions at this stage. It should also be noted that the issues raised concern people in all faith-based communities. Just as DVA perpetrators are not confined to specific social groups, there is no evidence to suggest that spiritual abuse and DVA are limited to specific faith communities. Certainly, media representations might suggest a higher prevalence of some forms of abuse within certain faith groups, such as child sexual abuse and the Catholic Church, but this has been challenged by recent cases arising from other faith contexts (see Chan, Tan, Ang, Nor, & Sharip, 2012).

Abuse of any kind does not take place in a social vacuum. It is culturally and historically framed, with understandings and experiences of the abuse and the responses to it being influenced by personal history and cultural heritage (see Kasturirangan, Krishnan, & Riger, 2004; Sanderson, 2008; Yan, Chan, & Tiwari, 2015). With situations of DVA, as research has repeatedly demonstrated, a person's background impacts on their experience and their perception of what has occurred (see Eurobarometer, 2010; Farriyal, Rassak, & Durocher, 2005; Sokoloff & Dupont, 2005). For many people, a central tenet of their personal and social identity relates to their belonging to a faith-based community and accordingly, there is a growing recognition of the need to better understand the role of faith in the commission and response to DVA.

DVA, Gender and Faith

The question of the gendered nature of DVA is covered elsewhere in this collection from a variety of perspectives and has a particular relevance to a discussion of faith and DVA. The authors recognise that DVA is experienced by both males and females within faith communities. Nonetheless, all published work identified to date has focused on a male to female perpetration of DVA within faith groups. This reflects the wider emphasis on female experiences of DVA currently evident in the UK society (Home Office, 2011). This, in turn, is supported by recorded statistics, which, in

2012–2013, highlighted that 4.9 million women compared to 2.7 million men were reported to have experienced DVA at some point in their lives since the age of 16 (Office of National Statistics, 2015). Whilst challenges to such statistics might be made concerning the gendered nature of disclosure (see Martin, Chap. 9, this volume), policy and practice reflect the high prevalence of DVA perpetrated against women. Echoing such data, a Church house publishing report states that, 'Domestic abuse is a gender-biased phenomenon: the incidents of abuse of women are very much more frequent and more severe' (2006, p. 16). This perspective is also prevalent in academic research and debate, such as Harne and Radford (2008) and Walby (1990) who locate DVA within patriarchal social structures that create and reinforce male dominance. DeKeseredy and Schwartz (2005) also suggest that male perpetrators receive patriarchal peer support from other men in their social networks, which help them to justify their actions. It may be that male victims are even more hidden than female victims in faith contexts. The construction of male and female roles and relationships within most major religions are largely stereotypical and may thus make the disclosure of female on male DVA extremely problematic and unlikely to occur. This further illustrates the interconnectedness of an individual's experience of DVA within their personal, faith, cultural and societal identity. Whilst this chapter will seek to broaden the debate, given the current challenges of reaching all victim voices, the literature that is referenced still primarily focuses on male to female DVA.

Gillum, Sullivan, and Bybee (2006) suggest that for individuals of faith and spirituality, their faith identity and faith community are integral components of their DVA experience. They argue that female victims, in particular, view their experience of abuse and recovery as being firmly connected to and shaped by their faith context. The researchers did not explore this factor as a gender-specific phenomenon, noting simply that faith communities can play both negative and positive roles in women's experiences of DVA. They state 'some of these communities have minimised, denied or enabled abuse, whereas others have provided much needed social support, practical assistance and spiritual encouragement' (Gillum et al., 2006, p. 240). Arguably, at face value, these factors are not particular to gender, but additional research may be useful to explore their application further.

Beyond the immediate faith-based environment is the interaction with the wider context of community. This considers the importance of the interplay of the faith-based group, organisation or community with the larger local community, region, town or city. This is of particular relevance where the faith-based community is different, separate and/or disparate from the other dominant communities within the region. In such situations, a person experiencing spiritual abuse and DVA within an 'isolated' community is likely to feel further disconnected and alone. The people they engage with on a daily basis within their own faith-based community may condone or dismiss the DVA, but disclosure outside of the immediate faith community may also appear unrealistic. The perceptions of and responses to faith communities by wider societal networks can also have a direct impact on those seeking help and recovery. Desai and Haffajee (2011) provide an example of a Muslim woman who was experiencing DVA and felt unable to disclose to her immediate family. She thought that she may be able to disclose to her non-Muslim friends, but then became concerned that this may reinforce their already negative preconceptions of Islam and the role of men. Therefore, she chose to stay silent. It is very unlikely that this example is an isolated case. Whilst some work around DVA in faith-based communities is occurring, which seeks to understand the role of faith in individuals' experiences of DVA, perpetrator behaviours and effective responses to DVA, it has tended to focus on particular perceptions of certain faiths, some of which are stereotypical. A much more detailed range of research and a broader dialogue need to be initiated. This chapter now continues to go some way towards pursuing this aim.

Spiritual Abuse and DVA

The recently revised Home Office definition of DVA broadens the scope of recognised DVA experiences and has been widely adopted (Home Office, 2013). In contrast, spiritual abuse is still a relatively unknown and rarely recognised form of abuse. Indeed, recent research with more than 500 individuals attending Christian churches identified that only 37 % of respondents had heard of the term spiritual abuse (Oakley & Kinmond, 2014). The definitions offered by respondents also illustrated limited understandings of the term. Academic work in this arena has only recently been presented and published (Gubi & Jacobs, 2009; Oakley & Kinmond, 2013a; Ward, 2011), which further demonstrates the paucity of academic debate on this subject.

It is pertinent here, therefore, to begin with a definition of spiritual abuse. The following is a current definition that has been adopted by several academics and practitioners across the UK. It stems from qualitative and quantitative research, undertaken by the authors (see Kinmond & Oakley, 2015; Oakley, 2009; Oakley & Kinmond, 2014). Spiritual abuse is concerned with the:

> Coercion and control of one individual by another in a spiritual context. The target experiences Spiritual Abuse as a deeply emotional personal attack. This abuse may include: manipulation and exploitation, enforced accountability, censorship of decision making, requirements for secrecy and silence, pressure to conform, misuse of scripture or the pulpit to control behaviour, a requirement of obedience to the abuser, the suggestion that the abuser has a "divine" position, and isolation from others, especially those external to the abusive context (Oakley & Kinmond, 2013a, p. 21).

It is widely accepted that DVA, by its nature, includes both psychological and emotional abuse, and both forms of abuse are central to spiritual abuse. There are two other significant ways in which DVA and spiritual abuse are linked. The first is where an individual who has a personal faith and belongs to a faith organisation is experiencing DVA in the domestic situation. In such circumstances, spiritual beliefs can be used as a tool of abuse, for example, restricting access to worship and using faith as a weapon of control (Church house publishing, 2006). The second is where an individual who has a personal faith is experiencing DVA and the faith context to which they belong is also spiritually abusive. The following issues are central to both of these conjoint forms of DVA and spiritual abuse.

Intentionality

An issue at the centre of the discussion of any form of abuse is the concept of intentionality. This highlights that the perpetration of the abuse is a deliberate act and that the abuser is cognisant of both the actions and the consequences of the actions. Intentionality has been explored in other forms of abuse, such as the abuse of older people. Nandlal and Wood (1997) draw a distinction between the intention to behave in a particular manner and a realisation that the behaviour will have a negative impact, which is not always evident. Within DVA, Sanderson (2008) notes an underlying motivation and desire to control a partner and thus, in this case the DVA is seen as intentional behaviour. Although the underpinning motivation for the control of another can be multifarious and highly complex, if perceived in this way, the links between spiritual abuse and DVA might become more obvious. Certainly, there are some individuals who are said to exhibit psychopathic traits and/or have been characterised as having an abusive personality (Dutton, 2007; Jacobsen & Gottman, 1998). In cases that are seen to fit this analysis, the intentionality to control, harm and abuse may be clearer. In many forms of abuse, however, the perpetrator's intentions are apparent and some time and effort are spent in preparation of the subsequent abuse. McAlinden (2006) documented the grooming processes involved in child sexual abuse and notes how this often includes the family of the child being abused, in order to avoid detection and make disclosures of the abuse less likely to be believed. The intentionality of the abuser in the grooming process is clear. Arguably, in other situations, particularly those framed within a context that promotes patriarchy, the individual motivation behind the DVA might be less straightforward.

The notion of intentionality is relevant to discussions of both DVA and spiritual abuse, although, to date, work in the area of spiritual abuse has given only sparse attention to this topic. However, when it is addressed, it is often suggested that in most cases abusers may be unaware or naive about the impact of their behaviour on others (Blue, 1993; Oakley, 2009; Oakley & Kinmond, 2013a). There is little evidence so far of individual intentionality in spiritual abuse and those who spiritually abuse others are often convinced that they are obeying God or other deities and that their behaviour is justified and necessary (Enroth, 1994). Patterns of spiritually abusive behaviour can occur over a period, and an individual may be presented with a large amount of evidence that illustrates the impact of their behaviour, but they still may be unable to reflect on this as a reality (Oakley, 2014). In this context, there is an argument that any continuation of the behaviour, after the individual has been informed that it is damaging and abusive, constitutes a move towards a greater degree of intentionality. The complexities of intentionality are beyond any pithy conclusion here, but certainly are an area worthy of further research and deeper consideration.

Sacred Texts and Teaching

In any discussion of DVA and spiritual abuse, there is a clear need to explore the topic of sacred texts and teaching. It is also important to understand how powerful sacred texts are to individuals of faith. They contain teaching on which individuals base their beliefs, behaviour and life choices. It is vital not to under-estimate the role that sacred texts can play in experiences of abuse and of particular relevance here is how they can be utilised as a tool in the commission of DVA and spiritual abuse.

Within the experience of spiritual abuse, sacred texts are often used out of their original context, to coerce an individual into behaving in a particular manner (Oakley, 2009, 2015; Oakley & Kinmond, 2013a). There are also many examples of the use of sacred texts across religions to support acts of DVA. Levitt and Ware (2006) questioned religious leaders about their interpretation of scriptures and noted that almost all of them believed that teachings could be and often were 'misinterpreted to subjugate women and justify [DVA]' (Levitt & Ware, 2006, p. 1177). Miles (1999) spoke to victims of DVA in a healthcare setting and recorded that in cases where spiritual abuse and DVA were connected, 'in each case the perpetrator had cited Scripture to justify his abusive behavior' (Miles, 1999, p. 33). Perhaps, the greater concern is that 'each of the victims herself [also] offered biblical explanations for why she "deserved" punishment' (Miles, 1999, p. 33). It should be noted that original interpretations of key sacred texts rarely allow for DVA. The Prophet Muhammad, for example, did not condone violence against women and insisted that they be treated with respect (Abugideiri, 2011). However, many sacred texts contain teachings about women, which have been used to justify male violence, including the Bible, the Qur'an and the Holy Vedas (Koepping, 2011). It is noted, for example, that verses in the Qur'an have been interpreted to suggest that men have superiority over women, whilst other interpretations state that the intention of the text is to promote relationships of honour and dignity (Levitt & Ware, 2006). Koepping (2011) emphasises the use of biblical texts as tools of DVA perpetrated in Christian communities. She argues, in particular, that the use of verses such as 'wives obey your husbands' (Ephesians 5:22) enable those committing DVA against women to justify their actions. She continues that whilst there are also male victims of DVA within these communities, there is no biblical support for female to male violence to be found in the Scriptures. Therefore, women within these faith communities are especially vulnerable to becoming victims of DVA.

In the study conducted by Levitt and Ware (2006), 91 % of the faith leaders questioned raised concerns that teachings on submission can be used to support abusive behaviour. Whilst some leaders suggested this happened only in cases where teachings were distorted, others suggested that teaching on submission generally created 'unbalanced power dynamics that increase the chances of [DVA]' (Levitt & Ware, 2006, p. 1186). These apparently 'justified' power differences may leave women vulnerable to abuse. Linked to work on submission is the discourse of obedience, which is common in many faith contexts (Oakley, 2009). Many faith communities include teachings on obedience to leadership, which can be interpreted as faith leadership, but also leadership within a domestic situation, often traditionally male. In cases where faith leaders manage their role with care and concern for individuals, this may present few difficulties, but when they do not, it can lead to abuse, both directly in the form of spiritual abuse and also indirectly as a context to the commission of DVA. If a discourse of obedience to leadership is advanced, both in terms of faith leaders and 'the head of the household' in a domestic situation, it can lead to an expectation that people should submit and be obedient to the 'leader' at all times. As a consequence, such obedience may become normalised so that, as Koepping (2011) and Gillum et al. (2006) reflect, many religious leaders do not recognise that women in their congregations are experiencing DVA. Alternatively, as Koepping (2011) continues, it may also lead to some ministers recognising the DVA, but choosing not to speak out about the issue.

Nason-Clark (2004) notes the high importance given to the status of marriage across many faith communities and the focus on the promise to stay together until death. It is noted that this can severely hinder women who may be seeking to leave and/or terminate violent relationships, either temporarily or permanently. Similarly, Dahm's (2011) research found that 71 % of participants suggested that the church's teachings on marriage and divorce present obstacles to victims of DVA. Nason-Clark (2001) states that the discourse of reconciliation in many major religions and sacred texts may be part of the reason why many women in faith communities stay in abusive relationships. However, conversely, it may also serve to act as a form of motivation for abusers in faith communities to seek help.

A further concern that has been raised about a teaching that is central to many faiths is the topic of suffering, which has been argued to 'encourage compliant and passive responses by women suffering in abusive relationships' (Church house publishing, 2006, p. 20). In the Christian faith, the suffering of Jesus is held as an example to followers and verses such as 'to share in his suffering' (1 Peter 4 v13) are used to create an understanding that suffering may be a positive aspect of the faith journey. Often individuals are encouraged to endure suffering courageously as part of their faith and thus it 'undermines people's recognition of the evils being done to them and implants masochistic attitudes of acceptance, or even celebration, of their afflictions' (Church house publishing, 2006, p. 20). In this context, those experiencing DVA may find it hard to distinguish between suffering and abuse.

The teachings on suffering are linked to those on forgiveness, which are foundational to most faiths. If handled appropriately, some individuals have found this to be a helpful principle in later stages of DVA recovery processes, helping them to move forward. However, great concern has also been raised about teachings on forgiveness across all major faiths, where the requirements to forgive can be placed above the necessity to ensure the safety of the individual experiencing the abuse. When victims of DVA disclose abuse within faith communities, it is essential that the first response is not to require forgiveness and a return to the abuser (Nyakudya, 2015). Teachings that focus on forgiveness as the initial response to disclosure are often found to originate from harmful theologies and discourses (Church house publishing, 2006). In such discourses, self-denial is seen as a higher form of spirituality, which requires the individual to forgive the perpetrator and not to take action against him or her. Such a position dismisses other key discourses across sacred texts of justice, safety and protection (Church house publishing, 2006).

DVA in a Spiritually Abusive Context

The issues discussed previously in this chapter are pertinent to a situation where an individual is experiencing DVA in the context of a spiritually abusive environment. If individuals are victimised within a context of spiritual abuse, they may often experience the misuse of scriptures both within their domestic situation and within their faith community. They are also unlikely to be encouraged to explore the sacred texts and spiritual meanings for themselves. This often puts them in an even more vulnerable position, where they are unable to discern whether texts are being falsely used to control their behaviour. In addition to the use of sacred texts, however, there are other key characteristics of spiritual abuse, which relate to incidents of DVA. It should be noted that many of the 'rules' discussed here are not explicitly stated as part of a faith community practice, but rather are implicit and often only clearly identified once they are seen to have been broken.

Unity

There are several faith-based discourses, which seem to present particular issues for victims of DVA within spiritually abusive contexts that can be used by perpetrators to justify their behaviour. For example, for Christian-based faiths, there are key biblical discourses such as that of unity, which can be used positively to encourage responsibility for one another and promote supportive, caring behaviour from all individuals in the faith context. However, this discourse can also be presented in a manner that silences individuals who may have concerns about the behaviours of others. It can be seen that if someone speaks out, they are threatening unity and it is only positive views that should be shared (Oakley & Kinmond,

2014). In a situation of DVA, this could effectively silence a victim who fears that speaking out will be negatively received and may just result in an increased level of danger towards them without any supportive intervention (Oakley, 2014).

Censorship

The spiritually abusive faith context is also dominated by a requirement of censorship. Individuals will be aware that asking questions and raising issues will be negatively evaluated as threatening unity (Oakley, 2009; Oakley & Kinmond, 2013a). Rules of secrecy and silence are common in these systems, and individuals within such faith contexts will learn not to share concerns or criticisms openly. Again, positive explanations for censorship will be provided, such as maintaining unity or promoting a positive and encouraging environment. Any disclosure of DVA may be very difficult, with further positive explanations for censorship usually centred on the unity of the marriage and family relationships. When the two forms of abuse are set within one individual experience, the power of censorship is compounded to create a culture that acts voraciously to prevent disclosure, with the sharing of concerns about abusive behaviour potentially being constructed as the promotion of disunity (Oakley, 2015).

Conformity

A further characteristic of spiritual abuse is conformity. In a spiritually abusive context, individuals will often be required to conform to specific patterns of behaviour and commitment (Oakley, 2009, 2015; Oakley & Kinmond, 2013a). Pressure can be applied to force individuals into increasing their level of engagement with the faith community, with it being suggested that to do so is a measurement of their faith and commitment to God or other faith deities (Oakley, 2009; Oakley & Kinmond, 2013a). For a victim of DVA existing within a spiritually abusive community, the consequences of conformity can be twofold. Individuals may spend extended periods within the abusive DVA relationship, with all external relationships only occurring within the context of the spiritually abusive community, with any contact outside of that environment becoming severely restricted. Consequently, there will be limited possibilities for disclosure and support outside of the immediate personal and community context. However, these are also the sites of the DVA and spiritual abuse and the individual, therefore, remains in a vicious circle and profoundly disempowered (Oakley, 2015).

Divine Position

The notion of divine position is a unique feature of spiritual abuse. The idea that an individual has been divinely appointed as a leader and should be respected at all times is a key element of some experiences of spiritual abuse (Oakley, 2014; Oakley & Kinmond, 2013a). Arguably, there are some parallels to be made here with patriarchal views of masculinity, wherein the male assumes the mantle as 'head' of a household. As Young (2005) comments, in this patriarchal logic, the male role puts others, usually women and children, in a subordinate position of dependence and obedience. However, such a position does not hold the same value or connotation as 'divinity'. Situations in which the two come together in a very powerful way are evidenced in some cases where the 'divine' is combined with the 'head' of a household and a faith leader is also the perpetrator of the DVA. This can be a particularly toxic mix for anyone at the receiving end of the abuse, as they may struggle to challenge either position. It is unlikely that individuals in a 'divine' position will experience DVA themselves and attempts to victimise them may be limited and impotent. However, faith leaders are in a revered position and able to challenge views around DVA, support victims and alter faith perceptions and responses to this form of abuse. The concept of the divine position can, therefore, be very useful if the reaction of the faith leader is positive, condeming DVA and can greatly assist in raising awareness and responding to DVA more constructively (Oakley, 2014).

Isolation

This chapter has already described how individuals in a spiritually abusive context may become increasingly committed to their faith context and therefore, by default, more isolated from external sources of support. Internal isolation and being ostracised within the faith community are also key features of spiritual abuse (Oakley & Kinmond, 2013a). Individuals have described the use of isolation as a method of control. Those who conform to the 'rules' of the faith community will achieve a sense of belonging and acceptance, whereas those who do not, often experience periods of intense isolation within the spiritually abusive context (Oakley, 2009). Disclosure of DVA, in particular, may be seen to be unacceptable, resulting in strategies that systemically shun and ignore the victim within the faith community.

Coercion and Control

Coercion and control recently became a feature of the Home Office definition of DVA and new legislative powers in the UK (Home Office, 2013). This follows several years of work and research by people such as Stark (2007) who identify coercion and control as systematic patterns of behaviours, which seek to oppress and control the victim. The distorted application of all of the aforementioned discourses and factors can contribute to profound experiences of coercion and control, which have also been described by many who have experienced spiritual abuse (Oakley, 2009; Oakley & Kinmond, 2013a, 2013b). Individuals report being pressured into behaving in particular ways. Often, victims are required to be accountable to those abusing them and this accountability may include sharing details of all of their decision-making and life choices. Victims also describe experiences of exploitation and manipulation. Controlling behaviours are often rationalised by the perpetrator by expressing positive motivations behind them, making it difficult for victims to identify that they are being coerced and/or to make any attempt to try to resist. For individuals experiencing DVA within a spiritually abusive faith context, features of coercion and control will be very familiar as they move between the domestic domain and faith community environments. They will be cognisant of a culture of control from their experiences outside of the immediate home. Identifying DVA as abuse may be especially challenging in such circumstances, as the coercion and control felt in other parts of their spiritually abusive experience may result in their 'normalisation' of the abuse encountered at home (Oakley, 2015).

Leaving

Exiting a relationship in which DVA has occurred has been reported to be extremely problematic across all victim groups (Shurman & Rodriguez, 2006). Many individuals find it impossible to leave for a complex variety of financial, psychological and emotional reasons. Similarly, victims of spiritual abuse report that leaving an abusive faith context is deeply challenging, with some describing the experience akin to a bereavement (Oakley, 2009). The impact of leaving a faith community cannot be under-estimated and needs to be more fully understood by statutory and non-statutory support services interacting with victims of DVA. Leaving a faith context can affect an individual's personal relationships, social support networks and financial resources and has a personal impact on their faith and belief. For many individuals, faith and belief are part of their core being, and exiting communities associated with these beliefs can trigger profound issues of self-concept and identity. There may be a myriad of consequences for a victim of DVA who leaves a faith community, which must be fully considered and addressed by the interventions available.

The Positive Role of Faith and Faith Communities in Responding to DVA

This chapter has thus far illustrated the ways in which the experience of DVA may be compounded by belonging to a faith community, especially one in which spiritual abuse is occurring. However, it would be an unbalanced picture to merely present the negative role that faith can play in experiences of DVA. This section of the chapter, therefore, will explore the positive aspects of belonging to faith-based communities and holding a personal faith in the context of surviving DVA, arguing for greater inclusion of faith representation in multi-agency working. Various works highlight the significant role faith communities and personal faith can play in the response to and recovery from DVA. For example, Fallot's (1997) work with abused women showed that most of them reported their spirituality to be a key aspect in their survival and recovery in a number of ways, including seeing God as a trustworthy refuge. Nason-Clark (2001) reflects on the importance of spirituality on psychological well-being and notes that the support of a faith community and congregation can be a key factor in achieving a positive outcome. Further, Gillum et al. (2006) suggest that many victims turn to religious organisations or families for comfort and support, following an experience of DVA. Indeed, there are many suggestions throughout the literature that faith and spirituality may be important in 'growing through' trauma (Hood, Spilka, Hunsberger, & Gorsuch, 1996; Pargament, Smith, Koenig, & Perez, 1998; Shaw, Joseph, & Linley, 2005), although it is acknowledged that when someone has experienced spiritual abuse, this process needs to be approached cautiously (Kinmond & Oakley, 2015).

Nason-Clark (2004) notes that faith leaders are key players and hold an important role in the effective response to DVA. One aspect of this role is the ability of faith leaders to teach sacred texts in ways which illustrate that DVA cannot be supported within that faith belief. For example, Levitt and Ware (2006) suggest that leaders can ensure that congregations are aware that scriptures advocate equality within marriage. Abugideiri (2011) highlights the powerful public declaration signed by a group of Imams, which stated their unified position against DVA. A similar gesture was made in 2014 by a group of faith leaders in Coventry signing a proclamation, thereby standing against DVA across their faith communities (Karmelwellness, 2014).

Levitt and Ware (2006) further illustrate the direct role that religious leaders can play in supporting women and responding effectively to DVA. They note the importance of ensuring that interactions with abused women do not reinforce the discourses of dominance occurring in abusive relationships. They continue that leaders must guard against the use of such discourses in order to support women in the transition from victim to survivor. Within Islam, Abugideiri (2011) reflects that faith leaders are in a position to encourage effective responses, such as supporting the victim to contact the police if they are feeling threatened and reassuring them that disclosure outside the faith community is appropriate. The faith leader may, as discussed earlier, exacerbate and perpetuate the abuse; however, they also clearly have a powerful opportunity to raise awareness of this form of abuse and to challenge and shape their faith community's response.

Intervention

Abugideiri (2011) suggests that faith communities may be the site of multiple resources for individuals who experience DVA. The community may be able to provide a safe haven and other practical support to a victim. Certainly, many religious communities do offer some support services, or have close links with external DVA specialist services. However, a greater involvement from faith communities in the development of multi-agency working has the potential to enhance and develop effective practice. As previously noted, many people report that their personal faith has sustained them through experiences of DVA (Nason-Clark, 2004); therefore, it is vital that there is recognition of this and the facility for these individuals to pursue their faith when they have exited the DVA situation. Gillum et al. (2006) note that for many women survivors of DVA, experiencing a welcoming, caring, faith-orientated source of support provided foundations for feelings of hope and healing.

Furthermore, as has already been noted, for many individuals, spirituality is an important part of their self-identity, and additional spiritual distress can be a consequence of experiencing DVA. Therefore, spiritual healing, supported by a faith community, may be a necessary part of their recovery. There are indications, however, that many domestic violence refuges and mainstream support services currently distance themselves from discussions of spirituality. This may be due to limited resources, the diversity of religious and spiritual beliefs that may be encountered and concerns about misunderstanding or intruding on an individual's spiritual privacy (Boehm et al., 1999 cited in Gillum et al., 2006). However, the concern with interventions that fail to facilitate and support spirituality and faith beliefs is that they may result in a physical healing but may leave individuals of faith without any form of spiritual healing. It is suggested, therefore, that effective responses to DVA need to consider how components of spirituality are accommodated. This might include greater liaison with faith leaders, who then work in partnership with DVA refuges and other support services, or the provision of support and transport to attend safe places of worship. Gillum et al. (2006) further argue that there is a need for all faith leaders to undertake training in the area of DVA, in order to understand the dynamics of this form of abuse, how it may manifest itself within their particular faith community and to promote effective responses. Nason-Clark (2001) reflects that for women from close-knit faith communities, disclosure is much more likely and this can be met by a discreet, informal and supportive response.

Practice

There are a number of common factors to be considered when working with issues of both spiritual abuse and DVA and, indeed, a combination of the two forms of abuse. Firstly, two key issues need to be raised in relation to wider societal responses to spiritual abuse in particular. The first is the limited understanding of spiritual abuse, even by people within faith communities themselves (Oakley & Kinmond, 2014), which makes its detection problematic. The second issue, however, relates to other strongly held negative public perceptions and views of particular religions or faith communities, or indeed all faiths. This can result in a very negative response to an individual who experiences abuse within a faith community. Some people may assert that individuals who choose to belong to, or associate themselves with a religious organisation deserve the abuse that then occurs (Oakley, 2009; Oakley & Kinmond, 2013a). It can be anticipated then that many people who have experienced spiritual abuse will remain silent, not wishing to trigger this negative reaction. Such a situation also finds resonance more generally with the prevailing context of DVA in the past century, where victims were blamed for their own victimisation. For individuals experiencing DVA, but with nowhere to turn for help, further damage and interpersonal trauma are evoked by not being able to discuss the issues openly and, thus, the abused person continues to suffer in isolated silence.

Most people who have been spiritually abused never seek support or counselling (Oakley & Kinmond, 2014). Following an abusive experience, in what they had previously assumed to be a 'safe' religious place, it is unsurprising perhaps that many find it difficult to trust anyone with their story. Whilst training across health and social care agencies on DVA has improved, there are currently very limited, patchy examples of training on spiritual abuse for counsellors or other professionals. Thus, individuals may find it challenging to find any support service provider who is cognoscente of the facts of spiritual abuse, or experienced in working with the nature of trauma caused by the complexity of its dynamics (Oakley & Kinmond, 2013a). That said, things are starting to change and there are some key issues for consideration for practitioners who work directly with the individual who has experienced spiritual abuse and/or DVA in a faith-based context.

Firstly, it is important to note that engaging with individuals who have experienced spiritual abuse and DVA may not be straightforward. They may start out by hoping and believing that they are ready to explore the hurt and trauma incurred, but then either find the experience too challenging and painful to continue or become very afraid of possible consequences for themselves or others. All of these reasons may then result in their withdrawal from the service, sometimes without notice. Some people will seek support for other apparent reasons and then later disclose their abusive experience. They may recall the experience and realise its significance, but may choose not to share it initially because they are not 'ready' to do so, or may not trust the support provider at first to handle the matter sensitively. Others may engage in practical support, but may never discuss the experience of spiritual abuse or DVA. This lack of disclosure can be related to the extreme trauma of the abuse, which has led to a process of 'protective denial'[2] (Sgroi, 1989). Some individuals will

---

[2] Protective Denial-This involves a utilisation of the coping strategies of defence that the individual used at the time of the abuse, but which then have become habitual patterns of behaviour and psychological functioning (Sgroi, 1989).

repress some or all of the memories of the abuse, which may then emerge as flashbacks if the memory is triggered. Such triggers can be as innocuous as a word, phrase, smell or music. However, the impact of these triggers can be immense for the abused person, sending them spiralling back into the experience of the trauma. Anyone working with someone who has experienced spiritual abuse and DVA generally needs to work sensitively and be vigilant to these possibilities.

Individuals may also respond by denying the importance of the abuse, dissociating any emotions from the memory of the experience. They may assert publically that it was not an important episode in their life and may possibly chastise themselves for ever having become involved in the faith community and/or relationship. Such reactions may be misconstrued publicly as flippancy. However, the private response may be far more dark and troubled. These individuals are unlikely to engage readily in support for spiritual abuse and/or DVA. Interventions must be client-centred and practitioners must not seek to force the issue, which, if pursued rigorously, may echo the oppressive behaviours of coercion they have experienced previously. However, key principles of safeguarding and safe-working for both the abused individual and the support provider should be followed at all times (Kinmond & Oakley, 2015).

Conclusion

This chapter has explored the intersectionality between DVA and spiritual abuse and has argued the importance of reviewing the two forms of abuse as interconnected and co-constructed. It has sought to demonstrate similarities in both the active compounds of both forms of abuse and in the personal impact on the individual. Whilst recognising the distinct challenges facing victims of DVA and spiritual abuse, there is clearly value to be had in generating stronger relationships between DVA agencies and faith organisations. Working in partnership will contribute to the protections and interventions available to address DVA within faith-based communities. There is currently only a very limited evidence base of practice in this area and a dearth of published empirical work. However, this chapter has synthesised relevant academic material to foster further dialogue and raise awareness. It is hoped, this will motivate others to continue to develop knowledge, practice and services in this little understood, but critically important, field.

References

Abugideiri, S. E. (2011). *A perspective on domestic violence in the Muslim community*. Retrieved October 29, 2015, from http://www.faithtrustinstitute.org/resources/articles/domestic-violence

Association of Chief Police Officers (ACPO). (2012). *Clare's law – The Domestic Abuse Disclosure Scheme*. Retrieved October 29, 2015, from http://www.gmp.police.uk/content/WebAttachments/88A190F67550078780257A71002E5DC8/$File/claire's%20law%20other%20people%20booklet.pdf

Blue, K. (1993). *Healing spiritual abuse – how to break free from bad church experiences*. Downers Grove, IL: Intervarsity Press.

Chan, L. F., Tan, S., Ang, J., Nor, N., & Sharip, S. (2012). A case of sexual abuse by a traditional faith healer: Are there potential preventions? *The Journal of Child Sexual Abuse, 21*(6), 613–620.

Church house publishing. (2006). *Responding to domestic abuse, guidelines for those with pastoral responsibilities*. Retrieved October 29, 2015, from https://www.churchofengland.org/our-views/marriage,-family-and-sexuality-issues/domestic-abuse.aspx

Dahm, C. W. D. (2011). *Parishes: Let's stop ignoring domestic violence*. Retrieved October 29, 2015, from http://www.uscatholic.org/church/2011/08/lets-stop-ignoring-domestic-violence

DeKeseredy, W. S., & Schwartz, M. D. (2005). Masculinities and interpersonal violence. In M. Kimmel, R. W. Connell, & J. Hearn (Eds.), *The handbook of studies on men and masculinities*. Thousand Oaks, CA: SAGE.

Desai, S., & Haffajee, Z. (2011). Breaking the silence: Reclaiming Qur'anic interpretations as a tool for empowerment and liberatory praxis for dealing with domestic violence Canadian Muslim communities. *Canadian Woman Studies, 29*, 127–134.

Dutton, D. G. (2007). *The abusive personality* (2nd ed.). New York: Guilford Press.

Enroth, R. M. (1994). *Recovering from churches that abuse*. Michigan: Zondervan.

Eurobarometer. (2010). *Domestic violence against women. Eurobarometer 344 survey*. Retrieved October 29, 2015, from http://ec.europa.eu/public_opinion/archives/ebs/ebs_344_en.pdf

Fallot, R. D. (1997). Spirituality in trauma recovery. In M. Harris & C. L. Landis (Eds.), *Sexual abuse in the lives of women diagnosed with severe mental illness* (pp. 337–355). Amsterdam: Harwood Academic.

Farriyal, F., Rassak, J., & Durocher, J. (2005). Attitudes of Pakistani men to domestic violence: A study from Karachi, Pakistan. *The Journal of Men's Health and Gender, 2*(1), 49–58.

Gillum, T. L., Sullivan, C. M., & Bybee, D. I. (2006). The importance of spirituality in the lives of domestic violence survivors. *Violence Against Women, 12*(3): 240–250.

Gubi, P. M., & Jacobs, R. (2009). Exploring the impact on counsellors of working with spiritually abused clients. *Mental Health, Religion and Culture, 12*(2), 191–204.

Harne, L., & Radford, J. (2008). *Tackling domestic violence. Theories, policies and practice*. Maidenhead: Open University Press.

Home Office. (2011). *Call to end violence against women and girls: Action plan*. London: HM Government.

Home Office. (2013). *Home Office Circular 003/2013: New government domestic violence and abuse definition*. Retrieved July 22, 2015, https://www.gov.uk/government/publications/new-government-domestic-violence-and-abuse-definition

Hood, R., Spilka, B., Hunsberger, B., & Gorsuch, B. (1996). *The psychology of religion* (2nd ed.). New York, NY: Guilford Press.

Jacobsen, N., & Gottman, J. (1998). *Breaking the cycle: New insights into violent relationships*. London: Bloomsbury.

Karmelwellness. (2014). *Tackling domestic violence and abuse in faith communities*. Conference Report, 20 November 2014. Retrieved October 29, 2015, from http://kahrmelwellness.com/coventry-conference/

Kasturirangan, A., Krishnan, S., & Riger, S. (2004). The impact of culture and minority status on women's experience of domestic violence. *Trauma, Violence, and Abuse, 5*(4), 318–332.

Kinmond, K., & Oakley, L. (2015). Working safely with spiritual abuse. In P. M. Gubi (Ed.), *Spiritual accompaniment and counselling*. London: Jessica Kingsley.

Koepping, E. (2011). Silence, collusion and sin: Domestic violence among Christians across Asia. *Madang, 15*, 49–74.

Levitt, H. M., & Ware, K. (2006). "Anything with two heads is a monster": Religious leaders' perspectives on marital equality and domestic violence. *Violence Against Women, 12*(12), 1169–1190.

McAlinden, A. (2006). "Setting 'em up": Personal, familial and institutional grooming in the sexual abuse of children. *Journal of Social and Legal Studies, 15*, 2–25.

Miles, A. (1999). When faith is used to justify abuse. *American Journal of Nursing, 99*, 32–35.

Nandlal, J. M., & Wood, L. A. (1997). Older people's understanding of verbal abuse. *Journal of Elder Abuse and Neglect, 9*, 17–31.

Nason-Clark, N. (2001). Woman abuse and faith communities: Religion, violence and provision of social welfare. In P. Nesbitt (Ed.), *Religion and social policy* (pp. 128–145). Oxford: Alta Mira Press.

Nason-Clark, N. (2004). When terror strikes at home: The interface between religion and domestic violence. *Journal for the Scientific Study of Religion, 43*(3), 303–310.

Nyakudya, K. (2015). A model for tackling domestic violence in faith communities. *Leeds National Training Day*, 12 February 2015. Leeds Beckett University, Karmelwellness.

Oakley, L. R. (2009). *The experience of spiritual abuse in the UK Christian church.* Unpublished PhD Thesis, Manchester Metropolitan University, UK.

Oakley, L. R. (2014). DVA and spiritual abuse. *DVA in faith communities conference*. 24 June 2014. Derby: Karmelwellness.

Oakley, L. R. (2015). The relationship between spiritual abuse and DVA. *Leeds National Training Day*, 12 February 2015. Leeds Beckett University, Karmelwellness.

Oakley, L. R., & Kinmond, K. S. (2013a). *Breaking the silence on spiritual abuse.* Basingstoke: Palgrave Macmillian.

Oakley, L. R., & Kinmond, K. S. (2013b). Spiritual abuse: A challenge for safeguarding practice in church. *CARING*. Churches Child Protection Advisory Service.

Oakley, L. R., & Kinmond, K. S. (2014). Developing safeguarding policy and practice for spiritual abuse. *Journal of Adult Protection, 16*(2), 87–95.

Office of National Statistics. (2015). *Crime statistics. Focus on violent crime and sexual offences 2012/13 release.* Retrieved October 24, 2015, from http://www.ons.gov.uk/ons/rel/crime-stats/crime-statistics/focus-on-violent-crime-and-sexual-offences--2012-13/rpt---chapter-4---intimate-personal-violence-and-partner-abuse.html#tab-conclusions

Pargament, K. I., Smith, B. W., Koenig, H. G., & Perez, L. M. (1998). Patterns of positive and negative religious coping with major life stressors. *Journal for the Scientific Study of Religion, 37*, 710–724.

Sanderson, C. (2008). *Counselling survivors of domestic abuse.* London: Jessica Kingsley.

Sgroi, S. M. (1989). Stages of recovery for adult survivors. In S. M. Sgroi (Ed.), *Vulnerable populations: Vol 2. Sexual abuse treatment for children, adult survivors and persons with mental retardation.* Lexington: Lexington Books.

Shaw, A., Joseph, S., & Linley, A. (2005). Religion, spirituality, and posttraumatic growth: A systematic review. *Mental Health, Religion and Culture, 8*(1), 1–11.

Shurman, L. A., & Rodriguez, C. M. (2006). Cognitive-affective predictors of women's readiness to end domestic violence relationships. *Journal of Interpersonal Violence, 21*(11), 1417–1497.

Sokoloff, N., & Dupont, I. (2005). Domestic violence at the intersections of race, class, and gender. Challenges and contributions to understanding violence against Marginalized women in diverse communities. *Violence Against Women, 11*(1), 38–64.

Stark, E. (2007). *Coercive control: How men entrap women in personal life.* New York, NY: Oxford University Press.

Walby, S. (1990). *Theorizing patriarchy.* Oxford: Basil Blackwell.

Ward, D. (2011). The lived experience of spiritual abuse. *Mental Health, Religion and Culture, 14*(9), 899–915.

Yan, E., Chan, K., & Tiwari, A. (2015). A systematic review of elder abuse in Asia. *Trauma, Violence, and Abuse, 16*(2), 199–219.

Young, I. M. (2005). The logic of masculinist protection: Reflections on the current security state. In M. Friedman (Ed.), *Women and citizenship* (pp. 15–34). New York, NY: Oxford University Press.

11

Housing: More Than Just Bricks and Mortar. Domestic Abuse Interventions Within the Housing Sector

Gudrun Burnet

Introduction

Having secure and safe accommodation has endured as a practical priority in the response to domestic abuse since it entered public consciousness in the UK from the 1950s onwards. However, the role of the housing sector has evolved over time, with changes in private ownership, tenancy rights and increased understandings of the impact of domestic abuse and the vulnerabilities of those experiencing it. This chapter is informed by the author's professional role with Peabody Housing Association[1], and highlights recent developments, which place housing in a central position as a potential first responder to situations of domestic abuse. The chapter will chart how this position has been reached by providing a brief

---

[1] Peabody was founded in 1862 by the American banker and philanthropist George Peabody. The organisation currently owns and manages more than 27,000 homes across London with more than 80,000 residents.

G. Burnet (✉)
Peabody Housing Association, London, UK

© The Editor(s) (if applicable) and The Author(s) 2016
S. Hilder, V. Bettinson (eds.), *Domestic Violence*,
DOI 10.1057/978-1-137-52452-2_11

overview of the historical developments of refuge provision and the challenges this pathway has incurred. The discussion then moves to an exploration of contemporary housing issues, such as the transition between short-term and long-term accommodation and securing stability for individuals and their children. In addition, changes to legislation, definitions and interpretations of 'vulnerability' and priority housing need are variably applied and the requirement for broader professional understandings of the impact of domestic abuse is emphasised. Convincing housing providers and their partners that the sector has responsibilities to honour, relating to the prevention, detection and cessation of domestic abuse, has also been met with some ambivalence and the chapter concludes by suggesting how further improvements might be made.

From Small Beginnings

Having somewhere safe to go in order to escape from situations of abuse at home was the initial focus of the feminist activist movement, which brought domestic abuse issues to the fore (Pascall, Lee, Morley, & Parker, 2001). Survivors of domestic abuse assisted other women in fleeing the family home, by using the legal provisions for squatters' rights and utilising empty houses and buildings as places of sanctuary.[2] A recognition of this trend and the need for something more formal to occur led to the opening of the first official refuge in Chiswick in 1971 and the establishment of the charities Refuge and Women's Aid. This was revolutionary at the time, as it formally symbolised the reality that many women were simply not safe in their own homes and placed the issue of domestic abuse into the public arena. The need for emergency refuge accommodation continued and expanded during the 1980s and 1990s. However, the physical capacities and the additional support services offered by refuges often varied. They were also not uniformly supported by local authori-

---

[2] Section 6 of the Criminal Law Act 1977 covers the occupation of property and was implemented to stop landlords and property owners using force to evict tenants. The 'Squatters Movement' utilised the law to prevent their forcible eviction from properties. This changed with clause 144 of the Legal Aid, Sentencing and Punishment of Offenders Act, which made it a criminal offence to squat in a property in England and Wales, punishable by up to 6 months imprisonment and fines up to £5000.

ties, resulting in a geographical lottery of service provision (Coy, Kelly, & Foord, 2009; see Turgoose, Chap. 6, this volume). Other additional criteria limited women's access to refuge, such as upper age limits for male children, the lack of capacity to accommodate large families, restrictions on accepting women with mental health and substance misuse issues and women in paid employment being unable to access housing benefit or afford the refuge rent costs (Coy et al., 2009, p. 45).

The situation has deteriorated further with the impact of the economic downturn and recent budget cuts, having a dramatic impact on the number of refuge places available nationwide. Women's Aid reported that between 2010 and 2014, the number of specialist refuge services had decreased from 187 to 155, with a bed space shortfall of 1727 (32 %) (Women's Aid's, 2014). Whilst the government responded to the National 2014 'Refuge SOS Campaign' led by Women's Aid with two further injections of monies, issues of longer term sustainability continue to impact negatively on the quantity and quality of this form of emergency intervention (Women's Aid's, 2014). It is known that the point of separation in a relationship can be a trigger for an escalation in violence within many situations of domestic abuse and can lead to incidents of stalking, harassment and murder (Richards & SafeLives, 2015). The security of having access to emergency accommodation is, therefore, paramount and can result in the need for location sites to change on a relatively regular basis. It is also important that other support agencies understand the confidential nature of such addresses and ensure they are not disclosed to the perpetrator directly or via a third party. The temporary nature of refuge facilities, however, renders them challenging as an environment for families in terms of trying to realise other positive changes and they were originally envisaged as a short-term 'stop gap' only. However, the difficulties in finding appropriate move-on accommodation have long endured, with ever shifting legal boundaries and variable definitions of vulnerability and homelessness (see Pascall et al., 2001; Websdale & Johnson, 1998).

Significant developments occurred via the *Domestic Violence and Matrimonial Proceedings Act* 1976, the *Domestic Proceedings and Magistrates Court Act* 1978 and the *Housing (Homeless Persons) Act* 1977. The first two pieces of legislation provided women with an option to stay in their own home with the aid of injunctions, and the latter enabled an approach to be made to a local authority to register as homeless as a result of the risk of harm posed to the individuals in their existing accommodation. However, Maidment (1983) argued that the promises provided by the legislative reforms were not fulfilled in practice, and the ways in which the legal provisions were interpreted often left women and children inadequately protected. The introduction of the *Housing Act* 1996 further restricted access to local authority accommodation, with tougher rules of eligibility and assessment pertaining to the right to recourse to public funds. Many individuals experiencing domestic abuse found that their homelessness applications were met with some scepticism and in some cases with refusal. Although some later concessions were made, the new rules resulted in issues, particularly for migrant women who had entered the UK as a result of their marriage to a UK citizen, but who were then forced to flee the relationship because of domestic violence (Southall Black Sisters, 2015).

Permanent, safe accommodation is essential to obtain employment, access education or further training and for the development of independent living skills. Without a safe place to live, all other positive efforts may be severely hampered and the well-being of individuals who have experienced abuse and of their children may be further impaired (Websdale & Johnson, 1998). To this extent, Websdale and Johnson (1998) argued that the impact of acquiring appropriate, safe, long-term housing was potentially more powerful as a tool for recovery from abuse than the pursuit of criminal prosecutions against the perpetrator or civil injunctions, and should therefore be prioritised. However, Kelly, Sharpe, and Klein (2014) observe that an individual's right to have a safe place to live, established in the early stages of feminist campaigns, is just one of the priorities that have been eroded over time, 'prolonging and complicating the process of rebuilding lives'(Kelly et al., 2014, p. 57). In their 2011–2014 study, which examined the barriers and economic costs for individuals seeking to secure safety from further violence and abuse, housing was the most prevalent issue identified by 100 female participants interviewed. This remained to be the case during further contact with the women over a 3-year period, highlighting that there were still concerns not only over the provision of an immediate place of safety, but also in relation to attempts to transfer to more stable, longer term accommodation. At the conclusion of their research, Kelly et al. (2014) reported that 60 % of the participants had secured social housing; however, many of the women had experienced several changes of address, with many having moved more than twice (56 %) and some having moved five or more times (5 %). A number of possible reasons are likely to have resulted in this state of transiency, such as the perpetrator becoming aware of the new location, difficulties in securing schooling, needing to be near work, affordability and short-term tenancies. However, for professionals with limited understandings of domestic abuse, this type of pattern can often be misconstrued and may work against the individual when assessments of need for practical support are undertaken. Women have reported that some housing officials did not appear to believe their accounts of domestic abuse and that they were perceived to be making claims simply to advance their position on a waiting list (Kelly et al., 2014, p. 58).

Homelessness. Legislation, the Role and Practice of Local Authorities

Barron (2009) (cited by the Department of Communities and Local Government (DCLG), 2010, p. 24) found that 41 % of women in refuges had left their abusive partner at least once before their first admission to a refuge. Binney, Harkell, and Nixon (1981) had also found that securing safe move-on accommodation was vital, with 59 % of the women surveyed advising that 'problems with accommodation' were a primary reason for their return to an abusive partner. The act of leaving an abusive situation is fraught with challenges and risks, resulting in many individuals struggling to make that initial break. However, when they do, they are then faced with an 'obstacle race' of homelessness legislation (Robson, 1981), which exacerbates their situation further. Despite legislative changes that are professed to have improved responses to situations of accommodation crisis, structural issues such as limited housing stock have not been addressed, resulting in what Loveland (1994, p. 331) describes as an 'exercise in legislative deceit'. In April 2003, the government introduced the Supporting People Programme (HM Government, 2003), which ring-fenced funds for housing-related support for families experiencing domestic abuse. However, by 2009, this ring-fencing had been removed. Since April 2010, housing support relating to situations of domestic abuse has been funded by the payment of area-based grants to local authorities, with local commissioners then determining how the money is to be distributed locally. Spending has reduced overall and as highlighted previously, specialist accommodations such as refuge places have decreased. Quick-fix injections of additional government funds have occurred, but with limited impact on women's safety in the longer term. It is advocated, therefore, that the approach to housing support needs to pursue a coordinated community model, with a more holistic view of refuge provision, local authority responsibilities, floating support and outreach services (Kelly et al., 2014).

Establishing 'Priority Need'

In November 2010, the DCLG commissioned a report by the Centre of Housing Policy at the University of York to examine the assistance provided to households at risk of domestic abuse, who are accepted as homeless under the relevant legislation, the funding of accommodation and housing-related support services for households at risk of domestic abuse and sanctuary scheme services[3] which served to assist households at risk of domestic abuse to remain in their own homes. The study found that 13 % of all applicants accepted as homeless were recorded as having lost their last settled accommodation due to being unable to remain in a violent relationship (6820 applicants). However, of that number, only 1760 (3 %) were recorded as a 'priority need' for rehousing. Overall, the number of people who have been accepted onto the homelessness register has decreased dramatically over recent years. It is likely that changes in local authority practices have impacted on this figure, with an emphasis on other 'housing

---

[3] Sanctuary schemes vary by region, but generally consist of local authority provisions for increased security measures to be installed at the accommodation. This can include extra locks, reinforced doors and, in severe cases, a panic room having a phone line that is directly linked to the police. Permission is required from the property landlord/owner, and sanctuary schemes are not appropriate in cases in which the property is jointly owned. They may also not deter a perpetrator in very high-risk cases, resulting in an individual becoming a 'prisoner in their own home'.

options' including sanctuary schemes, rent deposit schemes and tenancy sustainment services. However, it may also be the case that successfully achieving a formal homelessness status has become more difficult.

The Housing Act 1996 and *Homelessness Act* 2002 established that an individual has the right to approach any local authority and declare himself or herself homeless if remaining in the existing accommodation could lead to harm or violence. The local authority will then assess any such application via a number of set criteria, which will determine whether the person is legally homeless and eligible for assistance, the priority need status, whether the individual has become homeless intentionally and whether the individual has a local connection (Shelter, 2014). However, whilst the accompanying code of guidance stipulates that domestic violence is indeed a priority need, geographical variants in the provision of suitable housing can result in very different outcomes for families experiencing domestic abuse. Significantly, the code of guidance is not legally binding and allows for considerable discretion. The housing professionals responsible for making these assessments are, therefore, put in challenging positions, with limited accommodation options available and may thus struggle to support some individuals and their families. Fearn (2015) recently highlighted that pressures such as these can lead to acts of 'gatekeeping' and unethical practices. She details a High Court Order made in March 2015, issued to Southwark Council who had been referring homeless people directly to the private rented sector rather than assessing them under housing and homelessness legislation. They would then not be apparent in the collection of official homelessness data in that region. It was clear this practice had been established because of shortages in social housing and the pressures to keep accepted homelessness applications at a minimum.

It should also be noted that whilst local authorities have always been able to offer applicants a property in the private sector if they are formally accepted as being homeless, up until October 2012 (DCLG, 2012), the applicants could refuse this offer if they were willing to wait in temporary accommodation until something more suitable was found in the local authority housing stock. However, changes in 2012 now limit the opportunity for such a refusal. Applicants may, therefore, be put in a position where they are faced with the potential for more rapid increases in rental rates, more limited protections and the tenancy insecurities that are generally associated with the private rented sector. However, for the local authorities, it provides a further opportunity to secure a more rapid decrease in homelessness figures.

Crisis (2014) examined the treatment of those presenting as single homeless across several different local authority areas. A significant variation was found in the response from local authority areas and 'gatekeeping' was also identified. A total of 29 of 87 people were turned away from local authority housing departments without any assessment of their housing need. Crisis also found that many frontline staff were described as unhelpful, disrespectful and lacking in empathy, with some not even mentioning the opportunity for the individual to make a homelessness application. Providing evidence of a priority need has been a particular issue for those experiencing domestic abuse. As discussed in more detail in this volume by Bishop, Chap. 4, the case of *Yemshaw v Hounslow London Borough Council* (Herring, 2011) established that the definition of domestic violence includes the commission of emotional and psychological abuse and this should be applied when considering housing need. However, despite developments in the criminal prosecution of domestic abuse, which now includes an offence of coercive, controlling behaviour, understandings of the complexities of domestic abuse by non-specialist agencies such as housing, have remained very limited. Local authorities and housing providers have often relied on tangible, robust evidence of physical assault and have routinely asked the individuals affected by abuse to provide crime reference numbers or other forms of evidence from the police. This is despite the code of guidance stipulating that it is not the individual's responsibility to prove his or her case. Securing safe accommodation is highlighted as the initial priority, with the full application to be considered thereafter (DCLG, 2006).

The situation in England and Wales is not unique. In 2005, researchers conducting a study in New York (Anti-Discrimination Centre of Metro New York, 2005) initiated contact with housing coordinators in various districts, posing as individuals who had experienced domestic abuse, to assess the providers approach and strategy to support. In all, 20 % of the providers contacted in the study raised 'stereotypical concerns' about the applicants' 'mental stability' and the extent to which it may impact other residents and staff safety in an accommodation placement. A further

27.5 % advised that they were unable to provide any accommodation, or following an initial assessment, did not follow the application any further. The study by Kelly et al. (2014) also highlighted other disparities in the perspectives that may be held by housing professionals and those who have experienced domestic abuse. 'They were like, if you're desperate, you 'll take it' (Kelly et al., 2014, p. 61); however individual applicants were concerned to acquire accommodation which ensured the long-term safety of their families and ended the insecurity and chaos that their children, in particular, may have experienced previously. Many individuals may seek to ensure that their children's schooling is not disrupted, whilst others may want to move to a new borough to reduce the possibility that the perpetrator will be able to discover the new address. Finding new schools and supporting children's needs is, therefore, often of paramount concern in any housing application made. Again, this requires the housing professional to have an open and honest engagement with the applicant, an informed awareness of the relevant issues and key assessment skills to determine the best course of action in each individual case. The reality is often that people will be required to make very quick decisions about the suitability of a housing offer, which is dramatically life changing, leaving everything they know behind them to live somewhere new, surrounded by strangers. The pressures on the allocation system leaves very little space for reflection, resulting in a subsequent realisation for many applicants that the initial placement is totally unsuitable.

There is evidence that in cases where the individual has the support of a professional advocate, there is more likelihood of success in accessing various forms of intervention including housing (see Robinson and Payton, Chap. 10, this volume). Kelly et al. (2014) found that verification of the individual's situation via a women's organisation, referral from a Multi-Agency Risk Assessment Conference (MARAC) or support from a local member of parliament or councillor often resulted in more effective and timely responses from the housing sector. However this relies on the person wishing to engage with these other strategies and the disclosure of the abuse to other parties, in order that the 'professional' may substantiate the claim. Individuals will have been experiencing abuse for a long time before accessing support and will continue to endeavour to resolve their situation on their own without engaging in more formal interventions. The magnitude of the decision to leave must not be underestimated; however, once this step is taken, there are clearly a number of distressing obstacles that may be encountered before safe accommodation is finally secured.

Property and Tenancy Rights

Property and tenancy rights add a further layer of complexity to the housing response in situations of domestic abuse. In some cases, perpetrators can use tenancy rights as a tool of control, with individuals being forced to become a joint tenant to limit their rights to residency, or a further tenancy following any separation. Perpetrators may refuse to sign over a tenancy if the relationship ends and in some cases, terminate the tenancy without their partner's knowledge, leaving them homeless. The ownership of a property is also subject to legal differences between a couple's status as 'joint tenants' and 'tenants in common', which may also impact later rights to occupancy and the division of monies resulting from a sale. Such issues are virtually impossible to navigate without good legal guidance and support and can take a considerable length of time to resolve. In a case highlighted by Kelly et al. (2014, p. 62), a woman fleeing a situation of domestic abuse was a property owner. The perpetrator, however, had forged documents to mortgage her property, whilst continuing to reside there himself. The woman was left paying a mortgage on her own flat, rent for her new accommodation and the legal fees required to resolve the matter and evict her ex-partner. The situation continued for six months. Whilst the police have powers for the temporary removal of a perpetrator from the family home via the measures provided by Domestic Violence Protection Notices and Domestic Violence Protection Orders (see Burton this volume, Chap. 1), the longer term picture is far bleaker. Local authorities and housing providers very rarely take steps to remove perpetrators from a rented property and to secure an eviction would rely heavily on evidence provided by the individual experiencing abuse. This is something that many individuals would be unwilling to provide, for fear of further negative repercussions. Indeed, it is often the case that tenants have not been the ones to disclose the abuse to the housing provider in the first instance, but other complaints have been received from neighbours regarding noise nuisance, drunken behaviour and fighting. Issues can then be mistakenly dealt with as anti-social behaviour concerns, rather than identifying a situation where domestic abuse is the root cause. Ross (2007) highlights examples in a US study where this has then resulted in the individuals experiencing abuse being the ones evicted from their own homes.

In 2013, Clarke and Wydall evaluated a pilot project in North Yorkshire, which adopted a very different approach to tenancies and domestic abuse scenarios and sought to keep those experiencing abuse safe in their own homes. The project consisted of 12 statutory and voluntary sector agencies and provided support to all parties via three main pathways of intervention: the provision of advocacy for individuals experiencing abuse, support for children and young people and accommodation and key work for perpetrators whilst attending the Integrated Domestic Abuse Programme (IDAP, see Hilder and Freeman Chap. 13, this volume). For the individuals experiencing abuse, there were four very positive outcomes: respite from daily fear or anxiety, an avoidance of the upheaval of leaving the family home, being able to retain existing support networks, which, in turn, resulted in a reduced feeling of isolation and a greater sense of empowerment. Perpetrators were held accountable for their actions by being required to leave, but were also supported in trying to achieve stability elsewhere. This study offered a more holistic, positive approach in comparison with experiences elsewhere of women and children being placed in male hostels, being directed to unaffordable rented accommodation and often having to make stark choices between paying their rent or buying food (Kelly et al., 2014).

Tenancy Support and Independent Living

For many individuals experiencing domestic abuse, a lack of financial control and monetary independence is a feature of the abuse incurred. Individuals may discover that rent arrears have been accumulated in their name, but may lack complete knowledge of their own financial affairs as a result of the dynamics of an abusive relationship. They may be unable to answer the most basic questions posed about their finances by professionals and lack any access to independent funds, or indeed possess the experience and skills to begin to resolve their situation without further assistance and support. If individuals have rent arrears, they may be prevented from being granted a management transfer, priority banding or registering for home-swapping schemes. Navigating these processes is challenging enough in any circumstances, let alone in situations of distress, by individuals who may have little prior experience of managing their own affairs.

The benefits system is equally complex. The award of Universal Credit to a named member of a household to cover other household members' entitlements has raised particular issues for those who have experienced domestic abuse, as they are forced to make new fresh claims in their own name. In the initial stages of a separation, a person may also need to make an application for dual housing benefit in order to ensure that the rent is paid for both homes, permanent and temporary. Housing Benefit Regulation 7 (6) (a) states that Housing Benefit can be paid on two homes for a maximum period of 52 weeks if a claimant has left the permanent residence because of a fear of violence, but where there is a clear intention to return to the former home. It is not acceptable to claim for temporary accommodation provided by a relative. If there is no intention to return to the former residence, then dual payments can continue only for four weeks to cover the notice period, which the claimant would usually be expected to honour (Housing Benefit Regulations, 2006). Clearly, for some individuals experiencing domestic abuse, a return to the family home is unrealistic, and they will be seeking a long-term move to independency. However the declaration of no 'intention to return' may place them in further financial difficulties in the first instance. For those left with the single occupancy of a joint property, further financial disadvantages and penalties may occur. For example, the under-occupancy charge, otherwise known as the 'bedroom tax', may apply. Whilst exemption may be sought from this charge on compassionate grounds, such an application is likely to take some significant time to process. Overall, there appears to be a very real contradiction in homelessness, housing and welfare benefit laws, which appear to have limited regard of the realities of people's lives who experience domestic abuse. The provision of knowledgeable, proactive and empathetic frontline staff, therefore, becomes essential to assist individuals in circumnavigating this minefield of bureaucracy.

Even in cases where a new property is secured, individuals may face ongoing difficulties relating to their finances. Some people will have left their former family home at a point of crisis, with very little chance of transporting many of their personal belongings and therefore, they are faced with the prospect of starting from scratch. The abolition of community grants in April 2013 as a result of the *Welfare Reform Act 2012* has further exacerbated difficulties in being able to obtain even the most basic items required for setting up a home, with the capacity for professional discretion in making such decisions having been significantly reduced. This can result in individuals staying in temporary accommodation for longer, even though this may prove more expensive for the local authority in terms of higher housing benefit payments.

Despite some good intentions, the history of local authority housing support for individuals experiencing domestic abuse has, therefore, been one where vulnerable individuals have been required to justify their right to safety and support, with many being denied access. However, safe housing has remained central to the success of all other agency interventions in scenarios of domestic abuse and is frequently raised as an issue in the multi-agency strategies identified by the police, health and specialist domestic violence and abuse support agencies. It was time for a cultural change and for housing providers to move centre stage nationally in the response domestic abuse.

Housing as a Primary Responder to Situations of Domestic Abuse

Peabody provides housing to a diverse range of tenants and adopts a proactive stance to the support that should be offered to ensure the sustainability of tenancies and healthy communities. In 2007, Peabody identified a need to expand their Community Safety Team, which deals with high-level anti-social behaviour, including situations of domestic abuse. An expansion in recruitment led to the introduction of greater expertise pertaining to domestic abuse and violence against women and girls. This triggered a review of Peabody tenancy case files, with just four registered cases of domestic abuse at that time. This was clearly at odds with national figures on the prevalence of domestic abuse and warranted further investigation. It also became apparent that there were issues around resident safety and tenancy breakdowns pertaining to situations of domestic abuse that the organisation had either not recognised, or was ill-equipped to deal with. This identified a need for changes in the organisation's level of knowledge and expertise as well as operational policies and practice. The key priorities identified by Peabody included a significant increase in awareness and understandings of domestic abuse issues by both staff and residents. Staff also needed to be appropriately trained on safeguarding issues to be able to support families, providing information on the options and assistance available from both housing and other agencies as part of a coordinated community response.

One of the first major initiatives introduced by Peabody was the use of the Domestic Abuse, Stalking and Honour Based Violence Risk Identification Checklist (DASH) (Richards & SafeLives, 2015). All frontline housing staff were trained in its use as a step to making onward referrals to local MARACs and other agency support. The importance of housing sector contributions to multi-agency approaches to addressing domestic abuse is now widely recognised, although the sector's active engagement in processes such as MARAC remains very varied nationally. Managing the contribution and commitment to such forums requires good engagement skills with the individuals experiencing the abuse, perpetrators and professional agency partners, together with robust administrative systems that ensure confidentially is maintained. Peabody developed a bespoke case management framework, which enabled staff to organise the various strands of support, intervention and procedure required to support a family where domestic abuse occurs. An evaluation mechanism was also incorporated to ascertain residents' views of the outcome of their case and the support they had received from Peabody. In 2007, Peabody also funded an Independent Domestic Violence Advisor post, to further assist tenants who may be subject to the MARAC process (see Robinson and Payton, Chap. 12, this volume).

The organisation's transfer policy was reviewed, with the implementation of a weekly Priority Move Panel to approve cases for priority transfers and to allocate void properties to families experiencing domestic abuse who needed to be moved urgently. Peabody also adopted a presumptive stance that urgent requests were to be taken as genuine with a far lower burden of proof than that which might be required by other housing providers. The introduction of the DASH assessment process and trained Community Safety Officers greatly assisted with this organisational change. The new approach sought to respect the individual's account and support the employee's assessment of risk over any evidence of police contact, which, in many cases, was not forthcoming. A Domestic Abuse Checklist was also implemented to ensure Community Safety Officers provided relevant information at the first point of contact with those experiencing abuse, relating to safety information, national helplines and practical advice.

Peabody's Vulnerable Resident policy now also includes a clause to ensure that repairs to properties where domestic abuse has occurred are made promptly to make the home secure again as soon as possible. A budget is also provided to explore the need for extra security measures where there is an ongoing risk of harm from the perpetrator's potential return, working alongside local authority teams to ensure that equipment such as safety alarms are fitted as appropriate. All tenancy case work pertaining to domestic abuse is monitored by monthly case reviews to ensure a consistency of practice across the organisation. The initiatives put in place to improve residency work also triggered reflections on the wellbeing of staff and changes to policy and practice in terms of supporting staff who may be experiencing abuse have also been made.

Staff Training

Changes to policies and procedures are likely to have a limited impact unless the commitment and capacity of staff to implement them effectively is also established. Peabody's first staff training priority pertained to the specialist Community Safety Team, who would serve as first responders and advisors to staff and residents on issues of domestic abuse. Awareness and procedural training, as relevant to various staff roles, was then cascaded out to a wider network of frontline staff including Neighbourhood Managers, Letting officers, Revenues officers, Welfare Benefit officers, Tenancy and Family Support officers and Call Centre staff. Domestic Abuse awareness training is also now a standard component on the generic induction training for all new Peabody staff. Following on from this, it was acknowledged that maintenance staff, for example, surveyors or gas engineers, often had unique access to properties and would see evidence of damage caused, such as punch marks in walls, door locks fixed on the outside of bedroom doors and door locks damaged on the inside of bathroom doors. Whilst there was clearly no expectation that maintenance operatives would directly intervene in any manner, by simply raising their awareness of domestic abuse issues, there was a marked increase in the organisation's capacity to spot matters that may be of more significant concern. Whilst a delicate balance with tenancy rights to privacy must always be maintained, this training and the other developments described have seen a marked increase in realising opportunities for earlier intervention and prevention.

Public Awareness

As these advancements have occurred, Peabody has recognised that housing professionals are in a unique position of engagement with residents experiencing abuse. In cases where an individual's immediate priority may be the securement of somewhere safe to go, housing staff may be perceived as a far less intimidating and potentially more helpful point of disclosure than other agencies such as the police and children's services. The proactive stance promoted by Peabody, therefore, also needs to ensure that the unique characteristics of the sector are not lost. If a disclosure to a member of housing staff is seen as an inevitable gateway to a more complex array of agency involvement, then many individuals will not want to engage. The approach to the support offered, therefore, needs to be as client-centred as possible, ensuring that residents are fully involved in any decisions made.

Work has also been undertaken to provide guidance to Peabody residents on how to report domestic abuse concerns, encouraging a consideration of whether presenting issues such as noise nuisance or anti-social behaviours may indeed have a more particular underlying cause. All external and internal Peabody communications have been reviewed in relation to the new domestic abuse strategy, with relevant information being provided in welcome packs for new residents and awareness raising and contact detail posters being displayed on all noticeboards and reception areas across the estates. Public awareness raising campaigns have occurred both internally across the Peabody community and externally, engaging with the mass media in all its many forms at national and international levels. This has promoted the central role that the housing sector must play in reducing the prevalence and harm caused by domestic abuse. This has led, amongst other things, to the author sitting as the representative for housing on the National Violence Against Women and Girls stakeholder panel and supporting Home Office policy development relating to housing and Adolescent to Parent Violence and Abuse.

Positive Impact and Ongoing Challenges

Since the introduction of the measures described previously, the reporting levels to Peabody of incidents of domestic abuse have increased by 1425 % over an 8-year period, now with a consistent 25 % of all cases being dealt with by the Community Safety Team at any one time resulting from issues of domestic abuse. An independent evaluation is also being undertaken with those residents experiencing abuse who have received support from Peabody, to see where further improvements could be made. The latest figures show that in 2014–2015, the number of Peabody residents experiencing abuse who were satisfied with the organisational response to domestic abuse cases was 72.7 % and the figures for 2015–2016 so far show that this has increased to 90 %. It is encouraging that other housing providers and local authorities are also now developing practice in this area and at the time of writing this chapter, a further 41 Housing Providers had been trained nationwide by Peabody.

That said, it remains very apparent that some housing sector professionals had not anticipated this particular development aspect of their role, nor indeed did they see it as core function of their position. As a result, some have struggled to accept some of the links being advocated and for example, that consideration might be given to practical issues such as rent arrears being connected to issues of financial abuse and control. This is unsurprising perhaps, considering the length of time it has taken to highlight domestic abuse as a societal concern. This type of reticence is also not unique to the housing sector and the significant improvements still required within other professions, such as the police, are well documented, where more traditional associations with victim work and the pursuit of reductions in the risk of harm to the public remain (HMIC, 2014). However, for the housing sector, as with the police, the moral obligation to act upon safeguarding concerns, including those associated with domestic abuse, needs to be firmly embedded into the ethos of all staff roles, functions and recruitment processes across the whole organisation.

Conclusion

The Way Forward

The Domestic Abuse Housing Alliance (DAHA),[4] co-founded by Peabody, brings together skills from the housing sector, social enterprise and the specialist domestic violence and abuse support services sector, recognising the crucial role that housing plays in the prevention and reduction of the harm caused by domestic abuse. DAHA has developed an accreditation process, examining service delivery nationally across the housing sector, highlighting best practice and establishing minimum standards for housing providers to address issues of safety for those experiencing domestic abuse. Although still in its infancy, since DAHA's inception in September 2014 and at the time of writing this chapter, six housing providers had undertaken the first phase of the accreditation process, with a further 100 expressions of interest.

---

[4] The DAHA brings together Peabody, the social business Gentoo Group, and the charity Standing Together against Domestic Violence, who share a long-standing commitment to tackling domestic abuse, partnership working and sharing best practice.

The domestic abuse specialist support sector has seen the development of national standards, core principles and accreditation processes in other areas of service delivery, such as the development of national standards for specialist support services (Women's Aid, 2014) and the accreditation of programme work with perpetrators (RESPECT, 2015). The benefit and impact of such benchmarks has been felt in a number of ways, which DAHA would hope to replicate within the housing sector. Firstly, it establishes some common principles that all providers should adopt, utilising strategies that have been proven to work effectively, yet with some remaining scope for adaption to ensure that methods respond to local needs and contexts. A level of standardisation, however, also serves to reduce some of the 'geographical lottery' experience that housing residents may otherwise encounter in terms of the response to issues of domestic abuse. Staff increase their expertise, skills and confidence knowing that they are adopting methods that are viewed as current best practice and subject to ongoing evaluation and impact monitoring. Practice will, therefore, continue to develop as the broader breadth of knowledge of issues of domestic abuse continues to expand. A business case can also be made as opportunities for earlier intervention and prevention are realised, reducing the need for some individuals to access longer term recovery services at a later stage. The turnover of housing stock and management of rent arrears may also be more effectively addressed.

There is, however, no room for complacency. The starting point for many housing providers, who now recognise their responsibilities in relation to domestic abuse, will be a one-dimensional analysis of the experiences of women being abused by men. The diverse manifestations of abuse that may be shaped by a vast range of other identity and contextual factors may still fall foul to misinterpretation or dismissal. As this chapter has illustrated, the housing sector and particularly those providing move-on accommodation and long-term tenancies, have always been integral to an effective response to domestic abuse. However, formerly, as partnership forums have developed, housing was viewed as a practical resource only, just bricks and mortar. This chapter and the work of Peabody, strongly advocate that the housing sector is very much more than this and work must continue to realise the sector's full potential as a first responder in situations of domestic abuse.

References

Anti-Discrimination Centre of Metro New York. (2005). *Adding insult to injury: Housing discrimination against survivors of domestic violence*. New York: Anti-Discrimination Centre of Metro New York.
Binney, V., Harkell, G., & Nixon, J. (1981). *Leaving violent men: Study of refuges and housing for abused women*. Bristol: Women's Aid Federation.
Clarke, A., & Wydall, S. (2013). Making safe: A coordinated community response to empowering victims and tackling perpetrators of domestic violence. *Social Policy and Society, 12*(3), 393–406.
Coy, M., Kelly, L., & Foord, J. (2009). *Map of gaps. The postcode lottery of violence against women support services in Britain*. London: End violence against women and equality and human rights commission.
Crisis. (2014). *Turned away: The treatment of single homeless people by local authority homelessness services*. London: Crisis.
Department of Communities and Local Government (DCLG). (2006). Homelessness code of guidance for council. London: DCLG.
Department of Communities and Local Government (DCLG). (2010). *Meeting the needs of households at risk of domestic violence in England: The role of accommodation and housing-related support services*. York: University of York.
Department of Communities and Local Government (DCLG). (2012). *Homelessness (Suitability of Accommodation) (England) Order 2012 – Government's response to consultation*. London: DCLG.
Domestic Proceedings and Magistrates Court Act 1978 c 22. Retrieved October 25, 2015, from http://www.legislation.gov.uk/ukpga/1978/22/contents
Domestic Violence and Matrimonial Proceedings Act 1976 c22. Retrieved October 25, 2015, from http://www.legislation.gov.uk/ukpga/1978/22/contents
Fearn, H. (2015). *The scandal of councils turning away the homeless is finally being exposed.* 27th February 2015. Retrieved October 25, 2015, from http://www.theguardian.com/housing-network/2015/feb/27/council-gatekeeping-scandal-homeless-exposed
Her Majesty's Inspectorate of Constabulary (HMIC). (2014). *Everyone's Business: Improving the police response to domestic abuse*. London: HMIC.

Herring, J. (2011). The meaning of domestic violence: Yemsham vs London borough of hounslow. *Journal of Social Welfare and Family Law, 33*(3), 297–304.
HM Government. (2003). The supporting people programme. London: Communities and Local Government Committee. Retrieved October 25, 2015, from http://www.publications.parliament.uk/pa/cm200809/cmselect/cmcomloc/649/64904.htm
Homelessness Act 2002 c7. Retrieved October 24, 2015, from http://www.legislation.gov.uk/ukpga/2002/7/contents
Housing (Homeless Persons) Act 1977 c48. Retrieved October 25, 2015, from http://www.legislation.gov.uk/ukpga/1977/48/contents/enacted
Housing Act 1996. Retrieved October 25, 2015, from http://www.legislation.gov.uk/ukpga/1996/52/contents
Housing Benefit Regulations 2006. no213. Retrieved October 25, 2015, from http://www.legislation.gov.uk/uksi/2006/213/contents/made
Kelly, L., Sharpe, N., & Klein, R. (2014). *Finding the costs of freedom.* London: CWASU and Solace Women's Aid.
Loveland, I. (1994). "Cathy sod off." The end of homelessness legislation. *Journal of Social Welfare and Family Law, 16*(4), 367–389.
Maidment, S. (1983). Domestic violence and the law: The 1976 Act and its aftermath. *The Sociological Review, 31*(1), 4–25.
Pascall, S., Lee, S. J., Morley, R., & Parker, S. (2001). Changing housing policy: Women escaping domestic violence. *Journal of Social Welfare and Family Law, 23*(3), 293–309.
RESPECT. (2015). *Domestic violence prevention programmes.* Retrieved October 27, 2015, from http://www.respectphoneline.org.uk/pages/domestic-violence-prevention-programmes.html
Richards, L., & SafeLives. (2015). (formerly CAADA) *Domestic Abuse Stalking and Harassment (DASH) risk assessment tool.* Retrieved October 25, 2015, from http://www.safelives.org.uk/node/462
Robson, P. (1981). The homeless persons' obstacle race Parts I and II. *Journal of Social Welfare Law, 3*((5) and (6)) 1–15 and 65–82.
Ross, K. (2007). Eviction, discrimination, and domestic violence: Unfair housing practices against domestic violence survivors. *Women's Law Journal, 18*, 249–268.
Shelter. (2014). *How to apply as homeless.* Retrieved October 25, 2015, from http://england.shelter.org.uk/get_advice/homelessness/help_from_the_council_when_homeless/how_to_apply_as_homeless

Southall Black Sisters. (2015). *Abolish the no recourse to public funds campaign.* Retrieved October 25, 2015, from http://www.southallblacksisters.org.uk/campaigns/abolish-no-recourse-to-public-funds/

Websdale, N., & Johnson, B. (1998). Reducing woman battering: The role of structural approaches. *Social Justice, 24*(67), 54–81.

Women's Aid. (2014). *Cuts in refuge services puts vulnerable women and children at risk.* Retrieved October 25, 2015, from http://www.womensaid.org.uk/domestic-violence-press-information.asp?itemid=2944&itemTitle=Cuts+in+refuge+services+putting+vulnerable+women+and+children+at+risk&section=0001000100150001&sectionTitle=Press+releases

12

Independent Advocacy and Multi-Agency Responses to Domestic Violence

Amanda Robinson and Joanne Payton

Introduction

A timeline of domestic violence would stretch back for millennia. Centuries passed before the first laws against it were created; new agencies were founded to address the problem directly and existing agencies began crafting specific responses to help those affected. For most of this last half-century, responses to domestic violence have involved agencies working together far more often than in isolation. Whilst partnership approaches have frequently failed to live up to the exemplar of a well-oiled machine, pioneers recognised that the input of multiple agencies was particularly pertinent to the problem of domestic violence, which is a crime with multiple repercussions. The aim of this chapter is to

---

A. Robinson (✉)
School of Social Sciences, University of Cardiff, Cardiff, UK

J. Payton
Fuuse, Caerphilly, UK

© The Editor(s) (if applicable) and The Author(s) 2016
S. Hilder, V. Bettinson (Eds.), *Domestic Violence*,
DOI 10.1057/978-1-137-52452-2_12

interrogate the philosophy behind and the practice within multi-agency responses to domestic violence and to illustrate the importance of victim advocates. In the UK, 4.9 million women and 2.7 million men were reported to have suffered domestic violence in 2012–2013 (Office of National Statistics, 2015). Given that the nature and manifestation of abuse within intimate relationships is constantly evolving along with our understandings, the chapter also aims to critique and extend current conceptualisations of what effective responses to domestic violence look like in the 21st century.

The Development and Philosophy of Multi-Agency Responses

The identification of domestic violence as an issue that requires collaborative, community-level responses came very early in the development of policies arising at the inception of second-wave feminist activism in the 1970s and 1980s. Feminist attention to domestic violence was initially directed at criminalisation and the unlocking of the potential of the criminal justice system on behalf of victims. This was achieved via a reframing of violence within the family as criminal activity, which made criminal justice responses a possible resource. The first priorities for action were raising awareness and addressing the attitudes, behaviours and policies of the police in particular, as likely first responders to the most severe and blatant acts of violence. The development of mandatory arrest policies was seen as one way to counteract what was perceived to be an indefensible culture of negligence by statutory service providers (Buzawa, Buzawa, & Stark, 2012; Forell, 2013).

Over time, however, it became evident that even improved criminal justice measures were unlikely to address the issue of domestic violence adequately. Importantly, the vast majority of victimisation in relationships remains unreported to criminal justice agencies (Gracia, 2004). Furthermore, victims of domestic violence have complicated needs, which exceed the provisions of the criminal justice system, from the requirement for safe housing to the social and psychological rehabilitation of survivors and their children (Allen, Bybee, & Sullivan, 2005). In fact, it is hard to envisage how any single agency could deal with the diversity and complexity of victims' needs successfully. Research into domestic violence has benefited from contributions from psychology, sociology and criminology, amongst many other disciplines. Additionally, domestic violence responses intrude into the various remits of specialist non-government organisations (NGOs), housing authorities, the police, social services, children's services, health services, police and courts, as well as those dealing with mental health and substance addiction, according to the specific situations of each individual case. In the absence of a coordinated response, victims may be forced to locate disparate services under their own initiative, which can be exhausting and also assumes that they are able to access them and can identify their utility to their circumstances. This may not be the case for many victims who, amongst many other potential barriers, may have their movements restricted by their abuser, are unable to speak the dominant language or have a disability and/or lack knowledge of the services available to them. The process of identifying, understanding and rectifying this reality unites all multi-agency approaches working on behalf of victims.

The first incarnation of a coordinated victim-centred approach was developed in Duluth, Minnesota. The two main philosophical tenets of what has come to be known as the 'Duluth Model' are identified in the title of this chapter: multi-agency collaboration and victim advocacy. Agencies across the whole system must be involved in a community-driven response. Their policies and procedures must be not only interwoven, but also developed from the experiences of victims themselves and those who advocate for them, also addressing perpetrator behaviours via specialist programmes (see Hilder and Freeman, Chap. 13, this volume). The voices of victims and victim advocates are essential to the Duluth Model, which established a way of formalising interactions between police, local courts and NGOs dealing with domestic violence in order to produce effective 'joined up' solutions. This approach is now known as the Coordinated Community Response (CCR). It was the success of Duluth's trailblazing CCR, a partnership between Domestic Abuse Intervention Programs (DAIP) and city and county criminal justice agencies, established in 1980, which led to its implementation across the state of Minnesota in 1991 and its continued influence worldwide.[1]

Following Minnesota's lead, CCRs were introduced into practice across the USA, with notable examples in Colorado Springs, Portland, Baltimore, San Francisco and Omaha (Muftić & Bouffard, 2007). These examples of effective partnership working to tackle domestic violence quickly became influential globally. The World Health Organisation recommended specifically that 'interventions should cover and be coordinated between a range of different sectors' (Krug, Dahlberg, Mercy, Zwi, & Luzano, 2002, p. 110). Across the Atlantic, policy and legal instruments were being designed to encourage the formation of multi-agency partnerships, for domestic violence as well as other social problems. A report from the London School of Tropical Medicine notes their development across Europe, including in Germany, Belgium, Spain and The Netherlands (Bacchus, 2013). The following excerpt from a British domestic violence organisation signals the centrality of partnership working:

> The essence of partnership is a joint understanding of the purpose of the partnership. When the partnership is created to tackle domestic violence this becomes even more crucial. The reality of the victim experience, the cultural complexities and the prevalence make this a very difficult subject to tackle. Victims are often blamed, and people and partnerships tend not to understand domestic violence or accept its scale. Additionally, it affects almost every aspect of our society and requires every organisation that "deals with people" to be involved. (Standing Together Against Domestic Violence, 2011, p. 12)

Currently, the infrastructure to support partnership approaches to tackling crime in the community is embedded into all local areas in England and Wales (Berry, Briggs, Erol, & van Staden, 2009) and serves as both impetus and reminder that no one agency can effectively deal with

---

[1] On October 14, 2014 the Duluth Model's 'Coordinated Community Response to Domestic Violence', a partnership between DAIP and criminal justice agencies of the City of Duluth and St. Louis County, was named the world's best Domestic Violence policy. Of 25 international nominations, the 'Duluth Model' was the only policy to be awarded the Future Policy Gold Award (see www.theduluthmodel.org).

complex community safety and crime issues. *The Crime and Disorder Act 1998* mandated collaboration between 'responsible authorities', namely the police, local authorities, fire and rescue authorities, probation service and health, in the task of reducing local crime and anti-social behaviour issues. Community Safety Partnerships (formerly Crime and Disorder Reduction Partnerships) were set up as part of the Act to develop and implement strategies for reducing crime and improving public safety. They illustrate the trend towards inter-organisational collaboration identified by Kelman, Hong, and Turbitt (2011) as one of the central features in contemporary public management. Partnership and notions of 'joined up' government and interagency working have become established terminology, used to describe 'the aspiration to achieve horizontally and vertically coordinated thinking and action', which underlies a wide range of contemporary policies (Pollit, 2003, p. 35).

Despite the widespread prevalence of multi-agency initiatives such as CCRs, there are no implementation protocols (Klevens, Baker, Shelley, & Ingram, 2008), making it difficult to empirically evaluate their outcomes and impacts. Indeed, initiatives in a particular area are inherently 'bespoke', as different places will have different social histories and resources to consider. In short, there can be variability in the levels of coordination, the community and the responses applied within any CCR. Yet, the philosophical core and necessary elements of such approaches can be identified, even if their implementation differs across locations. Key components in the approach taken to domestic violence include identifying connections between controlling behaviours and abuse, acknowledging gendered patterns of perpetration; offering support and advocacy to women, educating abusers to help them change their behaviours and combining criminal redress with coordinated community responses based in risk assessment and the victim's perception of danger (Pence & McMahon, 1997).

Importantly, both support and protection for victims and sanctions and interventions for perpetrators need to be incorporated into a community-based approach. In recent years, the service provision landscape in the UK has very much emphasised the provision of protective and rehabilitative measures in a 'support' model, rather than in a punitive 'control' model (Mahapatro, 2014). The 'support' model generally reflects victims' own desires, of which the paramount requirement is often security for themselves and their children, rather than justice or retribution against the perpetrator. However, this landscape may be set to change, with more coordinated and targeted approaches for perpetrators being developed, such as the Domestic Abuse Task Force in Scotland and the identification and management of priority domestic abuse perpetrators in Wales (HMIC, 2014a; Robinson & Clancy, 2015). This chapter will now consider how various agencies attempt the complicated business of responding effectively in partnership to domestic violence.

The People and the Practice

Multi-agency responses are increasingly being developed, or identified, as good practice in dealing with domestic violence cross-culturally, being recommended by the World Health Organisation, the Council of Europe and within the UK, the Home Office, Welsh Government and National Institute of Clinical Excellence (NICE). The idea of collaboration and 'joined up' approaches may be widely endorsed, but it raises important questions about how these ideas are translated into practice. Multi-agency approaches can combine decision making on victim protection measures, the promotion of offender accountability and the coordination and evaluation of existing services. They can also respond to changing needs by developing new approaches, providing legal and social support services to victims and ultimately changing the social tolerance for domestic violence through the demonstration of a united front against abuse (Shepherd & Pence, 1999). It is important to recognise, therefore, that there are both strategic and operational activities associated with multi-agency work on domestic violence. The day-to-day activities for those involved may operate on either, or both of these levels.

Many models of multi-agency practice are likely to be in operation, even within a single geographic area, involving different combinations of professionals, each with their own aims and objectives. Many of these interagency networks will focus specifically on domestic violence victims as clients, whilst others will provide a different type of service that touches on their experience in some way. In England and Wales, it is likely that most cities will have a Specialist Domestic Violence Court (SDVC) (see Bettinson Chap. 5, this volume), a Multi-Agency Risk Assessment Conference (MARAC) forum, a specialist domestic violence organisation where Independent Domestic Violence Advisors (IDVAs) and other types of victim advocates may be based and a Sexual Assault Referral Centre (SARC). There is also likely to be a domestic violence forum, which is often part of the local Community Safety Partnership (CSP) and other specialised interventions. Therefore, it is more accurate to think of any specific illustration of multi-agency work on domestic violence as just one of many examples within a given region. Given the aims of this chapter, the focus here will be on a couple of the 'prescriptions' that are known to make exceptionally good use of the multi-agency 'ingredient' in more detail.

In England and Wales, responses at a community level have been expanded by the growth of the MARAC approach developed in Cardiff in 2003 (Robinson, 2004). As championed by the national domestic violence charity Coordinated Action Against Domestic Abuse (CAADA),[2] with funding and support from the Home Office, MARACs have become the mainstream intervention for a subset of cases deemed to be at high risk.[3] Practice within MARACs is deemed valuable by the professionals directly involved, as illustrated in a media report:

> One man has recently made threats to his pregnant partner which focus the attention of the panel very tightly on what is instantly grasped as a grave and immediate danger.... Action by action, the panel try to wrap a series of protective measures around the victim and just as importantly, her child and unborn baby. This is the rationale behind the process: by sharing information held by individual agencies about a couple's history, the full extent of the risk becomes better understood and, hopefully, effective measures can be put in place to reduce the danger. (Tickle, 2014)

---

[2] In February 2015, Coordinated Action Against Domestic Abuse (CAADA) changed its name to SafeLives, which 'better reflects our mission to make sure that all families are safe from domestic abuse' (see http://www.safelives.org.uk/).

[3] This determination follows the use of the DASH risk assessment checklist, which involves a structured judgement approach (i.e., scoring of risk factors plus use of professional judgement by practitioners). See Robinson (2010) for an overview of the process.

The MARAC approach, combined with other local interagency initiatives, has, broadly speaking, shifted partnership practice from being ad hoc and discretionary to becoming routine and coordinated. Research on MARACs undertaken by Robinson and Tregida (2007) indicated that women valued the multi-agency support they received and four out of ten women whose cases had been dealt with by a MARAC, had experienced no further violence. All of those victims who reported that the violence had ceased attributed the change to their own decision making, suggesting that victims perceive themselves as primary agents for change, even within the multi-agency framework (Robinson & Tregida, 2007).

Criticisms of MARACs, however, include the strong reliance on the mechanisms of risk management and their managerial nature, which can be considered disempowering to the victim, who is external to the process (Wilson, 2013). An evaluation of MARACs sponsored by the Home Office found that 97 % of practitioners and stakeholders believed the MARAC model was very, or fairly, effective (Steel, Blakeborough, & Nicholas, 2011). Some accept the MARAC model, but call for greater flexibility in practice. For example, the Iranian and Kurdish Women's Rights Organisation (IKWRO), a specialist charity supporting Middle Eastern and North African women, has called for a more restricted form of MARAC, composed of only the most essential partners such as the police, the referring agency and housing bodies and in cases where a child is at risk, social services. This is to deal with the under-recognised, but extremely high-risk, phenomenon of 'honour'-based violence. It is thought that the high levels of collaboration amongst potential perpetrators of such crimes calls for both a higher level of urgency and a more conservative attitude to information sharing (Payton, 2014). IKWRO's founder Diana Nammi explains that:

> One of the problems is that due to a wide network of relatives who could potentially be involved, we need to double up on information security. It's not unknown for relatives to use their professional abilities to help the family track down a fugitive from family violence. We need to be able to be sure that information which goes through any MARAC will not end up endangering a client. (private communication)

The UN special rapporteur Manjoo (2014) observes that NGO representation at MARACs is crucial in many cases, particularly for cases involving women from ethnic minorities, who have diverse needs that are not adequately catered to, or fully comprehended by, mainstream services. Unfortunately, however, NGOs are not recompensed for participation in a MARAC and whilst NGOs, particularly those working on behalf of minority women, have been facing further severe funding cuts as a result of austerity measures (see Turgoose, Chap. 6, this volume), the resource implications of attendance at a series of MARACs can be profoundly felt.

The most frequently expressed and probably most significant limitation of MARACs is that they prioritise some cases for a more intensive and integrated response, which means that certain individuals can obtain a level of service, which others cannot access. Not everyone is created equal under the MARAC model, which is based on a framework of risk assessment that designates individuals at high, medium and low risk. Risk-based interventions stand and fall on the efficacy of the tools by which risk is assessed and the skills and training of those applying them. There are inherent challenges in making such a system work effectively (Robinson, 2010). Despite this, the prioritisation function of MARACs can be seen as its greatest strength, in terms of mobilising resources promptly for those in the most serious situations. Paradoxically, however, prioritisation based on risk assessment can also be seen to detract attention and resources away from interventions based at other levels, 'risk has become a tool for funnelling and rationing the service response to a widespread and complex social problem' (Stanley & Humphreys, 2014, p. 79) It must be acknowledged that both positive and negative consequences are likely to flow from this. The dynamic nature of risk may be neglected and the rapid escalations in harm, which may occur, overlooked. A risk-based approach that provides adequately for individuals at all levels of risk and that can effectively identify and respond to risk levels that change over time is, therefore, ripe for development.

The pivotal figure in the MARAC approach is the IDVA whose key role is victim advocacy. CAADA (2010) found that the MARAC and IDVA combination could achieve up to 60 % decrease in violence, and using conservative measures, calculated from this that every one pound spent on MARACs saved six pounds in public money. The IDVA is the cornerstone of the MARAC's activities, keeping the interests of the victim central to the proceedings. If the other parties around the table are in the business of providing services, the IDVA is the person who requests them, through outlining the needs of their client. IDVAs should be independent, professional and trained, aware of local resources and options, provide crisis intervention and safety planning informed by risk assessment and coordinate services on behalf of victims, with the key objectives being to reduce the risk posed and increase safety (Coy & Kelly, 2011; Howarth, Stimpson, Barran, & Robinson, 2009; Robinson, 2009).

IDVAs and representatives of the police, both of whom have a direct responsibility to deal with domestic violence, are among those most likely to attend a MARAC, but this approach can include a multitude of other agencies, from specialist NGOs for minorities, to social housing (Steel et al., 2011). One IDVA described her role as follows:

> It's a bit like being the eyes, the ears and the voice for our clients, but also negotiating with other professionals ... say for example it's a situation with housing or Social Services and I'm aware that their response is wrong. Then what I will do is get in touch and explain to them – this is what your duty is, and negotiate: "this is what the client needs, this is actually what you should be doing" ... And then if you don't get the appropriate response then you look at what the other options are. So that would be legal options, because often when we are turned down by Social Services I would get a solicitor to challenge them under judicial review. (Coy & Kelly, 2011, p. 26)

This indicates the persistence of the IDVA in accessing support for the victim, which may be beyond the capacity of the victim at that time. The IDVAs do not only keep the focus of the intervention on the victim, but they act as a means to ensure that each participant agency across the collective takes responsibility for its actions, rather than allowing them to become dissipated across the group. They serve as a champion for victim rights, both in individual cases and with the potential to challenge local policy and practice more generally. 'IDVAs were seen, in a positive way, as whistle-blowers and enabling quality assurance checks on the policy and practice of statutory agencies' (Robinson, 2009, p. 18). These kinds of activities can be understood as 'institutional advocacy'. The independence of the IDVA is vital for delivering both individual and institutional advocacy. Thus, many of these positions are funded and managed through NGOs, which provide some independence, but often without the security of statutory services funding and subject to the unreliability of external commissioning patterns (see Turgoose, Chap. 6, this volume).

Extensive research has been able to identify victim advocacy as a key ingredient for producing positive change. An early study conducted in the USA found that access to an advocate led to increased social support and improved quality of life for victims (Sullivan & Bybee, 1999). These findings were echoed by further studies suggesting a range of observable improvements to the well-being of both victims and their children attributed to advocacy including increased safety, decreased abuse, improved access to community resources, decreased depression and stress and better parenting (see NICE, 2014; Shorey, Tirone, & Stuart, 2014). Even more notable is the relationship between the amount of support received and its impact. The more services accessed by a victim, the higher the likelihood of achieving safety, which is identified from a multi-site evaluation of IDVA services by Howarth and Robinson (2015). This suggests the victim advocate has a very valuable role as a gateway to services, as well as a mediator and a representative of the client. It is as a representative, however, where the victim advocate's role needs to be pursued with some delicacy; if a client is exhausted, for example, particularly by the prospect of re-disclosing experiences of abuse to multiple professionals. However, the daunting prospect of attending meetings with a variety of other agencies and the possibility that they may need to argue assertively for restricted resources, may well be something that the victim is grateful to relinquish to someone else. The success of the interaction depends on a healthy and respectful relationship being developed between the client and the advocate in which the wishes and best interests of the client are clearly understood and articulated. This is no mean feat for either party considering the psychological demands of violence and trauma (Payne, 2007; Peled, Eisikovits, Enosh, & Winstok, 2000).

The value of independence as a defining feature of IDVAs and other professionals delivering advocacy within a multi-agency context highlights the fact that such distinctiveness from the other partners can be perceived as healthy. It is also precisely because there are a range of perspectives involved that a partnership can be seen as greater than the sum of its parts. However, the goals and measures of success amongst those representing the agencies at the partnership table are important aspects to consider. A lack of agreement can interfere with effective practice. If the goal of the criminal justice system is to prevent recidivism, the goals of the community sector revolve around the prevention of re-victimisation (Maxwell & Robinson, 2013), linked but non-identical categories. As Hester (2011) has observed, there are several distinct understandings of the gendered nature of domestic violence, which can create contradictions and conflicts in multi-agency working. For instance, child protection workers may see the safety of the child as the mother's priority and ultimate responsibility regardless of the situation within the household (see Little and Garland, Chap. 7, this volume).

There can also be conflicts arising between the institutional cultures and the capacities of various agencies, where some only deal with cases designated as 'high risk' in contrast to others that also address other risk levels. There is also a variation in focus on the victim or the perpetrator between agencies. Some regard achieving immediate safety as the end point for intervention, whereas others wish to work towards establishing an improved quality of life for the victim (Stanley & Humphreys, 2014). Directing resources towards high-risk cases saves lives; however, these cases represent an egregious sub-sample of domestic violence experiences. The vast majority of cases are characterised by a pattern of sub-lethal but recurrent abusive behaviours, resulting in profound issues of psychological distress (Tuerkheimer, 2004). The 'science' behind risk assessment processes is also still relatively new. This raises concerns about whether the high number of decisions that are based on it each year are reliable and justified. Basing service provision on metrics developed from homicide risks could also restrict the implementation of services, which, if delivered at an earlier stage, could prevent further abuse and an escalation to the high-risk category. As Coy and Kelly (2011) note, IDVAs can feel torn when they cannot refer cases designated at standard or medium risk to MARAC even though they believe that person is in need of support. Therefore, ideally, the practice of building and putting into place an evidence-based multi-agency protection plan tailored to the victim's circumstances should be more routinely available to cases meeting a wider range of risk profiles.

Working Together to Maximise Impact

A multitude of barriers have been identified with regard to collaborative work, such as large caseloads, a lack of appropriate services, incomplete data, a lack of knowledge of competing or overlapping services, gaps in screening, a lack of resources and a failure to consider the political bases of each agency. It is also important to be aware of power imbalances between participating agencies, where the agendas of larger organisations can dominate (Hague, 2000). NICE (2014) has recently undertaken a comprehensive review of research into domestic violence responses across health and social care. In 2012, NICE began a process of commissioning and interpreting evidence from five systematic reviews of research into guidance for health and social care professionals. A total of 17 recommendations to promote effective practice were published in 2014, along with the evidence-based assertion (p. 6) that 'Working in a multi-agency partnership is the most effective way to approach the issue at both an operational and strategic level'.[4] The further promotion of participation in 'local strategic multi-agency partnership to prevent domestic violence and abuse' was also recommended by the research, which found moderate support for partnership working to reduce violence, increase referrals and provide victim support using a variety of measures (see also Maxwell & Robinson, 2013; Shorey et al., 2014). It is hoped that the recognition of domestic violence as a health issue will expand multi-agency work and strengthen the 'support' model of dealing with abuse. A greater commitment from the healthcare sector will be a welcome improvement, particularly in terms of widening access to specialist domestic violence support to those victims who initially seek contact and advice from health practitioners.

---

[4] The full guidance and supporting documentation can be found at: www.nice.org.uk/guidance/ph50

Community responses to social issues are perceived to be effective when the collaboration is inclusive, diverse and active, maximising their operational synergy (Allen, 2005). As a result, victims of domestic violence can be referred to a variety of services, which can help them in the short, medium and long term. Initial responses to a crisis situation can evolve into sustained contact with statutory and voluntary agencies, engaging in a long-term management of risk and providing services from counselling to help with education, training or employment. However, the multi-agency approaches already discussed here all rely on an initiating factor, such as a police call-out, or a disclosure to prompt a referral. A gathering of professionals from various sectors is, therefore, only partially representative of a community, where often informal relationships are far more salient than professional ones (Wilcox, 2006). A truly community-based long-term response to domestic violence must reach beyond professional organisations, because for most people, their first disclosure of abuse is to a friend, colleague or family member rather than a person working in a formal capacity (Sylaska & Edwards, 2014). These social networks may include resources that individuals can use to deal with, extricate themselves from and/or seek support with abusive situations. Informal networks also have many benefits that are not apparent amongst professional providers, such as flexibility, proximity, responsiveness and a lack of reliance on state or donor funding. Informal networks do not have any 'case closure' mechanism and so present a greater possibility of providing valuable ongoing support and monitoring. Whilst it must be remembered that some families and communities may also be involved in the commission of acts of abuse (see Oakley and Kinmond, Chap. 10, this volume), many people have been able to draw upon the positive support of their friends, relatives and neighbours during and after their experiences of domestic violence (Taket, O'Doherty, Valpied, & Hegarty, 2014). Initiatives such as 'Cocoon Watch' have been also deployed where, with the victim's consent, the community network is used as a reporting strategy to supplement the victim's own ability to notify any abusive and violent episodes to the police (HMIC, 2014b; Robinson, 2004).

A coordinated community response that goes beyond the initial point of crisis intervention also has the potential to cast its net even wider (Pennington-Zoellner, 2009). Few community-level interventions into domestic violence, for example, have engaged satisfactorily with employers, even though domestic violence is a major cause of lost revenue because of absences from work, employee turnover and decreased productivity in the workforce. Harassment and stalking can often take place at the workplace, and a strategy is required to ensure the victim's safety. Under *the Employment Rights Act 1996*, a company can be held liable if an employee uses workplace collateral in the commission of such a crime, such as using office resources and time, in order to harass a former partner. In cases where an employee has made a disclosure indicating a fear of harm, the employer also has a legal responsibility to ensure her or his safety. There are, therefore, moral, legal and financial motives for employers to engage more fully in coordinated responses to the issue of domestic violence to ensure appropriate policies and practices are in place. This may extend to employers' responsibilities for the health and safety of their employees, be it physical or emotional, under the *Health and Safety at Work Act* 1974 and *the Management of Health and Safety at Work Regulations* 1999. The provision by employers of counselling services and other forms of support may also assist individuals in regaining their confidence, recovering from any trauma and being able to return to work.

The faith and spiritual needs of victims of domestic violence are discussed extensively by Oakley and Kinmond, Chap. 10, in this volume. Religious language and ideas may have been militated by an abuser (Ellison, Bartowski, & Anderson, 1999) and some faith communities may themselves be spiritually abusive and controlling. Some faith leaders seek to reinforce entrenched patriarchal values and may seek to blame the victim and/or insist on the maintenance of a marriage even when it is abusive (Knickmeyer, Levitt, & Horne, 2010; Pyles, 2007). However, victims with a strong faith may also require support from faith leaders and faith community members who are better informed and proactive in the condemnation of domestic violence to assist their recovery.

The majority of women entering shelters have accompanying children (Poole, Beran, & Thurston, 2008) and interventions for children are also an important consideration in the provision of support. Individuals with children may benefit from advice in parenting, given that children within abusive households may be traumatised and may imitate unhealthy patterns of behaviour (see Little and Garland, Chap. 7, this volume). Further trauma can also be transmitted through child contact with the perpetrator, including the manipulation of children to report upon or abuse the resident parent by proxy. Engaging with a community-partnership approach to intervention can lead to an improved tailoring of child protection and support measures.

Moreover, a fully 'joined up' response would incorporate prevention and awareness-raising strategies at a primary level, directed, for instance, at young people through educational institutions. This was the source of some contention recently in Wales, where proposals for reform included the teaching of 'healthy relationships' as part of the core educational curriculum, which was supported by advocates against domestic violence and forced marriage. The original legislative proposals for *the Violence against Women, Domestic Abuse and Sexual Violence (Wales) Act* 2015 included a requirement for one staff member in every school to receive specialist training on domestic violence, sexual bullying, consent, female genital mutilation and forced marriage. Extensive campaigning from a variety of individuals and organisations ensured that these provisions were maintained despite some considerable opposition. The evidence for early intervention to examine young people's expectations of relationships and knowledge of available resources can have long-term effects in terms of reducing violence (O'Leary & Slep, 2012; see also Crowther-Dowey, Gillespie and Hopkins, Chap. 8, this volume). Furthermore, it provides a place to address some emerging issues, such as the use of social media in young people's relationships, which can include online abuse (Yahner, Dank, Zweig, & Lachman, 2015) and can familiarise young people with the indicators of abusive relationships (Renold, 2012).

Evaluating Impact

Research that seeks to evaluate collaborative working presents various challenges (Wandersman & Florin, 2003) and contemporary studies have tended not to focus on the more peripheral elements of a whole-community approach, such as women's access to civil injunctions, healthcare and child support (Shorey et al., 2014). It may prove difficult to separate the effects of collaborative working from individual factors relating to local situations and characteristics. Good practice may not travel across different regions and local efforts to understand the prevalent issues across large cities and rural areas alike need to be made (Standing Together Against Domestic Violence, 2011, p. 7) Whilst several studies have compensated for this by conducting multi-site research, it is difficult to isolate the effects of multi-agency working (Maxwell & Robinson, 2013). Indications of success are often drawn from evidence of reduced levels of risk and recidivism, within standard assessment schema. However, this may not bear any close relation to the victim's level of satisfaction or security. As Coy and Kelly (2011) note, a victim facing hospitalisation because of poor mental health as a result of sustained abuse, may be considered a success in terms of securing their safety, but demonstrates a very poor level of satisfaction by every other measure of their well-being (2011, p. 50). At a more granular level, given the complex interactions that take place, it is difficult to isolate the compounding effects of a single agency or individual response in the context of coordinated partnership (Salazar, Emshoff, Baker, & Crowley, 2007). The role of MARACs and IDVAS, for example, are inextricably linked, which makes it very difficult to discern between the positive impacts of individual advocacy from the effects of multi-agency working. The complexity of collaborative work may provide strong and responsive networks, but it is not necessarily a balanced arrangement, and the workload and resources required may be unevenly spread across the parties involved.

Conclusion

Multi-agency responses appear to be an effective way of combining the capacities of all of the relevant agencies within a local area. It is fitting that domestic violence, as a crime that has major impact on the community, is one that takes a coordinated community approach to address it. Independent advocacy for the victim appears to be a vital component, providing a situation in which the advocate acts as a proxy between the client and the formal agencies as the central pivot of the multi-agency approach, organising and collating casefile data, liaising between agencies and linking between agencies and the client.

However, it is important to recognise the limits of current arrangements, to encourage continued innovation and improvement in the response to domestic violence. The proliferation of a multi-agency system designed to deal effectively with the most high-risk cases of domestic violence is an important achievement and one that was unimaginable a decade ago. The interagency relationships built and supported within the MARAC system may also be useful in the long-term management of the most severe cases of violence and abuse within a community. However, MARACs should also consider the contextual issues of each case and be more flexible in their format, for example, where a more restricted range of partners may be appropriate to ensure more limited disclosures. Those cases that do not meet the MARAC threshold may also lose out on the benefits of collaborative working because of differing cut-off points for support between agencies, high demands for resources and/or a failure to identify ongoing needs. The demand for a clear multi-agency model of working for *all* victims is the most poignant critique of current MARAC arrangements. Whilst other coordinated community responses may go some way towards achieving this, it is currently the risk model that dominates agency decisions about the level of involvement required, particularly from those in the statutory sector. It would appear, therefore, that there is scope for further reflection and development to ensure that all of those individuals who are affected by the issues of harm raised here are given the best possible chance of a life free from violence.

References

Allen, N. E. (2005). A multi-level analysis of community coordinating councils. *American Journal of Community Psychology, 35*(1–2), 49–63.

Allen, N. E., Bybee, D. I., & Sullivan, C. M. (2005). Battered women's multitude of needs: Evidence supporting the need for comprehensive advocacy. *Violence Against Women, 10*(9), 1015–1035.

Bacchus, L. J. (2013). *Health sector responses to domestic violence: Promising intervention models in primary and maternity health care settings in Europe*. London: London School of Hygiene and Tropical Medicine.

Berry, G., Briggs, P., Erol, R., & van Staden, L. (2009). *The effectiveness of partnership working in a crime and disorder context: A rapid evidence assessment.* London: Home Office.

Buzawa, E. S., Buzawa, C. G., & Stark, E. (2012). *Responding to domestic violence: The integration of criminal justice and human services* (4th ed.). Los Angeles: SAGE.

CAADA. (2010). *Saving lives, saving money: MARACs and high risk domestic abuse.* Bristol: CAADA.

Coy, M., & Kelly, L. (2011). *Islands in the stream: An evaluation of four London independent domestic violence advocacy schemes.* London: Child and Woman Abuse Studies Unit, London Metropolitan University.

Crime and Disorder Act 1998 c37. Retrieved October 29, 2015, from http://www.legislation.gov.uk/ukpga/1998/37/contents

Ellison, C. G., Bartowski, J. P., & Anderson, K. L. (1999). Are there religious variations in domestic violence? *Journal of Family Issues, 20*(1), 87–113.

Employment Rights Act 1996 c18. Retrieved October 29, 2015, from http://www.legislation.gov.uk/ukpga/1996/18/contents

Forell, C. (2013). Stopping the violence: Mandatory arrest and police tort liability for failure to assist battered women. *Berkeley Journal of Gender, Law and Justice, 6*(2), 215–262.

Gracia, E. (2004). Unreported cases of domestic violence against women: Towards an epidemiology of social silence, tolerance, and inhibition. *Journal of Epidemiology and Community Health, 58*(7), 535–537.

Hague, G. (2000). *Reducing domestic violence: What works? Multi-agency fora.* London: Home Office.

Health and Safety at Work Act 1974. Retrieved October 29, 2015, from http://www.hse.gov.uk/legislation/hswa.htm

Her Majesty's Inspectorate of Constabulary. (2014a). *Everryone's business: Improving the police response to domestic violence.* London: HMIC.

Her Majesty's Inspectorate of Constabulary. (2014b). *West Yorkshire Police's approach to tackling domestic abuse.* London: HMIC.

Hester, M. (2011). The three planet model: Towards an understanding of contradictions in approaches to women and children's safety in contexts of domestic violence. *British Journal of Social Work, 41*(5), 837–853.

Howarth, E., & Robinson, A. L. (2015). Responding effectively to women experiencing severe abuse: Identifying key components in a British advocacy intervention. *Violence Against Women.* Retrieved October 29, 2015, from http://vaw.sagepub.com/content/early/2015/08/05/1077801215597789.abstract

Howarth, E., Stimpson, L., Barran, D., & Robinson, A. (2009). *Safety in numbers: A multi-site evaluation of independent domestic violence advisor services*. London: Hestia Trust.

Kelman, S., Hong, S., & Turbitt, I. (2011). Are there managerial practices associated with the outcomes of an interagency service delivery collaboration? Evidence from British Crime and disorder Reduction Partnerships. *Journal of Public Administration Research and Theory, 23*(3), 609–630.

Klevens, J., Baker, C. J., Shelley, G. A., & Ingram, E. M. (2008). Exploring the links between components of coordinated community responses and their impact on contact with intimate partner violence services. *Violence Against Women, 14*(3), 346–358.

Knickmeyer, N., Levitt, H., & Horne, S. G. (2010). Putting on Sunday best: The silencing of battered women within Christian faith communities. *Feminism & Psychology, 20*(1), 94–113.

Krug, E. G., Dahlberg, L. L., Mercy, J. A., Zwi, A. B., & Luzano, R. (2002). *World report on violence on health*. Geneva: World Health Organisation.

Mahapatro, M. (2014). Control and support models of help-seeking behavior in women experiencing domestic violence in India. *Violence and Victims, 29*(3), 464–475.

Management of Health and Safety at Work Regulations 1999 No. 3242. Retrieved October 29, 2015, from http://www.legislation.gov.uk/uksi/1999/3242/contents/made

Manjoo, R. (2014). *Special Rapporteur on violence against women finalizes country mission to the United Kingdom and Northern Ireland and calls for urgent action to address the accountability deficit and also the adverse impacts of changes in funding and services*. Retrieved August 12, 2015, from http://www.ohchr.org/en/newsevents/pages/displaynews.aspx?newsid=14514&

Maxwell, C. D., & Robinson, A. L. (2013). *Can interventions reduce recidivism and re-victimisation following adult intimate partner violence incidents?* Washington, DC: Forum on Global Violence Prevention, Institute of Medicine, National Academy of Sciences.

Muftić, L. R., & Bouffard, J. A. (2007). An evaluation of gender differences in the implementation and impact of a comprehensive approach to domestic violence. *Violence Against Women, 13*(1), 46–69.

NICE. (2014). *Domestic violence and abuse: How health services, social care and the organisations they work with can respond effectively*. Retrieved October 29, 2015, from https://www.nice.org.uk/guidance/ph50

O'Leary, K. D., & Slep, A. M. S. (2012). Prevention of partner violence by focusing on behaviors of both young males and females. *Prevention Science, 13*(4), 329–339.

Office of National Statistics. (2015). *Crime statistics. Focus on violent crime and sexual offences 2012/2013 release.* Retrieved October 24, 2015, from http://www.ons.gov.uk/ons/rel/crime-stats/crime-statistics/focus-on-violent-crime-and-sexual-offences--2012-13/rpt---chapter-4---intimate-personal-violence-and-partner-abuse.html#tab-conclusions

Payne, B. K. (2007). Victim advocates perceptions of the role of health care workers in sexual assault cases. *Criminal Justice Policy Review, 18*(1), 81–94.

Payton, J. L. (2014). "Honor", collectivity and agnation: Emerging risk factors in "honor"-based violence. *Journal of Interpersonal Violence, 29*(15), 2863–2883.

Peled, E., Eisikovits, Z., Enosh, G., & Winstok, Z. (2000). Choice and empowerment for battered women who stay: Towards a constructivist model. *Social Work, 45*(1), 9–25.

Pence, E. L., & McMahon, M. (1997). *A coordinated community responses to domestic violence.* Minnesota: DAIP.

Pennington-Zoellner, K. (2009). Expanding "community" in the community response to intimate partner violence. *Journal of Family Violence, 24*, 539–545.

Pollit, C. (2003). Joined-up government: A survey. *Political Studies Review, 1*(1), 34–49.

Poole, A., Beran, T., & Thurston, W. E. (2008). Direct and indirect services for children in domestic violence shelters. *Journal of Family Violence, 23*(8), 679–686.

Pyles, L. (2007). The complexities of the religious response to domestic violence – Implications for faith-based initiatives. *Affilia-Journal of Women and Social Work, 22*(3), 281–291.

Renold, E. (2012). *Boys and girls speak out: A qualitative study of children's gender and sexual cultures (age 10–12).* Cardiff: Cardiff University; NSPCC; Children's Commissioner for Wales.

Robinson, A. L. (2004). *Domestic violence MARACs (Multi-Agency Risk Assessment Conferences) for very high right victims in Cardiff, Wales: A process and outcome evaluation.* Cardiff: Cardiff University.

Robinson, A. L. (2009). *Independent domestic violence advisors: A multisite process evaluation funded by the Home Office.* Cardiff: School of Social Sciences, Cardiff University.

Robinson, A. L. (2010). Risk and intimate partner violence. In H. Kemshall & B. Wilkinson (Eds.), *Good practice in risk assessment and risk management* (3rd ed.). London: Jessica Kingsley Publishers.

Robinson, A. L., & Clancy, A. (2015). *Development of the Priority Perpetrator Identification Tool (PPIT) for domestic abuse*. Cardiff: Cardiff University.

Robinson, A. L., & Tregida, J. (2007). The perceptions of high-risk victims of domestic violence to a coordinated community response in Cardiff, Wales. *Violence Against Women, 13*(11), 1130–1148.

Salazar, L. F., Emshoff, J., Baker, C. K., & Crowley, T. (2007). Examining the behavior of a system: An outcome evaluation of a coordinated community response to domestic violence. *Journal of Family Violence, 22*, 631–641.

Shepherd, M. F., & Pence, E. L. (1999). *Coordinating community responses to domestic violence: Lessons from Duluth and beyond*. Thousand Oaks: SAGE.

Shorey, R. C., Tirone, V., & Stuart, G. L. (2014). Coordinated community response components for victims of intimate partner violence: A review of the literature. *Aggression and Violent Behavior, 19*(4), 363–371.

Standing Together Against Domestic Violence. (2011). *In search of excellence: A guide to effective domestic violence partnerships*. London: Standing Together Against Domestic Violence.

Stanley, N., & Humphreys, C. (2014). Multi-agency risk assessment and management for children and families experiencing domestic violence. *Children and Youth Services Review, 75*(1), 78–85.

Steel, N., Blakeborough, L., & Nicholas, S. (2011). *Supporting high-risk victims of domestic violence: A review of Multi-Agency Risk Assessment Conferences (MARACs)*. London: Home Office.

Sullivan, C. M., & Bybee, D. I. (1999). Reducing violence using community-based advocacy for women with abusive partners. *Journal of Consulting and Clinical Psychology, 67*(1), 43–53.

Sylaska, K. M., & Edwards, K. M. (2014). Disclosure of intimate partner violence to informal social support network members: A review of the literature. *Trauma Violence & Abuse, 15*(1), 3–21.

Taket, A., O'Doherty, L., Valpied, J., & Hegarty, K. (2014). What do Australian women experiencing intimate partner abuse want from family and friends? *Qualitative Health Research, 24*(7), 983–996.

Tickle, L. (2014). Domestic violence: How services come together to support high risk victims. *The Guardian*, November 25, 2014.

Tuerkheimer, D. (2004). Recognizing and remedying the harm to battering: A call to criminalize domestic violence. *Journal of Criminal Law and Criminology, 94*(4), 971–972.

Violence Against Women, Domestic Abuse and Sexual Violence (Wales) Act 2015 anaw 3. Retrieved October 29, 2015, from http://www.legislation.gov.uk/anaw/2015/3/contents/enacted

Wandersman, A., & Florin, P. (2003). Community interventions and effective prevention. *American Psychologist, 58*, 441–448.

Wilcox, P. (2006). Communities, care and domestic violence. *Critical Social Policy, 26*(4), 722–747.

Wilson, A. (2013). *Racism, surveillance, and managing gender violence in the UK*. Retrieved August 1, 2015, from https://www.opendemocracy.net/5050/amrit-wilson/racism-surveillance-and-managing-gender-violence-in-uk

Yahner, J., Dank, M., Zweig, J. M., & Lachman, P. (2015). The co-occurrence of physical and cyber dating violence and bullying among teens. *Journal of Interpersonal Violence, 30*(7), 1079–1089.

13

Working with Perpetrators of Domestic Violence and Abuse: The Potential for Change

Sarah Hilder and Caroline Freeman

Introduction

The historical challenges of recognising domestic violence and abuse (DVA) as a social issue and public concern are well known. A position that broadly contends that strategies of protection, prevention and intervention are required to support victims in situations of DVA is now generally undisputed across the UK and wider European community. However, many of the risk assessment and safety planning structures adopted to date have pursued a victim-centred approach, which has led to insufficient attention being given to the role of DVA perpetrators and their capacity for behavioural change. 'Criminalising' DVA behaviours and establishing a symbolic recognition of their severity, established via

S. Hilder (✉)
Community and Criminal Justice Division,
De Montfort University, Leicester, UK

C. Freeman
FreeVa, Leicester, UK

© The Editor(s) (if applicable) and The Author(s) 2016
S. Hilder, V. Bettinson (eds.), *Domestic Violence*,
DOI 10.1057/978-1-137-52452-2_13

legal provisions and sanctions, dominated earlier campaigns for greater protection. However, one of the ramifications of such an approach was that the view of the perpetrator became one-dimensional, based predominantly on the level of threat that they posed and with little, if any, sense of their responsibilities for reducing risks in the future.

Measures to contain, exclude and restrain the perpetrator are essential tools for protection at various stages in many cases of DVA, although they only serve to manage a risk of harm for a specified period. Many individuals who use DVA will continue to have relationships, or some form of contact with their victims, or they will move on to form new intimate relationships. Therefore, a willingness to explore the potential for perpetrator rehabilitation, changes in their behaviour and reductions in risk in the longer term remains vital, as it does for other forms of violent and sexual offending. This realisation has now been acknowledged internationally, most recently by Article 16 of the Council of Europe (Istanbul) Convention on preventing violence against women and domestic violence (Council of Europe, 2011). This instrument identifies the need for programmes of intervention, which teach non-violent behaviours to perpetrators, to be established alongside and in coordination with specialist services for victims. However, 'what works' with DVA perpetrators in this respect remains a matter of some perplexity and contention.

Reflecting the dominance of the focus given to heterosexual male perpetrators of DVA, this chapter commences by providing a brief overview of perpetrator programme developments in the UK, which seek to establish behavioural change, highlighting the diverging approaches that are apparent in the statutory and voluntary sectors. It examines developments in understandings of the complex nature of DVA and the impact of academic discourse and theoretical concepts on perpetrator work. The ongoing controversy as to whether a gendered perspective has a place in perpetrator interventions is highlighted, together with arguments for broader understandings of the ways in which a diverse range of identity factors may shape experiences of and responses to DVA. Some of the key challenges of programme evaluation and perpetrator engagement are noted, with a particular focus on how success is measured and the limited availability of any robust evidence of programme effectiveness. The chapter concludes with a discussion of referral agency responsibilities and suggestions for the developments needed to increase and sustain perpetrator engagement in programme work and longer term relapse prevention.

An Overview of Perpetrator Programme Development in the UK

As the profile of violence against women in the domestic sphere increased from the 1970s onwards, working with perpetrators of DVA was not originally seen to be a priority, desirable or even realistic. There were commonly held assumptions, particularly from pro-feminist groups, that the protection of women from violent men was the paramount concern and that the potential for rehabilitation and positive change in perpetrator behaviour was extremely limited (Harne & Radford, 2008). Other stakeholders have also been sceptical about the impact of perpetrator programmes, but due more to the lack of any strong evidence of the effectiveness of existing programmes (Morran, 2013) rather than any condonation of the ultimate aim of changing perpetrator behaviours.

The majority of DVA perpetrator programmes are group work-orientated and adopt cognitive behavioural or psycho-educational approaches, although the prevalence of individual one-to-one therapies is also increasing. The Duluth Model, which first incorporated a perpetrator programme into its coordinated response to DVA in Minnesota in the late 1970s (Pence & Paymar, 1993), continues to be the most renowned and widely adopted approach. However, its efficacy is viewed to be less potent if the gendered analysis of power and control, for which it is known, is adopted in isolation from an integrated agency approach, which includes victim safety support strategies and police liaison (Phillips, Kelly, & Westmarland, 2013). The late 1980s onwards saw the development of the DVA perpetrator programme CHANGE in Scotland and the Domestic Violence Intervention Programme (DVIP) in London. Perpetrator programmes were originally run by the voluntary sector, informed by specialist DVA services for victims and adopted the Duluth, gendered approach, locating DVA within patriarchal societal structures (Mullender & Burton, 2001). As other programmes were instigated in other parts of the UK, the National Practitioner's Network for Domestic Violence Intervention Programmes (1992–2010) emerged as an informal body, which sought to share and develop best practice in working with perpetrators to change behaviours and reduce the risk of harm to victims. It served as the forerunner to RESPECT, a national organisation establishing a statement of principles and minimum standards for voluntary sector Domestic Violence Perpetrator Programmes (DVPPs) in 2004. The accreditation of programmes is central to RESPECT's present day remit, although there is a clear change in its mandate, which now includes the support of male victims, the development of female perpetrator programmes, interventions for those in abusive LGB and/or T relationships and work with young people at risk of experiencing DVA behaviours. Elsewhere, other voluntary sector perpetrator programmes that adopt a gender-neutral approach to addressing violence in intimate relationships have emerged. Some have utilised motivational interviewing techniques (Farrell & Young, 2015) and make links to a wider range of psychological studies, which explore the value and impact of a therapeutical alliance.[1]

Within the criminal justice system, the Probation Service took a primary role in addressing DVA perpetrator behaviours from the late 1990s onwards, strongly influenced by wider developments in statutory accredited offending behaviour programmes, which favoured cognitive behavioural methods. Whilst the Integrated Domestic Abuse Programme (IDAP) adopted by probation provides a gendered analysis perspective to work with DVA perpetrators, other accredited probation programmes, such as the Community Domestic Violence Programme (CDVP), Building Better Relationships and the more recent Building Healthy Relationships programme do not assume a gendered connection. From 2000 onwards, court mandated perpetrator programmes were delivered entirely by the Probation Service, with a small handful of prisons also running the Building Better Relationships programme. By 2005, the Probation Service had trained its own personnel to run IDAP as an 'in

---

[1] For more information on the therapeutical alliance, see 'Alternatives to Violence Therapy Project' Norwegian Centre for Violence and Traumatic Stress (2014). A study of process outcomes of therapy of men who seek help for their use of violence: http://www.nkvts.no/en/Pages/ProjectInfo.aspx?prosjektid=1281

house' provision, with specialist DVA services partnerships maintained to provide victim support contact. Court mandated and non-court mandated programme provisions started to pursue quite different pathways. For the statutory sector, this was very much influenced by mainstream criminal justice practice, which favoured a rational calculator model.[2]

Following a further period of restructuring in 2014, the National Probation Service of England and Wales became subject to yet further demands for greater efficiency and cost-effectiveness, which influenced tendencies to favour shorter, brief therapy interventions. The 'Transforming Rehabilitation' (Ministry of Justice, 2013) agenda and the delegation of medium- to low-risk offending behaviour work to the newly formed private Community Rehabilitation Companies (CRCs) introduced yet another dimension to DVA perpetrator work. There are concerns that the dynamics of DVA and the potential for a rapid escalation in the level of harm posed are not well served by offender management structures, which separate levels of risk in this manner, across two different organisations. CRCs may not be best equipped to recognise and respond to any swift amplification of seriousness (Gilbert, 2013), although some regional CRCs may turn to the specialist DVA sector and form new alliances in the future to develop practice in this area. However, different strategies for the resourcing of DVA programme interventions are likely to occur, and further geographical variants may materialise.

For DVPPs in the voluntary and community sector, the challenges of commissioning frameworks have been keenly felt. An increase in recent times of DVPP referrals emanating from the family courts, Children and Family Court Advisory and Support Services (CAFCASS), local authority children's services and self-referrals by perpetrators has also been apparent. Often couched as early intervention perpetrator work, this diversity of pathways onto a DVPP raises a number of important issues, not the least of which is how the threshold point for a criminal prosecution of DVA is determined and by whom. Care must be taken to ensure that victims remain supported and empowered to pursue a legal redress,

---

[2] Rational Calculator Model, emanating from rational choice theory, also known as rational action theory, assumes that the commission of criminal acts is self-determined and purposeful to maximise individual pleasure and achievement. Less attention is given to the social construction of crime and the role of socio-political factors and structural inequalities. See Clarke and Felson (1997).

whether it be a criminal prosecution or civil injunction, but arguably this becomes more challenging in the context of a 'whole family' approach to DVA intervention (see Little and Garland, Chap. 7, this volume). The expanding array of DVA perpetrator work across criminal justice, civil court and social care functions may also result in some perpetrators acquiring a sense of quite profound injustice due to their perceptions of differential treatment. The implications for perpetrator engagement are revisited later in this chapter. Firstly, however, this discussion turns to the expanding array of theoretical understandings of DVA and their links to the content of perpetrator programmes.

Linking Theory to Practice

Kemshall, Kelly, Wilkinson, and Hilder (2015) provide some insight into the range of theoretical approaches, which have been adopted to work with violent offenders and more specifically, perpetrators of DVA. They cite Babcock, Tharp, Sharp, Heppner and Stanford (2014), who highlight the importance of recognising the differences between DVA where the violence utilised is instrumental and other scenarios where the harm caused is as a result of reactive and expressive violence (see also Kemshall et al., 2015, p. 10).

Instrumental and Expressive Typologies of DVA

Instrumental violence, where behaviours have an underpinning purpose, aims to dominate the victim and has been linked latterly to Stark's (2007) more detailed work on the use of coercion and control and Johnson's (2008) typology of intimate terrorism. Here, the perpetrator utilises a range of strategies in a systematic manner to oppress and intimidate the victim. Expressive violence, on the other hand, can be linked to concepts of anger management and Johnson's (2008) typology of situational couple violence, where the violence and abuse are reactions to an emotional trigger and are characterised more by a lack of self-control. Initially, perpetrator work, particularly within the statutory sector, often addressed

DVA as a form of expressive violence only, with male offenders often being sent on anger management courses. For some of the perpetrators, who were indeed using expressive violence, this may well have been a useful course of action. However, as understandings of coercive forms of DVA have increased and the psychological impact of DVA is more fully understood, the intimate terrorist image of a DVA perpetrator has tended to dominate in policy and professional practice. It is now more routinely recognised that DVA may involve a broader range of coercive behaviours, which may, or may not, include direct physical and sexual assault. Treating this form of DVA as an anger management problem is unhelpful at best and dangerous at worst, as escalating risk factors may not be noted and the realities of the victim's experience are not addressed.

However, expressive violence can also be very serious and may result in victim fatality. In this respect, De Wall, Anderson, and Bushman (2011) further developed the General Aggression Model and applied it to situations of DVA with some success. The model focused on expressive elements demonstrated by the perpetrator, the cognitive inputs leading to a violent episode, affective and arousal routes and outcomes of decision-making processes. DVA cases can be further complicated by an intertwining of instrumental and expressive violence within one relationship. In some cases, the victims may also respond to their situation with violent resistance, whereby the victims themselves use violence in an attempt to manage and/or resist the oppressive, instrumental violence of the perpetrators (Johnson, 2008). Robinson, Clancy, and Hanks (2014) highlight that whilst serial offending is not always an indication of high risk, it is important that relationships between frequency, severity and impact are fully understood. A series of incidents, which, if considered individually, may appear to be of low-level severity, but which are occurring at a high-level frequency, can cause significant psychological damage (Stark, 2009).

Emerging from Johnson's (2008) typologies, Friend, Cleary-Bradley, Thatcher, and Gottman (2011) evaluated a screening tool for identifying different types of DVA, by comparing couples who were identified via the use of the tool as experiencing situational violence, to a previously collected sample of "characterologically" (intimate terrorist) violent couples, distressed non-violent couples and situationally violent couples. Significantly, they found that physical violence domains were closely comparable in severity across all of the DVA types, be it an expressive or instrumental category, but psychological violence domains were far more prevalent in the characterological scenarios. What this suggests is that although the level of physical violence across a number of cases may appear to be very similar, the type of DVA that is actually occurring may be very different. Currently, risk assessment processes tend to focus on escalating patterns of physical and sexual assault as indicators of a high risk of harm and these, in turn, often inform the type of intervention that may be undertaken with a perpetrator. The instrumental or expressive function of the violence can be overlooked and in particular, the harm caused by severe instrumental psychological abuse, where there is no physical or sexual contact, remains unlikely to attract a high-risk assessment or a programme referral. A number of programme providers have recognised that there will be a diversity of DVA 'types' within any one perpetrator programme cohort and have sought to try and accommodate a range of possible typology variations in the strategies utilised. This is often characterised by a broader-based approach to the gendered analysis of the DVA, combined with an exploratory approach to individual concepts of identity, masculinity and the function of the DVA for each participant (RESPECT, 2015a).

Johnson (2008) notes that taking a gendered approach to work with men displaying expressive situational couple violence appears to do no harm and they are the most likely to complete DVA programmes, whatever the underpinning ideology. He also suggests that those demonstrating the systematic controlling, coercive forms of DVA, the intimate terrorists, fall into two categories: anti-social, where violence is also used elsewhere and 'emotionally dependent', where violence and abuse are only utilised at home against their partner. Johnson cites Saunders (1996) who found that cognitive behavioural interventions, which also incorporated a feminist perspective to address the gendered nature of the attitudes, thoughts and behaviours exhibited by perpetrators, were twice as effective for the anti-social category. However, a more individualistic psychodynamic approach was twice as effective for those who were seen as emotionally dependent. These categorisations by Johnson mirror the differentiations of 'generalists' and 'specialists', which have been utilised in work with sex offenders for some time (Soothill, Francis, Sanderson, & Ackerley, 2000). The concepts may prove to have some mileage in the development of a more targeted range of perpetrator programmes, investigating Johnson's observations in more detail and the value of 'generalist' and 'specialist' approaches for DVA.

Attachment theory discourses call for conjoint work and other forms of individually assessed psychological interventions have prevailed in other perpetrator literature (see Bowen, Gilchrist, & Beech, 2005; RESPECT, 2015b). Representing the commission of DVA as some form of psychological disorder, however, has been met with some resistance, particularly by those active in early feminist campaigns, which sought to bring to the fore the intimate partner terrorism that occurred in heterosexual relationships, committed by males. Psychological discourses of dependency, poor ego functioning, low self-esteem, unresolved conflicts and emotional repression have been seen to reduce the perpetrator's sense of responsibility for their actions and the benefits gained from it (Harne & Radford, 2008). Mullender and Burton (2001) also highlight the limitations of a response, which focuses on cognitive skills deficits with perpetrators who may function in a positive and reasoned manner in other aspects of their life.

Gender, Intersectionality and Perpetrator Programmes

The analytical model, developed by the Domestic Abuse Intervention Project, Duluth, Minnesota, USA (DAIP, 2015), seeks to illustrate the gendered nature of the strategies of control employed in situations of DVA, where the male perpetrator utilises power resources that are not uniformly accessible to women. For example, the ability to exercise economic control in a relationship is more easily achievable for a man, whilst average national incomes for males and females continue to be disparate. The gendered power at the centre of the Duluth wheel is also mediated by other societal structures such as law, religion and cultural discourses of masculinity, male dominance and gendered defined roles (Harne & Radford, 2008; see also Bishop, Chap. 4; Martin, Chap. 9; Oakley and Kinmond Chap. 10, this volume).

These issues may manifest differently depending on the patriarchal community, cultural and religious context within which the DVA occurs, but are also set within broader societal frameworks where messages regarding the gendered 'place' of women may still abound. Perpetrators are seen to draw upon sexist attitudes, gender stereotypes and misogyny, which are still inherent in modern society. Women can be seen as responsible for upholding family honour and the 'respectable' image of family life, with the 'shame' of any disclosure of DVA bearing heavily upon them rather than the perpetrator, sometimes to the point of their total destruction and murder (Home Affairs Committee, 2008). Pro-feminist approaches to interventions with heterosexual male perpetrators aim to enable an individual to recognise that DVA is purposeful and that they can make a decision to be non-violent. Gendered stereotypes and rationales that may be put forward to justify the DVA are examined, and the symbolic function, status and/or reward that the DVA represents for perpetrator are addressed, usually via a combination of cognitive behavioural and educational approaches.

More latterly aspects of this gendered analysis of DVA and in particular, an investigation of constructions of masculinity are being incorporated into earlier prevention and intervention work with young people, as discussed elsewhere in this volume (Crowther-Dowey, Gillespie and Hopkins, Chap. 8). The impact of mentoring support is also being examined with high-risk, heterosexual male perpetrators of DVA, as an opportunity for positive prosocial modelling and a reconstruction of more positive concepts of masculinity (Walker, 2015). A gendered role perspective has also been seen as useful when examining the experiences of male victims. The impact of DVA for male victims is often dismissed because of gendered assumptions that males should not 'allow' themselves to be at the receiving end of controlling abusive behaviours, particularly if they are exhibited by females, and should simply 'toughen up' (Martin, Chap. 9, this volume). Thus, a gendered understanding of DVA does not, as is commonly purported, deny heterosexual or gay male victim experiences and concepts of hegemonic masculinity are particularly relevant to both (Gadd, 2004). It is also important to consider women as agents of violence, both against men and within same-sex relationships. This is supported in England and Wales by the Home Office definition of DVA, which identifies that it cuts across gender and sexuality (Home Office, 2013). However, understandings of the extent to which commonalities and differences exist in the commission of DVA across different types of intimate partner relationships remain in their infancy. The largest body of research evidence, to date, about the use of abusive behaviours in lesbian, gay, bisexual and/or transgender (LGB and/or T) relationships, the Coral Project, is discussed elsewhere in this volume (Barnes and Donovan, Chap. 14). However, it remains to be the case that very little is known about female violence more generally, let alone in the domestic sphere, although certain characteristic trends have been identified (see Hester, 2009; Kemshall et al., 2015). Practitioners and academics who advocate for a gender-neutral approach to DVA perpetrator work have argued its transferability to work with female perpetrators. Resourcing a universally transferable programme option is also clearly more appealing for funders than a series of more specialised approaches. Until further research has been undertaken to determine the most effective strategies for working with female DVA perpetrators, practitioners are often forced to retreat to a 'something is better than nothing' position, which sees them apply male perpetrator programme principles in one-to-one work with women.

It has been argued that this gendered analysis of DVA leads to interventions based on an ideology rather than evidence. Dixon, Archer and Graham-Kevan (2012) argue that there is recognition in psychological literature that understandings of behaviours are rooted in the individual and for a DVA perpetrator, for example, they may be linked to fears of abandonment, distorted methods for resolving conflict or an incapacity to manage difficult emotions. They contend that without this individual functional assessment, it is impossible to intervene and the criminogenic need principle of any intervention will not be met. However, they continue, that it should not be assumed that this function is linked to patriarchal values (Dixon et al., 2012). Brownridge (2009) states that a feminist position, which supposes a universal heightened potential of DVA occurring towards all females, is understandable considering how long it has taken to get gender equality issues established within the DVA debate. However, he argues that this generalisation denies the diverse experiences of DVA that occur. A more sophisticated analysis of gender has been called for, which seeks to understand how gender is differentially constructed in everyday relations and activities (Westmarland & Kelly, 2013).

Others have advocated a much broader understanding of intersectionality and the multiple factors other than gender that impact on definitions, risks, experiences, consequences and responses to the violence and abuse that occur between intimate partners (Brownridge, 2009). Black women, for example, are over-represented in rates of severe violence and femicide, which has mainly been attributed by Sokoloft and Dupont (2005) to socio-economic differences and financial strains (as cited by Brownridge, 2009). Whilst Brownridge (2009) agrees that addressing patriarchal structures and sexual proprietary attitudes in broader society is important in reducing DVA, collective attitudes, beliefs and dynamics within smaller communities also need to be examined, particularly for those communities that function in a more isolated manner. Broader theoretical positions on perceptions of risks within society highlight that DVA will be recognised as a concern only in cases where there are jointly held sensitivities, which agree that it is harmful and unacceptable (Douglas 1966 as cited in Denney, 2005). The victim's voice is unlikely to be heard, and the perpetrator's behaviour will not be condemned and addressed if interactions at familial, community and cultural levels support such conduct (see Oakley and Kinmond, Chap. 10, this volume). The significance of environmental and contextual factors will, of course, vary in their relevance to each individual situation of DVA, but have the potential to provide further insight into both perpetrator and victim behaviours. Whilst these factors are included to some extent in risk assessment tools, addressing the specific ways in which a DVA perpetrator may target and exploit such factors is not always fully understood.

Johnson (2008) states that the ongoing contentions between those at opposing ends of the gendered approach to DVA are unhelpful. He suggests that it merely needs to be recognised that different types of DVA can occur and that an understanding of these differences is vital to ensure that the approach to intervention is effective. To dismiss the knowledge accumulated from feminist models to date would be foolish, but an openness to new ideas and the application and combination of alternative frameworks may also have something very positive to offer.

Desistance from DVA

The theoretical discourse of desistance is more familiar in its application to general offending and sexual offending patterns. However, it also has a place in theoretical understandings and practical responses to DVA. Here, the focus turns from risk assessment and causation, towards an exploration of why some perpetrators stop being violent. Walker, Bowen, and Brown (2013) undertook a critical review of desistance literature and examined 15 different studies that looked directly at the cessation of DVA by heterosexual men. They highlight the challenges of a desistance perspective, which focuses on protective factors rather than risk and criminogenic needs. This includes the pursuit of human and instrumental goods that lead to the formation of a long-term non-offending identity. It has been shown that some men do stop committing acts of DVA, and their aggression is not stable (Walker et al., 2013). This refutes the assumption supported by early research evidence, that once violence has been used, it will always continue, escalating in frequency and severity. Walker et al. (2013) found that perpetrators with shorter histories of violence, which was less severe, had a greater probability of desistance, supporting an argument for early intervention and prevention strategies.

When seeking to secure a cessation from DVA, desistance frameworks do not necessarily prioritise the need to address attitudes, beliefs and cognitive skills over other changes in the perpetrator's situation. Desistance factors, which have been found to inhibit the commission of general offending patterns, include relationship stability, although clearly with DVA the intimate relationship is also the site of the harmful behaviour. The 'quality' of a relationship is, therefore, brought more keenly into focus (Walker et al., 2013). Those specialist perpetrators who are only violent and abusive in the family home have been found to be more likely to desist than generalists, who demonstrate a wide range of violent and anti-social behaviour, both within the domestic sphere and in other social contexts. This indicates that developing or sustaining positive interactions outside of the domestic relationship may be conducive to positive change within the intimate relationship. There are also indications that in cases where perpetrators make a public disclosure to family or friends of their motivation to address their DVA behaviours, they are more likely to do so (Fagan, 1989 as cited by Walker et al., 2013). This can again be linked to their investment in building wider social capital and support as a catalyst for personal change.

Perpetrator accounts of the positive changes they have been able to make are generally not relied upon in research. However, Morran (2013) highlights that to totally dismiss them would mean that an understanding of long-term desistance is incomplete and methods established to facilitate agency, personal change and growth rendered inadequate. Morran (2013) interviewed a small sample of 11 perpetrators over a period of 2–7 years following perpetrator programme completion. The study sought to examine the concepts of maturity, agency, social bonds, networks and personal narrative, which are prevalent in desistance literature and explored their resonance with the DVA perpetrators over time. All of the participants referred to powerful patriarchal attitudes in their formative years and a lack of any encouragement to develop positive emotional literacy skills in their early development and formative relationships. This had then extended into their expectations of adult relationships. They highlighted their adoption of primary desistance techniques to stop their use of controlling behaviours in the short-term, but also the need to work on a secondary, permanent desistance from DVA, which was aligned to a changing personal narrative and the sense of 'becoming a different person'. Self-regulation was seen as important and the negative impact of oppressive constructions of masculinity, power and control were acknowledged. Developing new interests, positive engagements with others and new social groups were also valued. Whilst strong conclusions should not be drawn from such a small-scale study, the observations suggest that perpetrator interventions that rely on participation on behavioural change programmes as a singular strategy are likely to have a limited impact. Desistance theorists contend that a more holistic approach to understanding an individual's journey towards a cessation of DVA needs to be pursued. This links to strength-based work, which examines personal narrative and agency, individual aspirations and how they might be positively (re)constructed and achieved (Ward, Mann, & Gannon, 2007), acknowledging that the legitimate pursuit of such goals is likely to result in the reduction of further illegal, harmful acts occurring.

The Challenges of Evaluation and Engagement

Evaluating the impact of DVA perpetrator programmes remains problematic. Studies undertaken are rife with varying definitions and terminologies, and measurements of success have tended to rely on evidence of recidivism and the further commission of violence alone (Gondolf, 2004). Low reporting rates for DVA and the attrition that is known to occur within the criminal justice system highlight concerns with this approach. Official data are likely to be inaccurate and may underestimate repeat acts of abuse (Mullender & Burton, 2001). Perpetrator self-report is also often considered to be unreliable, as highlighted previously (Morran, 2013) and devising longer term methods for effectively tracking impact remains challenging (Mullender & Burton, 2001).

Custody

Day, Richardson, Bowen, and Barnardi (2014) highlight that there have been few evaluations of prison-based DVA perpetrator work. A 2010 implementation study highlighted that only five Healthy Relationship Programmes were occurring in male prisons across the UK at that time (Bullock, Sarre, Tarling, & Wilkinson, 2010). Running programmes in prison has also proved to be particularly difficult in relation to the adoption of a coordinated response to DVA, ensuring that victims are also offered contact and support. This vital programme component has often been seen to be lacking in many of the prison-led programmes (Bullock et al., 2010). It is also the case that whilst the highest risk DVA perpetrators may receive a custodial sentence, it is likely to be relatively short in duration. This often prohibits participation in a relevant programme whilst in custody, should one be available. Opportunities to undertake DVA perpetrator interventions upon release may also be limited and in the UK, the post release community supervision of prisoners serving less than 12 months now falls to the newly formed private CRCs.

Day et al. (2014) continue that the challenges of providing effective interventions for DVA perpetrators in a custodial setting are further exacerbated by the failure to treat such offenders as a specific category.

Whilst the DVA context may be flagged up by the Police and the Courts, this does not always transfer to the prison context and such issues may not be made apparent by the index offence alone. Risk assessment tools, which examine general offending behaviour patterns, are not effective in identifying risks of DVA and, therefore, the number of DVA perpetrators within the prison setting is likely to be far higher than evidenced by official records. Her Majesty's Prison Service has also previously been permitted much greater discretion in the development of assessment suitability criteria for DVA perpetrator programmes, resulting in a very uneven approach to overall provision (Bullock et al., 2010). Studies have shown, however, that imprisonment can reinforce DVA behaviours, supporting misogynistic attitudes and with the perpetrators' absence from the domestic setting becoming an additional source of conflict (Day et al., 2014). The need to address the implementation and evaluation of effective work with perpetrators of DVA in the custodial setting is, therefore, essential.

Community

There are also a number of challenges in the delivery of perpetrator programmes in the community, both in the statutory and voluntary sectors. Owing to the lack of any significant body of evidence of effective practice in DVA perpetrator work, the Probation Service in England and Wales has retreated to its established 'What Works' position, favouring cognitive behavioural programmes that adhere to national statutory sector accredited programme rules. The difficulties of ascertaining the long-term impact of probation programme work also prevail and again tends to rely on recidivism data alone. Attendance at a court mandated programme running in the community is also set in the context of legal enforcement frameworks for non-compliance with a court order. Here, the offender manager's capacity for using discretion to accept absences from a perpetrator is limited and there are clear expectations that the programme must be completed within a prescribed timescale. Attrition rates on court mandated programmes can, therefore, occur as a result of enforcement proceedings, which are implemented without any significant flexibility, rather than there being a fundamental unwillingness to engage in DVA work from the perpetrator. The extent to which an offender manager can encourage an individual to consider the programme participation as part of a more holistic package of intervention, drawing on desistance frameworks, may also be limited by organisational constraints. Suitability for a programme intervention also needs to be carefully assessed, rather than being target driven, but there is evidence to suggest that referrals to programmes are not always appropriately made. Bowen's (2011) evaluation of a brief therapy, DVA perpetrator programme run by a probation area in 2009, identified that only limited psychological change was achieved in programme completers. More importantly, however, it was demonstrated that this may have been due in part to the substantial number of inappropriate referrals for perpetrators who would have benefitted from a more in-depth intervention.

Non-court mandated perpetrator programme work is now an integral part of the coordinated community response to DVA in England and Wales, and the HM Government strategy to End Violence Against Women and Girls (Home Office, 2011). Evaluations of impact are required to be built in to applications for the accreditation of community-based perpetrator programmes by RESPECT, which must all also include a support and intervention service for the victims of the perpetrators on the programme. Associated Partner Support Services, sometimes called Women's Safety Services, run parallel to the perpetrator programme and aim to make persistent and proactive contact with (ex-)partners to manage ongoing risks, provide support and updates on perpetrator group attendance and participation. One of most important features of this contact is the insight it provides into the 'reality' of the victim's situation. It may reveal contradictions in relation to the ongoing prevalence of abusive behaviours, which a perpetrator may have claimed to have changed. Conversely, where the perpetrator is making real changes and this is corroborated by the victim, programme staff can be more confident in the effectiveness of the work that is taking place. It also serves as a form of ongoing encouragement for the perpetrator for further engagement. Staff must also be alert, however, to the possibility of coerced collusion whereby honest disclosures are not made by the victim for fear of reprisals. This may relate to the victim's ongoing fear of the perpetrator and/

or the couple's joint fear that any disclosure of violent incidents may lead to further consequences for themselves and their children, such as the commencement of formal care proceedings. Disengagement, avoidance and minimisation may, therefore, emanate from the victim as well as the perpetrator.

Securing a long-term evaluation strategy is also often unrealistic for community-based DVPP providers, particularly in view of the short-term funding contracts that many are subject to. That said, the changing context for DVPP delivery within the voluntary and community sector, with an increase in referrals from children services and family courts, has seen a shift away from the former preoccupation with recidivism rates as the singular measurement of success. A key example of this is the Mirabal project, concluding in 2015, which explored perceptions of positive impact via various processes of data collection across 11 research sites and four DVPP locations within the UK. The research included interviews with DVA perpetrators, partners, programme staff and funders (Kelly & Westmarland, 2015). Whilst the findings of the study provide limited insight into long-term cessation from acts of DVA, they do offer new insights into how initial steps into primary desistance might be evaluated, with particular value being placed on the victim's perception of progress. The following areas were identified as key indicators of positive change: respect and effective communication; space for action, addressing coercion and isolation; safety from violence and abuse; safe positive shared parenting; the partner's enhanced awareness of self, others and the impact of their behaviours and safer healthier childhood experiences for the couple's children.

All of the programmes studies by Mirabal were bound by the integrity framework devised by RESPECT and combined cognitive behavioural strategies with opportunities for educational and reflective work on gendered assumptions. Within this framework, it is likely that certain methods of intervention remain more effective than others, or impact differentially on different types of perpetrator and different forms of DVA, as discussed previously. A further examination of these distinctions may prove to be beneficial. Motivations for attending programmes were examined, linked in particular to the varied referral pathways that have been identified in this chapter. Perpetrators typically saw programme completion either as a hurdle to be negotiated, for example, in the pursuit of child contact, or as an opportunity for positive change in the dynamics and quality of an existing relationship. Attrition rates were still an issue and the extent to which other external factors may positively assist or hinder the individual's participation on a programme and their longer term cessation from DVA would be a useful focus for future research.

Bowen and Gilchrist (2006) report a link between the individual's response to DVA programmes and personality and lifestyle characteristics such as irresponsibility, impulsivity, erratic patterns of employment and instability. This would suggest that there are psychological development issues and external contextual influences, which may impact on a perpetrator's capacity to address their DVA behaviours. Additional interventions outside of the programme delivery are, therefore, likely to be required by many perpetrators if any chance of full engagement is to be realised. Donovan and Griffiths (2015) found that pre-group commencement work with perpetrators of DVA was an important factor in sustaining the individual's commitment and securing a greater prospect of subsequent programme completion. However, they also found that staff from agencies making referrals to DVPPs often lacked the skills and confidence to engage with the perpetrators. Some may also be resistant to the suggestion that this needs to change, considering DVA to be a criminal matter only and beyond the remit of health and social care. The reliance of perpetrators on ongoing facilitator contact, after group completion, is also illustrated in Morran's (2013), albeit very small, study. This suggests that resourcing and evaluating a pilot approach that adopts a more comprehensive individualised case management strategy to working with perpetrators of DVA may prove useful, maximising opportunities for sustaining engagement and realising longer term positive change.

Conclusion

This chapter has highlighted some of the various types of DVA perpetrators' behaviours that may occur and the impact of various theoretical discourses on the approaches taken to behavioural change programme work. Whilst the challenges of determining what is effective in perpetrator programme content delivery continue, there are indications that a number of different approaches have significant potential, if they are targeted appropriately. Some refinement to assessment processes in order to ensure that a more detailed consideration is given to the type of DVA occurring, as well as the level of risk posed, may help to ensure that issues of severe psychological DVA are not overlooked. A gendered analysis remains relevant and useful in a vast number of DVA cases; however, an additional exploration of approaches to be taken with 'generalist' and 'specialist' perpetrators may also prove worthwhile. It is unrealistic to suggest that bespoke programmes may be devised to fully reflect the diverse range of complex DVA experiences that may occur, but a stronger intersectional approach is required for both court ordered and non-court mandated programmes. This should include the development of knowledge and expertise of effective interventions for female perpetrators and those in LGB and/or T relationships. More diverse understandings and appropriate responses to DVA perpetrators may also be better facilitated via a stronger consideration of desistance frameworks, which undertake a more individualised approach to the cessation of DVA. The perpetrator programme is then viewed as just one of a number of elements, which may assist the perpetrator in working towards establishing a non-offending identity. All of this suggests that a shift in thinking is required, which moves away from rigid notions of competing ideas for effective programme content, to one which considers a more holistic view of the individual perpetrator and the various potential agents of change.

The remit of the organisations referring the perpetrator to a programme is also significant and will, for a variety of reasons identified here, be likely to influence the individual's engagement with the group process. This moves towards a position that looks beyond the programme intervention, to the work and support required with the perpetrator before, during and after the programme. This additional 'case management' of a perpetrator is more established as a practice within the probation service, although it is not without its limitations there. The public protection, risk management agenda underpinning the criminal justice approach is also one that those working in non-government organisations, social care and family courts are unlikely to want to replicate. The weight of responsibility for providing the perpetrator with the best possibility for success whilst undertaking a DVPP currently appears to rest with the programme facilitators. Whilst they often undertake various extended roles in addition to the programme delivery (Kelly & Westmarland, 2015), it is unrealistic to assume that they can offer a comprehensive package of support to all of their participants, and further resources are likely to be required. However, strategies that may be perceived as offering practical help to DVA perpetrators are likely to be met with some opposition, particularly during times of austerity. Nonetheless, there is a growing recognition that as key referral agencies for DVPPs, social work and healthcare professional training needs to stretch beyond simply the recognition of DVA in terms of the harm caused and child protection issues that may arise, to a proactive stance of engagement with those perpetrating the abuse. A perpetrator programme can never be a panacea, which, if successfully completed, will prevent further DVA from occurring. However, the potential for effective, well-targeted, evidence-based programmes to be combined with a more comprehensive assessment and pursuit of the protective factors, which may assist in supporting an individual's long-term cessation from DVA, are certainly worthy of some continued exploration.

References

Bowen, E. (2011). *The rehabilitation of partner-violent men*. Chichester: Wiley-Blackwell.
Bowen, E., & Gilchrist, E. (2006). Predicting dropout of court-mandated treatment in a British sample of domestic violence offenders. *Psychology, Crime and Law, 12*(5), 573–587.
Bowen, E., Gilchrist, E. A., & Beech, A. R. (2005). An examination of the impact of community-based rehabilitation on the offending behaviour of male domestic violence offenders and the characteristics associated with recidivism. *Legal and Criminological Psychology, 10*(2), 189–209.
Brownridge, D. A. (2009). *Violence against women. Vulnerable populations*. London: Routledge.
Bullock, K., Sarre, S., Tarling, R., & Wilkinson, M. (2010). *The delivery of domestic abuse programmes. An implementation study of the delivery of domestic*

abuse programmes in probation areas and Her Majesty's Prison Service. London: Ministry of Justice Research Series 15/10.

Clarke, R. V., & Felson, M. (Eds.) (1997). *Routine activity and rational choice. Advances in criminological theory* (Vol. 5). New Brunswick, NJ: Transaction Books.

Council of Europe. (2011). *Council of Europe convention on preventing and combating violence against women and domestic violence*. Strasbourg: Council of Europe.

Day, A., Richardson, T., Bowen, E., & Barnardi, J. (2014). Intimate partner violence in prisoners: Towards effective assessment and intervention. *Aggression and Violent Behavior, 19*, 579–583.

De Wall, C. N., Anderson, C. A., & Bushman, B. J. (2011). The General Aggression Model: Theoretical extensions to violence. *Psychology of Violence, 1*(3), 245–258.

Denney, D. (2005). *Risk and society*. London: SAGE.

Dixon, L., Archer, J., & Graham-Kevan, N. (2012). Perpetrator programmes for partner violence: Are they based on ideology or evidence. *Legal and Criminological Psychology, 17*, 196–215.

Domestic Abuse Intervention Programmes (DAIP). (2015). *Home of the Duluth Model* (home page). Retrieved October 27, 2015, from http://www.theduluthmodel.org/about/index.html

Donovan, C., & Griffiths, S. (2015). Domestic violence and voluntary perpetrator programmes. Engaging men in the pre-commencement phase. *British Journal of Social Work, 45*, 1155–1171.

Farrell, M., & Young, N. (2015). The strength to change. *Therapy Today*. Retrieved October 24, 2015, from http://www.ignition-learn.co.uk/resources/document-library.php

Friend, D. J., Cleary-Bradley, R. P., Thatcher, R., & Gottman, J. M. (2011). Typologies of intimate partner violence: Evaluation of a screening instrument for differentiation. *Journal of Family Violence, 26*, 551–563.

Gadd, D. (2004). Evidence-led policy or policy-led evidence? Cognitive behavioural programmes for men who are violent towards women. *Criminal Justice, 4*(2), 173–197.

Gilbert, B. (2013). Public protection? The implications of Grayling's 'Transforming Rehabilitation' agenda on the safety of women and children. *British Journal of Community Justice, 11*(2–3), 123–134.

Gondolf, E. (2004). Evaluating batterer counseling programs: A difficult task showing some effects and implications. *Aggression and Violent Behaviour, 9*(6), 605–631.

Harne, L., & Radford, J. (2008). *Tackling domestic violence. Theories, policies and practice*. Maidenhead: Open University Press.

Hester, M. (2009). *Who does what to whom? Gender and domestic violence perpetrators*. Bristol: University of Bristol and Newcastle, Northern Rock Foundation.

Home Affairs Committee. (2008). *Domestic violence, forced marriage and "honour"-based violence*. Sixth Report of Session 2007–08 (1). London: Stationary Office.

Home Office. (2011). *Call to end violence against women and girls: Action plan*. London: HM Government.

Home Office. (2013). *Home Office Circular 003/2013: New government domestic violence and abuse definition*. Retrieved October 27, 2015, from https://www.gov.uk/government/publications/new-government-domestic-violence-and-abuse-definition

Johnson, M. (2008). *A typology of domestic violence. Intimate terrorism, violent resistance and situational couple violence*. New England: Northeastern University Press.

Kelly, L., & Westmarland, N. (2015). *Domestic Violence Perpetrator Programmes: Steps towards change: Project Mirabal final report*. London and Durham, NC: London Metropolitan University and Durham University.

Kemshall, H., Kelly, G., Wilkinson, B., & Hilder, S. (2015). *What works in work with violent offenders? An overview*. Leicester: De Montfort University.

Ministry of Justice. (2013). Transforming rehabilitation a revolution in the way we manage offenders. London: Her Majesty's Stationary Office.

Morran, D. (2013). Desisting from domestic abuse: Influences, patterns and processes in the lives of formerly abusive men. *The Howard Journal, 52*(3), 306–320.

Mullender, A., & Burton, S. (2001). Dealing with perpetrators. In J. Taylor-Browne (Ed.), *What works in reducing domestic violence? A comprehensive guide for professionals*. London: Whiting and Birch Ltd.

Norwegian Centre for Violence and Traumatic Stress. (2014). *Alternatives to Violence Therapy Project. A study of process outcomes of therapy of men who seek help for their use of violence*. Retrieved October 27, 2015, from http://www.nkvts.no/en/Pages/ProjectInfo.aspx?prosjektid=1281

Pence, E., & Paymar, M. (1993). *Education groups for men who batter: The Duluth Model*. New York: Springer.

Phillips, R., Kelly, L., & Westmarland, N. (2013). *Perpetrator programmes. A historical overview*. London and Durham, NC: London Metropolitan University and Durham University.

RESPECT. (2015a). *Domestic violence prevention programmes.* Retrieved October 27, 2015, from http://www.respectphoneline.org.uk/pages/domestic-violence-prevention-programmes.html

RESPECT. (2015b). *Respect briefing paper: Evidence base for interventions with domestic violence perpetrators.* Retrieved October 27, 2015, from http://respect.uk.net/research/our-briefing-papers-and-articles/

Robinson, A. L., Clancy, A., & Hanks, S. (2014). *Prevalence and characteristics of serial domestic abuse perpetrators: Multi-agency evidence from Wales.* [Project Report]. Retrieved October 20, 2015, from http://orca.cf.ac.uk/67542/

Soothill, K., Francis, B., Sanderson, B., & Ackerley, E. (2000). Sex offenders: Specialists, generalists – Or both? *British Journal of Criminology, 40*(1), 56–67.

Stark, E. (2007). *Coercive control: How men entrap women in personal life.* New York: Oxford University Press.

Stark, E. (2009). Rethinking coercive control. *Violence Against Women, 15*(12), 1509–1525.

Walker, K. (2015). *Mentoring difficult to treat high-risk intimate partner violence perpetrators.* In Proceedings of XXXIVth International Congress of Law and Mental Health, July 2015. Retrieved October 27, 2015, from https://www.ialmh.org/Amsterdam2013/Abstract%20Booklet%20-%202015-07-16.pdf

Walker, K., Bowen, E., & Brown, S. (2013). Desistance from intimate partner violence: A critical review. *Aggression and Violent Behavior, 18*, 271–280.

Ward, T., Mann, R., & Gannon, T. (2007). The Good Lives Model of offender rehabilitation: Clinical implications. *Aggression and Violent Behaviour, 12*, 87–107.

Westmarland, N., & Kelly, L. (2013). Why extending measurements of success in domestic violence perpetrator programmes matters for social work. *British Journal of Social Work, 43*, 1092–1110.

14

Developing Interventions for Abusive Partners in Lesbian, Gay, Bisexual and/or Transgender Relationships

Rebecca Barnes and Catherine Donovan

Introduction

It has long been recognised that effective responses to domestic violence and abuse (DVA) should not only prioritise the support, protection and empowerment of survivors, but should also strive to hold perpetrators accountable for their abuse and challenge their attitudes, beliefs and behaviour (Pence & Shepard, 1999). This emphasis has been reinforced by recent national policies such as the *Call to End Violence Against Women and Girls* (Home Office, 2011) in the UK, and on a European level via the Istanbul Convention, Article 16 (Council of Europe, 2011), which was implemented in August 2014 and has, to date, been ratified by 18 states (Council of Europe, 2015).[1]

---

[1] As of June 2015, Albania, Andorra, Austria, Bosnia and Herzegovina, Cyprus, Denmark, Finland, France, Italy, Malta, Monaco, Montenegro, Portugal, Serbia, Slovenia, Spain, Sweden and Turkey have ratified the Istanbul Convention (Council of Europe, 2015). The UK is yet to join this list.

R. Barnes (✉)
University of Leicester, Leicester, UK

C. Donovan
University of Sunderland, Sunderland, UK

© The Editor(s) (if applicable) and The Author(s) 2016
S. Hilder, V. Bettinson (eds.), *Domestic Violence*,
DOI 10.1057/978-1-137-52452-2_14

In the UK context, this approach applies equally, in principle, to DVA in lesbian, gay, bisexual and/or transgender (LGB and/or T)[2] relationships. Recent years have witnessed increasing legal protections for and recognition of, LGB and/or T individuals and relationships (*Civil Partnership Act,* 2004; *Equality Act,* 2010; *Marriage (Same Sex Couples) Act,* 2013). The Public Sector Equality Duty, introduced by the *Equality Act,* 2010, places a legal obligation on public sector agencies to provide appropriate responses to all service users where there is an evident need. This has been a key driver for the development of policy and practice regarding support for survivors of LGB and/or T DVA.

In parallel with these developments, domestic violence policy and legislation have also recognised DVA in LGB and/or T relationships. In England and Wales, the Home Office definition of domestic violence identifies that it cuts across gender and sexuality (Home Office, 2013). The *Domestic Violence, Crime and Victims Act,* 2004 clarified that civil remedies such as non-molestation orders are available to survivors in both same-sex and heterosexual relationships. In addition, the Home Office funds Broken Rainbow (2015), the only national voluntary organisation that specialises in providing support and advice throughout UK regarding LGB and/or T DVA. In various parts of the UK, specialist LGB and/or T DVA services exist and mainstream statutory and voluntary agencies have made progress in developing inclusive and appropriate responses to LGB and/or T survivors. To date, however, LGB and/or T perpetrators have been largely invisible within these, or other, developments.

This chapter reports on the findings from the Coral Project, a UK study,[3] which has produced the largest body of research evidence, to date, on the use of abusive behaviours in LGB and/or T relationships and practitioners' perspectives on effective responses to LGB and/or T perpetra-

---

[2] The term LGB and/or T recognises that transgender individuals may identify their sexuality as heterosexual and have limited affinity with being lesbian, gay and/or bisexual. Its use is also intended to capture those who identify their sexuality and/or gender identities using other, or no, labels, but who seek or have relationships that fall outside of normative understandings of male, female heterosexual relationships.

[3] The study, officially titled *Understanding the relationship practices of abusive partners in same sex and/or trans relationships and their implications for theory and practice,* ran from October 2012–2014 and was funded by the Economic and Social Research Council, grant number ES/J012580/1. The project was led by Catherine Donovan (PI) in collaboration with Rebecca Barnes (Co-I).

tors (Donovan, Barnes, & Nixon, 2014). Whilst original in its focus, this chapter is nonetheless underpinned by shared concerns reflected elsewhere in this collection, namely, the recognition of the importance of developing effective and appropriate responses to perpetrators of DVA (see Hilder and Freeman, Chap. 13) and a commitment to adopting an intersectional approach that interrogates experiences of DVA at the margins (see Martin, Chap. 9 and Oakley and Kinmond, Chap. 10, this volume).

The chapter begins by briefly reviewing what is known, currently about LGB and/or T DVA and the provision for perpetrators of DVA in the UK, focusing on behavioural change programmes and highlighting the gap in service delivery for LGB and/or T perpetrators. Next, the scope and methodology of the Coral Project is outlined and findings from the Coral Project's national survey indicating the demand for LGB and/or T perpetrator interventions are highlighted. The main analysis presents practitioners' perspectives on the needs of LGB and/or T perpetrators and the opportunities for and barriers to, developing inclusive and appropriate LGB and/or T perpetrator interventions. The chapter concludes by emphasising the importance of making progress with the development of inclusive interventions for LGB and/or T perpetrators, whilst acknowledging that there is a need more generally for an integrated response to LGB and/or T DVA, which requires input from a wider range of practice settings, such as counselling and youth work.

The Growing Evidence Base about LGB and/or T DVA

Whilst a growing body of research on DVA in lesbian and gay relationships and to a much lesser extent, in bisexual and/or trans relationships exists, it is important to acknowledge considerable reticence historically, amongst feminists and LGB and/or T scholars and activists alike to acknowledge LGB and/or T DVA. This continues to persist in some quarters and has stemmed from fears about taking attention away from men's violence towards women and destabilising the feminist, gender-based analysis of DVA and/or fuelling homo/bi/transphobia and reinforcing the pathologisation of LGB and/or T relationships (Barnes, 2011; Donovan & Hester, 2014; Ristock, 2002).

Nevertheless, research on DVA in LGB and/or T relationships has been emerging from the USA since the 1980s, initially through small-scale, psychological studies predominantly focusing on lesbian relationships. These early studies typically reported very high rates of DVA in lesbian relationships, yet provided little contextualisation to understand how the violence and abuse operated, whilst relying, by necessity, on self-selected non-random samples (Brand & Kidd, 1986; Lie & Gentlewarrier, 1991). Research on DVA in gay men's relationships developed slightly later and has remained less extensive. However, similar to research on lesbian DVA, most studies on DVA and gay males have been conducted from a psychological perspective and have reported high prevalence figures across a variety of types of abuse, with high rates also of bi-directional, or mutual abuse (Bartholomew, Regan, White, & Oram, 2008; Merrill & Wolfe, 2000). As with small-scale descriptive studies of DVA in lesbian relationships, a lack of qualitative contextualisation has inhibited an in-depth understanding of how violence and abuse are used and experienced in gay male relationships (see Martin, Chap. 9, this volume).

More comprehensive research into lesbians' experiences of DVA followed in the form of Renzetti's (1992) US mixed-methods study (n = 100), and Ristock's (2002) Canadian qualitative study of 102 lesbians who were predominantly survivors of lesbian partner abuse and 77 feminist practitioners involved in delivering DVA services. In addition to documenting extensive physical, psychological, emotional, financial and sexual abuse, both studies identify how sexuality and disclosure can be used to control and manipulate survivors, including threats to 'out' women to their families and employers (Renzetti, 1992; Ristock, 2002). Ristock's study was the first comprehensive study to adopt a more sociological approach, identifying various contextual factors, which either increase women's vulnerability to experiencing DVA or accentuate the barriers to help seeking; these include first relationships, the closet (disclosure), homophobia, racism and poverty, immigration and dislocation, previous abuse and substance misuse (Ristock, 2002). To date, there does not appear to have been a comparable in-depth qualitative study of DVA in male same-sex relationships.

Research on LGB and/or T DVA has been slower to develop in the UK, but the authors' own previous research has made important contributions here. The first comprehensive national UK study was Donovan, Hester, Holmes, and McCarry's (2006) comparative study of love and violence in both same-sex and heterosexual relationships (Donovan & Hester, 2014; Donovan et al., 2006). In their national LGB and/or T community survey (n = 746), 38 % of participants reported having experienced domestic abuse in a non-heterosexual, same-sex relationship, and a considerably larger percentage reported ever having experienced one or more incidents of physical, emotional, financial and/or sexually abusive behaviours. Donovan and Hester coined the concept of the 'public story' of DVA (Donovan & Hester, 2011, 2014) to draw attention to the implicit heteronormative assumptions about DVA, that contend that it concerns a bigger, stronger male perpetrator being physically violent towards a smaller, weaker female victim. Whilst this reflects the majority of DVA cases that are reported to the police and DVA agencies, it poses barriers to the recognition, by both survivors and practitioners, of forms of DVA that fall outside of this narrow story. This includes survivors of DVA in LGB and/or T relationships. Moreover, the public story can steer practitioners towards viewing LGB and/or T DVA through a particular lens, risking incorrect assumptions that the most 'masculine' partner in physique, appearance or demeanour will always be the abuser (Donovan & Hester, 2014). Donovan and Hester's research, as well as Barnes (2007) qualitative study of 40 lesbian DVA survivors, found that there are significant barriers to help seeking. These include a lack of recognition of the DVA because of the public story, not seeking formal support out of fear of homophobic or otherwise inappropriate responses and reports of mixed reactions when support was sought either informally or from agencies. Whilst both studies reported some positive, affirming responses, some survivors reported that they were not offered a service, or their experiences were minimised or they felt stigmatised because of their sexuality (Barnes, 2007, 2008; Donovan & Hester, 2011, 2014).

Research on trans DVA is sparser still, but Roch, Morton, and Ritchie's (2010) study of 60 trans participants, mostly located in Scotland, found that 80 % reported having experienced physical, emotional and/or sexual abuse from a current or former partner. Transphobic emotional abuse was the most frequently reported form of abuse, including a disregard for chosen names or pronouns, having to hide their trans identity from others being made to feel ashamed or guilty about their trans identity and being made to feel uncomfortable about their bodies. A quarter of the sample had not told anyone about their experiences, often because of shame or fears of prejudice, not wanting to out themselves or thinking that there were no suitable agencies to support them. Notably, quantitative studies of LGB and/or T DVA often suggest that DVA is more prevalent in LGB and/or T relationships than in heterosexual relationships. However, the aforementioned studies cannot be regarded as true prevalence studies because of their sampling methods and, in many cases, small sample sizes. Hence, using such studies to assess the comparative prevalence of DVA in LGB and/or T and heterosexual relationships yields inaccurate and potentially misleading claims (see Donovan & Hester, 2014). Despite these measurement issues, it is clear that LGB and/or T DVA exists and that research into its nature, correlates and impacts is growing, with strong evidence to show that its survivors are often invisible and not well served.

What is lacking, however, is in-depth academic evidence about the perpetrators of DVA in LGB and/or T relationships, such as their attitudes, motives and help-seeking experiences and needs. There are exceptions, and some small-scale US psychological studies have examined the personality characteristics of clinical samples of abusive lesbians (Coleman, 2002; Poorman & Seelau, 2001). More recently, predominantly in North America, psychological research has explored the correlation between minority stress experienced by LGB and/or T individuals as a result of their marginalised sexualities and/or gender identities and DVA victimisation and perpetration (Balsam & Szymanski, 2005; Mendoza, 2011). However, whilst correlations have been reported, it remains unclear as to why some who experience minority stress become victims of DVA, whilst others become perpetrators and others become neither (Donovan, 2015; Donovan & Hester, 2014). A qualitative study of the life stories of 12 lesbians in the USA, who have been abusive towards female partners and/or others, argues that an intersectional approach is needed, which takes into account multiple factors such as family history, ethnicity, class, experiences of coming out and substance misuse (Smith, 2011), thus developing a more holistic understanding of how and why abusive behaviours are enacted. Before outlining how the Coral Project sought to address this knowledge gap, the current provision of interventions for DVA perpetrators in the UK is outlined.

Current Provision for Perpetrators of DVA

Hilder and Freeman provide a fuller overview of the nature of current provisions available for perpetrators of DVA in the UK in Chap. 13 of this volume. In the UK, perpetrator provision remains a postcode lottery, with whole counties being without a voluntary perpetrator programme and capacity is often very limited. These gaps can be attributed not only to insufficient funding, but also to historical concerns about the risk of diverting funds from survivors to male perpetrators and scepticism regarding whether perpetrator programmes work (Phillips, Kelly, & Westmarland, 2013). To date, provision for perpetrators reflects the statistical reality of DVA; hence, interventions have been developed for (ostensibly) heterosexual men who have been violent and/or abusive towards their female partners. In the criminal justice system, there are no accredited programmes for LGB and/or T perpetrators and indeed, there are no accredited DVA interventions for any female perpetrators. However, some former Probation Trusts have developed non-accredited programmes for one-to-one work with LGB and/or T offenders. Voluntary programmes also focus primarily on male perpetrators of DVA towards female partners. However, as will be discussed later, a small minority do advertise or provide on request a service for female perpetrators, or LGB and/or T perpetrators, usually in the form of ad hoc one-to-one work, rather than group programmes. What becomes evident, then, is a clear lack of opportunities for LGB and/or T perpetrators to address their attitudes and behaviour and in turn, the harm which they are causing, or pose, to current, former or future partners and their children. The Coral Project sought to gather evidence to examine how this gap might be addressed.

The Coral Project

The Coral Project is the first UK study to focus specifically on researching the perpetration of DVA in LGB and/or T relationships. The two key questions which it sought to answer were as follows:

1. What are the similarities and differences in understandings of relationship expectations and dynamics and the use of abusive behaviours across gender and sexuality?
2. How can the accounts from abusive and/or violent partners in LGB and/or T relationships be used, in conjunction with what is known about interventions for heterosexual male perpetrators, to develop interventions to address their behaviour?

In addition to seeking to answer these questions and develop a set of good practice recommendations for practitioners, another fundamental aim was to design, test and evaluate a methodology for researching LGB and/or T perpetrators of DVA. The conventional channels for conducting perpetrator research, such as accessing clinical samples via existing voluntary male perpetrator programmes, or accessing convicted perpetrators via prisons or probation, were not available because of the absence or invisibility of LGB and/or T perpetrators in these settings, barring a few isolated cases. Therefore, a more creative, methodologically innovative strategy for locating and studying a sample of LGB and/or T people who have behaved abusively in their relationships was required.

The approach taken, after consultation with the Coral Project's steering group, was to first conduct a national LGB and/or T community survey. Adopting and adapting the COmparing Heterosexual and Same-sex Abuse in Relationships (COHSAR)[4] approach (Donovan & Hester, 2014), the survey was titled, 'What do you do when things go wrong in your same sex, bisexual and/or trans relationships?' and asked participants to self-report, from a checklist of potentially abusive physical, emotional, sexual and financial behaviours, which, if any, they had experienced or

---

[4] COHSAR—COmparing Heterosexual and Same sex Abuse in Relationships, Survey strategy as detailed in Donovan and Hester (2014).

14 Interventions for Abusive Partners in LGB and/or T Relationships

used either in their current or last relationship, or ever in any previous relationship. Participants were also asked about their relationship expectations, decision-making, conflict resolutions and help-seeking behaviour. An online survey was disseminated across the UK, supported by steering group members, to over 100 LGB and/or T and DVA organisations and across social media. More than 900 responses were received, with 872 usable responses. The survey included a pretested 'readiness for change' indicator (Rollnick, Heather, Gold, & Hall, 1992) to facilitate the second phase of the research, which involved semi-structured, in-depth interviews with participants whose survey responses indicated a previous use of abusive behaviours in an LGB and/or T relationship. The follow-up interviews sought more detailed accounts of relationship histories, relationship values, expectations and perceptions, motives for using 'abusive' behaviours and help-seeking experiences and needs. The purposive selection of interview participants required careful considerations of safety. Based on the information available, only those participants were selected who were no longer in an abusive relationship, and who demonstrated some reflection on their behaviour and either referred to having taken steps to change their behaviour, or recognised the need for this. A total of 36 face-to-face interviews were conducted across the UK, each lasting approximately two hours and were audio-recorded and transcribed.

In the practitioner phase of the study, semi-structured interviews were conducted with 23 practitioners involved in the design and/or delivery of either voluntary or criminal justice perpetrator interventions. Access to criminal justice practitioners first necessitated approval from the National Offender Management Service (NOMS). Interviews were conducted face-to-face and lasted 60–90 minutes. Questions focused on the interventions that practitioners currently delivered, whether there was any current provision for LGB and/or T perpetrators, perceptions of the kind(s) of intervention LGB and/or T perpetrators might need and the barriers to developing this work. The findings of these interviews are discussed later in this chapter. Subsequently, 8 focus groups were conducted with 53 practitioners from various practice settings, including youth work, sex and relationships education (SRE), DVA services and individual and relationship counselling. The focus groups set out to elicit participants' feedback on some of the preliminary findings from the research, using a pack of survey data and case studies. This aimed to stimulate an exploration as to whether the results differed from work that participants may be more familiar with, involving heterosexual individuals and relationships. Probes were made to investigate the possible implications of these findings for their own understandings, practice and the role that their sector could play in recognising and responding to DVA in LGB and/or T relationships. This latter phase of the research marked a shift from the original intention to conduct focus groups with providers of perpetrator programmes. This reflected the emergent findings, which highlighted the potential for multiple practice settings to offer 'relationship services', contributing to more integrated responses to LGB and/or T DVA. This is returned to briefly in this chapter's conclusion. The findings from the national survey are presented here first to establish the need to develop interventions that meet the needs of LGB and/or T perpetrators of DVA.

Evidencing the Need for LGB and/or T Perpetrator Interventions: Survey Findings

The existence of LGB and/or T perpetrators and the need for appropriate interventions for them can be inferred from previous research, which documents the existence of LGB and/or T survivors of DVA. Until now, however, there has been a lack of first-hand data concerning people who have experienced abusive behaviours in LGB and/or T relationships. One caveat, before presenting the survey data, is to explain the Coral Project's cautious use of the terms 'perpetrator' and 'abusive', respectively. The survey was a general community study and did not exclusively elicit data from perpetrators; therefore, it is not a survey of perpetrator views. Moreover, participants were asked to report behaviours that they had used or experienced, but not all of those who self-reported behaviours are perpetrators or survivors, respectively. Johnson's typology of relationship violence shows how violence can be used in a multitude of ways in relationships, namely, to control or punish, in self-defence, in retaliation and as situational couple violence, where violence may result from an escalation of conflict, but where the use of violence is aberrant and does not create a climate of control or fear in that relationship (Johnson, 2006). Self-report surveys of DVA, including the one reported here, are usually too blunt an instrument to disentangle the different contexts for 'abusive' behaviours (Donovan & Hester, 2014; Johnson, 2006). However, in the follow-up interviews, participants overwhelmingly described relationships where they were using 'abusive' behaviours in self-defence, retaliation, isolated cases of situational couple violence and in relationships that were volatile for other reasons or ending (Donovan et al., 2014). Thus, whilst the survey data indicate that some respondents were likely to be primary perpetrators of coercive control and DVA, those participants either did not volunteer to take part in the follow-up interviews or may have been filtered out for safety reasons. A challenge for researchers and practitioners alike is to foreground context and adopt a more nuanced approach to conceptualising and assessing the use of potentially 'abusive' behaviours in a particular relationship dynamic (see Donovan et al., 2014).

These caveats contextualise what might otherwise appear to be a disproportionately high level of DVA perpetration in LGB and/or T relationships. When combining physical, emotional, sexual and financial behaviours, 57 % of the survey sample (based on n = 791 who answered the question) reported having used at least one of the 69 listed behaviours in the past 12 months of their current or last relationship. In all, 11 % reported having used six or more behaviours in the same period, while 4 % reported having used 10 or more behaviours, which is more likely to be indicative of either someone who is a primary perpetrator of DVA or, perhaps conversely, a survivor using multiple tactics of self-defence.

The most commonly reported behaviour was the withdrawal of affection, reported by 27 % of the sample and a good example of the difficulties of basing any interpretations in survey data alone. Affection and intimacy might be withdrawn as a punishment for not being a 'good partner', intended to manipulate, control and/or denigrate a partner. Alternatively, affection might be withdrawn by someone who is experiencing DVA and feels fearful or mistrusting of, or betrayed by, their abusive partner. Further still, withdrawal of affection is common when a relationship is coming to an end and one or both partners have disinvested from the relationship, or no longer desire intimacy or sex with their partner. Other behaviours, which were amongst the most common, were less ambiguous: 12 % reported regularly insulting or putting their partner down, 12 % slapped or pushed their partner and 7 % required their partner to account for all their expenditure. For a general, albeit self-selected, LGB and/or T population survey rather than a study of a clinical sample, these figures and participants' willingness to disclose these behaviours are significant.

Additionally, considerable numbers of survey participants indicated that they had issues with trusting others (n = 204), anger (n = 118), needing to be in control (n = 109) and jealousy (n = 71). Further, in response to the readiness to change indicator, 37 % strongly agreed or agreed that 'my behaviour is a problem sometimes', whilst 15 % strongly agreed or agreed that 'I am at the stage now where I should think about changing my behaviour'. Taken together, there is clear evidence of LGB and/or T people's reflection on their behaviour within intimate relationships and an impetus for change. Whilst not all of these participants would be at the threshold for requiring a perpetrator intervention, some would be. The remainder of this chapter considers how to develop LGB and/or T perpetrator interventions as one such vehicle for attitudinal and behavioural change.

Practitioners' Perspectives on Developing LGBT Perpetrator Interventions

This section draws primarily on the interview data gathered from practitioners whose work involves the design and/or delivery of ostensibly heterosexual male perpetrator interventions via voluntary programmes, or the criminal justice system. Participants were working on a variety of different interventions, as highlighted earlier, with criminal justice practitioners placing greater emphasis on targeting individuals' criminogenic risk factors. All practitioners engaged to a greater or lesser extent with feminist principles, usually embedded in attitudinal and identity work. This involved challenging 'gender regimes' (Morris, 2009 cited in Kelly & Westmarland, 2015), unpicking ideas of male privilege and traditional but oppressive beliefs about masculinity and gendered relationship roles.

Participants' first-hand experience of working with LGB and/or T perpetrators was most often restricted to one or two cases, with some reporting no direct experience. Regardless of this, all were eager to develop this work in order to be able to work safely and effectively with LGB and/or T perpetrators and to offer an equal service. However, as a self-selecting sample who were likely to be motivated by an interest in this area of work, it may not be possible to generalise their eagerness to all perpetrator practitioners. Despite willingness to develop this work, the interviews highlighted numerous complexities and dilemmas regarding how to proceed with this, as well as some examples of innovative practice. Debates centred on programme philosophy and content evidence and expertise organisation and facilitation and demand and viability. Each of these is now addressed in turn.

Programme Philosophy and Content

A key question discussed in the interviews concerned the transferability of existing perpetrator interventions designed for heterosexual men to LGB and/or T perpetrators of DVA. Many of the cognitive-behavioural elements of existing programmes, including techniques such as 'time outs' and communication skills training, were considered unanimously to be valuable across gender and sexuality. However, practitioners were more divided regarding whether a programme rooted in a feminist, gendered analysis of DVA would be appropriate and also whether new content specific to LGB and/or T perpetrators would be required. Responses to this question of transferability stretched along a continuum and were influenced by practitioners' perceptions of whether LGB and/or T relationships and DVA were different from, or the same as, heterosexual relationships (this debate has been covered in greater detail in Donovan & Barnes, 2016 under review). At one end, some participants considered that behaving abusively and seeking power and control were generic human issues irrespective of gender and sexuality. As a result, bar some tweaking of case studies to include same-sex relationships, it was thought that existing interventions could be used almost 'off-the-shelf' with LGB and/or T perpetrators. At the other end of the continuum were practitioners who considered that a heavily gendered approach to working with heterosexual men may not be transferable to LGB and/or T perpetrators because gender operates differently in LGB and/or T relationships. For some practitioners, there were tensions between being strong advocates of a gendered approach and understanding all DVA as being rooted in power and control, but not being able to operationalise these principles without reference to heterosexual masculinity and femininity. Moreover, a minority of practitioners, including one who self-defined as a lesbian, anticipated that same-sex couples might organise their relationships in conventionally (heterosexually) gendered ways. The pervasiveness of both heteronormativity and relatedly, the public story of DVA, can, therefore, obscure more nuanced understandings of how gender and power might operate in LGB and/or T relationships. In the middle of the continuum were those who felt that elements of existing interventions were valuable, but would need to be supplemented with LGB and/or T-specific content regarding experiences of living as a part of a minority and the effects of homo/bi/transphobia.

Evidence and Expertise

Participants were extremely thoughtful but tentative in their attempts to grapple with the prospect of providing an intervention for a poorly served group, reflecting the uncharted territory of LGB and/or T perpetrator work. This was particularly problematic for three of the prison-based practitioners, all forensic psychologists, who emphasised the lack of knowledge about whether the risk factors for LGB and/or T perpetrators would be the same as for heterosexual men. Given that NOMS-accredited programmes are grounded in empirical evidence from quantitative studies that statistically demonstrate 'what works', the lack of corresponding evidence for LGB and/or T perpetrators was seen as a barrier to developing accredited programmes. Other practitioners in both criminal justice and voluntary programmes felt that the lack of evidence, guidance and training to develop this work raised concerns in terms of the effectiveness of any interventions for reducing DVA. Some practitioners were keenly aware of the potential to 'get it wrong' with LGB and/or T people because of a lack of knowledge about their lives and relationships. Fears about causing offence by using the wrong language, for example, were reflected in their perceptions of the readiness of their organisation to work inclusively with LGB and/or T perpetrators.

However, the lack of any specific evidence and expertise with LGB and/or T DVA was not considered by most practitioners to be insurmountable. Some practitioners indicated that the urgency to develop a response to LGB and/or T perpetrators meant that it was not feasible to wait for evidence to amass or for another agency to lead the way. Instead, an experimental approach was required to develop best practice from the bottom up. This is echoed in the Coral Project's recommendation that a pilot LGB and/or T DVA perpetrator intervention be designed, implemented and evaluated (Donovan et al., 2014). For example, Ben explained why his Probation Trust had adapted a one-to-one module for DVA perpetrators for use with LGB and/or T perpetrators:

> [I'd] felt for some time that the [name] programme wasn't so far away from being useful and relevant for people in same sex relationships and I argued that ... we should expand or adapt it to look at how it could be more relevant. At the same time [an LGB and/or T DVA project] was saying, 'Why aren't you offering [an] intervention as well?' and so I suppose from both sides, we're saying there ought to be an intervention and ... [we] managed to ... get the backing from head office so it had the Probation Trust devoting resources to setting this up. (Ben, criminal justice, probation)

To address knowledge gaps and concerns about being inclusive and sensitive, a few other practitioners reported that their agency, or they as individual practitioners, were working in partnership with specialist local LGB and/or T agencies to boost referrals, promote a specific service or receive guidance on inclusive language and resources. Whilst the emphasis here is on how practitioners working on perpetrator interventions can benefit from the input of LGB and/or T specialist agencies, the opportunities for skill-sharing and service improvement are reciprocal. LGB and/or T agencies are often presumed to have the expertise to deal with all issues that LGB and/or T people encounter, yet they rarely have specialist DVA expertise, or sufficient resources, to be able to work safely and effectively with either survivors or perpetrators.

Organisation and Facilitation

Discussion of the practicalities of running interventions for LGB and/or T perpetrators raised various conundrums. The first key debate concerned whether GB and/or T men could be integrated into existing groups of heterosexual men. Most practitioners felt that this would not be appropriate and that there was a need for tailored resources and contents. Concerns were raised that GB and/or T men may feel unsafe and reluctant to make disclosures in a group with heterosexual men and would, therefore, be unable to benefit from group work dynamics. Sarah explained:

> I think one of the really big benefits of group work is that you learn off other group members; if […] either you feel intimidated by another group work member or you completely personally disapprove of their lifestyle choices, that's going to affect how willing you are to sort of engage in that group work dynamic. (Sarah, criminal justice, probation)

Practitioners who considered that a mixed group of heterosexual, GB and/or T men could work were in the minority. They included those who suggested that it might be possible if the existing group of men were willing for this to happen. Others felt that the ideal would be to eliminate any divisions around sexuality and/or gender in group work, albeit recognising that this might not yet be feasible. Some also acknowledged that men participating on existing programmes, who are ostensibly heterosexual and have female partners, may be bisexual and/or having sex with men and either have not disclosed this to anyone or have not been asked about their sexuality. Three practitioners described situations where they had consciously included gay or trans men in a heterosexual men's group but had then undertaken separate one-to-one work with that man to explore issues specific to sexuality and gender identity that could not be disclosed in the group. In these instances, other programme participants were not aware of the men's sexuality or trans identity. Yet, there are concerns regarding whether this option can, therefore, only be open to those men who can 'pass' as a heterosexual, cisgendered male. Such selection criterion would be difficult and discriminatory to impose. There are also likely harms and implications for programme effectiveness if group members have to conceal and cannot properly explore a central feature of their identity and relationship(s).

Since for most practitioners, mixed arrangements such as those mentioned earlier, were considered unworkable, the discussion then turned to the practicalities of running a bespoke LGB and/or T intervention. The key debates here were whether there should be separate provision by gender or sexuality, whether it should follow the widely established model for heterosexual men's programmes of co-facilitation by a male and a female facilitator and whether the sexuality of the facilitators would be relevant. Responses were mixed, and in many cases inseparable from resourcing considerations, which are revisited later.

The question as to whether LGB and/or T perpetrators could participate in one combined group or would need to be split by sexuality and/or gender identity was not an issue that typically participants had considered in any depth before. This was due, in part, to the fact that in heterosexual DVA work, integrating men and women in a group work programme would be unthinkable. Practitioners most commonly suggested that some stratification would be required, with the most logical choice being to have separate male and female groups. However, some started to doubt the adequacy of this level of stratification once they started to consider further ambiguities. For example, they considered how being bisexual might differ from being a gay man or a lesbian and whether trans perpetrators would need a trans-specific group, or could participate alongside lesbian and bisexual women or gay and bisexual men.

Perceptions of the necessity of co-gendered facilitation of an LGB and/or T intervention were also mixed. Some who considered that this was not important also questioned its value and feasibility within heterosexual men's programmes, especially given some of the challenges of finding male facilitators. There were different views about the purpose that opposite gender co-facilitation served. Whilst some practitioners indicated that the rationale behind this was a modelling of respectful male, female relationships and female leadership, some participants felt that a respectful relationship being modelled between two men or two women could be equally valuable, even for groups of heterosexual men. However, others questioned whether there would be any value to, for example, having a male co-facilitator for a lesbian group programme. The question of whether the facilitators' gender would matter was also often linked to perspectives of the relevance of the facilitators' sexuality. Here, again, views were mixed. On the one hand, there were practitioners who thought that being a skilled facilitator was the priority and that facilitators would not usually disclose their sexuality in heterosexual men's groups. Others described being more open about their own relationships. Conversely, some practitioners thought that the particular barriers to LGB and/or T individuals accessing services meant that it would be valuable to have LGB and/or T facilitators in order to build trust and rapport. Lucy, interestingly, took a middle ground position, arguing that LGB and/or T staff would be important when starting up a programme, but that the need for this might lessen over time:

I think to start with it would also have to probably have, have a higher proportion of LGB or T um workers, as the frontline workers, even if, I don't think it makes a difference longer time down the line whether, you know, what sexuality or gender you are when you're delivering this work so long as you know what you're talking about and you can empathise, but I think at the beginning its about having that credibility and the trust thing. (Lucy, voluntary programme).However, despite varying perceptions about what would work and what would be the ideal best practice, it was clear that feasibility and resourcing would limit what could actually be provided, as considered in the next section.

Demand and Viability

Whilst participants were keen for their organisation to offer appropriate interventions for LGB and/or T perpetrators, their perceptions of whether this work could be developed were tempered by concerns regarding viability. For both voluntary and criminal justice programmes, the principal concerns were funding and the lack of LGB and/or T referrals. The issue of LGB and/or T perpetrators very rarely and in some cases never approaching their agency was one that practitioners identified as problematic, both in terms of the resourcing of a new intervention but also for determining the format that any potential intervention could take. In turn, there were doubts about the viability of group programmes, especially if these were split by sex and/or sexuality or gender identity. Distinctions were, therefore, made between what might be ideal, that is, a group work programme with two facilitators, which would enable peer support and challenge, and what might be the only viable option, namely, one-to-one work with a single facilitator. This dilemma was articulated by Sarah, a probation officer:

> The problem is that I know that there aren't the numbers so if you're looking at um dividing it up um gender-wise as well, you'd probably only be able to run a [group] programme once every five years which would be disproportionate to the individual who'd (laughter) committed the offence. (Sarah, criminal justice, probation)

Some participants reflected on the possible reasons behind this perceived low demand and spoke of how sexuality and/or gender identity could pose barriers to accessing services. For example, Ben explained:

> We have argued that until we're offering [an] intervention, we may not have a demand. So until people think that the criminal justice service, the police and the probation service, are going to offer any sort of meaningful support or interventions for them, then they're maybe not likely to pursue prosecution, to bother calling the police in the first place, to admit to being gay in the probation appointment. So the fact that we don't have much evidence of a treatment need or a demand, um doesn't seem a justifiable reason to not offer the resource. (Ben, criminal justice, probation)

Jack reinforced this approach, saying that a prerequisite for the success of a bespoke LGB and/or T intervention would be outreach services for LGB and/or T communities to clearly communicate that they would be understood and welcomed:

> I think there'd have to be a whole push on an LGBT programme, promoting it very much as LGBT friendly and specific and facilitators that are aware of LGBT-specific relationship dynamics and things like that. (Jack, LGBT DVA consultant/trainer)

Without active outreach to LGB and/or T communities, referrals will remain low, or non-existent. However, particularly under a regime of austerity, it is not viable to justify and plan for new service development if demand cannot be evidenced. The approach of Ben's Probation Trust is, therefore, unique in this regard. Elsewhere, most participants referred to developments being hindered by this 'chicken-and-egg' dilemma.

Conclusion

Developing inclusive, appropriate and effective responses to LGB and/or T perpetrators of DVA is vital as a matter of equality, to hold perpetrators accountable and to pursue the safety of previous, current and potential victims/survivors of DVA within LGB and/or T relationships. Having established that there is demand for, yet a lack of provision for, LGB and/or T perpetrators, this chapter has focused on responding to LGB and/or T perpetrators though attitudinal and behaviour change programmes. The interview data analysed show how practitioners already working on, or alongside, these programmes perceive the opportunities for and barriers to, developing LGB and/or T perpetrator interventions. What is notable and encouraging is the high level of motivation to implement LGB and/or T DVA work. However, it is clear that whilst the energy and dedication of practitioners who have developed their own expertise in this field is crucial in building further momentum, there also needs to be an organisational steer and investment to enable this to happen. The interviews with practitioners highlight the complexities surrounding the development of this practice, theoretically and practically. In some respects, more questions are posed than answers found. Indeed, until LGB and/or T interventions are designed, tested and evaluated, there will continue to be many grey areas regarding what 'best practice' for LGB and/or T perpetrator interventions looks like. Practitioners' eagerness to see this work develop was, however, tinged with a recognition that under the current climate of austerity and the outsourcing of probation work, including DVA interventions, certain challenges are apparent. Given the juxtaposition between the very low (visible) demand for LGB and/or T interventions and the much greater demand for expansion of provision for heterosexual male perpetrators, the development and resourcing of more specialised interventions is difficult to justify. It is hoped that the Coral Project's findings, as well as organisations' recognition of their responsibilities to provide equally accessible services, will help to maintain the impetus for the important work, which some practitioners have already undertaken.

However, whilst behaviour change programmes have been the main focus of this chapter, it is also proposed that relying on perpetrator services alone to respond to LGB and/or T perpetrators is too limited. As urgently as this work needs to develop, the reality is that the numbers of LGB and/or T perpetrators who will voluntarily approach, or be mandated to, a specific perpetrator intervention, will for the foreseeable future only represent the tip of the iceberg. Consequently, there is both the opportunity and the need for a much wider range of practice settings, including youth work, SRE and counselling, to contribute to an integrated response to LGB and/or T DVA. Practitioners who do not work explicitly with LGB and/or T perpetrators, but who may encounter them through their work, require training and support, which will enable them to become skilled in recognising and responding to LGB and/or T DVA (Donovan et al., 2014). As the survey findings infer, many of those individuals who use potentially 'abusive' behaviours, who want to have better relationships and who recognise a need to change their behaviour, are not at the threshold for a perpetrator intervention. Therefore, whilst inclusive, high quality and effective LGB and/or T perpetrator interventions should be developed for those who require them, good practice needs to develop across multiple sectors to work with a wider range of LGB and/or T service individuals in order to reduce the risk of potentially 'abusive' and controlling behaviours escalating and enable them to develop relationships 'skills' that are positive for themselves and their partners.

References

Balsam, K. F., & Szymanski, D. M. (2005). Relationship quality and domestic violence in women's same-sex relationships: The role of minority stress. *Psychology of Women Quarterly, 29*(3), 258–269.

Barnes, R. (2007). *Woman-to-woman partner abuse: A qualitative analysis*. Unpublished PhD Thesis, University of Nottingham, UK.

Barnes, R. (2008). "I still sort of flounder in a sea of non-language": The constraints of language and labels in women's accounts of woman-to-woman partner abuse. In K. Throsby & F. Alexander (Eds.), *Gender and interpersonal violence: Language, action and representation*. Basingstoke: Palgrave Macmillan.

Barnes, R. (2011). Suffering in a silent vacuum: Woman-to-woman partner abuse as a challenge to the lesbian feminist vision. *Feminism and Psychology, 21*, 233–239.

Bartholomew, K., Regan, K. V., White, M. A., & Oram, D. (2008). Patterns of abuse in male same-sex relationships. *Violence and Victims, 23*(5), 617–636.

Brand, P. A., & Kidd, A. H. (1986). Frequency of physical aggression in heterosexual and female homosexual dyads. *Psychological Reports, 59*, 1307–1313.

Broken Rainbow. (2015). Retrieved October 24, 2015, from http://www.brokenrainbow.org.uk (home page).

Civil Partnership Act 2004 c33. Retrieved October 14, 2015, from http://www.legislation.gov.uk/ukpga/2004/33/contents

Coleman, V. E. (2002). Treating the lesbian batterer: Theoretical and clinical considerations: A contemporary psychoanalytic perspective. *Journal of Aggression, Maltreatment and Trauma, 7*(1/2), 159–205.

Council of Europe. (2011). *Council of Europe convention on preventing and combating violence against women and domestic violence*. Strasbourg: Couencil of Europe.

Council of Europe. (2015). *Convention on preventing and combating violence against women and domestic violence (Istanbul Convention)*. Retrieved April 26, 2015, from www.coe.int/t/dghl/standardsetting/convention-violence/

Domestic Violence, Crime and Victims Act 2004 c28. Retrieved October 24, 2015, from http://www.legislation.gov.uk/ukpga/2004/28/contents

Donovan, C. (2015). Tackling inequality in the intimate sphere: Problematizing love and violence in same-sex relationships. In R. Leckey (Ed.), *After legal equality: Family, sex, kinship*. Abingdon: Routledge.

Donovan, C., & Barnes, R. (2016 under review). Making sense of discourses of sameness and difference in agency responses to abusive LGB and/or T partners. Manuscript submitted for publication.

Donovan, C., Barnes, R., & Nixon, C. (2014). *The Coral Project: Exploring abusive behaviours in lesbian, gay, bisexual and/or transgender relationships – Interim report*. Sunderland and Leicester: University of Sunderland and University of Leicester.

Donovan, C., & Hester, M. (2011). Seeking help from the enemy: Help-seeking strategies of those in same sex relationships who have experienced domestic abuse. *Child and Family Law Quarterly, 23*(1), 26–40.

Donovan, C., & Hester, M. (2014). *Domestic violence and sexuality: What's love got to do with it?* Bristol: Policy Press.

Donovan, C., Hester, M., Holmes, J., & McCarry, M. (2006). *Comparing domestic abuse in same sex and heterosexual relationships*. Sunderland and Bristol: University of Sunderland and University of Bristol.

Equality Act 2010 c15. Retrieved October 24, 2015, from http://www.legislation.gov.uk/ukpga/2010/15/contents

Home Office. (2011). *Call to end violence against women and girls: Action plan*. London: HM Government.

Home Office. (2013). *Home Office Circular 003/2013: New government domestic violence and abuse definition*. Retrieved April 26, 2015, from https://www.gov.uk/government/publications/new-government-domestic-violence-and-abuse-definition

Johnson, M. P. (2006). Conflict and control: Gender symmetry and asymmetry in domestic violence. *Violence Against Women, 12*(11), 1003–1018.

Kelly, L., & Westmarland, N. (2015). *Domestic violence perpetrator programmes: Steps towards change: Project Mirabal final report*. London and Durham, NC: London Metropolitan University and Durham University.

Lie, G. Y., & Gentlewarrier, S. (1991). Intimate violence in lesbian relationships: Discussion of survey findings and practice implications. *Journal of Social Service Research, 15*, 41–59.

Marriage (same sex couples) Act 2013 c30. Retrieved October 24, 2015, from http://www.legislation.gov.uk/ukpga/2013/30/contents/enacted/data.htm

Mendoza, J. (2011). The impact of minority stress on gay male partner abuse. In J. L. Ristock (Ed.), *Intimate partner violence in LGBTQ lives (pp. 169–181)*. London: Routledge.

Merrill, G. S., & Wolfe, V. A. (2000). Battered gay men: An exploration of abuse, help seeking, and why they stay. *Journal of Homosexuality, 39*(2), 1–30.

Pence, E. L., & Shepard, M. F. (1999). An introduction: Developing a coordinated community response. In M. F. Shepard & E. L. Pence (Eds.), *Coordinating community responses to domestic violence*. London: SAGE.

Phillips, R., Kelly, L., & Westmarland, N. (2013). *Domestic violence perpetrator programmes: An historical overview*. London and Durham, NC: London Metropolitan University and Durham University.

Poorman, P. B., & Seelau, S. M. (2001). Lesbians who abuse their partners: Using the FIRO-B to assess interpersonal characteristics. In E. Kaschak (Ed.), *Intimate betrayal: Domestic violence in lesbian relationships (pp. 87–106)*. London: The Haworth Press.

Renzetti, C. M. (1992). *Violent betrayal: Partner abuse in lesbian relationships*. London: SAGE.

Ristock, J. L. (2002). *No more secrets: Violence in lesbian relationships*. New York: Routledge.

Roch, A., Morton, J., & Ritchie, G. (2010). *Out of sight, out of mind? – Transgender people's experience of domestic abuse*. Edinburgh: LGBT Youth Scotland, Scottish Trans Alliance and Equality Network.

Rollnick, S., Heather, N., Gold, R., & Hall, W. (1992). Development of a short 'readiness to change' questionnaire for use in brief, opportunistic interventions among excessive drinkers. *British Journal of Addiction, 87*(5), 743–754.

Smith, C. (2011). Women who abuse their female intimate partners. In J. L. Ristock (Ed.), *Intimate partner violence in LGBTQ lives (pp. 131–152)*. London: Routledge.

Index

A

abuse support services, 191, 193, 244
   specialist domestic violence and, 194–6
abusive attitudes, prevention, 173–5
abusive behaviour, 68, 71, 155, 167, 186, 191, 208, 289, 305, 307, 317
   factors influencing, 159–61
   in LGB and/or T, 305, 306
   perpetrators of, 164
   prevention, 173–5
abusive relationship, interventions targeting, 164–6
abusive relationship, participant response, 167–75
   aggression and violence, 168–9
   bad relationships, 169–70
   causes problems in relationships, 170
   preventing abusive attitudes and behaviour, 173–5
   resolve bad/unhealthy relationship, 171–2
Advocacy, Support, Safety, Information and Services Together (ASSIST), 91
aggressive hyper-masculine culture, 174
All Party Parliamentary Group (APPG), 119
   on domestic violence, 125
   on sexual violence, 125
APPG. *See* All Party Parliamentary Group (APPG)

Note: Page number followed by 'n' refers to footnotes.

Index

ASSIST. *See* Advocacy, Support, Safety, Information and Services Together (ASSIST)
Associated Partner Support Services, 289
Attitudes towards Domestic Violence (ADV) questionnaire, 165
attitudes, young people, 161–3
AT v Hungary, 20n6
authorities, local, 233
   area-based grants to, 232
   and housing providers, 234, 236
   role and practice of, 231–2

B
Bail Act 1976, 49
BAMER women. *See* Black and Minority Ethnic and Refugee (BAMER) women
barring orders, 46, 49, 53
bisexual male victims, 189–90
Black and Minority Ethnic and Refugee (BAMER) women
   access to DVA services, 120
   refuges for, 121
black and minority ethnic (BME) community, 112
Black Liberation Movement, 110, 110n2
Black Panther Movement, 110n2
bodily harm, 70–1
British Bill of Rights, 32

C
CAADA. *See* Coordinated Action Against Domestic Abuse (CAADA)
CAFCASS. *See* Children and Family Court Advisory and Support Services (CAFCASS)
CAMHS. *See* Child and Adolescent Mental Health Service (CAMHS)
CCR. *See* Coordinated Community Response (CCR)
CDVP. *See* Community Domestic Violence Programme (CDVP)
CEDAW. *See* Convention on the Elimination of All Forms of Discrimination against Women (CEDAW)
CERP. *See* Court Estate Closure Programme (CERP)
Child and Adolescent Mental Health Service (CAMHS), 148
Children and Family Court Advisory and Support Services (CAFCASS), 277
Children's Act 1989, 113, 133
civil law, 72–3
civil legal aid, 73–4
CJS. *See* Criminal Justice System (CJS)
co-commissioning models, 116
coercion and control
   DVA, 215–16
   legal recognition of, 71–2
coercive behaviour, emotional abuse and, 159–60
coercive control, 65, 134
   strategy, 65
   violence, 62
COHSAR approach. *See* COmparing Heterosexual and Same-sex Abuse in Relationships (COHSAR) approach

Index   323

commissioning and DVA sector, 116–20
Committee of Ministers of the Council of Europe, 22n8
Community Domestic Violence Programme (CDVP), 276
Community Rehabilitation Companies (CRCs), 277
Community Safety Officers, 241
Community Safety Partnership (CSP), 253, 255
Community Safety Team, 239, 241, 243
COmparing Heterosexual and Same-sex Abuse in Relationships (COHSAR) approach, 304
Conflict Tactic Scale (CTS), 61, 61n2
Convention of Belem do Para, 21, 21n7
Convention on Preventing and Combating Violence against Women and Domestic Violence, 22, 26–7
Convention on the Elimination of All Forms of Discrimination against Women (CEDAW), 17–19
Committee, 20, 29, 159
Convention rights, 24
Coordinated Action Against Domestic Abuse (CAADA), 255, 255n2, 257
Coordinated Community Response (CCR), 115, 251, 252, 252n1
coordinated victim-centred approach, 251
Coral Project, 189, 304–6

Council of Europe Convention on Preventing and Combating Violence against Women and Domestic Violence, 1, 6–7, 16
Council of Europe Task Force to Combat Violence against Women, 26
Court Estate Closure Programme (CERP), 94
Courts Closure Programme, 82, 91, 96
CPS. *See* Crown Prosecution Service (CPS)
CRCs. *See* Community Rehabilitation Companies (CRCs)
The Crime and Disorder Act 1998, 114, 253
Crime and Disorder Reduction Partnership (CDRP) network, 114
Crime and Security Act 2010, 47, 97
Crime Reduction Programme, 164
Criminal Justice Act 2003, 98, 99
Criminal Justice and Court Services Act 2000, 115
Criminal Justice System (CJS), 66, 70–1, 81, 114, 115, 260, 276
criminal law, 48, 49
   in domestic violence, 55
Criminal Law Act 1977, 228n2
criminogenic needs principle, 115n5
Crown Office and Procurator Fiscal Service, 90
Crown Prosecution Service (CPS), 84, 88
CSP. *See* Community Safety Partnership (CSP)

CTS. *See* Conflict Tactic Scale (CTS)
cynicism, 91

D
DAHA. *See* Domestic Abuse Housing Alliance (DAHA)
DAIP. *See* Domestic Abuse Intervention Programs (DAIP)
DASH. *See* Domestic Abuse, Stalking and Honour Based Violence Risk Identification Checklist (DASH)
Department of Communities and Local Government (DCLG) commissioned report, 232
desistance from DVA, 285–6
dichotomy, public/private, 18
discrimination, 19, 191
domestic abuse, 90–1, 159–60, 164
 commissioner funding strategies for, 192
 court, Scottish, 90–1
 housing as primary responder to situations of, 239–41
Domestic Abuse Housing Alliance (DAHA), 244, 244n4, 245
Domestic Abuse Intervention Programs (DAIP), 251
Domestic Abuse Intervention Project, 281
Domestic Abuse Investigation Unit, 92
Domestic Abuse, Stalking and Honour Based Violence Risk Identification Checklist (DASH), 240, 241
 risk assessment checklist, 255n3
Domestic Abuse Task Force, 254
domestic and sexual violence, APPG on, 119–20
Domestic Proceedings and Magistrates Court Act 1978, 229
domestic violence
 APPG on, 125
 cross-government definition of, 68
 ECHR case law on, 23
 forums, 114
 historical weaknesses in policing of, 38–42
 as human rights issue, 17–18
 UN endorsement of, 21
domestic violence and abuse (DVA), 1–2, 81, 82, 93, 107, 108, 191
 health and social care agencies on, 220
 instrumental and expressive typologies of, 278–81
 intersectionality, 281–4
 LGB and/or T, 121, 299–306
 male perpetrators of, 274, 281, 282
 perpetrators, 204, 275, 276, 278, 279, 286, 302
 self-report surveys of, 307
domestic violence and abuse (DVA) perpetrator programmes, 98, 275, 281–4
domestic violence and abuse (DVA) sector, 125
 commissioning and, 116–20
 grass root beginnings of, 109–12
 political ideology of, 110
 professional autonomy of, 119
domestic violence and abuse (DVA) services
 BAMER women's access to, 120

mainstream establishment and expansion of voluntary, 116
Domestic Violence and Matrimonial Proceedings Act 1976, 229
Domestic Violence Crime and Victims Act 2004, 66, 298
Domestic Violence Family Intervention Worker (FIW), 133
Domestic Violence Intervention Programme (DVIP), 275
Domestic Violence Perpetrator Programme (DVPP), 276, 277, 290
Domestic Violence Protection Notice (DVPN), 7, 37, 46–50, 236
authorisation for, 51
police implementation of, 52
Domestic Violence Protection Orders (DVPOs), 7, 37, 46–51, 53–5, 97, 236
police implementation of, 52
Duluth Model, 251, 252n1, 275
DVA. *See* Domestic violence and abuse (DVA)
DVIP. *See* Domestic Violence Intervention Programme (DVIP)
DVPN. *See* Domestic Violence Protection Notice (DVPN)
DVPOs. *See* Domestic Violence Protection Orders (DVPOs)
DVPP. *See* Domestic Violence Perpetrator Programme (DVPP)

E

ECHR. *See* European Convention on Human Rights (ECHR)

ECtHR. *See* European Court of Human Rights (ECtHR)
emotional abuse, 191
and coercive behaviour, 159–60
Employment Rights Act 1996, 263
Ending Violence Against Women and Girls Strategy, 107
European Committee on Crime Problems (CDPC), 26, 27
European Convention on Human Rights (ECHR), 17–18, 22–5
European Court of Human Rights (ECtHR), 16, 18, 22, 25, 29
exosystem, 174
expressive violence, 278, 279

F

faith-based community, 9, 189, 204, 206, 217, 221
faith-based context, 220
faith-based discourse, 212
faith-based environment, 206
faith-based group, 206
Family Intervention Worker (FIW), 9, 133
managing communication with children and services, 147–50
research methodology, 141–2
role, 135–9, 146–50
Family Law Act 1996, 53, 72, 133
female violence, 64
femininity, societal expectations of, 64
feminist
analysis, 184
criminology, 184
feminist sociopolitical theory, 183–4
Finney, A., 160

Firebreak Project, 156, 156n1, 157, 166–7
FIW. *See* Family Intervention Worker (FIW)
Fox, C., 165
Francis, B., 189
Freeman, C., 10, 273, 303
Friend, D. J., 279

G
gay male victims, 189–90
gender
  asymmetrical, 161
  and faith, DVA, 204–6
  identity, trans, 197
  role expectations, legal constructions of, 62–5
  stereotypes, 190
gender-neutral approach, 5, 7, 28, 76, 184
gender–power relations, 184
Goekce v Austria , 20n6
Government Select Committee on Violence, 111

H
Health and Safety at Work Act 1974, 263
healthy relationships, participant response, 167–75
  aggression and violence, 168–9
hegemonic masculinity, 184, 185
Her Majesty's Crown Prosecution Service Inspectorate (HMCPSI), 41

Her Majesty's Inspectorate of Constabulary (HMIC), 7, 37, 42, 44, 52, 55, 81
  College of Policing, 44, 45
  inspection, 41, 42
  report, 85, 86, 93, 193
Hester, M., *Three planets model* , 136, 138
hierarchy of harm, 60
Hill and Van Colle and *Smith* , 42
Hill v Chief Constable of West Yorkshire (1989) AC, 53, 42n3
HMCPSI. *See* Her Majesty's Crown Prosecution Service Inspectorate (HMCPSI)
HMIC. *See* Her Majesty's Inspectorate of Constabulary (HMIC)
Homelessness Act 2002, 233
homelessness legislation, 231
Home Office, 40, 47, 85, 114, 134, 157, 165, 192, 254–6, 298
  circular, 40, 41, 46
  domestic violence and abuse definition by, 158, 191
  DVA definition by, 206, 215, 282
  guidance, 49
  policy development, 243
Housing Act 1996, 230, 233
Housing (Homeless Persons) Act 1977, 111, 229
housing, as primary responder, 239–41
Housing Benefit Regulation 7 (6), 238
housing law provision, 74–5
human rights, 17
  approach, 32

discourse, 16, 32
issue, domestic violence as, 17–18
violation, 16
human rights law, 17, 18, 22, 24–6
hyper-masculine culture, 161, 166, 174

I

ICCPR. *See* International Covenant on Civil and Political Rights (ICCPR)
ICESCR. *See* International Covenant on Economic, Social and Cultural Rights (ICESCR)
IDAP. *See* Integrated Domestic Abuse Programme (IDAP)
IDVA. *See* Independent Domestic Violence Advisor (IDVA); Independent Domestic Violence Advocate (IDVA)
IKWRO. *See* Iranian and Kurdish Women's Rights Organisation (IKWRO)
Independent Domestic Violence Advisor (IDVA), 10, 115, 140, 144–5, 240, 255, 258–9
for male victims, 182, 195
role, 265
Independent Domestic Violence Advocate (IDVA), 83, 85, 88–90
Independent Police Complaints Commission, 96
instrumental psychological abuse, 280
instrumental violence, 278
Integrated Domestic Abuse Programme (IDAP), 237, 276

Inter-American Convention on the Prevention, Punishment and Eradication of Violence, 21
International Covenant on Civil and Political Rights (ICCPR), 17
International Covenant on Economic, Social and Cultural Rights (ICESCR), 17
international human rights, 18
intersectionality, 163–4, 281–4
intimate partner violence (IPV), 84
Iranian and Kurdish Women's Rights Organisation (IKWRO), 256
Istanbul Convention, 1, 4, 16, 19, 26–31, 124

J

Jallow v Bulgaria, 20n6
Johnson, M., typologies of domestic violence, 186, 189, 278–81, 284, 306
Joint Protocol, 91, 93
Judicial Studies Board, 63
justice system, criminal, 66, 70–1, 81, 114, 115, 260, 276

L

LASPO. *See* Legal Aid, Sentencing and Punishment of Offenders Act 2012 (LASPO)
legal aid
criteria, 73–4
in England and Wales, 92
Legal Aid, Sentencing and Punishment of Offenders Act (LASPO), 73, 228n2

legal response, in England and Wales, 60
Legal Services Commission, 53
legislation, homelessness, 231
lesbian, gay, bisexual and/or transgender (LGB and/or T), 11, 189, 190, 192, 196, 276, 292, 298–305
lesbian, gay, bisexual and/or transgender (LGB and/or T) perpetrator interventions, 306–8
  demand and viability, 314–16
  evidence and expertise, 310–11
  organisation and facilitation, 312–14
  practitioners' perspectives on development, 308–9
  programme philosophy and content, 309–10
  survey findings, 306–8
LGB and/or T. *See* lesbian, gay, bisexual and/or transgender (LGB and/or T)
liberty
  crime, 60, 69
local authorities, 233
  area-based grants to, 232
  and housing providers, 234, 236
  role and practice of, 231–2
Local Government Act 2000, 24

M
macrosystem, 175
male victims
  American studies of, 194
  gay and bisexual, 89–190
  heterosexual, 187–9
  IDVA for, 182, 195
  police and judicial response to, 193–4
  policy approach, 191–3
  prevalence of, 182–3
  in same-sex relationships, 189
  trans, 190–1
Management of Health and Safety at Work Regulations 1999, 263
mandatory arrest policy development, 250
MAPPA. *See* Multi-Agency Public Protection Arrangements (MAPPA)
Maputo Protocol, 21
MARAC. *See* Multi Agency Risk Assessment Conference (MARAC)
masculinity, 190, 286
  hegemonic, 184, 185
McPherson v Secretary of State for the Home Department, 22
Michael and others v Chief Constable of South Wales and another, 41
microsystem, 174
Multi-Agency Public Protection Arrangements (MAPPA), 115
multi-agency responses, 254, 265
  development and philosophy of, 250–4
Multi-Agency Risk Assessment Conference (MARAC), 3, 45, 55, 73, 74, 115, 136, 140, 235, 240, 255, 257–8, 260
  criticisms of, 256
  evaluation of, 256
  NGO representation at, 257
  prioritisation function of, 257
  role, 265

N

National Assistance Act 1948, 24
National Health Service and
    Community Care Act 1990, 24
National Helpline for Male Victims,
    195
National Institute for Health and
    Care Excellence (NICE), 261
National Offender Management
    Service (NOMS), 305
National Practitioner's Network for
    Domestic Violence
    Intervention Programmes, 276
National Society for the Prevention
    of Cruelty to Children
    (NSPCC), 166
    Aggression Project, 173
National Steering Group, 95
National Violence Against Women
    and Girls, 243
National Women's Aid Federation
    (NWAF), 111
NICE. *See* National Institute for
    Health and Care Excellence
    (NICE)
NOMS. *See* National Offender
    Management Service (NOMS)
non-government organisations
    (NGOs), 42, 251, 257–9, 292
NSPCC. *See* National Society for the
    Prevention of Cruelty to
    Children (NSPCC)
NWAF. *See* National Women's Aid
    Federation (NWAF)

O

Offences Against the Person Act
    1861, 65n8

*Oxfordshire County Council v R and
    another*, 24

P

PCCs. *See* Police and Crime
    Commissioners (PCCs)
Peabody, 239, 240
Peabody's Vulnerable Resident policy,
    241
perpetrator
    tenancy rights, 236
    and victims, 190
perpetrator intervention, LGB and/
    or T
    demand and viability, 314–16
    evidence and expertise, 310–11
    organisation and facilitation,
        312–14
    practitioners' perspectives on
        development, 308–9
    programme philosophy and
        content, 309–10
    survey findings, 306–8
perpetrator programme
    development in UK, 275–8
    DVA, 98, 280–4, 287–91
Personal, Social Health and
    Citizenship Education
    (PSHCE), 164, 165
physical abuse, 191
physical violence, 60, 61, 68, 162,
    168, 279–80
Police and Crime Commissioners
    (PCCs), 193
Pre-Sentence Report (PSR), 99
priority need establishment, 232–6
private dichotomy, 18
pro-arrest policy, 40, 49

Probation Service, 2, 276
   in England and Wales, 288
property and tenancy rights, 236–7
pro-prosecution policies, 49
Protection from Harassment Act 1997, 67, 68
Protocol to the African Charter on Human and Peoples' Rights, 21
PSR. *See* Pre-Sentence Report (PSR)
psychiatric injury, 70, 70n9
psychological abuse, 188
   instrumental, 280
psychological harm, 72
psychological violence, 280
Public Sector Equality Duty, 125

R
rational action theory, 277n2
Rational Calculator Model, 277n2
READAPT (Relationship Education and Domestic Abuse Prevention Tuition) project, 165
RESPECT, 193, 276, 289, 290
REFUGE, 72n11, 110n2, 118, 119, 121, 228, 229
refuge movement, 111
regional treaties, 19
responsivity principle, 115n5
Rights of Women in Africa, 21
risk principle, 115n5
R v Chief Constable of Thames Valley Police , 97

S
sacred texts and teaching, 209–12
Safe Lives, 118

same-sex relationships, male victims in, 189
sanctuary schemes, 232n3
SARC. *See* Sexual Assault Referral Centre (SARC)
Scotland
   Domestic Abuse Task Force in, 254
   rise in police diversion, 92–4
   specialist domestic abuse courts, 91
Scottish domestic abuse courts, 90–1
Scottish Legal Aid Board, 92
Screening Assessment tools, 186n1
SDVC. *See* Specialist Domestic Violence Court (SDVC)
section 76 Serious Crime Act 2015, 134
Sentencing Guidelines Council, 98
Serious Crime Act 2015, 66, 71, 85
service provision, expansion of, 112–13
sex and relationships education (SRE), 305
sexual abuse, 162, 168, 188, 191, 204, 208, 300, 301
Sexual Assault Referral Centre (SARC), 255
sexual stereotypes, 63
sexual violence, 110n1, 123, 160, 192, 193
   APPG on, 125
situational couple violence, 61
Social Return on Investment (SRI) methodology, 116, 118
sociopolitical theory, feminist, 183–4
Southall Black Sisters group, 112
Spare Rib , 110n1

specialist domestic violence, and abuse support services, 194–6
Specialist Domestic Violence Court (SDVC), 8, 50, 82–4, 95, 115, 255
  case identification, 84–5
  core principle of, 88
  defence at, 92
  in England and Wales, 87, 91
  extending the scope of, 96–8
  implementation of, 90
  sentencing, 98–9
spiritual abuse, 213
  and DVA, 203, 206–9
SRE. *See* sex and relationships education (SRE)
Standing Together Against Domestic Violence, 165
Stark, E. Coercion and Control, 62–5, 134, 215, 278
Supporting People Programme, 231

T

tenancy rights
  perpetrators, 236
  property and, 236–7
tenancy support, and independent living, 237–9
Three planets model (Hester), 136, 138
Torres Rueda, S., 189
trans gender identity, 182, 189, 197, 298n2, 312
trans male victims, 190–1
transphobic emotional abuse, 301
Troubled Families policy, 137, 138

U

UK
  Bill of Rights, 32
  Refuge 'on track' referral system, 119
  'Troubled Families' policy, 137
UN
  endorsement of domestic violence, 21
  General Assembly Declaration on the Elimination of Violence against Women, 20
  human rights treaties, 29–31
  Special Rapporteur, 19, 20
  Universal Declaration of Human Rights, 17

V

Van Colle and *Smith* (2008) UKHL, 50, 42n3
VAWG. *See* violence against women and girls (VAWG)
victim-centred court, and IDVA, 88–90
victimisation, 45, 47, 53, 54, 61, 108, 158, 161, 187, 197, 219, 250, 302
  male, 9, 27, 182–4, 192, 195
  re-victimisation, 23, 25, 74, 260
victimology, 184
Victim's Charter in 1990, 119
violation, human rights, 16
violence against women, 21, 27, 28
violence against women and girls (VAWG), 157, 163
  infliction of, 159
  strategy, 123, 157

Violence against Women, Domestic Abuse and Sexual Violence (Wales) Act 2015, 264
violent abuse, 160
VK v Bulgaria, 20n6

W

Welfare Reform Act 2012, 239
women
 UN Special Rapporteur on violence against, 20
 violence against, 21, 27, 28
Women and Domestic Violence
 Convention on Preventing and Combating Violence against, 22, 26–7
 Council of Europe Convention on Preventing and Combating Violence against, 1, 6–7, 16

Women's Aid Federations, 111
Women's Aid National Quality Standards, 124
Women's Liberation Movement, 109, 111
Women's Safety Services, 289

Y

Yemshaw v Hounslow London Borough Council, 234
Yildirim v Austria, 20n6
young people
 attitudes of, 161–3
 domestic abuse and, 157–9
 towards abusive relationships, 161–3